2D EDITION

EQUAL EMPLOYMENT OPPORTUNITY LAW

DAVID P. TWOMEY

Professor of Law
School of Management
Boston College
Member of the Massachusetts
and Florida Bars

GJ86BA
PUBLISHED BY
SOUTH-WESTERN PUBLISHING CO.
CINCINNATI, OH   WEST CHICAGO, IL   DALLAS, TX   LIVERMORE, CA

ISBN: 0-538-80521-8

1 2 3 4 5 6 7 M 5 4 3 2 1 0 9

Printed in the United States of America

Preface

Over the past quarter century our society's concern for the unbiased treatment of the individual in the workplace has been expressed in a seeming minefield of statutes, amendments, court decisions, and agency regulations in which professionals in personnel and human resources management must daily operate. Actions by certain firms in violation of federal equal employment laws have cost those firms millions of dollars in damages paid in the form of back pay awards to individuals wrongfully deprived of employment or promotions. Personnel and human resources management professionals not only perform the important tasks of personnel work but also are relied upon to assure that company decisions are not contrary to law. In effect, these professionals often serve as the consciences of their organizations in regard to problems relating to human resources utilization.

Thus today's human resources managers must be conversant in the language and thinking of the law. Not only must they be prepared to initially evaluate company policy for compliance, they must also be able to work directly with lawyers to translate complex regulatory guidelines into workable company procedures (and not infrequently, to remold company procedures into a form compatible with newly established or revised guidelines). Indeed, in some instances these executives are called upon to prepare and present the firm's case before state and federal administrative agencies and arbitration tribunals.

While the basic human resources management/personnel administration textbooks recognize the need for a familiarity with the general precepts of equal employment law, historically they have provided but summary treatment of this complicated and continually changing subject. This short text is intended to supplement basic texts in the important subject area of equal employment opportunity law and related topics. This text is also intended for students studying the legal environment of business; business law; and specialized courses for women, minorities, and other individuals who are protected by these laws. Since, as future managers, students will be called upon to know the law and work directly with attorneys, this text presents a straightforward discussion of the law and its nuances and, in addition, utilizes actual court opinions. The language of these opinions is the language of lawyers and judges. It is a new language that students must come to understand in order to become effective managers and to keep pace with trends in employment law as they continue to evolve. To help ease the students' introduction to this specialized language, the opinions in the text have been edited. Discussion of extraneous issues and nonessential procedural points has been eliminated. Questions have been added at the end of each opinion to direct the students' attention to crucial facts, distinctions, and legal theories.

A selection of questions and case problems is presented at the end of each of the book's four parts. The questions are of the short-answer variety and are intended to highlight important concepts. The problems are derived from court and administrative agency decisions in real cases and offer students the opportunity to apply the legal principles set forth in the text to real-life situations. Citations at the end of each problem enable students with access to a law library to research how the problem was actually resolved.

I would like to express my appreciation to all those who have helped to make this book possible.

Suggestions for the improvement of this text will be cordially welcomed.

David P. Twomey
Boston College
Chestnut Hill,
Massachusetts

About the Author

David P. Twomey graduated from Boston College in 1962, earned his MBA at the University of Massachusetts at Amherst in 1963, and, after two years of business experience, entered Boston College Law School, where he earned his Juris Doctor degree in 1968.

While a law student, he began his teaching career serving as Lecturer in Finance and Marketing at Simmons College in Boston. He joined the faculty of the Boston College School of Management in 1968 as an assistant professor, was promoted to associate professor in 1971, was granted tenure in 1974, and was promoted to the rank of professor in 1978. Professor Twomey has written numerous books and articles on labor, employment, and business law topics. He has a special interest in curriculum development, serving three terms as chairman of his school's Educational Policy Committee. Professor Twomey was recently awarded the faculty Gold Key Award by one of the largest student organizations on campus for his "service and sacrifice to the Boston College Community." He is chairman of the Business Law Department.

Professor Twomey is a nationally known labor arbitrator, having been selected by the parties as arbitrator in numerous disputes throughout the country in the private and public sectors. He was recently appointed by the president of the United States to a Presidential Emergency Board whose reports formed the basis for new collective bargaining agreements between six railway unions and the nation's Class I railroads. He was elected to the National Academy of Arbitrators in 1979. Professor Twomey is a member of the Massachusetts, Florida, and federal bars. He lives in Quincy, Massachusetts, with his wife Veronica and their three children—Erin, David, and Kerry.

Contents

1 Fair Employment Practices: I

SECTION 1—INTRODUCTION

There are four major federal laws that regulate equal rights in employment. The Civil Rights Act of 1964, Title VII, as amended by the Equal Employment Opportunities Act of 1972, forbids employer and union discrimination based on race, color, religion, sex, or national origin. The Equal Pay Act of 1963 requires equal pay for men and women doing equal work. The Age Discrimination in Employment Act of 1967 as amended forbids discriminatory hiring practices against job applicants and employees over the age of 40. The Rehabilitation Act of 1973 protects persons with handicaps from discrimination by employers performing federal contract work.

Additionally, Executive Order 11246, which has the force and effect of a statute enacted by Congress, regulates contractors and subcontractors doing business with the federal government. This order forbids discrimination against minorities and women and in certain situations requires affirmative action to be taken to better employment opportunities for minorities and women.

This chapter and the two following chapters discuss the law of fair employment practices. Coverage includes the above statutes and executive order, the U.S. Constitution, and the court decisions construing them.

SECTION 2—TITLE VII AS AMENDED

The general purpose of Title VII of the Civil Rights Act of 1964 is the elimination of employer and union practices that discriminate against employees and job applicants on the basis of race, color, religion, sex, or national origin.

Prohibited Practices

Title VII forbids discrimination in hiring, terms or conditions of employment, union membership and representation, and in the referral of applicants by employment services. Title VII specifically forbids any employer to fail or refuse to hire, or to discharge or otherwise discriminate against, any individual with respect to compensation, terms, conditions, or privileges of employment or to limit, segregate, or classify employees in any way that would deprive or tend to deprive any individual of employment opportunity or otherwise adversely affect the individual's status as an employee due to race, color, religion, sex, or national origin.

A union is forbidden to exclude or expel from its membership or otherwise discriminate against any individual; to limit, segregate, or classify its membership; or to classify, fail, or refuse to refer for employment any individual in any way that would deprive or tend to deprive the individual of employment opportunities or would limit such employment opportunities or otherwise adversely affect the individual's status as an employee or as an applicant for employment because of race, color, religion, national origin, or sex. It is further unlawful for any employer or union to discriminate against an individual in any program established to provide apprenticeship or other training.[1]

The Equal Employment Opportunity Commission

Compliance with Title VII is achieved through the enforcement activities of the Equal Employment Opportunity Commission (EEOC). The Civil Rights Act of 1964, which created the EEOC, granted it the authority to investigate and conciliate grievances alleging racial, religious, national origin, or sex discrimination. Where there is a state or local agency with the power to act on allegations of discriminatory practices, the charging party must file the complaint with that agency. The charging party must then wait sixty days or until the termination of the state proceedings, whichever occurs first, before filing a charge with the EEOC. The commission then conducts an investigation to determine whether reasonable cause exists to believe that the charge is true. If such cause is found to exist, the EEOC attempts to remedy the unlawful practice through conciliation.

The EEOC handles its investigative and conciliation responsibilities through its Rapid Charge Processing System. (See Figure 1–1.) Under this system the charging party is interviewed by an equal opportunity specialist who counsels the charging party on EEOC procedures and assists in the writing of the charge. The charging party is asked to complete a questionnaire that asks for information such as the name, address, and telephone number of the employer; the name of the supervisor; the date that the alleged discrimination occurred; and the nature of the discrimination. After a charge is filed, the employer is notified and a fact-finding conference is convened. At this conference evidence is presented by both the charging party and the employer before the equal opportunity specialist who tries to work out a settlement, if appropriate, satisfactory to both sides.

---

[1]See Section 703 of the Civil Rights Act, printed in the Appendix of this textbook.

FIGURE 1–1   EEOC Rapid Charge Processing System

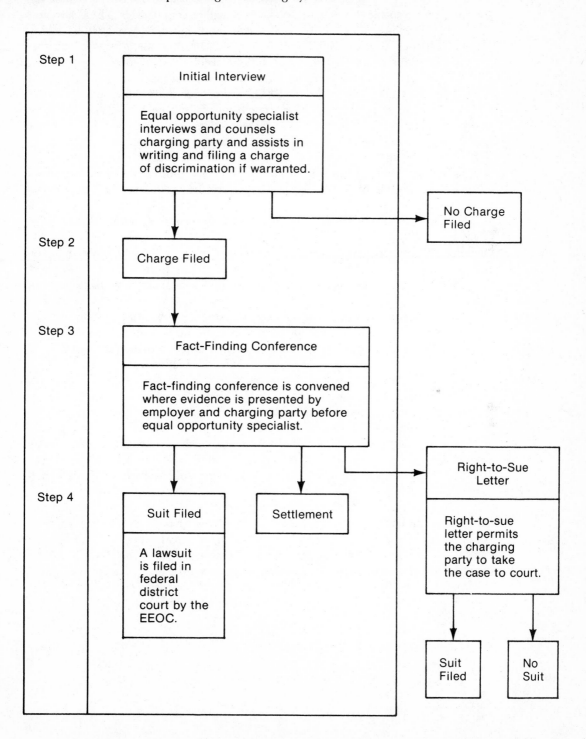

If the EEOC finds that there is reasonable cause to believe that discrimination has occurred and is unable to conciliate the charge, it will be considered by EEOC attorneys for possible litigation. If the EEOC decides to litigate the case, a lawsuit will be filed in federal district court. If the EEOC decides not to litigate the case, a right-to-sue letter will be issued that permits the charging party to take the case to court.

The Equal Employment Opportunities Act of 1972, which amended Title VII in several important areas, authorized the EEOC as described above to litigate court actions on behalf of the charging party when conciliation fails. The EEOC also was given authority under the 1972 amendments to bring class action suits and has exclusive authority to initiate and litigate allegations of a "pattern or practice" of discrimination. The 1972 act created the Office of General Counsel to the EEOC. The general counsel is appointed by the president with the advice and consent of the Senate. The general counsel is responsible for the conduct of litigation and the supervision of EEOC regional offices.

The amendments to Title VII significantly enlarge the class of persons under the act. State and local governments and their political subdivisions are now included in the act's definition of "persons," which makes them employers subject to the act.[2] The elimination of an exemption for educational institutions with respect to individuals whose work involves educational activities brings teachers and professional and nonprofessional staff members within the act's coverage. The amendments also lower from twenty-five to fifteen the number of employees required to bring their employer under the coverage of Title VII.[3] Labor unions with at least fifteen members are now subject to the law.[4] The inclusion within coverage of the act continues for all unions operating hiring halls and all employment agencies regardless of size.[5] Under the Presidential Civil Rights Reorganization Plan I of 1978, the EEOC was given responsibility formerly held by the Civil Service Commission for the handling of employment discrimination claims made by federal employees. Also under the 1978 plan, the EEOC took over from the Department of Labor the enforcement functions of the Equal Pay Act of 1963 and the Age Discrimination in Employment Act of 1967, as amended. Further, the EEOC is also responsible for administering Section 501 of the Rehabilitation Act of 1973, which prohibits the federal government, as an employer, from discriminating against handicapped persons.

The time limitation for filing charges with the EEOC is 180 days after the occurrence of the discriminatory act.[6] The time limit for filing charges is 300 days after the occurrence of the discriminatory act when the charging party is required to first file with a state or local agency.[7] After the conclusion of proceedings before the EEOC, the time limit for filing a civil lawsuit in a federal district court by an individual claiming a violation of Title VII is ninety days after receipt of a right-to-sue letter from the EEOC.[8] If an aggrieved individual does not meet the time limit of Title VII, the individual may

---

[2] 42 USC Section 701(a).
[3] 42 USC Section 701(b).
[4] 42 USC Section 701(e).
[5] 42 USC Section 701(e).
[6] 42 USC Section 701(e).
[7] 42 USC Section 706(e).
[8] 42 USC Section 706 (f)(1).

well lose the right to seek relief under the act. Limited exceptions exist where the time limits are considered "tolled" or suspended for equitable reasons. For example, in *Crown Corke Seal Co. v. Parker*[9] the Supreme Court decided that the ninety-day limitation period for filing a court action after receiving a right-to-sue notice from the EEOC was tolled because of the filing of a class action suit by others where Parker was a member of the class.

The remedial powers of federal courts deciding Title VII actions may include an injunction against the unlawful practice and the issuance of affirmative orders that may include reinstatement or the hiring of employees with or without back pay. However, the 1972 amendments limit back pay orders to a period of two years prior to the filing of the charge.[10]

Disparate Treatment and Disparate Impact Theories of Discrimination

The Supreme Court has created two legal theories under which a plaintiff may prove a case of unlawful employment discrimination: disparate treatment and disparate impact. (See Figure 1–2.) A *disparate treatment* claim exists where an employer treats some

FIGURE 1–2   Unlawful Discrimination Under Title VII

Preferential treatment in employment decisions on the basis of: Race Color Religion Sex National Origin	
DISPARATE TREATMENT THEORY	**DISPARATE IMPACT THEORY**
Nonneutral practice or Nonneutral application	Facially neutral practice and Neutral application
Requires proof of discriminatory motive	Does not require proof of discriminatory motive
	Requires proof of adverse effect on protected group and Employer is unable to show that practice is job related

---

[9]103 S. Ct. 2393 (1983). See also Zipes v. TWA, 455 U.S. 385 (1982), where the Supreme Court held that the filing period is not a jurisdictional prerequisite and is subject to equitable waiver, estoppel, and tolling.
[10]42 USC Section 706(g).

people less favorably than others because of their race, color, religion, sex, or national origin. Proof of the employer's discriminatory motive is critical in a disparate treatment case. A *disparate impact* claim exists where an employer's facially neutral employment practices, such as hiring or promotion examinations, which make no adverse reference to race, color, religion, sex, or national origin and are neutrally applied, have a significantly adverse or disparate impact on a protected group, *and* the employment practice in question is not shown to be job related by the employer. Under the disparate impact theory it is not a defense for an employer to demonstrate that the employer did not intend to discriminate. Highly technical rules exist concerning the burdens of proof and production for these two types of Title VII cases. Treatment of these rules is deferred to the next chapter so that the intervening text and materials may provide a foundation to better understand the basis and application of these rules.

SECTION 3—RACE AND COLOR

The legislative history of Title VII of the Civil Rights Act demonstrates that a primary purpose of the act is to provide fair employment opportunities for black Americans. The terms *race* and *color* as used in the act clearly apply to blacks, and thus the protections of the act are applied to blacks based on race or color. However, the word *race* as used in the act applies to all members of the four major racial groupings: white, black, native American, and Oriental. Native Americans can file charges and receive the protection of the act on the basis of national origin, race, or in some instances color. Orientals may file discrimination charges based on race, color, or in some instances national origin. Although not a common situation, whites are also protected against discrimination because of race and color. For example, two white professors at a predominately black university were successful in discrimination suits against the university where it was held that the university discriminated against them based on race and color in tenure decisions.[11]

Types of Charges

Approximately 80 percent of the employment discrimination charges filed with the EEOC allege discrimination on the basis of race and color.[12] These charges deal with allegations of failure to hire or failure to promote because of racial discrimination, as well as allegations of discipline and discharges because of discrimination based on race and color.

Employment Atmosphere

The EEOC has determined that an employer is responsible for maintaining a working environment free of racial intimidation. Under this determination, for example, the employer must not tolerate racial or ethnic jokes by employees.[13]

---

[11]Turgeon v. Howard University, 32 FEP 927 (D.C. DC 1983).
[12]Analysis of charges received, 1980–82, collected from the 15th, 16th, and 17th EEOC Annual Reports (issued 1981–83).
[13]EEOC Dec. 72–0957, 4 FEP 837 (1972).

Grooming Policy

The courts have upheld evenhanded employer grooming policies, even where it has been argued that the employer's policy infringed on black employees' cultural identification.[14]

Arrest and Conviction Inquiries

In *Gregory v. Litton Systems Inc.*,[15] the Ninth Circuit Court of Appeals upheld a district court's order for damages and attorneys' fees awarded pursuant to Title VII of the Civil Rights Act. It was stipulated that Litton's decision not to hire Gregory as a sheet metal worker was predicated upon Gregory's statement in Litton's employment questionnaire that he had been arrested fourteen times and not upon any consideration of convictions. The trial court held, and it was approved on appeal, that Litton's employment questionnaire, which required each applicant to reveal the applicant's arrest record, was discriminatory against black job seekers. It was held that Litton had not demonstrated that it had any reasonable business purpose for asking prospective employees about their arrest records.

The EEOC has taken the position that review of arrest records is irrelevant. The EEOC has also maintained that convictions cannot always be regarded as relevant to the ability of an individual to perform a job. The burden of proof is on the employer to justify inquiries into an applicant's arrest-conviction record. The EEOC has ruled that an employee's false answer to an inquiry regarding an arrest-conviction record did not justify discharge.[16] The EEOC relied on statistics showing that in some areas racial minorities are arrested and convicted substantially more frequently than Caucasians and found that "the foreseeable impact of respondent's arrest-conviction inquiry is that a substantially disproportionate percentage of those persons rejected or discharged because of the inquiry either because they answered in the affirmative, not at all, or falsely, will be Negro. In these circumstances the arrest-conviction policy is unlawful, absent a showing of business necessity."

The EEOC in this particular decision found that "business necessity" was not involved since the charging party had performed satisfactorily during an eighteen-month period of employment prior to the discovery of the false statement in the job application. Business necessity would clearly allow an employer to reject an applicant for a security-sensitive position based on the applicant's criminal record for theft.

Residency Requirements

In the *U.S. v. Villages of Elmwood Park and Melrose Park* case presented in this section, the court struck down the villages' respective three- and five-year residency requirements for consideration for police and fire fighting positions. These requirements were found

---

[14]In Brown v. D.C. Transit, 523 F.2d 725, 10 FEP (D.C. Cir. 1975), the U.S. Court of Appeals for the District of Columbia held that a grooming policy barring muttonchops and long sideburns did not deprive black bus drivers of their racial identity so as to constitute a Title VII violation.

[15]472 F.2d 631 (9th Cir. 1972).

[16]Decision of EEOC No. 72–1460, 1972 CCH Employment Practice Guide 6341.

to be artificial, arbitrary, and unnecessary barriers to employment that were unrelated to measuring job capabilities; thus they were prohibited by Title VII.

Specific Cases

Throughout the chapter specific cases will illustrate instances of racial discrimination as to initial hiring, transfer, promotions, and terminations. For example, in the *Griggs v. Duke Power* decision, which is presented in this section, an employer was found to have discriminated against blacks as to transfers and hiring by the use of tests and its educational requirement of a high school diploma, both of which were not job related.

● **Griggs v. Duke Power Company**
Supreme Court of the United States, 401 U.S. 424 (1971).

BURGER, C. J.
We granted the writ in this case to resolve the question whether an employer is prohibited by the Civil Rights Act of 1964, Title VII, from requiring a high school education or passing of a standardized general intelligence test as a condition of employment in or transfer to jobs when (a) neither standard is shown to be significantly related to successful job performance, (b) both requirements operate to disqualify Negroes at a substantially higher rate than white applicants, and (c) the jobs in question formerly had been filled only by white employees as part of a long-standing practice of giving preference to whites.

Congress provided, in Title VII of the Civil Rights Act of 1964, for class actions for enforcement of provisions of the Act and this proceeding was brought by a group of incumbent Negro employees against Duke Power Company. All the petitioners are employed at the Company's Dan River Steam Station, a power generating facility located at Draper, North Carolina. At the time this action was instituted, the Company had 95 employees at the Dan River Station, 14 of whom were Negroes; 13 of these are petitioners here.

The District Court found that prior to July 2, 1965, the effective date of the Civil Rights Act of 1964, the Company openly discriminated on the basis of race in the hiring and assigning of employees at its Dan River plant. The plant was organized into five operating departments: (1) Labor, (2) Coal Handling, (3) Operations, (4) Maintenance, and (5) Laboratory and Test. Negroes were employed only in the Labor Department where the highest paying jobs paid less than the lowest paying jobs in the other four "operating" departments in which only whites were employed. Promotions were normally made within each department on the basis of job seniority. Transferees into a department usually began in the lowest position.

In 1955 the Company instituted a policy of requiring a high school education for initial assignment to any department except Labor, and for transfer from the Coal Handling to any "inside" department (Operations, Maintenance, or Laboratory). When the Company abandoned its policy of restricting Negroes to the Labor Department in 1965, completion of high school also was made a prerequisite to transfer from Labor to any other department. From the time the high school requirement was instituted to the time of trial, however, white employees hired before the time of the high school education requirement continued to perform satisfactorily and achieve promotions in the "operating" departments. Findings on this score are not challenged.

The Company added a further requirement

for new employees on July 2, 1965, the date on which Title VII became effective. To qualify for placement in any but the Labor Department it became necessary to register satisfactory scores on two professionally prepared aptitude tests, as well as to have a high school education. Completion of high school alone continued to render employees eligible for transfer to the four desirable departments from which Negroes had been excluded if the incumbent had been employed prior to the time of the new requirement. In September 1965 the Company began to permit incumbent employees who lacked a high school education to qualify for transfer from Labor or Coal Handling to an "inside" job by passing two tests—the Wonderlic Personnel Test, which purports to measure general intelligence, and the Bennett Mechanical Comprehension Test. Neither was directed or intended to measure the ability to learn to perform a particular job or category of jobs. The requisite scores used for both initial hiring and transfer approximated the national median for high school graduates. *

The District Court had found that while the Company previously followed a policy of overt racial discrimination in a period prior to the Act, such conduct had ceased. The District Court also concluded that Title VII was intended to be prospective only and, consequently, the impact of prior inequities was beyond the reach of corrective action authorized by the Act.

The Court of Appeals was confronted with a question of first impression, as are we, concerning the meaning of Title VII. After careful analysis a majority of that court concluded that a subjective test of the employer's intent should govern, particularly in a close case, and that in this case there was no showing of a discriminatory purpose in the adoption of a diploma and test requirements. On this basis, the Court of Appeals concluded there was no violation of the Act.

The Court of Appeals reversed the District

Court in part, rejecting the holding that residual discrimination arising from prior employment practices was insulated from remedial action. The Court of Appeals noted, however, that the District Court was correct in its conclusion that there was no finding of a racial purpose or invidious intent in the adoption of a high school diploma requirement or general intelligence test and that these standards had been applied fairly to whites and Negroes alike. It held that, in the absence of a discriminatory purpose, use of such requirements was permitted by the Act. In doing so, the Court of Appeals rejected the claim that because these two requirements operated to render ineligible a markedly disproportionate number of Negroes, they were unlawful under Title VII unless shown to be job-related. We granted the writ on these claims.

The objective of Congress in the enactment of Title VII is plain from the language of the statute. It was to achieve equality of employment opportunities and remove barriers that have operated in the past to favor an identifiable group of white employees over other employees. Under the Act, practices, procedures, or tests neutral on their face, and even neutral in terms of intent, cannot be maintained if they operate to "freeze" the status quo of prior discriminatory employment practices.

The Court of Appeals' opinion, and the partial dissent, agreed that, on the record in the present case, "whites register far better on the Company's alternative requirements" than Negroes. ** This consequence would appear to be directly traceable to race. Basic intelligence must have the means of articulation to manifest itself fairly in a testing process. Because they are

---

*The test standards are thus more stringent than the high school requirement, since they would screen out approximately half of all high school graduates.

**In North Carolina, 1960 census statistics show that, while 34% of white males had completed high school, only 12% of Negro males had done so. U.S. Bureau of the Census of Population: 1960, Vol. 1, Characteristics of the Population, Part 35, Table 47.

Similarly, with respect to standardized tests, the EEOC in one case found that use of a battery of tests, including the Wonderlic and Bennett tests used by the Company in the instant case, resulted in 58% of whites passing the tests, as compared with only 6% of the blacks.

Negroes, petitioners have long received inferior education in segregated schools and this Court expressly recognizes these differences in *Gaston County v. United States*, 395 U.S. 285 (1969). There, because of the inferior education received by Negroes in North Carolina, this Court barred the institution of a literacy test for voter registration on the ground that the test would abridge the right to vote indirectly on account of race. Congress did not intend by Title VII, however, to guarantee a job to every person regardless of qualifications. In short, the Act does not command that any person be hired simply because he was formerly the subject of discrimination, or because he is a member of a minority group. Discriminatory preference for any group, minority or majority, is precisely and only what Congress has proscribed. What is required by Congress is the removal of artificial, arbitrary, and unnecessary barriers to employment when the barriers operate invidiously to discriminate on the basis of racial or other impermissible classification.

Congress has now provided that tests or criteria for employment or promotion may not provide equality of opportunity merely in the sense of the fabled offer of milk to the stork and the fox. On the contrary, Congress has now required that the posture and condition of the job-seeker be taken into account. It has—to resort again to the fable—provided that the vessel in which the milk is proffered be one all seekers can use. The Act proscribes not only overt discrimination but also practices that are fair in form, but discriminatory in operation. The touch-stone is business necessity. If an employment practice which operates to exclude Negroes cannot be shown to be related to job performance, the practice is prohibited.

On the record before us, neither the high school completion requirement nor the general intelligence test is shown to bear a demonstrable relationship to successful performance of the jobs for which it was used. Both were adopted, as the Court of Appeals noted, without meaningful study of their relationship to job-performance ability. Rather, a vice president of the Company testified, the requirements were instituted on the Company's judgment that they generally would improve the overall quality of the work force.

The evidence, however, shows that employees who have not completed high school or taken the tests have continued to perform satisfactorily and make progress in departments for which the high school and test criteria are now used. The promotion record of present employees who would not be able to meet the new criteria thus suggests the possibility that the requirements may not be needed even for the limited purpose of preserving the avowed policy of advancement within the Company. In the context of this case, it is unnecessary to reach the question whether testing requirements that take into account capability for the next succeeding position or related future promotion might be utilized upon a showing that such long-range requirements fulfill a genuine business need. In the present case the Company has made no such showing.

The Court of Appeals held that the Company had adopted the diploma and test requirements without any "intention to discriminate against Negro employees." We do not suggest that either the District Court or the Court of Appeals erred in examining the employer's intent; but good intent or absence of discriminatory intent does not redeem employment procedures or testing mechanisms that operate as "built-in headwinds" for minority groups and are unrelated to measuring job capability.

The Company's lack of discriminatory intent is suggested by special efforts to help the undereducated employees through Company financing of two-thirds the cost of tuition for high school training. But Congress directed the thrust of the Act to the *consequences* of employment practices, not simply the motivation. More than that, Congress has placed on the employer the burden of showing that any given requirement must have a manifest relationship to the employer in question.

The facts of this case demonstrate the inadequacy of broad and general testing devices as well as the infirmity of using diplomas or degrees as fixed measures of capability. History is filled with examples of men and women who rendered highly effective performance without the conventional badges of accomplishment in terms of certificates, diplomas, or degrees. Diplomas and tests are useful servants, but Congress has mandated the commonsense proposition that they are not to become masters of reality.

The Company contends that its general intelligence tests are specifically permitted by Section 703(h) of the Act. That section authorizes the use of "any professionally developed ability test" that is not "designed, intended *or used* to discriminate because of race. . . ." (Emphasis added.)

The Equal Employment Opportunity Commission, having enforcement responsibility, has issued guidelines interpreting Section 703(h) to permit only the use of job-related tests. The administrative interpretation of the Act by the enforcing agency is entitled to great deference. See *e.g., United States v. City of Chicago,* 400 U.S. 8 (1970). . . . Since the Act and its legislative history support the Commission's construction, this affords good reason to treat the guidelines as expressing the will of Congress. . . .

Nothing in the Act precludes the use of testing or measuring procedures, obviously they are useful. What Congress has forbidden is giving these devices and mechanisms controlling force unless they are demonstrably a reasonable measure of job performance. Congress has not commanded that the less qualified be preferred over the better qualified simply because of minority origins. Far from disparaging job qualifications as such, Congress has made such qualifications the controlling factor, so that race, religion, nationality, and sex become irrelevant. What Congress has commanded is that any tests used must measure the person for the job and not the person in the abstract.

The judgment of the Court of Appeals is, as to that portion of the judgment appealed from, reversed.

CASE QUESTIONS

1. What is the question before the Supreme Court?
2. What was the objective of Congress in the enactment of Title VII?
3. Would the Court order the case against the employer to be dismissed if it found that the employer had adopted the diploma and test requirements without any intention to discriminate against minority employees?
4. As a result of the *Griggs* decision, may employers insist that both minority and white job applicants meet the applicable job qualifications by the use of testing or measuring procedures?

U.S. v. Villages of Elmwood Park and Melrose Park
United States District Court, Illinois, 43 FEP 995 (1987).

[These actions were filed by the United States in December 1985 alleging a pattern or practice of unlawful discrimination in employment against black persons by the villages of Elmwood Park and Melrose Park in violation of Title VII of the Civil Rights Act of 1964. The United States moved for summary judgment on the issues of liability and prospective relief. The villages of Elmwood Park and Melrose Park are near the western boundary of the city of Chicago and are located within Cook County. According to the 1980 census, the labor force for Cook County is 20.7 percent black and for the Chicago standard metropolitan statistical area it is 16.2 percent black. No blacks live in Elmwood Park and twenty-four blacks live in Melrose Park. Both villages have a residency requirement of at least three years for police and fire fighter applicants. The purposes of the require-

ment were said to be to "help its own" in granting employment opportunities and to maintain pride in the community through hiring individuals who live there. Most recruiting is done on a word-of-mouth basis.]

MARSHALL, D. J.

. . . In *Griggs v. Duke Power Co.*, 401 U.S. 424, 431 (1971) the Supreme Court ruled that Title VII of the Civil Rights Act of 1964, as amended, "proscribes not only overt discrimination, but also practices that are fair in form, but discriminatory in operation." Thus, employment practices that are shown to have a discriminatory impact on a group protected under Title VII, notwithstanding an absence of discriminatory intent, are prohibited unless shown to have a "manifest relationship to the employment in question." *Id.* at 432.

As the Court went on to say in *Griggs*, "Good intent or absence of discriminatory intent does not redeem employment practices . . . which operate as 'built-in headwinds' for minority groups and are unrelated to measuring job capability." . . .

In this case, the undisputed facts show that the practices of Elmwood Park and Melrose Park have had an overwhelmingly discriminatory impact. Elmwood Park has no black persons in its resident civilian labor force. Melrose Park has 24 out of 11,000 persons. Their durational residence requirements for police officer and firefighter applicants exclude all black persons residing in Cook County and the metropolitan statistical area from employment in those categories in Elmwood Park and Melrose Park. The "philosophy" of the defendants to favor resident applicants over non-resident applicants for all other positions similarly disfavors all black persons in [the] labor market from employment. These practices are precisely the kind of "artificial, arbitrary and unnecessary barriers" which are "unrelated to measuring job capability" that congress prohibited in enacting Title VII. *Griggs v. Duke Power Co.*, supra, at 431, 432. The effect of these durational residency requirements and

the "philosophy" of favoring resident applicants over non-resident applicants reduces the proportion of blacks in the relevant labor force from approximately 13% and 18% (the percentages of black persons employed privately in the communities) to zero. Thus, all black persons are effectively barred from consideration for employment by the defendants. Unless these practices are necessary to the efficient operation of the defendants, they are unlawful. None of the reasons advanced by the defendants validate the requirements. Both defendants seek to help "our own". But helping "our own" only exacerbates the situation when all of "our own" are white. *Local 53 Asbestos Workers v. Vogler*, 407 F.2d 1047 (5th Cir. 1969).

"Pride in the community" is advanced as a reason. Perhaps there is a modicum of justification which requires residency for incumbent employees, i.e., after employment is effected, but we are at a loss to comprehend community pride as a valid condition precedent to employment. We note that there is no claim that a resident could perform the job more efficiently.

In addition to their use of durational residence requirements for police and firefighter applicants and their preferences for residence for all other village jobs, the defendants use "word of mouth" as the sole method of recruiting applicants for municipal vacancies. This is an additional barrier to black employment. It appears that there are no blacks living in Elmwood Park and only a handful in Melrose Park. In these circumstances, local networking will not convey information of job opportunities to non-whites. A word of mouth recruitment system limits information about job openings to the friends and relatives of incumbent employees and given the all white nature of the defendants' work forces, disproportionately deprives qualified black applicants of the information they need to apply for village jobs.

In short, the employment requirements and techniques used by the defendant Villages have had the effect of excluding all blacks from consideration for employment and actual employment in the two communities. The justifications advanced by defendants for these patently discriminatory employment practices are no justification at all. Indeed, if anything, they call into question the good faith of the defendants. The United States of America is entitled to summary judgment under the disparate impact analysis on the issues of liability and prospective relief. . . .

It is so ordered.

CASE QUESTIONS

1. Because of the residency requirements, what percentage of blacks were effectively barred from consideration for employment by the villages?
2. Assess the fairness of the villages' recruiting procedures.
3. Did the court agree that the villages had presented valid justification for their residency requirements?

SECTION 4—RELIGION

Under Section 701(j) employers have a duty to accommodate their employees' or prospective employees' religious practices. Under Section 702 religious organizations are exempt from Title VII prohibitions against discrimination on the basis of religion.

Employer's Duty to Accommodate

The 1972 amendments added to Title VII a definition of *religion* in Section 701(j), which provides:

> The term "religion" includes all aspects of religious observance and practice, as well as belief, unless an employer demonstrates that he is unable to reasonably accommodate to an employee's or prospective employee's religious observance or practice without undue hardship on the conduct of the employer's business.

Most cases involving allegations of religious discrimination revolve around the determination of whether an employer has made reasonable efforts to accommodate its employees' religious beliefs. The 1972 definition includes all aspects of religious observance, practice, and belief, so as to require employers to make reasonable accommodations for employees whose religion may include observances, practices, and beliefs, such as Friday evening and Saturday religious observances, that differ from the employer's requirements regarding schedules or other business-related employment conditions. Failure to make accommodation is unlawful unless an employer can demonstrate that it cannot reasonably accommodate such beliefs, practices, or observances without undue hardship in the conduct of its business. The Supreme Court considered such an issue in *Trans World Airlines, Inc. v. Hardinson.*[17] The Court of Appeals for the Eighth Circuit had ruled that TWA had not satisfied its duty to accommodate Hardinson's religious views, which kept him from working Saturdays. Specifically, the court of appeals found that TWA could have permitted Hardinson to work a four-day week despite the fact that this would have caused shop functions to suffer unless TWA had breached its seniority system or incurred overtime expense by keeping someone on the job. The Supreme Court reversed, holding that TWA made reasonable efforts to accommodate Hardinson, and to force it to comply with the court of appeals ruling would have created an undue hardship on TWA. Under *Hardinson* the employer and union need not violate

---

[17]432 U.S. 63 (1977).

a seniority provision of a valid collective bargaining agreement, the employer has no obligation to impose undesirable shifts on nonreligious employees, and the employer has no obligation to call in substitute workers if such accommodation would require more than *de minimis* cost.

Where an employer is called upon to make reasonable accommodations for the religious practice of an employee, both the employer and the employee may make proposals to achieve this accommodation. In *Ansonia Board of Education v. Philbrick*[18] Ronald Philbrick, a teacher, sued his school board because the school board's accommodation to his need to take six days off each school year for the holy days of his religion was to allow him to take three paid religious observance days granted him under the teachers' collective bargaining contract and three unpaid leave days. He had proposed as the appropriate accommodation that he take the three paid religious leave days plus three paid personal business leave days or that he pay the cost of a substitute teacher for the three days at $30 per day thus enabling him to receive his regular pay of $130 for each of these days. The Second Circuit agreed with Philbrick, holding that Title VII requires the employer to accept the employee's proposal unless it causes undue hardship to the employer's business. The Supreme Court held that the Second Circuit was in error and that the employer meets its obligation under Section 701(j) when it demonstrates that it has offered a reasonable accommodation to the employee which removes the conflict between the employment requirement and the religious practices of the individual. The extent of the undue hardship to the employer's business is only an issue when the employer claims it is unable to offer a reasonable accommodation without hardship.

Religious Organization Exemption

Section 702 of Title VII permits religious societies to grant hiring preferences in favor of members of their religion. The *Feldstein v. The Christian Science Monitor* decision, presented in this section, is an example of the application of Section 702. Section 702 provides in pertinent part that:

> This title shall not apply . . . to a religious corporation, association, educational institution, or society with respect to the employment of individuals of a particular religion to perform work connected with the carrying on by such corporation, association, educational institution, or society of its activities.

In *Mormon Church v. Amos*, presented in this section, the Supreme Court upheld the constitutionality of the Section 702 exemption, holding that Section 702 was not in violation of the Establishment Clause of the First Amendment. Thus the Mormon church was allowed to terminate a building engineer, who had worked at its nonprofit gymnasium for sixteen years, because he failed to maintain his qualifications for church membership. The decision to terminate was made on the basis of religion by the religious organization and was thus exempted from the Title VII prohibition against religious discrimination.

Section 703(e)(2) provides an exemption for educational institutions to hire employees of a particular religion if the institution is owned, controlled, or managed by a particular religious society. The exemption is a broad one and is not restricted to the religious activities of the institution.

---

[18]42 FEP 359 (1986).

Feldstein v. The Christian Science Monitor
United States District Court, 30 FEP 1842 (E.D. Mass. 1983).

[In January 1979 Mark Feldstein inquired at the Christian Science Monitor *whether there would be job openings on its news reporting staff upon his graduation from college in June. At that time, Feldstein was a college student interested in pursuing a career in journalism. Upon making his inquiry, Feldstein was instructed to contact the personnel department of the church, where he was asked if he was a member of the Christian Science church. He indicated that he was not and was informed that he would stand little, if any, chance of becoming employed by the* Monitor *as a reporter, as only Christian Scientists were hired except in the rare circumstance that no qualified member of the church was available. Feldstein nevertheless requested and obtained an employment application for a reporter's position. The employment application, used for positions throughout the church, contained several questions relating to religious practice, including "Are you . . . a member of the Mother Church? A branch Church member? Class taught?"; "Are you free from the use of liquor, tobacco, drugs, medicine?"; "Do you subscribe to the Christian Science periodicals?"; and "Are you a daily student of the lesson-sermon?" Inquiries were also directed to the applicant's present and past religious affiliation. References were sought from "two Christian Scientists who can comment on your character and your practice of Christian Science." The application closed with the following statement:*

The First Church of Christ, Scientist, may by law apply the test of religious qualifications to its employment policies. Those who meet this requirement and are otherwise qualified will be hired, promoted, and transferred without regard to their race, national origin, sex, color, or age.

Feldstein filed his application with the church in March 1979, together with a copy of his curriculum vitae, letters of recommendation, and a portfolio of newspaper articles that he had written.

In April he was notified by a church personnel representative that his application for employment as a reporter had been rejected. Feldstein alleged that his application for employment was not given a full consideration because he was not a Christian Scientist.]

MAZZONE, D. J.

Title VII of the Civil Rights Act of 1964 was originally passed as an expression of Congress' laudable intention to eliminate all forms of unjustified discrimination in employment, whether such discrimination be based on race, color, religion, sex, or national origin. This posed a sharp question under the Establishment Clause of the First Amendment to the United States Constitution as to whether Congress could properly regulate the employment practices, and specifically the preference of co-religionists, of religious organizations in matters related to their religious activities. As a result, the original Title VII contained an exemption from the operation of Title VII's proscriptions with respect to the employment of co-religionists to perform work related to the employer's religious activity. Church-affiliated educational institutions were also permitted to hire on the basis of religion.

In 1972, a number of amendments to Title VII were proposed in an effort to alter and expand the existing exemption for religious organizations. . . .

. . . Title VII was amended to eliminate the qualification that only religious activities of religious organizations would be exempt from suit based on religious discrimination. Section 702 provides, as a result of the 1972 amendment:

This subchapter shall not apply . . . to a religious corporation, association, educational institution, or society with respect to the employment of individuals of a particular religion to perform work connected with the carrying on by such corporation, association, educational institution or society of its activities.

It is clear that the disposition of this matter turns on two key issues: first, whether the Monitor is a religious activity of a religious organization and therefore within the limited exemption provided by Congress in the Civil Rights Act of 1964; and second, if it is not a religious activity of a religious organization, whether the 1972 amendment to Title VII excluding from the scope of Title VII *all* activities of whatever nature of a religious organization is constitutional in light of the requirements of the Free Exercise and Establishment Clauses of the First Amendment.

It is self-evident, as well as uncontested, that the First Church of Christ, Scientist is a religious organization. The status of the Christian Science Publishing Society and of the Monitor is less clear. The plaintiff has argued that the Monitor is a highly regarded and impartial newspaper carrying news stories, articles, features, columns and editorials that are secular in nature and content. The defendants take exception to this characterization of the Monitor and make reference to a number of facts in support of their position that the newspaper is a religious activity of a religious organization and therefore exempt from regulation under Title VII. . . .

The deed of trust of the Publishing Society declares as its purpose "more effectually promoting and extending the religion of Christian Science." . . .

The plaintiff does not contest that the Christian Science Church is intimately involved with the management, the day-to-day operations and the financial affairs of the Monitor. Paragraph 5 of his complaint states in part:

Defendant First Church of Christ, Scientist is a nonincorporated religious association. . . . Control of the Church is vested in a Board of Directors who serve in accordance with terms set out in the Church Manual. *Pursuant to the* Church Manual, the Board has ultimate authority for and responsibility over the policy and operations of the Monitor. . . .

. . . A religious activity of a religious organization does not lose that special status merely because it holds some interest for persons not members of the faith, or occupies a position of

respect in the secular world at large. Though the "wall between church and state" is not absolute, I am nevertheless unwilling to involve the federal court in what is ultimately an internal administrative matter of a religious activity.

While fully crediting the plaintiff's statements that the Monitor holds itself out as an objective and unbiased reporter of world news and events, I cannot ignore the close and significant relationship existing between the Christian Science Church, the Publishing Society and the Monitor; or the declared purpose, both at the time of its founding and until the present, of the Monitor to promulgate and advance the tenets of Christian Science. I find the conclusion inescapable that the Monitor is itself a religious activity of a religious organization, albeit one with a recognized position and an established reputation in the secular community.

Having concluded that the Monitor is a religious activity of a religious organization, I find that the constitutionality of that part of Section 702 of Title VII, 42 U.S.C. § 2000e-1, that extends the exemption provided for religious organizations, to *all* their activities, secular and religious, is simply not here implicated.

Because I find that the Monitor is a religious activity of a religious organization, I find that it is permissible for the Monitor to apply a test of religious affiliation to candidates for employment. Therefore, I find as a matter of law that the defendants have not committed an unlawful employment practice under the Civil Rights Act of 1964. The defendants' motion for summary judgment is granted and the complaint is dismissed.

So ordered.

CASE QUESTIONS

1. Does the *Christian Science Monitor* violate Title VII by giving preference to Christian Scientists when hiring reporters for the newspaper?
2. Does Section 702 of Title VII allow religious societies to hire coreligionists for secular activities as opposed to religious activities?

Mormon Church v. Amos

Supreme Court of the United States, 107 S. Ct. 2862 (1987).

[*Mayson worked for sixteen years as a building engineer at the Mormon church's Deseret Gymnasium in Salt Lake City. He was discharged from this job because he failed to qualify for a "temple recommend," which is only issued to individuals observing the church's standards, such as regular church attendance; tithing; and abstinence from coffee, alcohol, and tobacco. A class action suit was brought on behalf of Mayson, Amos, and others claiming that Section 702 was in violation of the Establishment Clause of the First Amendment when construed to allow religious employers to discriminate on religious grounds in hiring and tenure for nonreligious jobs. The district court held that Section 702 was unconstitutional as applied to secular activities, and it reinstated Mayson with back pay.*]

WHITE, J.

This Court has long recognized that the government may (and sometimes must) accommodate religious practices and that it may do so without violating the Establishment Clause. It is well established, too, that "[t]he limits of permissible state accommodation to religion are by no means co-extensive with the noninterference mandated by the Free Exercise Clause." There is ample room under the Establishment Clause for "benevolent neutrality which will permit religious exercise to exist without sponsorship and without interference." At some point, accommodation may devolve into "an unlawful fostering of religion," but this is not such a case, in our view. . . .

Lemon [*v. Kurtzman*, 403 U.S. 602 (1971),] requires first that the law at issue serve a "secular legislative purpose." This does not mean that the law's purpose must be unrelated to religion—that would amount to a requirement "that the government show a callous indifference to religious groups," and the Establishment Clause has never been so interpreted. Rather, *Lemon's* "purpose" requirement aims at preventing the relevant governmental decisionmaker—in this case, Congress—from abandoning neutrality and acting with the intent of promoting a particular point of view in religious matters. . . .

After a detailed examination of the legislative history of the 1972 amendment, the District Court concluded that Congress' purpose was to minimize governmental "interfer[ence] with the decision-making process in religions." We agree with the District Court that this purpose does not violate the Establishment Clause.

The second requirement under *Lemon* is that the law in question have "a principal or primary effect . . . that neither advances nor inhibits religion." Undoubtedly, religious organizations are better able now to advance their purposes than they were prior to the 1972 amendment to § 702. But religious groups have been better able to advance their purposes on account of many laws that have passed constitutional muster: for example, the property tax exemption at issue in *Walz v. Tax Comm'n, supra,* or the loans of school books to school children, including parochial school students, upheld in *Board of Education v. Allen,* 392 U.S. 236 (1968). A law is not unconstitutional simply because it *allows* churches to advance religion, which is their very purpose. For a law to have forbidden "effects" under *Lemon,* it must be fair to say that the *government itself* has advanced religion through its own activities and influence. As the Court observed in *Walz,* "[F]or the men who wrote the Religion Clauses of the First Amendment the 'establishment' of a religion connoted sponsorship, financial support, and active involvement of the sovereign in religious activity." . . .

Appellees argue that § 702 offends equal protection principles by giving less protection to the employees of religious employers than to the employees of secular employers. Appellees rely on *Larson v. Valente*, 456 U.S. 228, 246 (1982), for the proposition that a law drawing distinctions on religious grounds must be strictly scrutinized. But *Larson* indicates that laws discriminating *among* religions are subject to strict scrutiny, *ibid.*, and that laws "affording a uniform benefit to *all* religions" should be analyzed under *Lemon*, 456 U.S., at 252. In a case such as this, where a statute is neutral on its face and motivated by a permissible purpose of limiting governmental interference with the exercise of religion, we see no justification for applying strict scrutiny to a statute that passes the *Lemon* test. The proper inquiry is whether Congress has chosen a rational classification to further a legitimate end. We have already indicated that Congress acted with a legitimate purpose in expanding the § 702 exemption to cover all activities of religious employers. To dispose of appellees' Equal Protection argument, it suffices to hold—as we now do—that as applied to the nonprofit activities of religious employers, § 702 is rationally related to the legitimate purpose of alleviating significant governmental interference with the ability of religious organizations to define and carry out their religious missions.

It cannot be seriously contended that § 702 impermissibly entangles church and state; the statute effectuates a more complete separation of the two and avoids the kind of intrusive inquiry into religious belief that the District Court engaged in in this case. . . .

The judgment of the District Court is reversed, and the case is remanded for further proceedings consistent with this opinion.

It is so ordered.

CASE QUESTIONS

1. Why was Mayson fired from his job?
2. Does Section 702 allow a religious organization to refuse to hire or to continue in employment individuals that are not members of the religious organization where the positions involved are nonreligious jobs?
3. Why did Congress enact Section 702?

SECTION 5—SEX

The amendment adding the word *sex* to Section 703 of Title VII of the Civil Rights Act was adopted one day before the House passed the act. It was added without legislative hearings and with little debate.[19] As a result, the courts do not have the benefit of a fully developed legislative history to be referred to in interpreting cases relating to sex discrimination. Courts therefore apply the plain and ordinary meaning of the word *sex*, and under such application employers who discriminate against female or male employees because of their sex are held to be in violation of Title VII.

Height, Weight, and Physical Ability Requirements

Under the *Griggs v. Duke Power* decision, an employer must be ready to demonstrate that criteria used to make an employment decision that has a disparate impact on women,

---

[19]The amendment adding the word *sex* was offered by Congressman Howard Smith of Virginia, then chairman of the Rules Committee, who was an opponent of Title VII. The amendment was adopted by a majority, most of whom later voted against Title VII. Apparently it was thought that the amendment adding the word *sex* might kill the entire legislation.

such as minimum height and weight requirements, are in fact job-related. All candidates for a position requiring physical strength must be given an opportunity to demonstrate their capability to perform the work. Women cannot be precluded from consideration just because they have not traditionally performed such work. In *Boyd v. Ozark Airlines*[20] a woman contended that the airline's minimum height requirement for pilots discriminated against her on the basis of sex. The evidence established that the airline's 5-foot-7-inch minimum height requirement had a disparate impact on women. While the court agreed that minimum height requirements for the position of pilot are valid, it held that the airline's requirements were excessive and ordered the airline's height requirements lowered to 5 feet 5 inches.

Pregnancy-Related Benefits

Title VII arguments concerning the matters of disability due to pregnancy and loss of competitive seniority due to pregnancy have been considered by the United States Supreme Court. In the landmark case of *General Electric v. Gilbert*,[21] the Supreme Court held that a disability plan which did not cover pregnancy was not violative of Title VII absent any indication that the exclusion of pregnancy benefits was a pretext for discriminating against women. However, in *Nashville Gas v. Satty*[22] the Court held that a company policy which deprived female workers of their competitive seniority upon their return from maternity leave was violative of Title VII. In distinguishing *General Electric v. Gilbert*, the Court stated: "Here, by comparison, the [employer] has not merely refused to extend to women a benefit that men cannot and do not receive, but has imposed on women a substantial burden that men need not suffer."

In 1978 Title VII was amended by adding to Section 701 a new subsection (k), which clarified that the prohibitions against sex discrimination in the act include discrimination in employment based on pregnancy, childbirth, or related medical conditions. The intent of the amendment was to reverse the *Gilbert* decision that disability plans that exclude pregnancy do not discriminate on the basis of sex in violation of the act. The amendment prevents employers from treating pregnancy, childbirth, and related medical conditions in a manner different from the treatment of other disabilities. Thus women disabled due to pregnancy, childbirth, or other related medical conditions must be provided with the same benefits as other disabled workers. This includes temporary and long-term disability insurance, sick leave, and other forms of employee benefit programs. An employer who does not provide disability benefits or paid sick leave to other employees is not required to provide them for pregnant workers. Under the 1978 law benefits do not have to be provided for abortion except where it is necessary to preserve the life of the mother or where medical complications have arisen from an abortion.[23]

---

[20]419 F. Supp. 1061 (E.D. Mo. 1976).
[21]423 U.S. 822 (1976).
[22]434 U.S. 136 (1977).
[23]The Pregnancy Disability Act of 1978, Pub. L. 95–522 (1978).

In *Newport News Shipbuilding and Dry Dock Co. v. EEOC*[24] the employer amended its health insurance plan after the Pregnancy Disability Act of 1978 to provide for benefits for pregnancy-related conditions for its female employees, with the plan providing for less extensive benefits for the wives of male employees. The Supreme Court held that such a plan discriminated against married male employees since their benefits package was less than that provided to married female employees, which was contrary to the Pregnancy Disability Act. The dissent argued that the Pregnancy Disability Act plainly speaks of female employees affected by pregnancy and says nothing about spouses of male employees.

Pension-Related Benefits

In the case of pension plans, employers have sometimes required their female employees to pay more into pension plan funds because, as a class, women outlive men and therefore receive benefits for a longer period of time. This practice was held to be in violation of Title VII by the Supreme Court in *City of Los Angeles v. Manhart*.[25] The Court reasoned that although the generalization that women live longer than men was true, it was an insufficient reason for burdening those women to whom the generalization did not apply. Since it could not be known to whom the generalization did apply while an employee was alive, it could not be used to justify requiring larger payment from any female employee.

In *Arizona Annuity Plans v. Norris*[26] the Supreme Court followed its *Manhart* ruling in holding that the pension annuity plans administered for employees of the state of Arizona, which pay a woman lower monthly retirement benefits than a man who has made the same contribution, were in violation of Title VII, constituting discrimination on the basis of sex.

Homosexuals and Transsexuals

The EEOC and the courts have uniformly held that Title VII does not prohibit employment discrimination against homosexuals.[27] The EEOC and the courts have determined that the word *sex* as used in Title VII means a person's gender and not the person's sexual orientation.

The courts have also uniformly held that Title VII's ban on sex discrimination in employment practices does not encompass discrimination against transsexuals. This was the holding of the U.S. Court of Appeals for the Eighth Circuit in *Sommers v. Budget Marketing*. The *Sommers* decision, which contains a discussion of the meaning and application of the word *sex* as used in Title VII, is presented in this section.

---

[24]103 S. Ct. 2622 (1983).
[25]435 U.S. 702 (1978).
[26]103 S. Ct. 3492 (1983).
[27]Blum v. Gulf Oil Corp., 597 F.2d 936, 20 FEP 108 (5th Cir. 1979).

Audra Sommers, a/k/a Timothy K. Cornish v. Budget Marketing Inc.
United States Court of Appeals, Eighth Circuit, 667 F.2d 748 (1982).

PER CURIAM:

Sommers claims to be "female with the anatomical body of a male."* Inasmuch as Sommers refers to herself in the feminine gender, this court will likewise do so. As Audra Sommers, appellant was hired by Budget on April 22, 1980, to perform clerical duties. On April 24, 1980, Sommers's employment was terminated. Budget alleged Sommers was dismissed because she misrepresented herself as an anatomical female when she applied for the job. It further alleged that the misrepresentation led to a disruption of the company's work routine in that a number of female employees indicated they would quit if Sommers were permitted to use the restroom facilities assigned to female personnel. After exhausting administrative remedies, Sommers brought action against Budget, alleging that she had been discharged on the basis of sex in violation of Title VII of the Civil Rights Act of 1964. . . .

. . . Sommers's amended complaint claimed she had been discriminated against because of her status as a female, that is, a female with the anatomical body of a male, and further stated that sexual conversion surgery had not been performed. Sommers nonetheless argued that the court should not be bound by the plain meaning of the term "sex" under Title VII as connoting either male or female gender, but should instead expand the coverage of the Act to protect individuals such as herself who are psychologically female, albeit biologically male. In response,

Budget argued that Title VII provided no relief for a person like Sommers.

. . . The court entered summary judgment in favor of Budget. Sommers contends on this appeal that the district court erred in concluding that Title VII coverage did not extend to those discriminated against because of their transsexuality and therefore erred in awarding summary judgment to Budget. We disagree.

. . . Although this circuit has not previously considered the issue raised on this appeal, we are in agreement with the district court that for the purposes of Title VII the plain meaning must be ascribed to the term "sex" in absence of clear congressional intent to do otherwise. Furthermore, the legislative history does not show any intention to include transsexualism in Title VII. The amendment adding the word "sex" to the Civil Rights Act was adopted one day before the House passed the Act without prior legislative hearing and little debate. It is, however, generally recognized that the major thrust of the "sex" amendment was towards providing equal opportunities for women.

Also, proposals to amend the Civil Rights Act to prohibit discrimination on the basis of "sexual preference" have been defeated. Three such bills were presented to the 94th Congress and seven were presented to the 95th Congress. Sommers's claim is not one dealing with discrimination on the basis of sexual preference. Nevertheless, the fact that the proposals were defeated indicates that the word "sex" in Title VII is to be given its traditional definition, rather than an expansive interpretation. Because Congress has not shown an intention to protect transsexuals, we hold that discrimination based on one's transsexualism does not fall within the protective purview of the Act.

We are not unmindful of the problem Sommers faces. On the other hand, Budget faces a

---

*A medical affidavit submitted by Sommers stated that a psychological female with anatomical features of a male is one type of transsexual but that transsexualism is not voluntarily assumed and is not a matter of sexual preference. A transsexual has been described as an individual who is mentally one sex but physically of the other. Annot., 63 A.L.R.3d 1199, n. 1 (1975), or as one born with the anatomical genitalia of one sex but whose self-identity is of the other sex. Annot., 78 A.L.R.3d 19, 54 (1977).

problem in protecting the privacy interests of its female employees. According to affidavits submitted to the district court, even medical experts disagree as to whether Sommers is properly classified as male or female. The appropriate remedy is not immediately apparent to this court. Should Budget allow Sommers to use the female restroom, the male restroom, or one for Sommers's own use?

Perhaps some reasonable accommodation could be worked out between the parties. The issue before this court is not whether such an accommodation can be reached. Rather, the issue is whether Congress intended Title VII of the Civil Rights Act to protect transsexuals from discrimination. As explained above, we hold that such discrimination is not within the ambit of the Act.

The decision of the district court granting summary judgment in favor of the employer is affirmed.

CASE QUESTIONS

1. What did Sommers claim?
2. Does the Title VII ban on sex discrimination encompass discrimination based on transsexualism?

SECTION 6—EMPLOYER LIABILITY FOR SEXUAL HARASSMENT

In the mid-1970s the first sexual harassment cases appeared. The early cases generally held that actions taken by an employer against an employee were not based on the employee's sex but rather on whether the employee would acquiesce to sexual demands made by an employer and as such did not fall under the protection of Title VII.[28] Public awareness of the extensive problems relating to sexual harassment in the workplace became a major media issue in the late 1970s. The trend of the early court decisions was quickly reversed, and sexual harassment became generally recognized by the courts as a form of sex discrimination prohibited by Title VII.[29] On November 10, 1980, the EEOC issued *Sex Discrimination Guidelines* specifically dealing with the problem of sexual harassment. The guidelines define sexual harassment as follows:

> Unwelcome sexual advances, requests for sexual favors, and other verbal or physical conduct of a sexual nature constitute sexual harassment when (1) submission to such conduct is made either explicitly or implicitly a term or condition of an individual's employment, (2) submission to or rejection of such conduct by an individual is used as a basis for employment decisions affecting such individual, or (3) such conduct has the purpose or effect of unreasonably interfering with an individual's work performance or creating an intimidating, hostile, or offensive working environment.

The guidelines were immensely helpful in publicizing the problems relating to sexual harassment and in informing employers of their obligations. The guidelines are not administrative "regulations," and courts are not bound by the EEOC guidelines. However, the Supreme Court in *Griggs v. Duke Power Company* declared that EEOC guidelines should be shown "great deference" by the courts.[30] The courts then, and not

---

[28]In Tompkins v. Public Serv. Elec. & Gas Co., 422 F. Supp. 553 (D. N.J. 1976), the court held that sexual harassment did not constitute sexual discrimination under Title VII. So also, the same result was reached in Corne v. Bausch and Lomb, Inc., 390 F. Supp. 161 (D. Ariz. 1975), when a male supervisor made sexual advances toward female employees.

[29]See, e.g., Gerber v. Saxon Bus. Prod., Inc., 552 F.2d 1032 (4th Cir. 1977). See also Barnes v. Costle, 561 F.2d 983 (D.C. Cir. 1977).

[30]Griggs v. Duke Power Company, 401 U.S. 424, 433–434 (1971) and Bushey v. N.Y. Civ. Serv. Comm'n., 733 F.2d 220 at 225 (2nd Cir. 1984).

the EEOC, have the final voice in settling the legal issues involving sexual harassment in the workplace.[31]

Employer Liability for Sexual Harassment by Supervisors

There are two broad classifications of sexual harassment involving supervisors: quid pro quo cases and hostile working environment cases. Each type is discussed below.

1. *Quid pro quo sexual harassment.* Quid pro quo cases of sexual harassment are those cases in which sexual favors are either explicitly or implicitly required as a condition of employment in return for tangible job benefits such as obtaining employment, continued employment, promotion, a raise, or a favorable job evaluation.

   The leading case of quid pro quo harassment involved Paulette Barnes who had her job terminated after she refused her supervisor's sexual advances. The Court of Appeals for the District of Columbia Circuit, in *Barnes v. Costle*,[32] heard the argument made by the employer that Barnes was pursuing an improper legal theory. The employer argued that the action based on sex discrimination was improper since Barnes's supervisor terminated her job because she had refused sexual advances, not because she was a woman. The court responded:

   > But for her womanhood . . . [Barnes's] participation in sexual activity would never have been solicited. To say, then, that she was victimized in her employment simply because she declined the invitation is to ignore the asserted fact that she was invited only because she was a woman subordinate to the inviter in the hierarchy of agency personnel.[33]

   The court concluded that sex discrimination within the meaning of Title VII is not confined to disparate treatment solely limited to gender. Also, the court held that the employer was chargeable with the Title VII violations of its supervisor under the facts before it.

   It is now well settled that sexual harassment of an employee by a supervisor that affects tangible job benefits is sex discrimination in violation of Title VII, and such harassment gives rise to employer liability for the acts of the supervisor, regardless of whether the employer knew or should have known of the acts of the supervisor.[34]

2. *Hostile working environment.* The Court of Appeals for the District of Columbia Circuit extended the scope of its *Barnes* decision, in *Bundy v. Jackson*,[35] holding that a plaintiff may establish a violation of Title VII by proving that discrimination based on sex has created a hostile or abusive work environment.

---

[31]While men may also be victims of sexual harassment in the workplace (see discussion in David Huebschen v. Department of Health and Social Services, 716 F.2d 1167 [7th Cir. 1983]), data indicate that in most cases the perpetrators are men and the victims are women. However, the law applies to sexual harassment of males by females, of males by males, and of females by females.
[32]561 F.2d 983 (D.C. Cir. 1977).
[33]Id. at 990.
[34]See Horn v. Duke Homes, Inc., Div. of Windsor Mobile Homes, 755 F.2d 599, 604–606 (7th Cir. 1985); Craig v. Y&Y Snacks, Inc., 721 F.2d 77, 80–81 (3rd Cir. 1983); and Katz v. Dole, 709 F.2d 251, 255, n. 6 (4th Cir. 1983).
[35]641 F.2d 934, 24 FEP 1155 (D.C. Cir. 1981).

Unlike Paulette Barnes, Sandra Bundy was not terminated for refusing her supervisor's advances. Her claim in part stated that "conditions of employment" as set forth in Title VII include the psychological and emotional work environment. The sexually stereotyped insults and demeaning propositions to which she was subjected and which caused her anxiety illegally poisoned the work environment. The court of appeals set forth the following relevant fact pattern in its decision:

> The District Court's decision that sexual intimidation was a "normal condition of employment" in Bundy's agency finds ample support in the District Court's own chronology of Bundy's experiences there. Those experiences began in 1972 when Bundy, still a GS-5, received and rejected sexual propositions from Delbert Jackson, then a fellow employee at the agency but now its Director and the named defendant in this lawsuit in his official capacity. It was two years later, however, that the sexual intimidation Bundy suffered began to intertwine directly with her employment, when she received propositions from two of her supervisors, Arthur Burton and James Gainey.
>
> Burton became Bundy's supervisor when Bundy became an Employment Development Specialist in 1974. Shortly thereafter Gainey became her first-line supervisor and Burton her second-line supervisor, although Burton retained control of Bundy's employment status. Burton began sexually harassing Bundy in June 1974, continually calling her into his office to request that she spend the workday afternoon with him at his apartment and to question her about sexual proclivities. Shortly after becoming her first-line supervisor Gainey also began making sexual advances to Bundy, asking her to join him at a motel and on a trip to the Bahamas. Bundy complained about these advances to Lawrence Swain, who supervised both Burton and Gainey. Swain casually dismissed Bundy's complaints, telling her that "any man in his right mind would want to rape you," and then proceeding himself to request that she begin a sexual relationship with him in his apartment. Bundy rejected his request.[36]

The court held that Bundy had proven that she was a victim of sexual harassment in the context of a discriminatory work environment permitted by her employer. This sexual harassment, even if it did not result in a loss of tangible benefits, is illegal sex discrimination. The court stated that injunctive relief should be required. The court also ordered the agency's director to establish and publicize procedures whereby harassed employees could complain to the director immediately and confidentially. The director should promptly take all necessary steps to investigate and correct any harassment, including warnings and appropriate discipline directed at the offending party, and should generally develop other means of preventing harassment within the agency.

The court in *Bundy* provided injunctive relief and awarded attorney's fees to Bundy. However, compensatory and punitive damages against the employer are not available in so-called pure hostile environment cases, such as *Bundy*, where the complainant continues to work for the employer. Where the complainant demonstrates that a hostile work environment effected a constructive termination of employment, a back pay remedy may be in order.[37]

---

[36]24 FEP at 1156, 1157.
[37]Mitchell v. OsAir, Inc., 629 F. Supp. 636 (D.C. Ohio 1986).

3. *Employer defenses*. Not all workplace conduct that may be described as "harassment" is actionable under Title VII. For sexual harassment to be actionable it must be sufficiently severe or pervasive to alter the conditions of the victim's employment and create an offensive or abusive environment. In *Walter v. KFGO Radio*[38] the court intimated that employers will not be liable despite admittedly offensive conduct where the conduct does not create an offensive working environment.

An employer may successfully defend against a sexual harassment claim by showing that the conduct was "welcomed" by the complainant. In *Meritor Savings Bank v. Vinson*, presented in this section, the U.S. Supreme Court dealt with the matter of the complainant's "voluntary" participation in the claimed sexual episodes as a defense for the employer. The Court rejected the argument that voluntary conduct was a valid defense. The Court stated in part:

> The gravamen of any sexual harassment claim is that the alleged sexual advances were "unwelcome." 29 CFR § 1604 11(a)(1985). . . . The correct inquiry is whether respondent by her conduct indicated that the alleged sexual advances were unwelcome, not whether her actual participation in sexual intercourse was voluntary.

4. *Lack of notice to employer*. In the *Meritor Savings Bank v. Vinson* decision, the Court left open the final resolution of the question of whether the failure of the complainant to use the employer's established grievance procedure to give the employer notice, or to otherwise put the employer on notice of the misconduct, insulates the employer from liability for the wrongdoing of the supervisory employee in hostile environment cases.

It is submitted, based on EEOC *Sex Discrimination Guidelines* § 1604.11(f) and the Supreme Court's analysis of *Meritor's* grievance procedure, that an employer may avoid liability for hostile working environment sexual harassment by its supervisors where the employer affirmatively raises the subject, expresses strong disapproval, and advises employees how to raise the issue according to the following outline:

   a. Develops and implements an equal employment policy that specifically includes sexual harassment as a prohibited activity for which discipline up to and including discharge will be imposed. (The *Meritor* antidiscrimination policy did not specifically address sexual harassment.)
   b. Designates a responsible senior official to whom complaints of sexual harassment can be made. (The *Meritor* grievance procedure required the employee to first complain to her supervisor, who was the offending supervisor.)
   c. Investigates all complaints thoroughly and expeditiously.
   d. If a complaint is meritorious, the employer imposes appropriate and consistent discipline, depending on the seriousness of the offense.

In the *Avco* decision, presented in this section, flaws in the company's sexual harassment procedures, coupled with the egregious misconduct involved and a finding that the company should have known of prior incidents by the supervisor, resulted in a decision against the employer.

---

[38] 26 FEP 982 (D.N.D. 1981).

Employer Liability for Co-Worker Sexual Harassment

Co-worker sexual harassment certainly exists today, yet court cases charging this form of discrimination are not very common. Most employers are aware of the problems of sexual harassment and now have procedures through which employees can rectify co-worker sexual harassment. Under the rules of conduct of many employers, the co-worker may be subject to discipline up to and including discharge for the sexual harassment of fellow workers in the form of sexual flirtations, propositions, or other sexually degrading conduct.[39]

Currently an employer is not vicariously liable for a co-worker's sexual harassment unless it fails to take remedial action against the activities of which it knew or should have known.[40] Courts refuse to impose vicarious liability because the co-worker usually has no authority over the harassed person, and thus the wrongful actions cannot occur within the scope of the co-worker's employment and cannot be imputed to the employer. In *Kyriazi v. Western Electric Co.*,[41] where three male co-workers teased and tormented the complainant, Kyriazi, and made wagers concerning her virginity, the court found that Kyriazi's supervisors were aware of the harassment and made no attempt to discipline the co-workers involved. Not only did the court find the employer liable for violating Title VII for this and other employer-imputed conduct, the court, under state law claims made by Kyriazi, assessed $1,500 in punitive damages against each of the co-workers and explicitly prevented the employer from indemnifying these employees for their punitive damages.

Employer Liability for Sexual Harassment of Nonemployees

An employer may be held to have violated Title VII of the Civil Rights Act of 1964 if it permits its employees to be subjected to sexual harassment by nonemployees. In such a case the burden of proof would be on the complainant to show that the harassment in question created a hostile or abusive work atmosphere and that the employer knew or should have known of the harassment and failed to take reasonable measures to prevent it.

Presently, sexual harassment by nonemployee cases relate to employers requiring employees to wear sexually provocative uniforms where the employers should reasonably know that wearing the uniforms would subject the employees to sexual harassment by

---

[39]See for example AT&T's affirmative action policy statement, which contains a section prohibiting sexual harassment. Under this section "sexually harassing conduct in the workplace, whether committed by supervisors or non-supervisory personnel, is also prohibited. This includes: repeated, offensive sexual flirtations, advances, propositions, continual or repeated verbal abuse of a sexual nature; graphic verbal commentaries about an individual's body; sexually degrading words used to describe an individual; and the display in the workplace of sexually suggestive objects or pictures." In the AT&T and IBEW arbitration decision AAA 327–3, arbitrator Robins upheld a five-day suspension concerning an offensive action in violation of the company's sexual harassment policy that the perpetrator believed to be a joke which would be seen as amusing by the individual who was the object of the action. See also Greyhound Lines, Inc. and IAM, AAA 325, p. 1, upholding discipline for "boisterous, profane or vulgar language."

[40]E.g., Katz v. Dole, 709 F.2d 251 at 256 (4th Cir. 1983) and Henson v. City of Dundee, 682 F.2d 897 at 905 (11th Cir. 1982).

[41]461 F. Supp. 894 (D.N.J. 1978) enforced by 465 F. Supp. 1141 (D.N.J. 1979), modifying and enforcing 476 F. Supp. 335 (D.N.J. 1979).

nonemployees. In *EEOC v. Sage Realty Co.,*[42] where a female lobby attendant was required to wear a uniform that resulted in her being subjected to sexual propositions and lewd comments by passersby, the court found that the employer, Sage, had violated Title VII of the act. The court accepted the principle that an employer may impose "reasonable" dress requirements but held that the employer did not have the unfettered discretion to force employees to wear sexually provocative uniforms.

---

[42]EEOC v. Sage Realty Corp., 25 E.P.D. ¶31,529 (SDNY 1981).

Meritor Savings Bank v. Vinson
Supreme Court of the United States, 40 FEP 1822 (1986).

[Mechelle Vinson (respondent) brought this action against Sidney Taylor, a vice-president and branch manager of Meritor Savings Bank, and the bank (petitioners) claiming that during her four years at the bank she had been constantly subjected to sexual harassment by Taylor in violation of Title VII. She testified to over forty instances of sexual favors successfully sought by Taylor from 1974 to 1977 when these activities ceased after she started going with a steady boyfriend. Taylor denied allegations of sexual activity. He contended instead that respondent made her accusations in response to a business-related dispute. The bank also denied respondent's allegations and asserted that any sexual harassment by Taylor was unknown to the bank and engaged in without its consent or approval. The district court denied relief, finding in part that:

If (respondent) and Taylor did engage in an intimate or sexual relationship during the time of (respondent's) employment with [the bank], that relationship was a voluntary one having nothing to do with her continued employment at [the bank] or her advancement or promotions at that institution.

The court of appeals reversed the district court. The Supreme Court granted certiorari.]

REHNQUIST, J.
. . . [I]n 1980 the EEOC issued guidelines specifying that "sexual harassment," as there de-

fined, is a form of sex discrimination prohibited by Title VII. . . .

Since the guidelines were issued, courts have uniformly held, and we agree, that a plaintiff may establish a violation of Title VII by proving that discrimination based on sex has created a hostile or abusive work environment. . . .

The question remains . . . whether the District Court's ultimate finding that respondent "was not the victim of sexual harassment," effectively disposed of respondent's claim. The Court of Appeals recognized, we think correctly, that this ultimate finding was likely based on one or both of two erroneous views of the law. First, the District Court apparently believed that a claim for sexual harassment will not lie absent an *economic* effect on the complainant's employment. ("It is without question that sexual harassment of female employees in which they are asked or required to submit to sexual demands as a *condition to obtain employment or to maintain employment or to obtain promotions* falls within protection of Title VII.") Since it appears that the District Court made its findings without ever considering the "hostile environment" theory of sexual harassment, the Court of Appeals' decision to remand was correct.

Second, the District Court's conclusion that no actionable harassment occurred might have rested on its earlier "finding" that "[i]f [respondent] and Taylor did engage in an intimate or sexual relationship . . . that relationship was a voluntary one." But the fact that sex-related conduct was "voluntary," in the sense that the complainant was not forced to participate against her will, is not a defense to a sexual harassment suit brought under Title VII. The gravamen of any sexual harassment claim is that the alleged sexual advances were "unwelcome." While the question whether particular conduct was indeed unwelcome presents difficult problems of proof and turns largely on credibility determination committed to the trier of fact, the District Court in this case erroneously focused on the "voluntariness" of respondent's participation in the claimed sexual episodes. The correct inquiry is whether respondent by her conduct indicated that the alleged sexual advances were unwelcome, not whether her actual participation in sexual intercourse was voluntary.

Petitioner contends that even if this case must be remanded to the District Court, the Court of Appeals erred in one of the terms of its remand. Specifically, the Court of Appeals stated that testimony about respondent's "dress and personal fantasies," which the District Court apparently admitted into evidence, "had no place in this litigation." The apparent ground for this conclusion was that respondent's voluntariness *vel non* in submitting to Taylor's advances was immaterial to her sexual harassment claim. While "voluntariness" in the sense of consent is not a defense to such a claim, it does not follow that a complainant's sexually provocative speech or dress is irrelevant as a matter of law in determining whether he or she found particular sexual advances unwelcome. To the contrary, such evidence is obviously relevant. The EEOC guidelines emphasize that the trier of fact must determine the existence of sexual harassment in light of "the record as a whole" and "the totality of circumstances, such as the nature of the sexual advances and the context in which the alleged incidents occurred." Respondent's claim that any marginal relevance of the evidence in question was outweighed by the potential for unfair prejudice is the sort of argument properly addressed to the District Court. In this case the District

Court concluded that the evidence should be admitted, and the Court of Appeals' contrary conclusion was based upon the erroneous, categorical view that testimony about provocative dress and publicly expressed sexual fantasies "had no place in this litigation." While the District Court must carefully weigh the applicable considerations in deciding whether to admit evidence of this kind, there is no *per se* rule against its admissibility.

Although the District Court concluded that respondent had not proved a violation of Title VII, it nevertheless went on to consider the question of the bank's liability. Finding that "the bank was without notice" of Taylor's alleged conduct, and that notice to Taylor was not the equivalent of notice to the bank, the court concluded that the bank therefore could not be held liable for Taylor's alleged actions. The Court of Appeals took the opposite view, holding that an employer is strictly liable for a hostile environment created by a supervisor's sexual advances, even though the employer neither knew nor reasonably could have known of the alleged misconduct. The court held that a supervisor, whether or not he possesses the authority to hire, fire, or promote, is necessarily an "agent" of his employer for all Title VII purposes, since "even the appearance" of such authority may enable him to impose himself on his subordinates. . . .

The EEOC suggests that when a sexual harassment claim rests exclusively on a "hostile environment" theory, however, the usual basis for a finding of agency will often disappear. In that case, the EEOC believes, agency principles led to

"a rule that asks whether a victim of sexual harassment had reasonably available an avenue of complaint regarding such harassment, and, if available and utilized, whether that procedure was reasonably responsive to the employee's complaint. If the employer has an expressed policy against sexual harassment and has implemented a procedure specifically designed to resolve sexual harassment claims, and if the victim does not take advantage of that procedure, the employer should be shielded from liability absent actual knowledge of the sexually hostile environment (obtained, e.g., by the filing of a charge with the EEOC

or a comparable state agency). In all other cases, the employer will be liable if it has actual knowledge of the harassment or if, considering all the facts of the case, the victim in question had no reasonably available avenue for making his or her complaint known to appropriate management officials." Brief for United States and Equal Opportunity Employment Commission as Amici Curiae, *26.*

This debate over the appropriate standard for employer liability has a rather abstract quality about it given the state of the record in this case. We do not know at this stage whether Taylor made any sexual advances toward respondent at all, let alone whether those advances were unwelcome, whether they were sufficiently pervasive to constitute a condition of employment, or whether they were "so pervasive and so long continuing . . . that the employer must have become conscious of [them]," Taylor v. Jones, 653 F.2d 1193, 1197–1199, 28 FEP Cases 1024, 1027 (CA8 1981) (holding employer liable for racially hostile working environment based on constructive knowledge).

We therefore decline the parties' invitation to issue a definitive rule on employer liability, but we do agree with the EEOC that Congress wanted courts to look to agency principles for guidance in this area. While such common-law principles may not be transferable in all their particulars to Title VII, Congress' decision to define "employer" to include any "agent" of an employer, 42 U.S.C. §2000e(b), surely evinces an intent to place some limits on the acts of employees for which employers under Title VII are to be held responsible. For this reason, we hold that the Court of Appeals erred in concluding that employers are always automatically liable for sexual harassment by their supervisors. For the same reason, absence of notice to an employer does not necessarily insulate that employer from liability.

Finally, we reject petitioner's view that the mere existence of a grievance procedure and a policy against discrimination, coupled with respondent's failure to invoke that procedure, must insulate petitioner from liability. While those facts are plainly relevant, the situation before us demonstrates why they are not necessarily dispositive. Petitioner's general nondiscrimination policy did not address sexual harassment in particular, and thus did not alert employees to their employer's interest in correcting that form of discrimination. Moreover, the bank's grievance procedure apparently required an employee to complain first to her supervisor, in this case Taylor. Since Taylor was the alleged perpetrator, it is not altogether surprising that respondent failed to invoke the procedure and report her grievance to him. Petitioner's contention that respondent's failure should insulate it from liability might be substantially stronger if its procedures were better calculated to encourage victims of harassment to come forward.

In sum, we hold that a claim of "hostile environment" sex discrimination is actionable under Title VII, that the District Court's findings were insufficient to dispose of respondent's hostile environment claim, and that the District Court did not err in admitting testimony about respondent's sexually provocative speech and dress. As to employer liability, we conclude that the Court of Appeals was wrong to entirely disregard agency principles and impose absolute liability on employers for the acts of their supervisors, regardless of the circumstances of a particular case.

Accordingly, the judgment of the Court of Appeals reversing the judgment of the District Court is affirmed, and the case is remanded for further proceedings consistent with this opinion.

It is so ordered.

CASE QUESTIONS

1. Is the fact that the sex-related conduct by an employee and her supervisor was "voluntary" a defense to a sexual harassment charge?
2. Was it proper for a trial court to consider evidence of sexually provocative speech or dress on the part of the complainant in a sexual harassment suit?
3. Did Taylor in fact make unwelcome sexual advances to Vinson?
4. What was wrong with the bank's nondiscrimination policy and grievance procedure?

Yates v. Avco Corporation
United States Court of Appeals, Sixth Circuit, 819 F.2d 630 (1987).

[Secretaries Charlotte Yates (Street) and Cheryl Mathis brought suit against their supervisor, Edwin Sanders, and Avco Corporation alleging sexual harassment under Title VII. Avco appealed the district court's finding that it was liable for the supervisor's actions.]

MARTIN, J.

I.

. . . Cheryl Mathis's relationship with Mr. Sanders began on terms she described as good, but it later became clear that Sanders sought some kind of personal relationship with her. Whenever Mathis was in his office he wanted the door to outside offices closed, and he began discussing very personal matters with her, such as the lack of a sexual relationship with his wife. He then began bombarding her with unwelcome invitations for drinks, lunch, dinner, breakfast, and asking himself to her house. Mathis made it clear that she was not interested in a personal relationship with her married boss. On a couple of occasions Sanders did in fact insist on coming to her apartment during the day and at those times Mathis asked a girlfriend from Avco to come with her.

Sanders also commented on Mathis's appearance, making lewd references to parts of her body. As Mathis rejected Sanders's advances, he would become belligerent. By the spring of 1983 Mathis began to suffer from severe bouts of trembling and crying which became progressively worse and eventually caused her to be hospitalized on two separate occasions, once for a week in June, 1983, and again in July for a few days. During this entire summer Mathis remained out on sick leave, not returning to work until September, 1983. She received her full pay until July 18, when her sick leave benefits expired. She was then compensated at the lesser "disability" rate of pay. When she returned from extended sick leave

in September, 1983, Mathis held the same job, title, grade and compensation rate and remained under Sanders's supervision.

As soon as she returned to work, Sanders's harassment resumed. He talked of "putting her on his mistress list" and made lewd jokes and comments. When Mathis resisted his advances Sanders became hostile, giving her more work than she could handle during her part-time hours. Once again she began to experience trembling, crying and emotional distress, and once again she was forced to seek medical help and did not work.

The other employee in this litigation, Charlotte Street, had been transferred to Sanders's supervision in June, 1983 while Cheryl Mathis was on sick leave. Sanders's behavior toward Street was similar to his behavior with Mathis. He incessantly asked her to lunch, dinner and drinks, mentioned sleeping together on more than one occasion, tried to discuss his and her personal relationships and made frequent sexually suggestive comments. He would call Street into his office "because [he] wanted to watch [her] walk out" and then make groaning sounds.

The harassment not only tormented Street and Mathis, it created hostility between them and other members of the department who apparently resented the plaintiffs' familiarity with Sanders. When Street could stand no more of this, she complained to Joe Baron, Manager of Personnel. In October, 1983, while Mathis was out on sick leave, Avco became aware that Mathis's emotional problems were connected to the work situation at Avco and questioned her. Avco then began an investigation of both complaints. During the initial part of the investigation Sanders continued in his job; however, he was later put on administrative leave pending a decision about his future with Avco. . . .

As a result of the Avco internal investigation Ed Sanders was found to have harassed employees, was drastically demoted, and received a substantial cut in salary. Though this meant Sanders would no longer be a supervisor, the plaintiffs were forced to endure unnecessary personal hardship to get to this stage. Both of their personnel files contained references to extended sick leave rather than giving any indication of the true reason for their absences. Even after Sanders was penalized, Avco refused to correct their personnel records. Though the company arranged an administrative leave for Sanders while he was under investigation, this same arrangement was never made for Mathis or Street. These discrepancies help to demonstrate that Avco's sexual harassment policy was not functioning properly nor implemented equitably.

II.

Pursuant to 42 U.S.C. §2000-e5(f)(5), the claims were referred to a magistrate on August 14, 1984, and a hearing was held in April 1985. The magistrate found that the plaintiffs had established a prima facie case against both defendants in that (1) as women they were members of a protected class; (2) they were subject to unwelcome sexual harassment, as it was not solicited and not desired; (3) the harassment was based on sex because there was no evidence that men were subjected to similar harassment; (4) because the harassment was sufficiently persistent and severe to affect the psychological well-being of the plaintiffs it affected a "term, condition, or privilege of employment;" and (5) a sufficient respondeat superior relationship existed to hold Avco liable for Sanders's actions. The magistrate found not only that Sanders had been given the authority to hire, fire and promote, but Avco had at least constructive knowledge of Sanders's behavior based on earlier allegations against him. Thus, he found both Sanders and Avco liable to Mathis and Street and ordered that they be awarded back-pay for the time they were out on sick leave, plus prejudgment interest; . . . that Avco correct the misleading impressions in the personnel files, including placing a copy of his report in the files; and that

Mathis and Street be awarded their expenses in bringing the action, including reasonable attorney's fees. . . .

III.

Avco . . . argues that the decision in *Meritor Sav. Bank, FSB v. Vinson*, 106 S. Ct. 2399, 2407–08 (1986), holds that traditional agency principles should be applied to questions of employer liability for harassment carried out by supervisors, and that consequently, the district court was in error. Though *Vinson* does adopt an agency standard, we find that under an agency theory and the facts of this case, Avco remains bound by Sanders's actions. . . . On the question of Mathis's back-pay for the time she was out on sick leave, we affirm. . . .

Unlike the situation the Supreme Court saw in *Vinson*, 106 S. Ct. 2399, there is no question that the sexual harassment complained of here did in fact occur and that the sexual advances were unwelcome. These factual findings are not disputed. The primary question here is whether as the district court found, Avco should be held responsible for its supervisor's acts. . . .

In this case Avco had a published procedure regarding sexual harassment. That procedure provided that the employee should report any conduct or circumstances which may constitute sexual harassment to the Employee Relations Department and to his immediate supervisor; that the Department would investigate complaints, determine corrective action and notify the supervisor of steps to be taken; and that the supervisor would promptly implement the corrective action. Though the intent of this policy was commendable, the facts of the case demonstrate that not only was it vague on paper, it was vague and ad hoc in its implementation and did not function effectively to eliminate harassment in the Avco Nashville plants.

First, the policy assumes that the supervisor is not the harasser, and gives the supervisor the responsibility for both reporting and correcting the harassment. Such a policy must necessarily discourage reporting and diminish an employee's faith in the system's ability to alleviate the problem when the supervisor is in fact the harasser.

Second, when Mathis and Street finally complained to Joe Baron about the harassment they were experiencing the matter was not dealt with effectively. Upon complaining, both Mathis and Street were told *not* to go to the EEOC, and that their complaints would be handled promptly within the company's harassment investigation framework. Taped testimony was taken and an investigation was begun, yet when Mathis and Street requested copies of their testimony their requests were denied. Street was told that if she felt uncomfortable continuing to work under Sanders's supervision while he remained under investigation, an administrative leave could be arranged. However, when Street went to Joe Baron seeking such a leave, she was told repeatedly just to call in sick. When she complained to Baron about the practice, he told her to get a note from her doctor to make the sick leave legitimate. When Street attempted to do that, her doctor correctly refused, telling her that her leave should be handled by the company. The "confidential" procedures of the department meant that the plaintiffs' personnel files documented excessive absenteeism, and for all intents and purposes Charlotte Street believed she was endangering her position as an Avco employee. In addition, Street was not free to explain to Sanders why she was absent from work. This resulted in one visit by Sanders to her house during which she was terrified that he might realize she was in fact at home and try to come in. Avco's policy of not placing documentation of sexual harassment in personnel files seems to protect only Avco and the harasser, rather than the affected employee. An effective anti-harassment policy does not operate this way.

Third, evidence was offered to indicate that Sanders harassed women as early as 1980. . . .

Though it is difficult to say unequivocally that Avco had actual notice of Sanders's behavior prior to Mathis's and Street's complaints in 1983, such a finding is not necessary. The magistrate found that Avco "knew, or upon reasonably diligent inquiry should have known, that Sanders

was sexually harassing the plaintiffs and other females." . . . The magistrate found at least constructive notice here, and we affirm that finding.

Here we have a company with a sexual harassment policy that did not function properly, coupled with a twenty-eight year supervisory employee who harassed women on a daily basis in the course of his supervision of them. Thus, even under traditional agency principles, Avco should be liable. The essential question in applying agency principles is whether the act complained of took place in the scope of the agent's employment. This determination requires an examination of such factors as *when* the act took place, *where* it took place, and whether it was *foreseeable*. *See generally* Restatement (Second) of Agency §§ 217–232 (1958). The Restatement specifically provides that even though an act is forbidden it may still be within the scope of employment. Restatement (Second) of Agency § 230. Here the harassment took place at the office, during working hours and was carried out by someone with the authority to hire, fire, promote and discipline the plaintiffs. There is no question that it was foreseeable. Had it not been, Avco would not have had a policy attempting to deal with it. Thus, none of the "agency factors" would indicate that Avco should be absolved of the responsibility for Sanders's actions.

Thus, we agree with the district court that the magistrate's finding that Avco at least reasonably should have known of Sanders's actions was not clearly erroneous. We believe that because Sanders was both an agent and supervisor of Avco, it is easier to impute his own knowledge to the Avco management. We also find that although Avco took remedial action once the plaintiffs registered complaints, its duty to remedy the problem, or at a minimum, inquire, was created earlier when the initial allegations of harassment were reported. In addition, although its remedial action with regard to the plaintiffs' complaint was prompt, it was not adequate. . . .

IV.

As we noted above, we do not believe that

the district court erred in awarding back-pay to Mathis for the time she was on sick leave. The award of back-pay is not the same as an award of damages for emotional distress which concededly is not recoverable under Title VII.

Because Mathis was forced to take extensive sick leave, she was compensated at a lower level than she would have been had she remained at work. We believe that she provided adequate proof that Sanders's behavior caused her absence from work and that the magistrate and district court properly ordered the company to compensate her.

V.

On the record before us we cannot recompute damages and we therefore remand to the district court for a recalculation of the damage award to both Mathis and Street in accordance with this opinion.

CASE QUESTIONS

1. Identify the harm caused by the supervisor's unlawful actions.
2. Evaluate the company's sexual harassment procedures.
3. Did the court of appeals find that Avco was not liable for the supervisor's misconduct?

SECTION 7—NATIONAL ORIGIN

National origin discrimination extends Title VII protection to members of all nationalities. As examples, national origin discrimination claims under Title VII have been brought on behalf of Spanish-surnamed persons; a person of Cajun descent; and persons of Hungarian, German, and Polish ancestry.[43]

The judicial principles that have emerged from cases involving other forms of employment discrimination are generally applicable to cases involving allegations of national origin discrimination. Thus physical standards such as minimum height requirements, which tend to exclude persons of a particular national origin because of the physical stature of the group, have been deemed unlawful where these standards cannot be justified by business necessity.[44]

Adverse employment decisions based on an individual's lack of English language skills have been considered violative of Title VII in those situations where the language requirement bears no demonstrable relationship to the successful performance of the job to which it is applied.

An employer may forbid bilingual sales employees to speak anything but English in sales areas while on the job according to the *Garcia v. Gloor*[45] decision. An expert witness testified that the Spanish language is the most important aspect of ethnic identification for Mexican-Americans. However, the court held that the discharge of Garcia was not discrimination based on national origin but rather a discharge because, having the ability to comply with the employer's "English-only" rule, he did not do so.

Title VII does not prohibit discrimination on the basis of citizenship where an employer has a rule against employment of aliens and the application of the rule is not a pretext for excluding persons of a particular national origin.[46]

---

[43]Roach v. Dresser Industries, 494 F. Supp. 215, FEP 1073 (W.D. La. 1980).

[44]Davis v. County of Los Angeles, 13 FEP 1217 (9th Cir. 1976) and League of United Latin American Citizens v. City of Santa Ana, 410 F. Supp. 873 (C.D. Calif. 1976).

[45]618 F.2d 264, 22 FEP 1403 (5th Cir. 1980).

[46]Espinoza v. Farah Manufacturing Co., 414 U.S. 86, 6 FEP 933 (1973).

SECTION 8—TITLE VII: SECTION 703 EXCEPTIONS

Section 703 of the act defines what employment activities are unlawful. This same section, however, also exempts several key practices from the scope of Title VII enforcement. The most important are the bona fide occupational qualification exception, the testing and educational requirement exception, and the seniority system exception.

Bona Fide Occupational Qualification Exception

Section 703(e) stipulates that it shall not be an unlawful employment practice for an employer to hire employees on the basis of their religion, sex, or national origin in those certain instances where religion, sex, or national origin is a bona fide occupational qualification (BFOQ) reasonably necessary to the normal operation of a particular enterprise. The so-called BFOQ clause is construed narrowly by the courts, and the burden of proving the business necessity for any such restrictive occupational qualifications is on the employer. The *Diaz* decision reported in this section exemplifies the narrow application of this statutory exception. It is important to note that there is no BFOQ exception for either race or color.

In *Dathard v. Rawlinson*[47] the Supreme Court, while recognizing that the BFOQ exception was meant to be an extremely narrow one, upheld as a BFOQ a male-only requirement for correctional counselor (guards) positions in male maximum security correctional institutions in Alabama. The Court referred to the substantial amount of testimony that the use of women as guards in "contact" positions under the existing conditions in Alabama maximum security male penitentiaries (which included 20 percent of the male prisoners being sex offenders housed throughout the facilities) would pose a substantial security problem directly linked to the sex of the prison guards.

In *Steele v. B.F. Goodrich Co.*[48] the company's policy of prohibiting fertile women from working on jobs involving a significant exposure to vinyl chloride was found to be a BFOQ. The administrative law judge rejected the argument that the company policy of excluding all women capable of bearing children from the job was an overly broad rule. The ALJ found that the policy was to protect unborn fetuses from developmental abnormalities at a time when they are most vulnerable and at a time the female employee is unlikely to know she is pregnant.

Testing and Educational Requirements

Section 703(h) of the act authorizes the use of "any professionally developed ability test [that is not] designed, intended, or used to discriminate." The Supreme Court held in *Griggs v. Duke Power Company* that employment testing and educational requirements must be "job related," that is, the employers must prove that the tests and educational requirements bear a demonstrable relationship to job performance. The Court ruled that

---

[47]433 U.S. 321, 15 FEP 10 (1977).
[48]Steele v. B.F. Goodrich Co., Ill Human Rights Comm., No. 1980 CF 0617 (November 17, 1982). But see Wright v. Olin Corp., 697 F.2d 1172, n. 21 (4th Cir. 1982), where the court considers the BFOQ exception in relation to the "disparate treatment/business necessity" theory and defense.

the employer's lack of intention to discriminate against blacks was irrelevant when the effect was to discriminate. As stated by the Supreme Court in *Griggs*, "What Congress has commanded is that any tests used must measure the person for the job and not the person in the abstract."[49]

The *Albemarle Paper Co. v. Moody* decision, which is reported in Section 11 of Part 2, demonstrates the requirement that where tests used by an employer have an adverse impact on a protected class under the act, the validation studies of these tests must be able to withstand strict scrutiny that they are job related. Validation studies demonstrate the job relatedness or lack thereof in the selection procedure in question.[50]

The two most common methods of test validation are *content validation* and *criterion-related validation.*

Content validation is the measure of how well a test correlates to the specific job tasks that make up the job. In order for the test to withstand the strict scrutiny that it may be subject to in court, a detailed *job analysis* must be conducted by the employer, thoroughly analyzing the component functions of the job in question and identifying the tasks that make up the important elements of the job. Tests must then be designed to measure performance in these important functions. An example of a selection procedure based on content validity is the administration of typing and shorthand tests for a candidate for a secretarial position. An example of a content-validated job-related physical agility test, agreed to in a consent decree between the state of Maine and the U.S. Justice Department, which the parties believe will lead to the hiring of more female state troopers, requires the following. Each applicant must be able to:

1. Push a standard size vehicle a distance of 12 feet on a level surface
2. Rescue an injured child from a school bus
3. Carry one end of a stretcher with a 175-pound mannequin a distance of 200 feet
4. Climb a flatbed truck; and
5. Run 1.5 miles in a designated time period[51]

Criterion-related validation is established by demonstrating that there is a significant positive correlation between success on the test (predictor) in question and comparative success on some measures of job performance (criteria). A *predictive* criterion validation study involves a test during the hiring process administered to a sample group with members of the sample group being selected without reference to their test scores. Later the actual job performance of the sample group is evaluated and compared to the test scores to see if the test accurately predicted performance. The *concurrent* criterion validation study involves the administration of a test to current employees, with their actual job performance being compared to their test scores to see if the test has validity. An example of a criterion-related validation study would be either a predictive or concurrent study to determine whether salespersons scoring higher on an intelligence test

---

[49]See p. 8 of this text for the opinion.
[50]The EEOC has published *Uniform Guidelines of Employee Selection Procedures*, which represents a summary statement of legal and validation standards for determining the proper use of tests and other selection procedures in order to assist employers and others to comply with federal law prohibiting discriminatory employment practices. 29 CFR § 1607 (1981).
[51]United States v. State of Maine, CA-83-0195P, May 26, 1983.

also tended to be among the better sales performers and whether this relationship was statistically significant.

Because of the fear of court rejection of employment tests in hiring practices and because of the expense involved in conducting job analyses, designing tests, and conducting validation studies, many employers abandoned the use of written tests. This is unfortunate since a properly designed test can be one of the least discriminatory ways of selecting employees.

A judicial trend is now evident whereby courts will accept prior court-approved validation studies developed for a different employer in a different state or region so long as it is demonstrated that the job for which the test was initially validated is essentially the same job function for which the test is currently being used. Thus a fire fighters test that had been validated in a study in California was accepted as valid when later used in Richmond, Virginia.[52] Such application is called *validity generalization*. It now appears that, based on the use of validity generalization, employers seeking to use employment tests may be able to rely on validation studies for like job classifications prepared by other employers in the same industry or by professional test developers.

Seniority System

Of the three major exceptions to Section 703, the one most important to workers is the seniority system exception found in Section 703(h). It provides that differences in employment conditions that result from a bona fide seniority system are sanctioned as long as the differences do not stem from an intention to discriminate. The term *seniority system* is generally understood to mean a set of rules that insure workers with longer years of continuous service for an employer a priority claim to a job over others with fewer years of service. Because such rules provide workers with considerable job security, organized labor has continually and successfully fought to secure seniority provisions in collective bargaining agreements.

In the *Teamsters v. United States* decision, reported in this section, the Court held that by virtue of Section 703(h), a bona fide seniority system does not become unlawful simply because it may perpetuate pre-Title VII discrimination. In *American Tobacco Company v. Patterson*[53] the Supreme Court held that Section 703(h) is applicable as well to bona fide seniority systems created after the passage of Title VII. As a result of the *American Tobacco* decision, even though a seniority system has a disparate or adverse impact on a protected class of persons under the act, such alone is insufficient to invalidate the seniority system. To invalidate a seniority system it has to be shown that the system is not bona fide because the *actual motive* of the parties in adopting the seniority system was to discriminate. In *Pullman-Standard v. Swint*[54] the Supreme Court recognized that adverse impact on minorities is part of the evidence to be considered by the trial court in reaching a finding of fact on whether there was a discriminatory intent.

In *Firefighters Local 1784 v. Stotts*, reported in this section, the city of Memphis planned to lay off employees due to budget cuts and had agreed with the city's unions

---

[52]Friend v. Leidinager, 588 F.2d 61, 18 FEP 1052 (4th Cir. 1978).
[53]456 U.S. 63, 28 FEP 713 (1982).
[54]456 U.S. 273, 28 FEP 1073 (1982).

that "seniority . . . shall govern layoffs and recalls." Minority fire fighters sought a court injunction preventing the layoffs based on seniority in order to protect the employment gains of minority fire fighters under court-approved consent decrees in 1974 and 1980. The district court approved and the court of appeals upheld a modified layoff plan that resulted in nonminority employees with more seniority than minority employees being laid off or reduced in rank. The Supreme Court reversed the lower courts, citing *Teamsters* as a precedent for its position that Section 703(h) permits, as in this case, the routine application of a seniority system absent proof of an intention to discriminate. The Supreme Court pointed out that there was no finding that any black protected from the layoffs had been an actual victim of discrimination and had received an award of competitive seniority.

Diaz v. Pan American World Airways, Inc.
United States Court of Appeals, Fifth Circuit, 442 F.2d 385 (1971).

TUTTLE, C. J.

This appeal presents the important question of whether Pan American Airlines' refusal to hire appellant and his class of males solely on the basis of their sex violates Section 703(a)(1) of Title VII of the 1964 Civil Rights Act. Because we feel that being a female is not a "bona fide occupational qualification" for the job of flight cabin attendant, appellee's refusal to hire appellant's class solely because of their sex does constitute a violation of the Act.

The facts in this case are not in dispute. Celio Diaz applied for a job as flight cabin attendant with Pan American Airlines in 1967. He was rejected because Pan Am had a policy restricting its hiring for that position to females. He then filed charges with the Equal Employment Opportunity Commission (EEOC) alleging that Pan Am had unlawfully discriminated against him on the grounds of sex. The Commission found probable cause to believe his charge, but was unable to resolve the matter through conciliation with Pan Am. Diaz next filed a class action in the United States District Court for the Southern District of Florida on behalf of himself and others similarly situated, alleging that Pan Am had violated Section 703 of the 1964 Civil Rights

Act by refusing to employ him on the basis of his sex; he sought an injunction and damages.

Pan Am admitted that it had a policy of restricting its hiring for the cabin attendant position to females. Thus, both parties stipulated that the primary issue for the District Court was whether, for the job of flight cabin attendant, being a female is a "bona fide occupational qualification (hereafter BFOQ) reasonably necessary to the normal operation" of Pan American's business.

The trial court found that being a female was a BFOQ. Before discussing its findings in detail, however, it is necessary to set forth the framework within which we view this case.

Section 703(a) of the 1964 Civil Rights Act provides, in part:

(a) It shall be an unlawful employment practice for an employer—
(1) to fail or refuse to hire or to discharge any individual, or otherwise to discriminate against any individual with respect to his compensation, terms, conditions, or privileges of employment, because of such individual's race, color, religion, sex or national origin. . . .

The scope of this section is qualified by Section 703(e) which states:

(e) Notwithstanding any other provision of this subchapter,

(1) it shall not be an unlawful employment practice for an employer to hire and employ employees . . . on the basis of his religion, sex, or national origin in those certain instances where religion, sex, or national origin is a bona fide occupational qualification reasonably necessary to the normal operation of that particular business or enterprise. . . .

Since it has been admitted that appellee has discriminated on the basis of sex, the result in this case turns, in effect, on the construction given to this exception.

We note, at the outset, that there is little legislative history to guide our interpretation. The amendment adding the word "sex" to "race, color, religion and national origin" was adopted one day before House passage of the Civil Rights Act. It was added on the floor and engendered little relevant debate. In attempting to read Congress' intent in these circumstances, however, it is reasonable to assume, from a reading of the statute itself, that one of Congress' main goals was to provide equal access to the job market for both men and women. Indeed, as this court in *Weeks v. Southern Bell Telephone and Telegraph Co.*, 408 F.2d 228 at 235 clearly stated, the purpose of the Act was to provide a foundation in the law for the principle of nondiscrimination. Construing the statute as embodying such a principle is based on the assumption that Congress sought a formula that would not only achieve the optimum use of our labor resources but, and more importantly, would enable individuals to develop as individuals.

Attainment of this goal, however, is, as stated above, limited by the bona fide occupational qualification exception in Section 703(e). In construing this provision, we feel, as did the court in *Weeks, supra,* that it would be totally anomalous to do so in a manner that would, in effect, permit the exception to swallow the rule. Thus, we adopt the EEOC guidelines which state that "the Commission believes that the bona fide occupational qualification as to sex should be interpreted narrowly." 29 CFR 1604.1(a). Indeed, close scrutiny

of the language of this exception compels this result. As one commentator has noted:

The sentence contains several restrictive adjectives and phrases: it applies only in those certain instances where there are bona fide qualifications reasonably necessary to the operation of that particular enterprise. The care with which Congress has chosen the words to emphasize the function and to limit the scope of the exception indicates that it had no intention of opening the kind of enormous gap in the law which would exist if [for example] an employer could legitimately discriminate against a group solely because his employees, customers, or clients discriminated against that group. Absent much more explicit language, such a broad exception should not be assumed for it would largely emasculate the act. (Emphasis added.) 65 Mich. L. Rev. (1967).

Thus, it is with this orientation that we now examine the trial court's decision. Its conclusion was based upon (1) its view of Pan Am's history of the use of flight attendants; (2) passenger preference; (3) basic psychological reasons for the preference; and (4) the actualities of the hiring process. . . .

We begin with the proposition that the use of the word "necessary" in Section 703(e) requires that we apply a business *necessity* test, not a business *convenience* test. That is to say, discrimination based on sex is valid only when the *essence* of the business operation would be undermined by not hiring members of one sex exclusively.

The primary function of an airline is to transport passengers safely from one point to another. While a pleasant environment, enhanced by the obvious cosmetic effect that female stewardesses provide as well as, according to the finding of the trial court, their apparent ability to perform the nonmechanical functions of the job in a more effective manner than most men, may all be important, they are tangential to the essence of the business involved. No one has suggested that having male stewards will so seriously affect the operation of an airline as to jeopardize or even minimize its ability to provide safe transportation from one place to another. Indeed the record discloses that many airlines including Pan Am have utilized both men and women flight cabin attendants in the past and Pan Am, even at the time of this suit, has 283 male stewards employed on some of its foreign flights.

We do not mean to imply, of course, that Pan Am cannot take into consideration the ability of *individuals* to perform the nonmechanical functions of the job. [These functions include providing reassurance to anxious passengers, giving courteous personalized service and, in general, making flights as pleasurable as possible.] What we hold is that because the nonmechanical aspects of the job of flight cabin attendant are not "reasonably necessary to the normal operation" of Pan Am's business, Pan Am cannot exclude *all* males simply because *most* males may not perform adequately. . . .

As the Supreme Court stated in *Griggs v. Duke Power Co.*, 401 U.S. 424 (1971), "the administrative interpretation of the Act by the enforcing agency is entitled to great deference." . . . Indeed, while we recognize that the public's expectation of finding one sex in a particular role may cause some initial difficulty, it would be totally anomalous if we were to allow the preferences and prejudices of the customers to determine whether the sex discrimination was valid. Indeed, it was, to a large extent, these very

prejudices the Act was meant to overcome. Thus, we feel that customer preference may be taken into account only when it is based on the company's inability to perform the primary function or service it offers.

Of course, Pan Am argues that the customers' preferences are not based on "stereotyped thinking," but the ability of women stewardesses to better provide the nonmechanical aspects of the job. Again, as stated above, since these aspects are tangential to the business, the fact that customers prefer them cannot justify sex discrimination.

The judgment is Reversed and the case is Remanded for proceedings not inconsistent with this opinion.

CASE QUESTIONS

1. What is the primary issue of the case?
2. How does the court construe the BFOQ exception in Section 703(e)?
3. When hiring flight cabin attendants, may an airline take into consideration the ability of individual males to perform the nonmechanical aspects of the job such as reassuring anxious passengers and making flights as pleasurable as possible?
4. Was the court persuaded by the airline's argument that passengers prefer female stewardesses?

Teamsters v. United States
Supreme Court of the United States, 431 U.S. 324 (1977).

STEWART, J.
This litigation brings here several important questions under Title VII of the Civil Rights Act of 1964, as amended, 42 U.S.C. Section 2000e *et seq.* (1970 ed. and Supp. V). The issues grow out of alleged unlawful employment practices engaged in by an employer and a union. The employer is a common carrier of motor freight

with nationwide operations, and the union represents a large group of its employees. The District Court and the Court of Appeals held that the employer had violated Title VII by engaging in a pattern and practice of employment discrimination against Negroes and Spanish-surnamed Americans, and that the union had violated the Act by agreeing with the employer to create and maintain a seniority system that perpetuated the effects of past racial and ethnic discrimination. . . .

The central claim . . . was that the company had engaged in a pattern or practice of discriminating against minorities in hiring so-called line drivers. Those Negroes and Spanish-surnamed persons who had been hired, the Government alleged, were given lower paying, less desirable jobs as servicemen or local city drivers, and were thereafter discriminated against with respect to promotions and transfers. In this connection the complaint also challenged the seniority system established by the collective-bargaining agreements between the employer and the union. . . .

[After finding that the employer had engaged in a pattern or practice of discriminating against minorities in hiring line drivers, the Supreme Court addressed the issue of whether the seniority system utilized by the employer was violative of Title VII.]

The District Court and the Court of Appeals also found that the seniority system contained in the collective-bargaining agreements between the company and the union operated to violate Title VII of the Act.

For purposes of calculating benefits, such as vacations, pensions, and other fringe benefits, an employee's seniority under this system runs from the date he joins the company, and takes into account his total service in all jobs and bargaining units. For competitive purposes, however, such as determining the order in which employees may bid for particular jobs, are laid off, or are recalled from layoff, it is bargaining-unit seniority that controls. Thus, a line driver's seniority, for purposes of bidding for particular runs and protection against layoff, takes into account only the length of time he has been a line driver at a particular terminal. The practical effect is that a city driver or serviceman who transfers to a line-driver job must forfeit all the competitive seniority he has accumulated in his previous bargaining unit and start at the bottom of the line-drivers' "board."

The vice of this arrangement, as found by the District Court and the Court of Appeals, was that it "locked" minority workers into inferior jobs and perpetuated prior discrimination by discouraging transfers to jobs as line drivers. While the disincentive applied to all workers, including whites, it was Negroes and Spanish-surnamed persons who, those courts found, suffered the most because many of them had been denied the equal opportunity to become line drivers when they were initially hired, whereas whites either had not sought or were refused line-driver positions for reasons unrelated to their race or national origin.

The linchpin of the theory embraced by the District Court and the Court of Appeals was that a discriminatee who must forfeit his competitive seniority in order finally to obtain a line-driver job will never be able to "catch up" to the seniority level of his contemporary who was not subject to discrimination. Accordingly, this continued, built-in disadvantage to the prior discriminatee who transfers to a line-driver job was held to constitute a continuing violation of Title VII, for which both the employer and the union who jointly created and maintain the seniority system were liable. . . .

Because the company discriminated both before and after the enactment of Title VII, the seniority system is said to have operated to perpetuate the effects of both pre- and post-Act discrimination. Post-Act discriminatees, however, may obtain full "make whole" relief, including retroactive seniority under *Franks v. Bowman*, 424 U.S. 747 without attacking the legality of the seniority system as applied to them. *Franks* made clear and the union acknowledges that retroactive seniority may be awarded as relief from an employer's discriminatory hiring and assignment policies even if the seniority system agreement itself makes no provision for such relief. 424 U.S., at 778–779. Here the Government has proved that the company engaged in a post-Act pattern of discriminatory hiring, assignment, transfer, and promotion policies. Any Negro or Spanish-surnamed American injured by those policies may receive all appropriate relief as a direct remedy for this discrimination.

What remains for review is the judgment that the seniority system unlawfully perpetuated the effects of *pre-Act* discrimination. We must decide, in short, whether Section 703(h) validates otherwise bona fide seniority systems that afford no constructive seniority to victims, discriminated against prior to the effective date of Title VII, and it is to that issue that we now turn.

The primary purpose of Title VII was "to assure equality of employment opportunities and to eliminate those discriminatory practices and devices which have fostered racially stratified job environments to the disadvantage of minority citizens." *McDonnell Douglas Corp. v. Green*, 411 U.S. 792, 800. . . . To achieve this purpose, Congress "proscribe[d] not only overt discrimination but also practices that are fair in form, but discriminatory in operation." *Griggs v. Duke Power Co.*, 421 U.S. 424, 431. Thus, the Court has repeatedly held that a prima facie Title VII violation may be established by policies or practices that are neutral on their face and in intent but that nonetheless discriminate in effect against a particular group. . . .

One kind of practice "fair in form, but discriminatory in operation" is that which perpetuates the effects of prior discrimination. As the Court held in *Griggs, supra:* "Under the Act, practices, procedures, or tests neutral on their face, and even neutral in terms of intent, cannot be maintained if they operate to 'freeze' the status quo of prior discriminatory employment practices." 401 U.S., at 430.

Were it not for Section 703(h), the seniority system in this case would seem to fall under the *Griggs* rationale. The heart of the system is its allocation of the choicest jobs, the greatest protection against layoffs, and other advantages to those employees who have been line drivers for the longest time. Where, because of the employer's prior intentional discrimination, the line drivers with the longest tenure are without exception white, the advantages of the seniority system flow disproportionately to them and away

from Negro and Spanish-surnamed employees who might by now have enjoyed those advantages had not the employer discriminated before the passage of the Act. This disproportionate distribution of advantages does in a very real sense "operate to 'freeze' the status quo of prior discriminatory employment practices." *Ibid.* But both the literal terms of Section 703(h) and the legislative history of Title VII demonstrate that Congress considered this very effect of many seniority systems and extended a measure of immunity to them.

Throughout the initial consideration of H.R. 7152, later enacted as the Civil Rights Act of 1964, critics of the bill charged that it would destroy existing seniority rights. The consistent response of Title VII's congressional proponents and of the Justice Department was that seniority rights would not be affected, even where the employer had discriminated prior to the Act. An interpretative memorandum placed in the Congressional Record by Senators Clark and Case stated:

Title VII would have no effect on established seniority rights. Its effect is prospective and not retrospective. Thus, for example, if a business has been discriminating in the past and as a result has an all-white working force, when the title comes into effect the employer's obligation would be simply to fill future vacancies on a non-discriminatory basis. He would not be obliged—or indeed, permitted—to fire whites in order to hire Negroes, or to prefer Negroes for future vacancies, or, once Negroes are hired, to give them special seniority rights at the expense of the white workers hired earlier. 110 Cong. Rec. 7213 (1964) (emphasis added).

A Justice Department statement concerning Title VII, placed in the Congressional Record by Senator Clark, voiced the same conclusion:

Title VII would have no effect on seniority rights existing at the time it takes effect. If, for example, a collective bargaining contract provides that in the event of layoffs, those who were hired last must be laid off first, such a provision would not be affected in the least by Title VII. This would be true even in the case where owing to discrimination prior to the effective date of the title, white workers had more seniority than Negroes. Id., *at 7207 (emphasis added)*. . . .

In sum, the unmistakable purpose of Section 703(h) was to make clear that the routine application of a bona fide seniority system would not be unlawful under Title VII. As the legislative history shows, this was the intended result even where the employer's pre-Act discrimination resulted in whites having greater existing seniority rights than Negroes. Although a seniority system inevitably tends to perpetuate the effects of pre-Act discrimination in such cases, the congressional judgment was that Title VII should not outlaw the use of existing seniority lists and thereby destroy or water down the vested seniority rights of employees simply because their employer had engaged in discrimination prior to the passage of the Act.

To be sure, Section 703(h) does not immunize all seniority systems. It refers only to "bona fide" systems, and a proviso requires that any differences in treatment not be "the result of an intention to discriminate because of race . . . or national origin. . . ." But our reading of the legislative history compels us to reject the Government's broad argument that no seniority system that tends to perpetuate pre-Act discrimination can be "bona fide." To accept the argument would require us to hold that a seniority system becomes illegal simply because it allows the full exercise of the pre-Act seniority rights of employees of a company that discriminated before Title VII was enacted. It would place an affirmative obligation on the parties to the seniority agreement to subordinate those rights in favor of the claims of pre-Act discriminatees without seniority. The consequence would be a perversion of the congressional purpose. We cannot accept the invitation to disembowel Section 703(h) by reading the words "bona fide" as the Government would have us do. Accordingly, we hold that an otherwise neutral, legitimate seniority system does not become unlawful under Title VII simply because it may perpetuate pre-Act discrimination. Congress did not intend to make it illegal for employees with vested seniority rights to continue to exercise those rights, even at the expense of pre-Act discriminatees. . . .

The seniority system in this case is entirely bona fide. It applies equally to all races and ethnic groups. To the extent that it "locks" employees into nonline-driver jobs, it does so for all. The city drivers and servicemen who are discouraged from transferring to line-driver jobs are not all Negroes or Spanish-surnamed Americans; to the contrary, the overwhelming majority are white. The placing of line drivers in a separate bargaining unit from other employees is rational, in accord with the industry practice, and consistent with NLRB precedents. It is conceded that the seniority system did not have its genesis in racial discrimination, and that it was negotiated and has been maintained free from any illegal purpose. In these circumstances, the single fact that the system extends no retroactive seniority to pre-Act discriminatees does not make it unlawful.

Because the seniority system was protected by Section 703(h), the union's conduct in agreeing to and maintaining the system did not violate Title VII. On remand, the District Court's injunction against the union must be vacated. . . .

It is so ordered.

CASE QUESTIONS

1. What was the theory embraced by the district court and the court of appeals with respect to the discrimination fostered by the company's seniority system?
2. What does the union claim was the central purpose behind Section 703(h) of Title VII?
3. According to the Court, for there to be a violation of Title VII, is it necessary to find discriminatory intent?
4. Does a bona fide seniority system become unlawful under Title VII simply because it may perpetuate pre-act discrimination?

Firefighters Local 1784 v. Stotts
Supreme Court of the United States, DLR No. 114, at D1 (June 13, 1984).

[Respondent Captain Carl Stotts, a black member of the Memphis, Tennessee, fire department, filed a class action in federal district court charging that the department and certain city officials were engaged in a pattern or practice of making hiring and promotion decisions on the basis of race in violation of Title VII of the Civil Rights Act of 1964. This action was consolidated with an action filed by respondent Private Fred Jones, also a black member of the department, who claimed that he had been denied a promotion because of his race. Thereafter, a consent decree was entered with the stated purpose of remedying the department's hiring and promotion practices with respect to blacks. Subsequently, when the city announced that projected budget deficits required a reduction of city employees, the district court entered an order preliminarily enjoining the department from following its seniority system of "last hired, first fired" based on citywide seniority with "bump down" rights in determining who would be laid off as a result of the budgetary shortfall, since the proposed layoffs would have a racially adverse effect and the seniority system was not a bona fide one. A modified layoff plan, aimed at protecting black employees so as to comply with the court's order, was then presented and approved, and layoffs pursuant to this plan were carried out. This resulted in white employees with more seniority than black employees being laid off when the otherwise applicable seniority system would have called for the layoff of black employees with less seniority. The court of appeals affirmed, holding that although the district court was wrong in holding that the seniority was not bona fide, it had acted properly in modifying the consent decree. The Supreme Court granted certiorari.]

WHITE, J.

The Court of Appeals held that even if the injunction is not viewed as compelling compliance with the terms of the decree, it was still properly entered because the District Court had inherent authority to modify the decree when an economic crisis unexpectedly required layoffs which, if carried out as the City proposed, would undermine the affirmative action outlined in the decree and impose an undue hardship on respondents. This was true, the court held, even though the modification conflicted with a bona fide seniority system adopted by the City. The Court of Appeals erred in reaching this conclusion.

Section 703(h) of Title VII provides that it is not an unlawful employment practice to apply different standards of compensation, or different terms, conditions, or privileges of employment pursuant to a bona fide seniority system, provided that such differences are not the result of an intention to discriminate because of race. It is clear that the City had a seniority system, that its proposed layoff plan conformed to that system, and that in making the settlement the City had not agreed to award competitive seniority to any minority employee whom the City proposed to lay off. The District Court held that the City could not follow its seniority system in making its proposed layoffs because its proposal was discriminatory in effect and hence not a bona fide plan. Section 703(h), however, permits the routine application of a seniority system absent proof of an intention to discriminate. *Teamsters v. United States*, 431 U.S. 324, 352 (1977). Here, the District Court itself found that the layoff proposal was not adopted with the purpose or intent to discriminate on the basis of race. Nor had the City in agreeing to the decree admitted in any way that it had engaged in intentional discrimination. The Court of Appeals was therefore correct in disagreeing with the District Court's holding that the layoff plan was not a bona fide application of the seniority system, and it would appear that the City could not be faulted for following the seniority plan expressed in its agreement with the Union. The Court of Appeals nevertheless held that the injunction was proper even though it conflicted with the seniority system. This was error.

To support its position, the Court of Appeals first proposed a "settlement" theory, *i.e.*, that the strong policy favoring voluntary settlement of Title VII actions permitted consent decrees that encroached on seniority systems. But at this stage in its opinion, the Court of Appeals was supporting the proposition that even if the injunction was not merely enforcing the agreed-upon terms of the decree, the District Court had the authority to modify the decree over the objection of one of the parties. The settlement theory, whatever its merits might otherwise be, has no application when there is no "settlement" with respect to the disputed issue. Here, the agreed-upon decree neither awarded competitive seniority to the minority employees nor purported in any way to depart from the seniority system.

A second ground advanced by the Court of Appeals in support of the conclusion that the injunction could be entered notwithstanding its conflict with the seniority system was the assertion that "[i]t would be incongruous to hold that the use of the preferred means of resolving an employment discrimination action decreases the power of a court to order relief which vindicates the policies embodied within Title VII, and 42 U.S.C. §§ 1981 and 1983." 679 F.2d, at 566. The court concluded that if the allegations in the complaint had been proved, the District Court could have entered an order overriding the seniority provisions. Therefore, the court reasoned, "[t]he trial court had the authority to override the Firefighters' Union seniority provisions to effectuate the purpose of the 1980 Decree." 679 F.2d, at 566.

The difficulty with this approach is that it overstates the authority of the trial court to disregard a seniority system in fashioning a remedy after a plaintiff has successfully proved that an employer has followed a pattern or practice having a discriminatory effect on black applicants or employees. If individual members of a plaintiff class demonstrate that they have been actual victims of the discriminatory practice, they may

be awarded competitive seniority and given their rightful place on the seniority roster. This much is clear from *Franks v. Bowman Transportation Co.*, 424 U.S. 947 (1976) and *Teamsters v. United States*, 431 U.S. 324 (1977). *Teamsters*, however, also made clear that mere membership in the disadvantaged class is insufficient to warrant a seniority award; each individual must prove that the discriminatory practice had an impact on him. 431 U.S., at 367–371. Even when an individual shows that the discriminatory practice has had an impact on him, he is not automatically entitled to have a non-minority employee laid off to make room for him. He may have to wait until a vacancy occurs, and if there are non-minority employees on layoff, the Court must balance the equities in determining who is entitled to the job. *Teamsters, supra*, 431 U.S., at 371–376. Here, there was no finding that any of the blacks protected from layoff had been a victim of discrimination and no award of competitive seniority to any of them. Nor had the parties in formulating the consent decree purported to identify any specific employee entitled to particular relief other than those listed in the exhibits attached to the decree. It therefore seems to us that in light of *Teamsters*, the Court of Appeals imposed on the parties as an adjunct of settlement something that could not have been ordered had the case gone to trial and the plaintiffs proved that a pattern or practice of discrimination existed.

Our ruling in *Teamsters* that a court can award competitive seniority only when the beneficiary of the award has actually been a victim of illegal discrimination is consistent with the policy behind § 706(g) of Title VII, which affects the remedies available in Title VII litigation. That policy, which is to provide make-whole relief only to those who have been actual victims of illegal discrimination, was repeatedly expressed by the sponsors of the Act during the congressional debates. Opponents of the legislation that became Title VII charged that if the bill were enacted, employers could be ordered to hire and promote persons in order to achieve a racially-balanced work force even though those persons had not been victims of illegal discrimination. Responding to these charges, Senator Humphrey explained the limits on a court's remedial powers as follows:

"No court order can require hiring, reinstatement, admission to membership, or payment of back pay for anyone who was not fired, refused employment or advancement or admission to a union by an act of discrimination forbidden by this title. This is stated expressly in the last sentence of Section 707(e) [enacted without relevant change as § 706(g)]. . . . Contrary to the allegations of some opponents of this title, there is nothing in it that will give any power to the Commission or to any court to require . . . firing . . . of employees in order to meet a racial 'quota' or to achieve a certain racial balance. That bugaboo has been brought up a dozen times; but is nonexistent." 110 Cong. Rec. 6549 (remarks of Sen. Humphrey). . . .

The Court of Appeals holding that the District Court's order was permissible as a valid Title VII remedial order ignores not only our ruling in *Teamsters* but the policy behind § 706(g) as well. Accordingly, that holding cannot serve as a basis for sustaining the District Court's order. . . .

We thus are unable to agree either that the order entered by the District Court was a justifiable effort to enforce the terms of the decree to which the City had agreed or that it was a legitimate modification of the decree that could be imposed on the City without its consent. Accordingly, the judgment of the Court of Appeals is reversed.

It is so ordered.

[Justice Blackmun, with whom Justices Brennan and Marshall joined, filed a dissenting opinion asserting that the case is moot since the injunction terminated prior to the Court's deliberations.]

CASE QUESTIONS

1. Does Section 703(h) permit the routine application of a seniority system absent proof of intention to discriminate?
2. Was the city's layoff plan adopted with the intent to discriminate on the basis of race?
3. Did the court-approved consent decree award black employees competitive seniority or modify the seniority system so that the district court was justified in enjoining the layoff of junior black employees?

Part Questions and Problems

1. What are the four major federal statutes dealing with the regulation of equal rights in employment?
2. State the general purpose of the Civil Rights Act of 1964.
3. What federal agency has the responsibility to achieve compliance with Title VII of the amended Civil Rights Act?
4. Continental Photo, Inc. is a portrait photography company. Alex Riley, a black man, applied for a position as a photographer with Continental. Riley submitted an application and was interviewed. In response to a question on a written application, Riley indicated that he had been convicted of forgery, a felony, six years prior to the interview and had received a suspended sentence. He also noted that he would discuss the matter with his interviewer if necessary. The subject of the forgery conviction was subsequently not mentioned by Continental's personnel director in his interview with Riley. Riley's application for employment was eventually rejected. Riley inquired as to the reason for his rejection by Continental. The personnel director, Geuther, explained to him that the prior felony conviction disclosed on his application and an unsatisfactory test score were the reasons for his rejection.

    Riley contended that the refusal to hire him because of his conviction record was actually discrimination against him because of his race in violation of Title VII. Riley felt that his successful completion of a five-year probation without incident and his steady work over the years qualified him for the job.

Continental maintained that since its photographers handle approximately $10,000 in cash per year, its policy of not hiring applicants whose honesty was questionable was justified. Continental's policy excluded all applicants with felony convictions.

What factors must be weighed in this case? Has Continental violated Title VII? Decide. Would the result be different if Riley had been a convicted murderer? [Continental Photo, Inc., 26 FEP 1799 (EEOC 1980)]

5. Sambo's Restaurants maintained a uniform grooming policy concerning each of its over one thousand establishments nationwide. The policy forbade restaurant managers and other restaurant personnel to wear facial hair, with an exception for a neatly trimmed mustache. Sambo's has consistently enforced this grooming policy since the restaurant chain's inception in 1957. Grooming standards similar to Sambo's were common in the restaurant industry. Sambo's felt that the grooming policy reflected the restaurant's public image as a family-oriented business where food was served under sanitary conditions.

Mohen S. Tucker was a member of the Sikh religion. The practice of Sikhism forbade the cutting or shaving of facial hair and also required the wearing of a turban that covered the head. In accordance with the dictates of his religion, Tucker wore a long beard. Tucker applied for a position as a Sambo's restaurant manager. While filling out the application, he was informed of the Sambo's grooming policy, which would require that he shave his beard or be denied the position. Tucker informed Sambo's that it was against his religion to shave his beard. Sambo's responded that no exceptions were allowed under the grooming policy for religious reasons and denied his application.

Tucker brought a court action through the EEOC, claiming that Sambo's had violated Title VII by refusing to accommodate his religious practice. Sambo's denied any religious discrimination.

What standard of review should be employed to decide this case? What factors will be relevant? Decide the case. [EEOC v. Sambo's of Georgia, Inc., 27 FEP 1210 (D.C. N.D. Ga. 1981)]

6. Mercy Health Center in Oklahoma City, Oklahoma, was a hospital that provided extensive medical services including obstetrical and gynecological care. The labor and delivery area of the hospital hosted an average of 148 deliveries a month. Forty to fifty percent of those births were life threatening to the mother or infant and were therefore classified as high risk. Staff nurses in the labor and delivery area were involved in extensive contact with the expectant mother. Their duties included assessment and examination of the mother, which consisted of frequent contact with the mother's body. In order to minimize the tension, fear, and stress that accompanies the labor and delivery experience, Mercy did not hire males for the position of staff nurse in the labor and delivery area. The hospital cited its paramount concern for the privacy and comfort of the mother as a basis for its policy. Mercy also conducted a survey of parents involved in prenatal classes and found that 60 to 70 percent of the mothers and a larger percentage of the fathers objected to the use of male nurses in the labor and delivery area.

Andre Fontain applied for a job as a staff nurse in the labor and delivery area at Mercy. Because of the policy, he was denied employment.

Through the EEOC, Fontain alleged that Mercy discriminated against him on the basis of sex in violation of Title VII. The hospital denied the charge of discrimination.

Has Mercy violated Title VII? If so, what defense, if any, is available to the hospital? Decide the case. [EEOC v. Mercy Health Center, 29 FEP 159 (D.C. W.D. Okla. 1982)]

7. DiMillo's Floating Restaurant on Long Wharf, Portland, Maine, ran a help-wanted ad in the *Portland Press Herald*, which read in part:

Bartenders/Cocktail Service, Experienced Only. Applicants must be able to wear uniforms sizes 8 to 12.

Complaints were made to the Maine Human Rights Commission. Antonio DiMillo defended the ad in a newspaper interview, expressing the view that all over the country the restaurant industry routinely hires waitresses based on their size. DiMillo was quoted as saying: "Do you go out to eat and drink? Do you like to see a fat big broad coming at you?"

Against whom, if anyone, does the ad discriminate? What responsibility, if any, does the newspaper have in publishing employment advertisements that are found to discriminate? [See page 13 of the *Portland Press Herald*, Vol. 121, No. 127, Thursday, November 18, 1982.]

8. Sylvia Hayes worked as a staff technician in the radiology department of Shelby Memorial Hospital, a county hospital located in Birmingham, Alabama. In early October 1980 Hayes was told by her physician that she was pregnant. When Hayes informed the doctor of her occupation as an X-ray technician, the doctor advised Hayes that she could continue working until the end of April as long as she followed standard safety precautions. On October 8 Hayes told Gail Nell, the director of radiology at Shelby, that she had discovered she was two months pregnant. On October 14 Hayes was discharged by the hospital. The hospital's reason for terminating Hayes was its concern for the safety of her fetus given the X-ray exposure that occurs during employment as an X-ray technician.

Hayes brought an action under Title VII claiming that her discharge was unlawfully based on her condition of pregnancy. She cited scientific evidence and the practice of other hospitals where pregnant women were allowed to remain in their jobs as X-ray technicians.

The hospital claimed that Hayes' discharge was based on business necessity. Specifically, the hospital claimed that the potential for future liability existed if an employee's fetus was damaged by radiation encountered at the workplace.

Has the hospital violated Title VII by discharging Hayes? What remedy, if any, is appropriate in this case? Decide the case. [Hayes v. Shelby Memorial Hospital, 29 FEP 1173 (D.C. N.D. Ala. 1982)]

9. Glenwood H. MacDougal, chairman of the Office Occupations Department at Northern Maine Vocational Technical Institute in Presque Isle, claimed that between September 1985 and September 1986 he received in the mail sexually suggestive items. Poems, letters, and cards were all signed "Love, Charlene." MacDougal's attorney stated that MacDougal became emotionally upset because of this, was forced to seek psychological counseling, and had been out of work for over six weeks due to these emotional problems. MacDougal brought suit against three female teachers at the institute, charging them with sexual harassment. MacDougal sought $1.6 million in damages.

The three teachers defended that there had been a history of good-humored practical jokes played by the faculty members at the school, that MacDougal himself participated, and that all they were doing was playing a practical joke on MacDougal. They claimed that they had no intention of harassing him.

Does the EEOC guidelines definition of sexual harassment apply to men? Assuming, for the sake of discussion, that men are protected from sexual harassment under the guidelines, was there a violation of the guidelines? What is the measure of damages in a case such as this? [MacDougal v. Gregg et al., the *Boston Herald*, Feb. 26, 1987, p. 23.]

10. A teenage female high school student named Salazar was employed part-time at Church's Fried Chicken restaurant. Salazar was hired and supervised by Simon Garza, the assistant manager of the restaurant. Garza had complete supervisory powers when the restaurant's manager, Garza's roommate, was absent. Salazar alleged that while she worked at the restaurant, Garza would refer to her and all other females by a Spanish term that she found objectionable. According to Salazar, Garza once purportedly made a lecherous

comment about Salazar's body and repeatedly asked her about her personal life. On another occasion, Garza allegedly physically removed eyeshadow from Salazar's face because he felt that it looked ugly. Salazar also claimed that one night she was restrained in a back room of the restaurant while Garza and another employee fondled her. Later that night, when Salazar told a customer about what had happened, she was fired. Salazar believed that she was fired because she disclosed this incident.

Salazar filed an action under Title VII against Garza and Church's Fried Chicken, Inc. alleging sexual harassment. The defendants moved for summary judgment. Garza, who has since stopped working at Church's, contended that even if Salazar's allegations were true, she had not established sexual harassment under Title VII. Church's, the corporate defendant, maintained that it should not be held liable under Title VII for Garza's harassment. Church's grounded its argument on the existence of a published "fair treatment policy" and a grievance procedure that was not invoked by Salazar.

If Salazar's allegations are true, has she stated an actionable case under Title VII? May Church's be held liable for Garza's actions? If the case proceeds to trial, what remedies may Salazar seek? [Salazar v. Church's Fried Chicken, Inc., 44 FEP 472 (S.D. Tex. 1987)]

2

Fair Employment Practices: II

SECTION 9—BURDEN OF PROOF

As stated previously, the Supreme Court has created two legal theories for a plaintiff to prove a case of unlawful discrimination: disparate treatment and disparate impact.

Disparate treatment is intentional employment discrimination where, for example, women are treated less favorably than men, or blacks are treated less favorably than whites. The burden of proof for disparate treatment cases is developed in this section.

Disparate impact is a theory of employment discrimination that focuses on the consequences of an employer's selection procedures for hiring and promotions. The theory was developed in the *Griggs v. Duke Power Company* decision. The practice occurs where an employer's facially neutral employment practices have a significantly adverse or disparate impact on a protected group, and the employer is unable to show that the practice is job related. Proof of a discriminatory motive is not required. The burden of proof for disparate impact cases is also developed in this section.

Proof in Disparate Treatment Cases

In *McDonnell Douglas Corp. v. Green*[1] the Supreme Court discussed how a prima facie showing of discrimination in the context of a disparate treatment case may be established. The plaintiff must show (1) that he or she belongs to a group protected from discrimination under Title VII on the basis of characteristics such as race, color, national origin,

---

[1] 411 U.S. 792 (1972).

sex, or religion; (2) that he or she applied and was qualified for a job for which the employer was seeking applicants; (3) that, despite being qualified, he or she was rejected; and (4) that, after he or she was rejected, the position remained open and the employer continued to seek applicants whose qualifications were similar to those of the plaintiff. Once such a prima facie case is established, the burden shifts to the employer to articulate some legitimate, nondiscriminatory reason for its action. If such a reason is forthcoming, then the plaintiff is afforded an opportunity to demonstrate by a preponderance of the evidence that the supposedly valid reasons for the employer's actions were in fact a cover-up or pretext for a discriminatory decision.

In *Furnco Construction Co. v. Waters*[2] the Supreme Court explained its *McDonnell Douglas* decision. The *Furnco* case concerned Title VII. Eight black bricklayers challenged the company's policy of not hiring "at the gate" but rather hiring only those workers whose quality could be attested to by the job supervisor. The company showed that 13.3 percent of the total work hours of the job were performed by black bricklayers while 5.7 percent of the bricklayers in the relevant labor force were minority group members. The Supreme Court remanded the case to the court of appeals. In *Furnco* the four-point inquiry of *McDonnell Douglas* did make out a prima facie case of discrimination, but such is not to be equated with an ultimate finding of fact as to a discriminatory refusal to hire. When the four points are met by the plaintiff, the employer must only show that it based its employment decision on a legitimate business consideration such as efficiency or safety and not on an illegitimate one such as race.

In *Board of Trustees of Keene State College v. Sweeney*[3] the Supreme Court remanded a decision to the U.S. court of appeals because it found that the court appeared to impose a heavier burden on the employer than that required by *McDonnell Douglas* and *Furnco*. The Court stated that there is a significant distinction between requiring an employer to merely articulate some legitimate, nondiscriminatory reason and requiring the employer to prove the absence of discriminatory motive. The Court held that the "employer's burden is satisfied if [it] simply explains what [it] had done or produces evidence of legitimate, nondiscriminatory reasons."

Confusion existed in the federal trial courts and appeals courts as to the precise nature of the shifts of burdens of proof and persuasion after the plaintiff made out a prima facie case under the *McDonnell Douglas* model. The *Burdine* decision, presented in this section, confirms that the employer rebuts a prima facie case by producing admissible evidence of a legitimate reason for its decision to reject the plaintiff. Legitimate, non-discriminatory reasons offered by an employer could be lesser comparative qualifications, inability to work in harmony with others, or violations of employer rules. Once a prima facie case is properly rebutted, the plaintiff can prevail by showing that the employer was motivated by a discriminatory reason or that the employer's reason is not believable. Under *Burdine*, then, the employer has an intermediate burden of production, but the ultimate burden of proving that the defendant-employer intentionally discriminated against the plaintiff remains with the plaintiff at all times.

The Supreme Court made an additional attempt to clarify its numerous decisions

---

[2] 438 U.S. 567 (1978).
[3] 439 U.S. 24, 18 FEP 520 (1978).

on proof in disparate treatment cases in *Postal Service v. Aikens*,[4] focusing in detail on its *McDonnell Douglas* and *Burdine* precedents. Under the *McDonnell Douglas-Burdine* model, as applied in *Aikens*, a three-stage process is followed. Stage 1 focuses on the plaintiff's burden to present sufficient evidence of discrimination to establish a prima facie case according to the elements set forth in *McDonnell Douglas*. At the end of the plaintiff's presentation of evidence, the district court may sustain the defendant-employer's motion to dismiss the case for lack of a prima facie case, and the case would be terminated. Stage 2 is reached if the court determines that the plaintiff has made out a prima facie case. At this stage the defendant must respond with evidence of a non-discriminatory reason for the plaintiff's rejection. Stage 3 is sometimes referred to as the "pretext" stage in reference to *Burdine*. As set forth in *Burdine*, the plaintiff has the right to offer additional evidence rebutting the employer's asserted reason for the rejection. Alternatively, the plaintiff may simply rely on the evidence of a discriminatory motive introduced as part of its prima facie case. However, it is at this third stage that the district court must reach the ultimate question of fact by deciding which party's explanation of the employer's motivation in rejecting the plaintiff for employment is to be believed. The court will weigh all the evidence of record in reaching its decision.

Proof in Disparate Impact Cases

In *Connecticut v. Teal*, presented in this section, the Supreme Court set forth a three-part analysis of disparate impact claims. The underlying theory was developed in the *Griggs v. Duke Power Co.* decision. The three-part analysis and an explanation of each part follows:

1. In order to make out a prima facie case, the plaintiff must prove that the facially neutral employment practice at issue had a significantly discriminatory impact. Thus the plaintiff must show by the use of statistical evidence that certain selection criteria or promotion criteria had an adverse impact on a minority group or women. In *Teal* the plaintiffs demonstrated that the state's test for promotion to supervisor had an adverse impact on blacks.
2. If the showing of discriminatory impact is made, the employer must then demonstrate that the requirement had a "manifest relationship to the employment in question." The quoted language is from the *Griggs* decision, and the inquiry under *Griggs* becomes whether the selection procedure in question is "job related" or otherwise constitutes a "business necessity." In *Teal* the state did not demonstrate that the examination for promotion to supervisor was job related.
3. Even in such a case where the employer shows that the test was job related, the plaintiff may prevail by showing that the employer was using the practice as a mere pretext for discrimination. This third step is, in effect, the intentional discrimination theory of disparate treatment that would be processed under the *McDonnell Douglas-Burdine* model. This step makes clear that a plaintiff(s) may proceed under one or both of the theories discussed in this section.

The Court in *Teal* refers back to the *Griggs* discussion of the legislative history of Title VII whereby it was concluded that Congress in adding Section 703(h) intended to make

---

[4] 108 S. Ct. 1478 (1983).

clear that tests that were job related would be permissible despite their disparate impact.

In *Watson v. Fort Worth Bank and Trust Co.*[5] the Supreme Court approved the use of disparate impact analysis to review hiring or promotion decisions based on subjective criteria such as personal interviews and performance appraisals. Previously disparate impact analysis had been limited to review of objective selection practices such as standardized tests and diploma requirements.

---

[5]47 FEP 102 (U.S. S. Ct. 1988).

Texas Department of Community Affairs v. Burdine
Supreme Court of the United States, 450 U.S. 248 (1981).

[Petitioner, the Texas Department of Community Affairs (TDCA), hired the respondent, Burdine, in January 1972 for the position of accounting clerk in the Public Service Careers Division (PSC). PSC provided training and employment opportunities in the public sector for unskilled workers. When hired, Burdine possessed several years' experience in employment training. She was promoted to Field Services Coordinator in July 1972. Her supervisor resigned in November of that year, and she was assigned additional duties. Although she applied for the supervisor's position of Project Director, the position remained vacant for six months.

PSC was funded completely by the United States Department of Labor. The Department was seriously concerned about inefficiencies at PSC. In February 1973 the Department notified the Executive Director of TDCA, B. R. Fuller, that it would terminate PSC the following month. TDCA officials, assisted by Burdine, persuaded the Department to continue funding the program, conditioned upon PSC reforming its operations. Among the agreed conditions were the appointment of a permanent Project Director and a complete reorganization of the PSC staff. After consulting with personnel within TDCA, Fuller hired a male from another division of the agency as Project Director. In reducing the PSC staff, he terminated Burdine along with two other employ-

ees, and retained another male, Walz, as the only professional employee in the division. It is undisputed that respondent had maintained her application for the position of Project Director and had requested to remain with TDCA. Burdine soon was rehired by TDCA and assigned to another division of the agency.

Burdine filed this suit in the United States district court alleging that the failure to promote and the subsequent decision to terminate her had been predicated on gender discrimination in violation of Title VII. After a bench trial, the district court held that neither decision was based on gender discrimination. The court relied on the testimony of Fuller that the employment decisions necessitated by the commands of the Department of Labor were based on consultation among trusted advisors and nondiscriminatory evaluation of the relative qualifications of the individuals involved. He testified that the three individuals terminated did not work well together and that TDCA thought that eliminating this problem would improve PSC's efficiency. The court accepted this explanation as rational and, in effect, found no evidence that the decisions not to promote and to terminate respondent were prompted by gender discrimination. The Court of Appeals for the Fifth Circuit reversed in part the holding of the district court that Fuller's testimony sufficiently had rebutted Burdine's prima facie case of

*gender discrimination in the decision to terminate
her employment at PSC. The court of appeals
reaffirmed its previously announced views that the
defendant in a Title VII case bears the burden of
proving by a preponderance of the evidence the
existence of legitimate nondiscriminatory reasons
for the employment action and that the defendant
also must prove by objective evidence that those
hired or promoted were better qualified than the
plaintiff. The Supreme Court granted certiorari.]*

POWELL, J.

The burden of establishing a prima facie case of
disparate treatment is not onerous. The plaintiff
must prove by a preponderence of the evidence
that she applied for an available position, for
which she was qualified, but was rejected under
circumstances which give rise to an inference of
unlawful discrimination. The prima facie case
serves an important function in the litigation: it
eliminates the most common nondiscriminatory
reasons for the plaintiff's rejection. As the Court
explained in *Furnco Construction Co. v. Waters*,
438 U.S. 567, 577 (1978), the prima facie case
"raises an inference of discrimination only because we presume these acts, if otherwise unex-
plained, are more likely than not based on the
consideration of impermissible factors." Establishment of the prima facie case in effect creates
a presumption that the employer unlawfully discriminated against the employee. If the trier of
fact believes the plaintiff's evidence, and if the
employer is silent in the face of the presumption,
the court must enter judgment for the plaintiff
because no issue of fact remains in the case.

The burden that shifts to the defendant,
therefore, is to rebut the resumption of discrimination by producing evidence that the plaintiff
was rejected, or someone else was preferred, for
a legitimate, nondiscriminatory reason. The defendant need not persuade the court that it was
actually motivated by the proffered reasons. It is
sufficient if the defendant's evidence raises a genuine issue of fact as to whether it discriminated
against the plaintiff. To accomplish this, the defendant must clearly set forth, through the in-

troduction of admissible evidence, the reasons
for the plaintiff's rejection. The explanation
provided must be legally sufficient to justify a
judgment for the defendant. If the defendant
carries this burden of production, the presumption raised by the prima facie case is rebutted, and
the factual inquiry proceeds to a new level of
specificity. Placing this burden of production on
the defendant thus serves simultaneously to meet
the plaintiff's prima facie case by presenting a
legitimate reason for the action and to frame
the factual issue with sufficient clarity so that the
plaintiff will have a full and fair opportunity to
demonstrate pretext. The sufficiency of the defendant's evidence should be evaluated by the
extent to which it fulfills these functions.

The plaintiff retains the burden of persuasion. She now must have the opportunity to demonstrate that the proffered reason was not the true
reason for the employment decision. This burden
now merges with the ultimate burden of persuading the court that she has been the victim of
intentional discrimination. She may succeed in
this either directly by persuading the court that
a discriminatory reason more likely motivated
the employer or indirectly by showing that the
employer's proffered explanation is unworthy
of credence.

In reversing the judgment of the District
Court that the discharge of respondent from PSC
was unrelated to her sex, the Court of Appeals
adhered to two rules it had developed to elaborate
the defendant's burden of proof. First, the defendant must prove by a preponderance of the
evidence that legitimate, nondiscriminatory reasons for the discharge existed. Second, to satisfy
this burden, the defendant "must prove that those
he hired . . . were somehow *better* qualified than
was plaintiff; in other words, comparative evidence is needed."

The Court of Appeals has misconstrued the
nature of the burden that *McDonnell Douglas*
and its progeny place on the defendant. We stated
in *Sweeney* that "the employer's burden is satisfied
if he simply 'explains what he was done' or 'pro-
duc[es] evidence of legitimate nondiscriminatory

reasons.' " It is plain that the Court of Appeals required much more: it placed on the defendant the burden of persuading the court that it had convincing, objective reasons for preferring the chosen applicant above the plaintiff. *

The court placed the burden of persuasion on the defendant apparently because it feared that "[i]f an employer need only *articulate*—not prove—a legitimate, nondiscriminatory reason for his action, he may compose fictitious, but legitimate, reasons for his actions." We do not believe, however, that limiting the defendant's evidentiary obligation to a burden of production will unduly hinder the plaintiff. First, as noted above, the defendant's explanation of its legitimate reasons must be clear and reasonably specific. This obligation arises both from the necessity of rebutting the inference of discrimination arising from the prima facie case and from the requirement that the plaintiff be afforded "a full and fair opportunity" to demonstrate pretext. Second, although the defendant does not bear a formal burden of persuasion, the defendant nevertheless retains an incentive to persuade the trier of fact that the employment decision was lawful. Thus, the defendant normally will attempt to prove the factual basis for its explanation. . . . Given these factors, we are unpersuaded that the plaintiff will find it particularly difficult to prove that a proffered explanation lacking a factual basis is a pretext. We remain confident that the *McDonnell Douglas* framework permits the plaintiff meriting relief to demonstrate intentional discrimination.

The Court of Appeals also erred in requiring the defendant to prove by objective evidence that the person hired or promoted was more qualified than the plaintiff. *McDonnell Douglas* teaches that it is the plaintiff's task to demonstrate that similarly situated employees were not treated equally. The Court of Appeals' rule would require the employer to show that the plaintiff's objective qualifications were inferior to those of the person selected. If it cannot, a court would, in effect, conclude that it has discriminated.

The court's procedural rule harbors a substantive error. Title VII prohibits all discrimination in employment based upon race, sex and national origin. "The broad, overriding interest, shared by employer, employee, and consumer, is efficient and trustworthy workmanship assured through fair and . . . neutral employment and personnel decisions." Title VII, however, does not demand that an employer give preferential treatment to minorities or women. 42 U.S.C. § 2000e–2(j). The statute was not intended to "diminish traditional management prerogatives." It does not require the employer to restructure his employment practices to maximize the number of minorities and women hired.

The views of the Court of Appeals can be read, we think, as requiring the employer to hire the minority or female applicant whenever that person's objective qualifications were equal to those of a white male applicant. But Title VII does not obligate an employer to accord this preference. Rather, the employer has discretion to choose among equally qualified candidates, provided the decision is not based upon unlawful criteria. The fact that a court may think that the employer misjudged the qualifications of the applicants does not in itself expose him to Title VII liability, although this may be probative of whether the employer's reasons are pretexts for discrimination.

In summary, the Court of Appeals erred by requiring the defendant to prove by a prepon-

---

*The court reviewed the defendant's evidence and explained its deficiency:

"Defendant failed to introduce comparative factual data concerning Burdine and Walz. Fuller merely testified that he discharged and retained personnel in the spring shakeup at TDCA primarily on the recommendations of subordinates and that he considered Walz qualified for the position he was retained to do. Fuller failed to specify any objective criteria on which he based the decision to discharge Burdine and retain Walz. He stated only that the action was in the best interest of the program and that there had been some friction within the department that might be alleviated by Burdine's discharge. Nothing in the record indicates whether he examined Walz' ability to work well with others. This court in East found such unsubstantiated assertions of 'qualification' and 'prior work record' insufficient absent data that will allow a true *comparison* of the individuals hired and rejected." 608 F.2d at 568, 21 FEP Cases at 979.

derance of the evidence the existence of non-discriminatory reasons for terminating the respondent and that the person retained in her stead had superior objective qualifications for the position. When the plaintiff has proved a prima facie case of discrimination, the defendant bears only the burden of explaining clearly the non-discriminatory reasons for its actions. The judgment of the Court of Appeals is vacated and the case is remanded for further proceedings consistent with this opinion.

It is so ordered.

CASE QUESTIONS

1. State the facts of this case.
2. After a prima facie case has been made out, what is the defendant's "burden"?
3. Under the *Burdine* rule is the employer required to prove by a preponderance of the evidence that the person hired, promoted, or retained was better qualified than the person who was rejected?
4. Under *Burdine* is an employer required to hire, promote, or retain a minority or female employee whenever this individual's objective qualifications are equal to those of white male applicants?

Connecticut v. Teal

Supreme Court of the United States, 457 U.S. 440 (1982).

BRENNAN, J.

We consider here whether an employer sued for violation of Title VII of the Civil Rights Act of 1964 may assert a "bottom line" theory of defense. Under that theory, as asserted in this case, an employer's acts of racial discrimination in promotions—effected by an examination having disparate impact—would not render the employer liable for the racial discrimination suffered by employees barred from promotion if the "bottom line" result of the promotional process was an appropriate racial balance. We hold that the "bottom line" does not preclude respondent-employees from establishing a prima facie case, nor does it provide petitioner-employer with a defense to such a case.

Four of the respondents, Winnie Teal, Rose Walker, Edith Latney, and Grace Clark, are black employees of the Department of Income Maintenance of the State of Connecticut. Each was promoted provisionally to the position of Welfare Eligibility Supervisor and served in that capacity for almost two years. To attain permanent status as supervisors, however, respondents had to participate in a selection process that required, as

the first step, a passing score on a written examination. This written test was administered on December 2, 1978, to 329 candidates. Of these candidates, 48 identified themselves as black and 259 identified themselves as white. The results of the examination were announced in March 1979. With the passing score set at 65,[*] 54.17 [percent] of the identified black candidates passed. This was approximately 68 percent of the passing rate for the identified white candidates.[**] The four respondents were among the blacks who

---

[*]The mean score on the examination was 70.4 percent. However, because the black candidates had a mean score 6.7 percentage points lower than the white candidates, the passing score was set at 65, apparently in the attempt to lessen the disparate impact of the examination.

[**]The following table shows the passing rates of various candidate groups:

Candidate Group	Number	No. Receiving Passing Score	Passing Rate (%)
Blank	48	26	54.17
Hispanic	4	3	75.00
Indian	3	2	66.67
White	259	206	79.54
Unidentified	15	9	60.00
Total	329	246	74.77

failed the examination, and they were thus excluded from further consideration for permanent supervisory positions. In April 1979, respondents instituted this action in the United States District Court for the District of Connecticut against petitioners, the State of Connecticut, two state agencies, and two state officials. Respondents alleged, *inter alia*, that petitioners violated Title VII by imposing, as an absolute condition for consideration for promotion, that applicants pass a written test that excluded blacks in disproportionate numbers and that was not job related.

More than a year after this action was instituted, and approximately one month before the trial, petitioners made promotions from the eligibility list generated by the written examination. In choosing persons from that list, petitioners considered past work performance recommendations of the candidates' supervisors and, to a lesser extent, seniority. Petitioners then applied what the Court of Appeals characterized as an affirmative action program in order to ensure a significant number of minority supervisors. Forty-six persons were promoted to permanent supervisory positions, 11 of whom were black and 35 of whom were white. The overall result of the selection process was that, of the 48 identified black candidates who participated in the selection process, 22.9 percent were promoted and of the 259 identified white candidates, 13.5 percent were promoted.*** It is this "bottom line" result, more favorable to blacks than to whites, that petitioners urge should be adjudged to be a complete defense to respondents' suit.

After trial, the District Court entered judgment for petitioners. The court treated respondents' claim as one of disparate impact under *Griggs v. Duke Power Co.*, 401 U.S. 424 (1971), *Albemarle Paper Co. v. Moody*, 422 U.S. 405 (1975), and *Dothard v. Rawlinson*, 433 U.S. 321 (1977). However, the court found that, although the comparative passing rates for the examination indicated a prima facie case of adverse im-

___

***The actual promotion of blacks was thus close to 170 percent that of the actual promotion rate of whites.

pact upon minorities, the result of the entire hiring process reflected no such adverse impact. Holding that these "bottom line" percentages precluded the finding of a Title VII violation, the court held that the employer was not required to demonstrate that the promotional examination was job related. The United States Court of Appeals for the Second Circuit reversed, holding that the District Court erred in ruling that the results of the written examination alone were insufficient to support a prima facie case of disparate impact in violation of Title VII. The Court of Appeals stated that where "an identifiable pass-fail barrier denies an employment opportunity to a disproportionately large number of minorities and prevents them from proceeding to the next step in the selection process," that barrier must be shown to be job related. We granted certiorari, and now affirm.

We must first decide whether an examination that bars a disparate number of black employees from consideration for promotion, and that has not been shown to be job related, presents a claim cognizable under Title VII. Section 703(a)(2) of Title VII provides in pertinent part:

It shall be an unlawful employment practice for an employer—
(2) to limit, segregate, or classify his employees or applicants for employment in any way which would deprive or tend to deprive any individual of employment opportunities or otherwise adversely affect his status as an employee, because of such individual's race, color, religion, sex, or national origin. 78 Stat. 255, as amended, 42 U.S.C. § 2000e–2(a)(2).

Respondents base their claim on our construction of this provision in *Griggs v. Duke Power Co.*, *supra*. Prior to the enactment of Title VII, the Duke Power Company restricted its black employees to the labor department. Beginning in 1965, the company required all employees who desired a transfer out of the labor department to have either a high school diploma or to achieve a passing grade on two professionally prepared aptitude tests. New employees seeking positions in any department other than labor had to possess both a high school diploma and a passing grade on these two examinations. Although these requirements applied equally to white and black employees and applicants, they barred employment opportunities to a disproportionate number of blacks. While there was no showing that the employer had a racial purpose or invidious intent in adopting these requirements, this Court held that they were invalid because they had a disparate impact and were not shown to be related to job performance:

[Title VII] *proscribes not only overt discrimination but also practices that are fair in form, but discriminatory in operation. The touchstone is business necessity. If an employment practice which operates to exclude Negroes cannot be shown to be related to job performance, the practice is prohibited.*

Griggs and its progeny have established a three-part analysis of disparate impact claims. To establish a prima facie case of discrimination, a plaintiff must show that the facially neutral employment practice had a significantly discriminatory impact. If that showing is made, the employer must then demonstrate that "any given requirement [has] a manifest relationship to the employment in question," in order to avoid a finding of discrimination. Even in such a case, however, the plaintiff may prevail, if he shows that the employer was using the practice as a mere pretext for discrimination.

Griggs recognized that in enacting Title VII, Congress required "the removal of artificial, arbitrary, and unnecessary barriers to employment" and professional development that had historically been encountered by women and blacks as well as other minorities.

Petitioners' examination, which barred promotion and had a discriminatory impact on black employees, clearly falls within the literal language of § 703(a)(2), as interpreted by *Griggs*. The statute speaks, not in terms of jobs and promotions, but in terms of *limitations* and *classifications* that would deprive any individual of employment *opportunities*. A disparate impact claim reflects the language of § 703(a)(2) and Congress' basic objectives in enacting that statute: "to achieve equality of employment *opportunities* and remove barriers that have operated in the past

to favor an identifiable group of white employees over other employees." When an employer uses a non-job-related barrier in order to deny a minority or woman applicant employment or promotion, and that barrier has a significant adverse effect on minorities or women, then the applicant has been deprived of an employment *opportunity* "because of . . . race, color, religion, sex, or national origin." In other words, § 703(a)(2) prohibits discriminatory "artificial, arbitrary, and unnecessary barriers to employment," that "limit . . . or classify . . . applicants for employment . . . in any way which would deprive or tend to deprive any individual of employment *opportunities*.". . .

In short, the District Court's dismissal of respondents' claim cannot be supported on the basis that respondents failed to establish a prima facie case of employment discrimination under the terms of § 703(a)(2). The suggestion that disparate impact should be measured only at the bottom line ignores the fact that Title VII guarantees these individual respondents the *opportunity* to compete equally with white workers on the basis of job-related criteria. Title VII strives to achieve equality of opportunity by rooting out "artificial, arbitrary, and unnecessary" employer-created barriers to professional development that have a discriminatory impact upon individuals. Therefore, respondents' rights under § 703(a)(2) have been violated, unless petitioners can demonstrate that the examination given was not an artificial, arbitrary, or unnecessary barrier, because it measured skills related to effective performance in the role of Welfare Eligibility Supervisor.

The United States, in its brief as *amicus curiae*, apparently recognizes that respondents' claim in this case falls within the affirmative commands of Title VII. But it seeks to support the District Court's judgment in this case by relying on the defenses provided to the employer in § 703(h). Section 703(h) provides in pertinent part:

"*Notwithstanding any other provision of this title, it shall not be an unlawful employment practice for an employer . . . to give and to act upon the results of any professionally developed ability test provided that such test, its administration or action upon the results is not designed, intended or used to discriminate because of race, color, religion, sex or national origin." 78 Stat. 257, as amended, 42 U.S.C. § 2000e–2(h).*

The Government argues that the test administered by the petitioners was not "used to discriminate" because it did not actually deprive disproportionate numbers of blacks of promotions. But the Government's reliance on § 703(h) as offering the employer some special haven for discriminatory tests is misplaced. We considered the relevance of this provision in *Griggs*. After examining the legislative history of § 703(h), we concluded that Congress, in adding § 703(h), intended only to make clear that tests that were *job related* would be permissible despite their disparate impact. A non-job-related test that has a disparate racial impact, and is used to "limit" or "classify" employees, is "used to discriminate" within the meaning of Title VII, whether or not it was "designed or intended" to have this effect and despite an employer's efforts to compensate for its discriminatory effect.

In sum, respondents' claim of disparate impact from the examination, a pass-fail barrier to employment opportunity, states a prima facie case of employment discrimination under § 703(a)(2), despite their employer's nondiscriminatory "bottom line," and that "bottom line" is no defense to this prima facie case under § 703(h).

Having determined that respondents' claim comes within the terms of Title VII, we must address the suggestion of petitioners and some *amici curiae* that we recognize an exception, either in the nature of an additional burden on plaintiffs seeking to establish a prima facie case or in the nature of an affirmative defense, for cases in which an employer has compensated for a discriminatory pass-fail barrier by hiring or promoting a sufficient number of black employees to reach a nondiscriminatory "bottom line." We reject this suggestion, which is in essence nothing more than a request that we redefine the protections guaranteed by Title VII.

Section 703(a)(2) prohibits practices that would deprive or tend to deprive "*any individual* of employment opportunities." The principal focus of the statute is the protection of the individual employee, rather than the protection of the minority group as a whole. Indeed, the entire statute and its legislative history are replete with references to protection for the individual employee.

In suggesting that the "bottom line" may be a defense to a claim of discrimination against an individual employee, petitioners and *amici* appear to confuse unlawful discrimination with discriminatory intent. The Court has stated that a nondiscriminatory "bottom line" and an employer's good faith efforts to achieve a nondiscriminatory work force, might in some cases assist an employer in rebutting the inference that particular action had been intentionally discriminatory: "Proof that [a] work force was racially balanced or that it contained a disproportionately high percentage of minority employees is not wholly irrelevant on the issue of intent when that issue is yet to be decided." But resolution of the factual question of intent is not what is at issue in this case. . . .

. . . Every *individual* employee is protected against both discriminatory treatment and against "practices that are fair in form, but discriminatory in operation." Requirements and tests that have a discriminatory impact are merely some of the more subtle, but also the more pervasive, of the "practices and devices which have fostered racially stratified job environments to the disadvantage of minority citizens."

In sum, petitioners' nondiscriminatory "bottom line" is no answer, under the terms of Title VII, to respondents' prima facie claim of employment discrimination. Accordingly, the judgment of the Court of Appeals for the Second Circuit is affirmed, and this case is remanded to the District Court for further proceedings consistent with this opinion.

It is so ordered.

Dissenting Opinion

POWELL, J., joined by BURGER, C. J., and REHNQUIST and O'CONNER, J. J.

. . . Our disparate impact cases consistently have considered whether the result of an employer's *total selection process* had an adverse impact upon the protected group. If this case were decided by references to the total process—as our cases suggest that it should be—the result would be clear. Here 22.9% of the blacks who entered the selection process were ultimately promoted, compared with only 13.5% of the whites. To say that this selection process had an unfavorable "disparate impact" on blacks is to ignore reality. . . .

. . . Employers need not develop tests that accurately reflect the skills of every individual candidate; there are few if any tests that do so. Yet the Court seems unaware of this practical reality, and perhaps oblivious to the likely consequences of its decision. By its holding today, the Court may force employers either to eliminate tests or rely on expensive, job-related testing procedures, the validity of which may or may not be sustained if challenged. For state and local governmental employers with limited funds, the practical effect of today's decision may well be the adoption of simple quota hiring. This arbitrary method of employment is itself unfair to individual applicants, whether or not they are members of minority groups. And it is not likely to produce a competent workforce. Moreover, the Court's decision actually may result in employers employing *fewer* minority members.

[A]s *private parties are permitted under Title VII itself to adopt voluntary affirmative action plans, . . . Title VII should not be construed to prohibit a municipality's using a hiring process that results in a percentage of policemen approximating their percentage of the local population, instead of relying on the expectation that a validated job-related testing procedure will produce an equivalent result, yet with the risk that it might lead to substantially less hiring.*

Finding today's decision unfortunate in both its analytical approach and its likely consequences, I dissent.

CASE QUESTIONS

1. State the three-part analysis courts apply to disparate impact claims.
2. Was the written examination taken by Teal, Walker, Latney, and Clark job related?
3. If a test is proven to be job related where the evidence shows a disparate impact on a minority group, does the *Teal* decision require the test to be invalidated?
4. Did the state of Connecticut intend to discriminate against Teal, Walker, Latney, and Clark?

SECTION 10—STATISTICAL CASES

In *Hazelwood School District v. United States*[6] the Supreme Court dealt with the matter of statistical proof in Title VII cases. The Hazelwood School District was formed by thirteen rural school districts outside of St. Louis, Missouri. Of the more than 19,000 teachers employed in the St. Louis area, 15.4 percent were black. This figure included the St. Louis City School District, which had a policy of attempting to maintain a 50 percent black teaching staff. Apart from the city district, 5.7 percent of the teachers in the county were black according to the 1970 census. In the 1972–73 school year Hazelwood employed 16 black teachers on its staff of 1107 (1.4 percent), and by the 1973–74 school year 22 of 1231 (1.8 percent) of the teachers were black. The attorney general of the United States brought a "pattern or practice" of discrimination suit against the school district. This suit was unsuccessful in the U.S. district court but successful in the U.S. court of appeals. The Supreme Court granted certiorari. In its decision the Court set forth certain principles for statistical cases and remanded the case for further proceedings.

---

[6]433 U.S. 299, 15 FEP 1 (1977).

Qualified Labor Market

A "population-workforce" comparison makes a statistical comparison of the percentage of blacks, Hispanics, or women in the population of a specific geographical area to the number of blacks, Hispanics, or women employed by a defendant employer. In *Hazelwood* the Supreme Court cautioned that the statistical data for such comparisons should be based on the "qualified" labor market. The Court stated:

> When special qualifications are required to fill particular jobs, comparisons to the general population (rather than to the smaller group of individuals who possess the necessary qualifications) may have little probative value.[7]

Relevant Geographic Area

The *Hazelwood* decision emphasized the importance of determining the relevant geographic area for statistical comparison purposes. The objective is to define the area from which applicants are likely to come, absent discrimination. Thus commuting patterns, availability of public transportation, and the geographic scope of the employer's recruiting practices are all relevant considerations. For example, if the employer recruits for executives on a nationwide basis, the relevant geographical area would be the entire country, and nationwide statistics would be applicable.

Relevant Time Frame

Hazelwood recognized the concept of "relevant time frame" statistics, which focuses on the employment decisions made during the relevant time period of the litigation rather than looking at "static" statistics. The relevant time period is after the effective date of Title VII. However, under the Supreme Court's *United Air Lines v. Evans*[8] decision, the Court considers discriminatory acts occurring before the charge-filing period to be the legal equivalent of acts occurring before the effective date of Title VII. Thus the relevant time frame for a Title VII case is the period starting three hundred days prior to the filing of a charge with the EEOC. For example, if an employer had few blacks in its work force but in the two years prior to the filing of a charge had hired blacks at a rate equal to or above the percentage of blacks in the work force of the area, the relevant time frame analysis would lead to a finding that Title VII was not violated even though a "static analysis"—which is simply the actual percentage of blacks employed in the employer's total work force on a given date regardless of hiring dates—would show a gross disparity. The *Evans* Court would consider the statistical significance of the static analysis, which would indicate the existence of past discrimination as "merely an unfortunate event in history which has no present legal consequences."

Sufficiency of Statistical Disparity

Ultimately in a statistical case a court is called upon to make determinations based on the statistical evidence before it. The Court in *Hazelwood* made it clear that the statistical

---

[7]433 U.S. 229, 308 n. 13, 15 FEP 1, 5 (1977).
[8]431 U.S. 553, 14 FEP 1510 (1977).

disparity must be a "gross" disparity in order for there to be a finding of discrimination based on the statistical evidence. The *Hazelwood* Court set forth a "standard deviations" analysis that has been followed by numerous lower courts. The Supreme Court did not resolve the discrimination issue before it in *Hazelwood* and remanded the case to the district court for further proceedings on the geographic scope of the relevant labor market utilizing the statistical methodology explained in *Castaneda v. Partida*.[9] Footnote 17 of the *Hazelwood* decision states:

> Indeed, under the statistical methodology explained in *Castaneda* . . . involving the calculation of the standard deviation as a measure of predicted fluctuations, the difference between using 15.4% and 5.7% as the areawide figure would be significant. If the 15.4% figure is taken as the basis for comparison, the expected number of Negro teachers, hired by Hazelwood in 1972–1973 would be 43 (rather than the actual figure of 10) of a total of 282, a difference of more than five standard deviations; the expected number in 1973–1974 would be 19 (rather than the actual figure 5) of a total of 123, a difference of more than three standard deviations. For the two years combined, the difference between the observed number of 15 Negro teachers hired (of a total of 405) would vary from the expected number of 62 by more than six standard deviations. Because a fluctuation of more than two or three standard deviations would undercut the hypothesis that decisions were being made randomly with respect to race, each of these statistical comparisons would reinforce rather than rebut the Government's other proof. If, however, the 5.7% areawide figure is used, the expected number of Negro teachers hired in 1972–1973 would be roughly 16, less than two standard deviations from the observed number of 10; for 1973–1974, the expected value would be roughly seven, less than one standard deviation from the observed value of 5; and for the two years combined, the expected value of 23 would be less than two standard deviations from the observed total of 15. . . .
>
> These observations are not intended to suggest that precise calculations of statistical significance are necessary in employing statistical proof, but merely to highlight the importance of the choice of the relevant labor market area.

Please note in footnote 17 that the Supreme Court has adopted a rule of thumb for the number of standard deviations that would undercut the hypothesis that the decisions were being made randomly with respect to race, etc., and that it is a greater than "two or three standard deviations" rule.

The binomial test used by the Supreme Court in *Castaneda* may be summarized in terms of a set of equations using the following symbols to represent the variables.[10] Thus,

n = number of binomial trials in a particular experiment
p = probability of a success on each trial
e = expected number of successes
o = observed number of successes
SD = standard deviation
Z = Z statistic or Z score, which is the number of standard deviations by which the number of successes actually observed differs from the number expected

---

[9]430 U.S. 482 (1977).
[10]See Sugrue and Fairley, *A Case of Unexamined Assumptions: The Use and Misuse of the Statistical Analysis of* Castaneda/Hazelwood *in Discrimination Litigation*, 24 B.C. Law Rev. 925 (1983).

1. In *Castaneda* the statistical analysis sought to assess if the shortage in the number of Mexican-Americans called to serve on grand juries in Hidalgo County, Texas, could have occurred by chance. The total number of persons selected for grand jury was 870; thus "n" = 870. Mexican-Americans made up 79.1% of the population from which grand jurors were drawn; thus "p" = .791. The actual number of Mexican-Americans selected for grand jury duty was 339; thus "o" = 339. To find the expected number of successes, multiply "n" times "p" (e = n × p): e = 870 × .791 = 688.

2. To calculate the standard deviation (SD), take the square root of the product of the number of trials, the probability of a success, and the probability of a failure (SD = $\sqrt{n \times p \times (1 - p)}$): SD = $\sqrt{870 \times .791 \times .209} = \sqrt{143.83}$ = 11.99.

3. To calculate the Z statistic or score, which is the number of standard deviations by which the number of successes actually observed differs from the number of successes expected, the numerator consists of the expected number minus the observed number or

$$Z = \frac{e - o}{SD} : Z = \frac{688 - 339}{11.99} = 29.1$$

A fluctuation of more than two or three standard deviations—that is a Z score of greater than 2 or 3—would undercut the hypothesis that the selection process was being made randomly with respect to national origin. In *Castaneda* the fluctuation was so great that the Court concluded that the statistical disparities established a prima facie case of discrimination against Mexican-Americans in the selection process.

In *EEOC v. Sears*[11] the Equal Employment Opportunity Commission brought a discrimination case against Sears that was based almost entirely on statistics. The case was the culmination of twelve years of work and expense on both sides. The trial lasted some ten months, and $3 million was paid in expert witness fees alone. The court decided the case against the EEOC, finding that the EEOC did not prove even one individual instance of discrimination by Sears. On appeal the EEOC contended that its statistical analysis showed that only sex discrimination could explain the predominance of males in the most lucrative sales jobs, while mostly females worked the lower-paying noncommission sales jobs. The court of appeals, however, determined that the EEOC's statistical evidence was flawed in that it inflated the percentage of qualified female applicants.[12] Moreover, the court of appeals held that the district court had properly credited Sears' defense that during the period of time in question, 1973 through 1980, women were historically not interested in the irregular hours, the compensation risks, and the products involved in commission sales.

As will be seen in Section 12, a voluntary affirmative action plan under the so-called *Weber* standards requires that an employer self-analysis be made as part of the plan to determine if and where conspicious racial or gender imbalances exist. An affirmative action plan may then seek to remedy such imbalances. It is very important that the self-analysis be conducted in accordance with the *Hazelwood* standards. In evaluating its work force to see if conspicuous racial or gender imbalances exist and in setting goals

[11]39 FEP 1652 (1986).
[12]45 FEP 1257 (7th Cir. 1988).

to remedy imbalances, the employer should take into account the number of women and minorities qualified for the individual positions in the relevant geographical area.[13]

SECTION 11—TITLE VII COURT-ORDERED REMEDIES

The remedial powers of federal courts deciding Title VII actions include injunctions against unlawful practices, affirmative orders requiring the reinstatement or the hiring of employees, and the awarding of back pay and seniority rights. The 1972 amendments limit back pay orders to a period of two years prior to the filing of the charge.[14]

Make-Whole Remedies for Victims

In the *Albemarle Paper Company* decision, reported in this section, the Supreme Court held that back pay should only be denied in limited situations and for reasons which would not frustrate the purposes of Title VII. The *Bowman* decision is an example of a remedy fashioned from legislative intent. There the Supreme Court held that the awarding of seniority rights was necessary to eradicate the effects of post-Title VII discrimination against black employees.

Court-Ordered Affirmative Action for Nonvictims

In *Sheet Metal Workers' Local 28 v. EEOC* the Supreme Court held that district courts were not limited to awarding preferential relief only to the actual victims of unlawful discrimination. The courts may order preferential relief, such as requiring the employer to meet goals and timetables for the hiring of minorities, where an employer or labor union has engaged in persistent and egregious discrimination or where it is necessary to dissipate the lingering effects of pervasive discrimination. The Court stated, however, that in the majority of Title VII cases where Title VII has been found to have been violated, the district court will need only to order the employer or union to cease the unlawful practices and award make-whole relief to the individuals victimized by those practices. The *Sheet Metal Workers* decision is presented in this section.

Award of Attorney's Fees

Section 706(k) of Title VII provides that the court in its discretion may allow the prevailing party, other than the EEOC and the United States, a reasonable attorney's fee. In *New York Gaslight Club Inc. v. Carey*[15] the Supreme Court held that a federal court may allow the prevailing party attorney's fees before a state administrative proceeding that Title VII requires federal claimants to invoke.

The Supreme Court in *Christiansburg Garment Co. v. EEOC*[16] set forth a standard that allows district courts the discretion to award attorney's fees to a prevailing defendant

---

[13]Please see Justice O'Conner's concurring opinion in Johnson v. Transportation Agency, 107 S. Ct. 1442, 1463 (1987).
[14] 42 USC Section 706(g).
[15]477 U.S. 54, 22 FEP 1642 (1980).
[16]434 U.S. 412 (1978).

where the plaintiff's case is "frivolous, unreasonable, or without foundation." In *Arnold v. Burger King Corporation*[17] the Fourth Circuit Court of Appeals affirmed an award of $10,744 in attorney's fees against an unsuccessful plaintiff in a race discrimination case. The plaintiff, Arnold, a black male, was employed as a manager of a Burger King when several female employees formally complained to management that Arnold had sexually harassed them. The complaints accused Arnold of various incidents of misconduct including propositions and acts of deliberate and suggestive physical conduct. Following the complaints, Arnold was discharged. He then filed a race discrimination charge with the EEOC. After the EEOC issued a right-to-sue letter, Arnold took his former employer to court, where his only evidence was testimony from several co-workers and friends attesting to his good character. Burger King cited evidence that the work force was half white and half black, that the number of blacks in management had risen, and that a white employee involved in a less severe sexual harassment incident was fired before Arnold. The district court ruled that Arnold's case was frivolous and groundless from the outset and dismissed the case. The district court also awarded the $10,744 in attorney's fees to be paid by Arnold, which fees were upheld by the court of appeals.

---

[17]32 FEP 1769 (4th Cir. 1983).

Albemarle Paper Company v. Moody
Supreme Court of the United States, 422 U.S. 405 (1975).

[Respondents, a certified class of present and former Negro employees, brought this action against petitioners, their employer, Albemarle Paper Co., and the employees' union, seeking injunctive relief against "any policy, practice, custom or usage" at the plant violative of Title VII of the Civil Rights Act of 1964, as amended by the Equal Employment Opportunity Act of 1972, and after several years of discovery moved to add a class back pay demand. At this trial, the major issues were the plant's seniority system, its program of employment testing, and back pay. The district court found that, following a reorganization under a new collective bargaining agreement, the Negro employees had been "locked" in the lower paying job classifications, and ordered petitioners to implement a system of plantwide seniority. The court refused, however, to order back pay for losses sustained by the plaintiff class under the discriminatory system, on the grounds that (1) Albemarle's breach of Title VII was found not to have been

in "bad faith" and (2) respondents had initially disclaimed interest in back pay and delayed making their back pay claim until five years after the complaint was filed, thereby prejudicing petitioners. The court also refused to enjoin or limit Albemarle's testing program, which respondents had contended had a disproportionate adverse impact on blacks and was not shown to be related to job performance. The court concluded that "personnel tests administered at the plant have undergone validation studies and have been proven to be job related." Respondents appealed on the back pay and preemployment test issues. The court of appeals reversed the district court's judgment.]

STEWART, J.

The District Court's decision must therefore be measured against the purposes which inform Title VII. As the Court observed in *Griggs v. Duke Power Co.*, the primary objective was a prophylactic one:

It was to achieve equality of employment opportunities and remove barriers that have operated in the past to favor an identifiable group of white employees over other employees.

Backpay has an obvious connection with this purpose. If employers faced only the prospect of an injunctive order, they would have little incentive to shun practices of dubious legality. It is the reasonably certain prospect of a backpay award that "provide[s] the spur or catalyst which causes employers and unions to self-examine and to self-evaluate their employment practices and to endeavor to eliminate, so far as possible, the last vestiges of an unfortunate and ignominious page in this country's history."

It is also the purpose of Title VII to make persons whole for injuries suffered on account of unlawful employment discrimination. This is shown by the very fact that Congress took care to arm the courts with full equitable powers. . . .

It follows that, given a finding of unlawful discrimination, backpay should be denied only for reasons which, if applied generally, would not frustrate the central statutory purposes of eradicating discrimination throughout the economy and making persons whole for injuries suffered through past discrimination. The courts of appeals must maintain a consistent and principled application of the backpay provision, consonant with the twin statutory objectives, while at the same time recognizing that the trial court will often have the keener appreciation of those facts and circumstances peculiar to particular cases.

The District Court's stated grounds for denying backpay in this case must be tested against these standards. The first ground was that Albemarle's breach of Title VII had not been in "bad faith." This is not a sufficient reason for denying backpay. Where an employer *has* shown bad faith—by maintaining a practice which he knew to be illegal or of highly questionable legality—he can make no claims whatsoever on the Chancellor's conscience. But, under Title VII, the mere absence of bad faith simply opens the door to equity; it does not depress the scales in the employer's favor. If backpay were awardable only

upon a showing of bad faith, the remedy would become a punishment for moral turpitude, rather than a compensation for workers' injuries. This would read the "make whole" purpose right out of Title VII, for a worker's injury is no less real simply because his employer did not inflict it in "bad faith." Title VII is not concerned with the employer's "good intent or absence of discriminatory intent" for "Congress directed the thrust of the Act to the *consequences* of employment practices, not simply the motivation." To condition the awarding of backpay on a showing of "bad faith" would be to open an enormous chasm between injunctive and backpay relief under Title VII. There is nothing on the face of the statute or in its legislative history that justifies that creation of drastic and categorical distinctions between those two remedies. . . .

[A synopsis of the remainder of the Court's opinion is as follows:

As is clear from *Griggs, supra,* and the Equal Employment Opportunity Commission's guidelines for employers seeking to determine through professional validation studies whether employment tests are job related, such tests are impermissible unless shown, by professionally acceptable methods, to be "predictive of or significantly correlated with important elements of work behavior which comprise or are relevant to the job or jobs for which candidates are being evaluated." Measured against that standard, Albemarle's validation study is materially defective in that (1) it would not, because of the odd patchwork of results from its application, have "validated" the two general ability tests used by Albemarle for all the skilled lines of progression for which the two tests are, apparently, now required; (2) it compared test scores with subjective supervisorial rankings, affording no means of knowing what job performance criteria the supervisors were considering; (3) it focused mostly on job groups near the top of various lines of progression, but the fact that the best of those employees working near the top of the lines of progression score well on a test does not necessarily mean that the test permissibly measures the qualifications of new workers entering lower level jobs; and (4) it dealt only with job-experienced white workers, but the tests themselves are given to new job applicants who are younger, largely inexperienced, and in many instances nonwhite.]

Accordingly, the judgment is vacated, and these cases are remanded to the District Court for proceedings consistent with this opinion.

It is so ordered.

Franks v. Bowman Transportation Co., Inc.
(Supplemental Case Digest—Title VII Remedies)
Supreme Court of the United States, 424 U.S. 747 (1976).

A trucking company had discriminated against blacks after the passage of Title VII by denying them employment as over-the-road drivers. In holding that a remedy which included seniority rights was necessary, the Court reviewed the legislative intent behind Section 706(g) of the Act.

Last term's *Albemarle Paper Company v. Moody*, 422 U.S. 405, 418 (1975), consistent with the congressional plan, held that one of the central purposes of Title VII is "to make persons whole for injuries suffered on account of unlawful employment discrimination." To effectuate this make-whole objective, Congress in Section 706(g) vested broad equitable discretion in the federal courts to order such affirmative action as may be appropriate, which may include, but is not limited to, reinstatement or hiring of employees, with or without backpay . . . , or any other equitable relief as the court deems appropriate. The legislative history supporting the 1972 Amendments of Section 706(g) of Title VII affirms the breadth of this discretion. The provisions of [Section 706(g)] are intended to give the courts wide discretion exercising their equitable powers to fashion the most complete relief possible. . . . [T]he Act is intended to make the victims of unlawful employment discrimination whole, and . . . the attainment of this objective . . . requires that persons aggrieved by the consequences and effects of the unlawful employment practice be so far as possible, restored to a position where they would have been were it not for the unlawful discrimination. Section-by-Section Analysis of H.R. 1746, accompanying the Equal Employment Opportunity Act of 1972—Conference Report, 118 Cong. Rec. 7166, 7168 (1972). This is emphatic confirmation that federal courts are empowered to fashion such relief as the particular circumstances of a case may require to effect restitution, making whole insofar as possible the victims of racial discrimination in hiring. Adequate relief may well be denied in the absence of a seniority remedy slotting the victim in that position in the seniority system that would have been his had he been hired at the time of his application. It can hardly be questioned that ordinarily such relief will be necessary to achieve the make-whole purposes of the Act.

CASE QUESTIONS

1. In *Albemarle* did a showing that the employer had not acted in bad faith relieve the employer from a back pay obligation?
2. Why did the district court in *Albemarle* refuse to order a back pay remedy?
3. Does the Supreme Court agree with the district court's ruling in *Albemarle* that it has unfettered discretion in fashioning a remedy?
4. According to the House Report quoted in the *Bowman* decision, what is the primary intention of Title VII?

Sheet Metal Workers' Local 28 v. EEOC
Supreme Court of the United States, 106 S. Ct. 3019 (1986).

[In 1975 the district court found the Sheet Metal Workers and its apprenticeship committee guilty of violating Title VII of the Civil Rights Act of 1964 by discriminating against nonwhite workers in recruitment, selection, training, and admission to the union. The court ordered the union to end their discriminatory practices, established a 29 percent nonwhite membership goal based on the percentage of nonwhites in the relevant labor pool in New York City to be achieved by July 1981, and ordered petitioners to implement procedures designed to achieve this goal under the supervision of a court-appointed administrator. Thereafter, the administrator proposed and the court adopted an affirmative action program. The court of appeals affirmed, with modifications. On remand, the district court adopted a revised affirmative action program and extended the time to meet the 29 percent membership goal. The court of appeals again affirmed. In 1982 and again in 1983, the district court found the union guilty of civil contempt for disobeying the court's earlier orders. The court imposed a $150,000 fine to be placed in a special Employment, Training, Education, and Recruitment Fund (Fund) to be used to increase nonwhite membership in the union and its apprenticeship program. The district court ultimately entered an amended affirmative action program establishing a 29.23 percent nonwhite membership goal to be met by August 1987. The court of appeals affirmed the district court's contempt findings (with one exception), the contempt remedies including the Fund order, and the affirmative action program with modifications holding that the 29.23 percent nonwhite membership goal was proper and did not violate Title VII or the Constitution. The union appealed. In this appeal the solicitor general of the United States and the union argued that the membership goal and other provisions giving nonwhites preference were prohibited by Section 706(g) of Title VII, which states that no court order "shall require the admission . . . of an individual or a member of a union . . . if such individual was refused admission . . . for any reason other than discrimination."]

BRENNAN, J.

Petitioners, joined by the Solicitor General, argue that the membership goal, the Fund order, and other orders which require petitioners to grant membership preferences to nonwhites are expressly prohibited by § 706(g), 42 U.S.C. § 2000e–5(g), which defines the remedies available under Title VII. Petitioners and the Solicitor General maintain that § 706(g) authorizes a district court to award preferential relief only to the actual victims of unlawful discrimination. They maintain that the membership goal and the Fund violate this provision, since they require petitioners to admit to membership, and otherwise to extend benefits to black and Hispanic individuals who are not the identified victims of unlawful discrimination. We reject this argument, and hold that § 706(g) does not prohibit a court from ordering, in appropriate circumstances, affirmative race-conscious relief as a remedy for past discrimination. Specifically, we hold that such relief may be appropriate where an employer or a labor union has engaged in persistent or egregious discrimination, or where necessary to dissipate the lingering effects of pervasive discrimination.

A

Section 706(g) states:

"If the court finds that the respondent has intentionally engaged in or is intentionally engaging in an unlawful employment practice . . . , the court may enjoin the respondent from engaging in such unlawful employment practice, and order such affirmative action as may be appropriate, which may include, but is not limited to, reinstatement or hiring of employees, with or without back pay . . . , or any other equitable relief as the court deems appropriate. . . . No order of the court shall require the admission or reinstatement of an individual as a member of a union, or the hiring, reinstatement, or promotion of an individual as an employee, or the payment to him of any back pay, if such individual was refused admission, suspended, or expelled, or was refused employment or advancement or was suspended or discharged for any reason other than discrimination on account of race, color, religion, sex, or national origin in violation of . . . this title." 42 U.S.C. § 2000e–5(g).

The language of § 706(g) plainly expresses Congress's intent to vest district courts with broad discretion to award "appropriate" equitable relief to remedy unlawful discrimination. *Teamsters v. United States*, 431 U.S. 324, 364 (1977); *Franks v. Bowman Transportation Co.*, 424 U.S. 747, 771 (1976); *Albemarle Paper Co. v. Moody*, 422 U.S. 405, 421 (1975). Nevertheless, petitioners and the Solicitor General argue that the last sentence of § 706(g) prohibits a court from ordering an employer or labor union to take affirmative steps to eliminate discrimination which might incidentally benefit individuals who are not the actual victims of discrimination. This reading twists the plain language of the statute.

The last sentence of § 706(g) prohibits a court from ordering a union to admit an individual who was "refused admission . . . for any reason other than discrimination." It does not, as petitioners and the Solicitor General suggest, say that a court may order relief only for the actual victims of past discrimination. The sentence on its face addresses only the situation where a plaintiff demonstrates that a union (or an employer) has engaged in unlawful discrimination, but the union can show that a particular individual would have been refused admission even in the absence of discrimination, for example because

that individual was unqualified. In these circumstances, § 706(g) confirms that a court could not order the union to admit the unqualified individual. In this case, neither the membership goal nor the Fund order required petitioners to admit to membership individuals who had been refused admission for reasons unrelated to discrimination. Thus, we do not read § 706(g) to prohibit a court from ordering the kind of affirmative relief the District Court awarded in this case.

B

The availability of race-conscious affirmative relief under § 706(g) as a remedy for a violation of Title VII also furthers the broad purposes underlying the statute. Congress enacted Title VII based on its determination that racial minorities were subject to pervasive and systematic discrimination in employment. "[I]t was clear to Congress that '[t]he crux of the problem [was] to open employment opportunities for Negroes in occupations which have been traditionally closed to them,' . . . and it was to this problem that Title VII's prohibition against racial discrimination in employment was primarily addressed." *Steelworkers v. Weber*, 443 U.S. 193, 203 (1979) (quoting 110 Cong. Rec. 6548 (1964) (remarks of Sen. Humphrey)). Title VII was designed "to achieve equality of employment opportunities and remove barriers that have operated in the past to favor an identifiable group of white employees over other employees." *Griggs v. Duke Power Co.*, 401 U.S. 424, 429–430 (1971); see *Teamsters, supra*, at 364–365; *Franks, supra*, at 763, 771; *Albemarle Paper*, at 417–18. In order to foster equal employment opportunities, Congress gave the lower courts broad power under § 706(g) to fashion "the most complete relief possible" to remedy past discrimination. *Franks, supra*, at 770; *Albemarle Paper, supra*, at 418.

In most cases, the court need only order the employer or union to cease engaging in discriminatory practices, and award make-whole relief to the individuals victimized by those practices. In some instances, however, it may be necessary to require the employer or union to take affirmative steps to end discrimination effectively to enforce Title VII. Where an employer or union has engaged in particularly longstanding or egregious discrimination, an injunction simply reiterating Title VII's prohibition against discrimination will often prove useless and will only result in endless enforcement litigation. In such cases, requiring recalcitrant employers or unions to hire and to admit qualified minorities roughly in proportion to the number of qualified minorities in the work force may be the only effective way to ensure the full enjoyment of the rights protected by Title VII. . . .

To summarize, many opponents of Title VII argued that an employer could be found guilty of discrimination under the statute simply because of a racial imbalance in his work force, and would be compelled to implement racial "quotas" to avoid being charged with liability. *Weber*, 443 U.S., at 205. At the same time, supporters of the bill insisted that employers would not violate Title VII simply because of racial imbalance, and emphasized that neither the Commission nor the courts could compel employers to adopt quotas solely to facilitate racial balancing. *Id.*, at 207, n. 7. The debate concerning what Title VII did and did not require culminated in the adoption of § 703(j), which stated expressly that the statute did not require an employer or labor union to adopt quotas or preferences simply because of a racial imbalance. However, while Congress strongly opposed the use of quotas or preferences merely to maintain racial balance, it gave no intimation as to whether such measures would be acceptable as *remedies* for Title VII violations.

Congress's failure to consider this issue is not surprising, since there was relatively little civil rights litigation prior to the adoption of the 1964 Civil Rights Act. More importantly, the cases that had been litigated had not resulted in the sort of affirmative-action remedies that, as later became apparent, would sometimes be necessary to eliminate effectively the effects of past discrimination. Thus, the use of racial preferences as a *remedy* for past discrimination simply was not an issue at the time Title VII was being considered. Our task

then, is to determine whether Congress intended to preclude a district court from ordering affirmative action in appropriate circumstances as a remedy for past discrimination. Our examination of the legislative policy behind Title VII leads us to conclude that Congress did not intend to prohibit a court from exercising its remedial authority in that way. Congress deliberately gave the district courts broad authority under Title VII to fashion the most complete relief possible to eliminate "the last vestiges of an unfortunate and ignominious page in this country's history," *Albemarle Paper*, 422 U.S., at 418. As we noted above, affirmative race-conscious relief may in some instances be necessary to accomplish this task. In the absence of any indication that Congress intended to limit a district court's remedial authority in a way which would frustrate the court's ability to enforce Title VII's mandate, we decline to fashion such a limitation ourselves.

C

Finally, petitioners and the Solicitor General find support for their reading of § 706(g) in several of our decisions applying that provision. Petitioners refer to several cases for the proposition that court-ordered remedies under § 706(g) are limited to make-whole relief benefiting actual victims of past discrimination. . . .

Petitioners claim to find their strongest support in *Firefighters v. Stotts*, 467 U.S. 561 (1984). . . .

Stotts discussed the "policy" behind § 706(g) in order to supplement the holding that the District Court could not have interfered with the city's seniority system in fashioning a Title VII remedy. This "policy" was read to prohibit a court from awarding make-whole relief, such as competitive seniority, backpay, or promotion, to individuals who were denied employment opportunities for reasons unrelated to discrimination. The District Court's injunction was considered to be inconsistent with this "policy" because it was tantamount to an award of make-whole relief (in the form of competitive seniority) to individual black firefighters who had not shown that the proposed layoffs were motivated by racial discrimination. However, this limitation on *individual* make-whole relief does not affect a court's authority to order race-conscious affirmative action. The purpose of affirmative action is not to make identified victims whole, but rather to dismantle prior patterns of employment discrimination and to prevent discrimination in the future. Such relief is provided to the class as a whole rather than to individual members; no individual is entitled to relief, and beneficiaries need not show that they were themselves victims of discrimination. In this case, neither the membership goal nor the Fund order required the petitioners to indenture or train particular individuals, and neither required them to admit to membership individuals who were refused admission for reasons unrelated to discrimination. We decline petitioners' invitation to read *Stotts* to prohibit a court from ordering any kind of race-conscious affirmative relief that might benefit nonvictims. This reading would distort the language of § 706(g), and would deprive the courts of an important means of enforcing Title VII's guarantee of equal employment opportunity.

D

Although we conclude that § 706(g) does not foreclose a district court from instituting some sorts of racial preferences where necessary to remedy past discrimination, we do not mean to suggest that such relief is always proper. While the fashioning of "appropriate" remedies for a particular Title VII violation invokes the "equitable discretion of the district courts," *Franks,* 424 U.S., at 770, we emphasize that a court's

judgment should be guided by sound legal principles. In particular, the court should exercise its discretion with an eye towards Congress's concern that race-conscious affirmative measures not be invoked simply to create a racially balanced work force. In the majority of Title VII cases, the court will not have to impose affirmative action as a remedy for past discrimination, but need only order the employer or union to cease engaging in discriminatory practices and award make-whole relief to the individuals victimized by those practices. However, in some cases, affirmative action may be necessary in order effectively to enforce Title VII. . . . [A] court should consider whether affirmative action is necessary to remedy past discrimination in a particular case before imposing such measures, and . . . the court should also take care to tailor its orders to fit the nature of the violation it seeks to correct. In this case, several factors lead us to conclude that the relief ordered by the District Court was proper. . . .

Affirmed.

CASE QUESTIONS

1. State the union's position on the meaning of Section 706(g).
2. Did the Court accept the union's interpretation of Section 706(g)?
3. In most cases involving Title VII violations, will the district courts require employers or unions to take affirmative steps to end such discrimination as was done in the *Sheet Metal Workers* case?
4. Did the *Stotts* decision maintain that court-ordered remedies should be limited to make-whole relief benefiting actual victims of past discrimination?

SECTION 12—CONSENT DECREES AND VOLUNTARY AFFIRMATIVE ACTION PLANS

Employers have an interest in affirmative action because it is fundamentally fair to have a diverse and representative work force. Moreover, affirmative action is an effective means of avoiding litigation costs associated with discrimination cases while at the same time preserving management prerogatives and preserving rights to government contracts. Employers, under affirmative action plans (AAPs), may undertake special recruiting and other efforts to hire and train minorities and women and help them advance within the company. However, the plan may also provide job preferences for minorities and women. Such aspects of affirmative action plans have resulted in numerous lawsuits contending that Title VII of the Civil Rights Act of 1964, the Fourteenth Amendment, or collective bargaining contracts have been violated. The Supreme Court has not been able to settle the many difficult issues before it with a clear and consistent majority. The Court has decided cases narrowly, with individual justices often feeling compelled to speak in concurring or dissenting opinions.

Private Sector AAPs

The Supreme Court, in the landmark *Griggs v. Duke Power Co.* decision, made a statement on discriminatory preferences and Title VII:

> The Act does not command that any person be hired simply because he was formerly the subject of discrimination, or because he is a member of a minority group. Discriminatory preference for any group, minority or majority, is precisely and only what Congress has proscribed. What is required by Congress is the removal of artificial, arbitrary, and unnecessary barriers to employment when the barriers operate invidiously to discriminate on the basis of racial or other impermissible classification.

In *McDonald v. Santa Fe Trail Transportation Co.*[18] the Supreme Court held that discrimination against whites was prohibited by Title VII. In *Regents of the University of California v. Bakke*[19] the Supreme Court held that Allan Bakke, an applicant for admission to the University of California Medical School at Davis, was denied admission to the school solely on racial grounds and that the Constitution forbids such.

It was in the above context that the Supreme Court considered the question of whether Title VII allows an employer and union in the private sector to implement an affirmative action plan that granted a racial preference to blacks where there was no finding of proven discrimination by a court but where there was a conspicuous racial imbalance in the employer's skilled craft work force. The Court decided this question in *Steelworkers v. Weber*, presented in this section. The Court held that the employer could implement such a plan under Title VII. It thus rejected the contentions of the white male plaintiff that the selection of junior black employees over more senior white male employees discriminated against the white males because of their color and was "reverse discrimination" contrary to Title VII. The Court majority chose not to define in detail a line of demarcation between permissible and impermissible affirmative action plans, but certain principles may be extracted from the majority opinion as to what is permissible:

1. The affirmative action must be in connection with a "plan."
2. There must be a showing that affirmative action is justified as a remedial measure. The plan then must be remedial to open opportunities in occupations closed to protected classes under Title VII or designed to break down old patterns of racial segregation and hierarchy. In order to make a determination that affirmative action is justified, the parties must make a self-analysis to determine if and where conspicious racial imbalances exist.

---

[18]427 U.S. 273, 12 FEP 1577 (1976).
[19]438 U.S. 265, 17 FEP 1000 (1978).

3. The plan must be voluntary.
4. The plan must not unnecessarily trammel the interests of whites.
5. The plan must be temporary.

The *Weber* decision is the cornerstone on which many subsequent Supreme Court decisions on affirmative action issues are structured.

Public Sector AAPs

In *Wygant v. Jackson Board of Education,*[20] where five judges wrote opinions on the issues before the Court, a sufficient number of justices supported various aspects of the concept of a public sector employer's right to implement a race-conscious affirmative action plan. However, the Court struck down a layoff preference for blacks as violative of the Fourteenth Amendment. Under *Wygant* a majority of the Supreme Court justices recognized affirmative action in the public sector as permissible where (1) there is convincing evidence of prior discrimination by the governmental unit involved (the affirmative action is justified as a remedial measure) and (2) the means chosen to accomplish the remedial purpose is "sufficiently narrowly tailored" to achieve its remedial purpose. A majority of justices concluded, however, that the layoffs were not sufficiently narrowly tailored to survived the Fourteenth Amendment challenge.

The plurality opinion rejected the theory that providing minority role models for minority students to alleviate societal discrimination justified the layoff preference provision for black teachers, saying that such is insufficient to justify racial classifications.

Most of the justices agreed that the public employer does not have to wait for a court finding that it has been guilty of past discrimination before it takes action. However, compelling evidence of past discrimination must be shown before affirmative action preferences may be implemented.

In *Johnson v. Santa Clara County Transportation,*[21] involving public sector affirmative action, the Supreme Court applied the *Weber* principles and upheld the public employer's decision under a voluntary AAP to promote a qualified woman over a more qualified man. It is thus evident that voluntary affirmative action is permissible in both the public and private sectors.

The Supreme Court has recently dealt with three types of specific issues involving public sector AAPs and has reached narrow determinations on those issues as follows:

1. *Consideration of sex in AAPs.* In the *Johnson v. Santa Clara County Transportation* decision, referred to above and presented in this section, the Supreme Court decided that the public employer did not violate Title VII by promoting a female employee to the position of dispatcher over a more qualified male employee under the terms of its voluntary affirmative action plan.
2. *Promotion quotas.* In *United States v. Paradise*[22] a sharply divided Court approved a promotion quota for the Alabama State Police requiring that one black state trooper be promoted for each white state trooper. The plurality opinion

---

[20]106 S. Ct. 1842 (1986).
[21]107 S. Ct. 1842 (1986).
[22]107 S. Ct. 1053 (1987).

found the quota "narrowly tailored" to serve its purpose. Justice Stevens, who cast the deciding vote, believed the relief to be proper because of the state agency's egregious past violations of the Equal Protection Clause.

3. *Layoff preferences.* In *Wygant v. Jackson Board of Education*[23] the Supreme Court struck down a layoff provision in a collective bargaining agreement that gave preferences to blacks. This provision was held to violate the Equal Protection Clause of the Fourteenth Amendment. The plurality opinion stated in part:

> While hiring goals impose a diffuse burden, often foreclosing only one of several opportunities, layoffs impose the entire burden of achieving racial equality on particular individuals, often resulting in serious disruption of their lives. That burden is too intrusive. We therefore hold that, as a means of accomplishing purposes that otherwise may be legitimate, the Board's layoff plan is not sufficiently narrowly tailored. Other, less intrusive means of accomplishing similar purposes—such as the adoption of hiring goals—are available.[24]

In reading Justice O'Connor's concurring opinion in *Wygant* in conjunction with the plurality decision, it is apparent that racially based layoff procedures are of dubious legality.

Consent Decrees

Citing *Steelworkers v. Weber*, the Supreme Court stated in *Firefighters Local 93 v. City of Cleveland*[25] that voluntary action available to employers and unions seeking to eradicate racial discrimination may include reasonable race-conscious relief that benefits individuals who are not actual victims of discrimination. In *Weber* the voluntary action was the private contractual agreement between the employer and the union. In *Firefighters Local 93* a federal district court approved a consent decree between the city of Cleveland and an organization of black and Hispanic fire fighters who brought suit against the city charging racial discrimination in promotions and assignments. The terms of a consent decree are arrived at through agreement of the parties to a lawsuit; the court reviews and approves it, and the decree is enforceable by the court. Local 93, while not a party to the lawsuit, was recognized as an intervenor. Local 93 did not approve of the consent decree, which set forth a quota system for the promotion of minorities over a four-year period. Local 93 had contended before the district court that "promotions based upon a criterion other than competence, such as a racial quota system, would deny those most capable from their promotions and deny . . . the City . . . the best possible fire fighting force."[26]

The Supreme Court rejected the union's argument that Section 706(g) of Title VII precludes the courts from approving consent decrees benefiting individuals who were not the actual victims of discrimination.

The importance of the *Local 93* decision is that while Section 706(g) restricts the district court's powers to order relief, such as hiring or promotion orders for individuals

---

[23]40 FEP 1321 (1986).
[24]Id. at 1326.
[25]106 S. Ct. 3063 (1986).
[26]Id. at 3068.

who have not actually suffered discrimination, a consent decree is not an "order of the court" according to the Supreme Court majority. Thus it may go beyond what a court could have ordered if the case had been litigated to its conclusion.

Union or Individual Challenges to Consent Decrees

The *Firefighters Local 93* decision recognized that unions and individuals who object to consent decrees remain free to challenge the decrees under the Equal Protection Clause of the Fourteenth Amendment and Section 703(a) and (d) of Title VII.

In the private sector where an employer has a collective bargaining contract with a union and enters into a consent decree with the EEOC that contains affirmative action job preferences in conflict with the seniority provisions of the collective bargaining contract, such may be later challenged by the union in a contract violation suit under Section 301 of the LMRA.[27]

Because consent decrees can be later challenged by individuals and unions on the basis of the Constitution, Title VII, and labor contracts, it is important that all interested parties be encouraged to participate in developing the agreement that serves as the basis of the decree so as to preclude further litigation.

---

[27]W. R. Grace & Co. v. Rubber Workers Local 759, 461 U.S. 757 (1983).

● Steelworkers v. Weber
Supreme Court of the United States, 443 U.S. 193 (1979).

[In 1974 petitioners United Steelworkers of America (USWA) and Kaiser Aluminum & Chemical Corp. (Kaiser) entered into a master collective bargaining agreement covering terms and conditions of employment at fifteen Kaiser plants. The agreement included an affirmative action plan designed to eliminate racial imbalances in Kaiser's craft work forces by reserving for black employees 50 percent of the openings in in-plant craft training programs until the percentage of black craft workers in a plant was commensurate with the percentage of blacks in the local labor force. This litigation arose from the operation of the affirmative action plan at Kaiser's Gramercy, Louisiana, plant where, prior to 1974, 1.83 percent of the skilled craft workers were black and the local work force was approximately 39 percent black. Pursuant to the national agreement, Kaiser, rather than continuing its practice of hiring trained outsiders, established a training program

to train its production workers to fill craft openings. Kaiser selected trainees on the basis of seniority and race so that at least 50 percent of the trainees were black until the percentage of black skilled craft workers in the plant approximated the percentage of blacks in the local labor force. During the plan's first year of operation, seven black and six white craft trainees were selected from the plant's production work force, with the most senior black trainee having less seniority than several white production workers whose bids for admission to the training program were rejected. Thereafter, respondent Brian Weber, one of those white production workers, instituted a class action in federal district court, alleging that because the affirmative action program had resulted in junior black employees receiving training in preference to senior white employees, respondent and other similarly situated white employees had been discriminated against in violation of the provisions of Section 703(a) and (d) of Title VII, which makes it unlawful to "discriminate . . . because of . . . race" in hiring and in the selection of apprentices for training programs. The district court held that the affirmative action plan violated Title VII, entered judgment in favor of the plaintiff class, and granted injunctive relief. The court of appeals affirmed, holding that all employment preferences based upon race, including those preferences incidental to bona fide affirmative action plans, violated Title VII's prohibition against racial discrimination in employment. The Supreme Court granted certiorari.]

BRENNAN, J.

We emphasize at the outset the narrowness of our inquiry. Since the Kaiser-USWA plan does not involve state action, this case does not present an alleged violation of the Equal Protection Clause of the Fourteenth Amendment. Further, since the Kaiser-USWA plan was adopted voluntarily, we are not concerned with what Title VII requires or with what a court might order to remedy a past proved violation of the Act. The only question before us is the narrow statutory issue of whether Title VII forbids private employers and unions from voluntarily agreeing upon bona fide affirmative action plans that accord racial preferences in the manner and for the purpose provided in the Kaiser-USWA plan. That question was expressly left open in *McDonald v. Sante Fe Trail Transp. Co.*, 427 U.S. 273 (1976), which held, in a case not involving affirmative action, that Title VII protects whites as well as blacks from certain forms of racial discrimination.

Respondent argues that Congress intended in Title VII to prohibit all race-conscious affirmative action plans. Respondent's argument rests upon a literal interpretation of § § 703(a) and (d) of the Act. Those sections make it unlawful to "discriminate . . . because of . . . race" in hiring and in the selection of apprentices for training programs. Since, the argument runs, *McDonald v. Santa Fe Trail Transp. Co.*, *supra*, settled that Title VII *forbids* discrimination against whites as well as blacks, and since the Kaiser-USWA affirmative action plan operates to discriminate against white employees solely because they are white, it follows that the Kaiser-USWA plan violates Title VII.

Respondent's argument is not without force. But it overlooks the significance of the fact that the Kaiser-USWA plan is an affirmative action plan voluntarily adopted by private parties to eliminate traditional patterns of racial segregation. In this context respondent's reliance upon a literal construction of § § 703(a) and (d) and upon *McDonald* is misplaced. It is a "familiar rule, that a thing may be within the letter of the statute and yet not within the statute, because not within its spirit, nor within the intention of its makers." The prohibition against racial discrimination in § § 703(a) and (d) of Title VII must therefore be read against the background of the legislative history of Title VII and the historical context from which the Act arose. Examination of those sources makes clear that an interpretation of the sections that forbade all race-conscious affirmative action would "bring about an end completely at variance with the purpose of the statute" and must be rejected.

Congress' primary concern in enacting the prohibition against racial discrimination in the Title VII of the Civil Rights Act of 1964 was with "the plight of the Negro in our economy." As Senator Clark told the Senate:

The rate of Negro unemployment has gone up consistently as compared with white unemployment for the past 15 years. This is a social malaise and a social situation which we should not tolerate. That is one of the principal reasons why the bill should pass.

. . . Accordingly, it was clear to Congress that "[t]he crux of the problem [was] to open employment opportunities for Negroes in occupations which have been traditionally closed to them," and it was to this problem that Title VII's prohibition against racial discrimination in employment was primarily addressed. . . .

Given this legislative history, we cannot agree with respondent that Congress intended to prohibit the private sector from taking effective steps to accomplish the goal that Congress designed Title VII to achieve. The very statutory words intended as a spur or catalyst to cause "employers and unions to self-examine and to self-evaluate their employment practices and to endeavor to eliminate, so far as possible, the last vestiges of an unfortunate and ignominious page in this country's history," *Albemarle Paper Co. v. Moody*, 422 U.S. 405 (1975), cannot be interpreted as an absolute prohibition against all private, voluntary, race-conscious affirmative action efforts to hasten the elimination of such vestiges. . . .

Our conclusion is further reinforced by examination of the language and legislative history of § 703(j) of Title VII. . . .

. . . The section provides that nothing contained in Title VII "shall be interpreted to *require* any employer . . . to grant preferential treatment . . . to any group because of the race . . . of such . . . group on account of" a de facto racial imbalance in the employer's work force. The section does *not* state that "nothing in Title VII shall be interpreted to *permit*" voluntary affirmative efforts to correct racial imbalances. The natural inference is that Congress chose not to forbid all voluntary race-conscious affirmative action. . . .

. . . In view of [the] legislative history and in view of Congress' desire to avoid undue federal regulation of private businesses, use of the word "require" rather than the phrase "require or permit" in § 703(j) fortifies the conclusion that Congress did not intend to limit traditional business freedom to such a degree as to prohibit all voluntary race-conscious affirmative action.

We therefore hold that Title VII's prohibition in § § 703(a) and (d) against racial discrimination does not condemn all private, voluntary, race-conscious affirmative action plans.

We need not today define in detail the line of demarcation between permissible and impermissible affirmative action plans. It suffices to hold that the challenged Kaiser-USWA affirmative action plan falls on the permissible side of the line. The purposes of the plan mirror those of the statute. Both were designed to break down old patterns of racial segregation and hierarchy. Both were structured to "open employment opportunities for Negroes in occupations which have been traditionally closed to them."

At the same time, the plan does not unnecessarily trammel the interests of the white employees. The plan does not require the discharge of white workers and their replacement with new black hirees. Nor does the plan create an absolute bar to the advancement of white employees; half of those trained in the program will be white. Moreover, the plan is a temporary measure. . . .

We conclude, therefore, that the adoption of the Kaiser-USWA plan for the Gramercy plant falls within the area of discretion left by Title VII to the private sector voluntarily to adopt affirmative action plans designed to eliminate conspicuous racial imbalance in traditionally segregated job categories. Accordingly, the judgment of the Court of Appeals for the Fifth Circuit is reversed.

So ordered.

[BRENNAN, J., delivered the opinion of the Court, in which STEWART, WHITE, MARSHALL, and BLACKMUN, J. J., joined. BLACKMUN, J., filed a concurring opinion. BURGER, C. J., filed a dissenting opinion. REHNQUIST, J., filed a dissenting opinion, in which BURGER, C. J., joined. POWELL and STEVENS, J. J., took no part in the consideration or decision of the cases.]

Dissenting Opinions

BURGER, C. J.

The Court reaches a result I would be inclined to vote for were I a Member of Congress considering a proposed amendment of Title VII. I cannot join the Court's judgment, however, because it is contrary to the explicit language of the statute and arrived at by means wholly incompatible with long-established principles of separation of powers. Under the guise of statutory "construction," the Court effectively rewrites Title VII to achieve what it regards as a desirable result. It "amends" the statute to do precisely what both its sponsors and its opponents agreed the statute was not intended to do.

When Congress enacted Title VII after long study and searching debate, it produced a statute of extraordinary clarity, which speaks directly to the issue we consider in this case. In § 703(d) Congress provided:

It shall be an unlawful employment practice for any employer, labor organization, or joint labor-management committee controlling apprenticeship or other training or retraining, including on-the-job training programs to discriminate against any individual because of his race, color, religion, sex, or national origin in admission to, or employment in, any program established to provide apprenticeship or other training.

Often we have difficulty interpreting statutes either because of imprecise drafting or because legislative compromises have produced genuine ambiguities. But here there is no lack of clarity, no ambiguity. The quota embodied in the collective-bargaining agreement between Kaiser and the Steelworkers unquestionably discriminates on the basis of race against individual employees seeking admission to on-the-job training programs. And, under the plain language of § 703(d), that is "an unlawful employment practice." . . .

REHNQUIST, J.

Contrary to the Court's analysis, the language of § 703(j) is precisely tailored to the objection voiced time and again by Title VII's opponents. Not once during the 83 days of debate in the Senate did a speaker, proponent or opponent, suggest that the bill would allow employers *voluntarily* to prefer racial minorities over white persons. In light of Title VII's flat prohibition on discrimination "against any individual . . . because of such individual's race," § 703(a),

42 U.S.C. § 2000e–2(a) [42 U.S.C.S. § 2000e–2(a)], such a contention would have been, in any event, too preposterous to warrant response. . . .

In light of the background and purpose of § 703(j), the irony of invoking the section to justify the result in this case is obvious. The Court's frequent references to the "voluntary" nature of Kaiser's racially discriminatory admission quota bear no relationship to the facts of this case. Kaiser and the Steelworkers acted under pressure from an agency of the Federal Government, the Office of Federal Contract Compliance, which found that minorities were being "underutilized" at Kaiser's plants. That is, Kaiser's work force was racially imbalanced. Bowing to that pressure, Kaiser instituted an admissions quota preferring blacks over whites, thus confirming that the fears of Title VII's opponents were well founded. Today, § 703(j), adopted to allay those fears, is invoked by the Court to uphold imposition of a racial quota under the very circumstances that the section was intended to prevent. . . .

CASE QUESTIONS

1. State the facts that led Kaiser to contract with the union concerning the affirmative action training program.
2. What did the Court state was the question before it?
3. Do you believe that the Supreme Court applied Section 703(d) as written by Congress in this case?
4. Does the Court set guidelines for what are permissible and impermissible affirmative action plans?

Johnson v. Santa Clara County Transportation Agency
Supreme Court of the United States, 107 S. Ct. 1442 (1987).

[In 1978 an affirmative action plan (Plan) for hiring and promoting minorities and women was voluntarily adopted by the Santa Clara County

Transportation Agency (Agency). The Plan provided inter alia that in making promotions to positions within a traditionally segregated job *classification in which women have been significantly underrepresented, the Agency was authorized to consider, as one factor, the sex of a qualified applicant. The Plan was intended to achieve a statistically measurable yearly improvement in hiring and promoting minorities and women in job classifications where they were underrepresented. The long-term goal was to attain a work force whose composition reflected the proportion of minorities and women in the area labor force. The Plan set aside no specific number of positions for minorities or women but required that short-range goals be established and annually adjusted to serve as the most realistic guide for actual employment decisions. When the Agency announced a vacancy for the position of road dispatcher, none of the 238 positions in the skilled craft worker job classification, which included the dispatcher position, was held by a woman. The qualified applicants for the position were interviewed. The Agency, pursuant to the Plan, ultimately passed over petitioner, Paul Johnson, and promoted a female, Diane Joyce. After receiving a right-to-sue letter from the EEOC, Johnson filed suit in federal court. The court held that the Agency had violated Title VII of the Civil Rights Act of 1964. The court found that Joyce's sex was the determining factor in her selection and that the Agency's Plan was invalid under the criterion announced in* Steelworkers v. Weber, 443 U.S. 193, *that the Plan be temporary. The court of appeals reversed.]*

BRENNAN, J.

The assessment of the legality of the Agency Plan must be guided by our decision in *Weber*. . . .

The first issue is therefore whether consideration of the sex of applicants for skilled craft jobs was justified by the existence of a "manifest imbalance" that reflected underrepresentation of women in "traditionally segregated job categories." In determining whether an imbalance exists that would justify taking sex or race into account, a comparison of the percentage of minorities or women in the employer's work force with the percentage in the area labor market or general population is appropriate in analyzing jobs that require no special expertise, see *Team-*

sters v. United States, 431 U.S. 324 (1977) (comparison between percentage of blacks in employer's work force and in general population proper in determining extent of imbalance in truck driving positions), or training programs designed to provide expertise, see *Weber, supra* (comparison between proportion of blacks working at plant and proportion of blacks in area labor force appropriate in calculating imbalance for purpose of establishing preferential admission to craft training program). Where a job requires special training, however, the comparison should be with those in the labor force who possess the relevant qualifications. See *Hazelwood School District v. United States*, 433 U.S. 299 (1977) (must compare percentage of blacks in employer's work ranks with percentage of qualified black teachers in area labor force in determining underrepresentation in teaching positions). The requirement that the "manifest imbalance" relate to a "traditionally segregated job category" provides assurance both that sex or race will be taken into account in a manner consistent with Title VII's purpose of eliminating the effects of employment discrimination, and that the interests of those employees not benefitting from the plan will not be unduly infringed. . . .

It is clear that the decision to hire Joyce was made pursuant to an Agency plan that directed that sex or race be taken into account for the purpose of remedying underrepresentation. The Agency Plan acknowledged the "limited opportunities that have existed in the past," for women to find employment in certain job classifications "where women have not been traditionally employed in significant numbers." As a result, observed the Plan, women were concentrated in traditionally female jobs in the Agency, and represented a lower percentage in other job classifications than would be expected if such traditional segregation had not occurred. Specifically, 9 of the 10 Para-Professionals and 110 of the 145 Office and Clerical Workers were women. By contrast, women were only 2 of the 28 Officials and Administrators, 5 of the 58 Professionals, 12 of the 124 Technicians, none of the Skilled Craft Workers, and 1—who was Joyce—

of the 110 Road Maintenance Workers. The Plan sought to remedy these imbalances through "hiring, training and promotion of . . . women throughout the Agency in all major job classifications where they are underrepresented."

As an initial matter, the Agency adopted as a benchmark for measuring progress in eliminating underrepresentation the long-term goal of a work force that mirrored in its major job classifications the percentage of women in the area labor market. Even as it did so, however, the Agency acknowledged that such a figure could not by itself necessarily justify taking into account the sex of applicants for positions in all job categories. For positions requiring specialized training and experience, the Plan observed that the number of minorities and women "who possess the qualifications required for entry into such job classifications is limited." The Plan therefore directed that annual short-term goals be formulated that would provide a more realistic indication of the degree to which sex should be taken into account in filling particular positions. The Plan stressed that such goals "should not be construed as 'quotas' that must be met," but as reasonable aspirations in correcting the imbalance in the Agency's work force. . . .

As the Agency Plan recognized, women were most egregiously underrepresented in the Skilled Craft job category, since *none* of the 238 positions was occupied by a woman. In mid-1980, when Joyce was selected for the road dispatcher position, the Agency was still in the process of refining its short-term goals for Skilled Craft Workers in accordance with the directive of the Plan. This process did not reach fruition until 1982, when the Agency established a short-term goal for that year of three women for the 55 expected openings in that job category—a modest goal of about 6% for that category. . . .

The Agency's Plan emphatically did *not* authorize . . . blind hiring. It expressly directed that numerous factors be taken into account in making hiring decisions, including specifically the qualifications of female applicants for particular jobs. Thus, despite the fact that no precise short-term goal was yet in place for the Skilled

Craft category in mid-1980, the Agency's management nevertheless had been clearly instructed that they were not to hire solely by reference to statistics. The fact that only the long-term goal had been established for this category posed no danger that personnel decisions would be made by reflexive adherence to a numerical standard.

Furthermore, in considering the candidates for the road dispatcher position in 1980, the Agency hardly needed to rely on a refined short-term goal to realize that it had a significant problem of underrepresentation that required attention. Given the obvious imbalance in the Skilled Craft category, and given the Agency's commitment to eliminating such imbalances, it was plainly not unreasonable for the Agency to determine that it was appropriate to consider as one factor the sex of Ms. Joyce in making its decision. The promotion of Joyce thus satisfies the first requirement enunciated in *Weber*, since it was undertaken to further an affirmative action plan designed to eliminate Agency work force imbalances in traditionally segregated job categories.

We next consider whether the Agency Plan unnecessarily trammeled the rights of male employees or created an absolute bar to their advancement. In contrast to the plan in *Weber*, which provided that 50% of the positions in the craft training program were exclusively for blacks, and to the consent decree upheld last term in *Firefighters v. Cleveland*, 478 U.S. ____ (1986), which required the promotion of specific numbers of minorities, the Plan sets aside no positions for women. The Plan expressly states that "[t]he 'goals' established for each Division should not be construed as 'quotas' that must be met." Rather, the Plan merely authorizes that consideration be given to affirmative action concerns when evaluating qualified applicants. As the Agency Director testified, the sex of Joyce was but one of numerous factors he took into account in arriving at his decision. The Plan thus resembles the "Harvard Plan" approvingly noted by JUSTICE POWELL in *University of California Regents v. Bakke*, 438 U.S. 265, 316–319 (1978), which considers race along with other criteria in determining admission to the college. As JUSTICE POWELL observed, "In such an admissions program, race or ethnic background may be deemed a 'plus' in a particular applicant's file, yet it does not insulate the individual from comparison with all other candidates for the available seats." *Id.*, at 317. Similarly, the Agency Plan requires women to compete with all other qualified applicants. No persons are automatically excluded from consideration; *all* are able to have their qualifications weighed against those of other applicants.

In addition, petitioner had no absolute entitlement to the road dispatcher position. Seven of the applicants were classified as qualified and eligible, and the Agency Director was authorized to promote any of the seven. Thus, denial of the promotion unsettled no legitimate firmly rooted expectation on the part of the petitioner. Furthermore, while the petitioner in this case was denied a promotion, he retained his employment with the Agency, at the same salary and with the same seniority, and remained eligible for other promotions. . . .

. . . In this case . . . substantial evidence shows that the Agency has sought to take a moderate, gradual approach to eliminating the imbalance in its work force, one which establishes realistic guidance for employment decisions, and which visits minimal intrusion on the legitimate expectations of other employees. Given this fact, as well as the Agency's express commitment to "attain" a balanced work force, there is ample assurance that the Agency does not seek to use its Plan to maintain a permanent racial and sexual balance. . . .

Affirmed.

Dissenting Opinion

JUSTICE SCALIA, with whom THE CHIEF JUSTICE joins, and with whom JUSTICE WHITE joins [in part], dissenting.

With a clarity which, had it not proven so unavailing, one might well recommend as a model of statutory draftsmanship, Title VII of the Civil Rights Act of 1964 declares:

"*It shall be an unlawful employment practice for an employer—*

"*(1) to fail or refuse to hire or to discharge any individual, or otherwise to discriminate against any individual with respect to his compensation, terms, conditions, or privileges of employment, because of such individual's race, color, religion, sex, or national origin; or*

"*(2) to limit, segregate, or classify his employees or applicants for employment in any way which would deprive or tend to deprive any individual of employment opportunities or otherwise adversely affect his status as an employee, because of such individual's race, color, religion, sex, or national origin.*" 42 U.S.C. § 2000e–2(a).

The Court today completes the process of converting this from a guarantee that race or sex will *not* be the basis for employment determinations, to a guarantee that it often *will*. Ever so subtly, without even alluding to the last obstacles preserved by earlier opinions that we now push out of our path, we effectively replace the goal of a discrimination-free society with the quite incompatible goal of proportionate representation by race and by sex in the workplace. . . .

After a two-day trial, the District Court concluded that Diana Joyce's gender was "*the determining factor*" in her selection for the position. Specifically, it found that "[b]ased upon the examination results and the departmental interview, [Mr. Johnson] was more qualified for the position of Road Dispatcher than Diane Joyce"; that "[b]ut for [Mr. Johnson's] sex, male, he would have been promoted to the position of Road Dispatcher"; and that "[b]ut for Diane Joyce's sex, female, she would not have been appointed to the position. . . ." The Ninth Circuit did not reject these factual findings as clearly erroneous, nor could it have done so on the record before us. We are bound by those findings under Federal Rule of Civil Procedure 52(a).

The most significant proposition of law established by today's decision is that racial or sexual discrimination is permitted under Title VII when it is intended to overcome the effect, not of the employer's own discrimination, but of societal attitudes that have limited the entry of certain races, or of a particular sex, into certain jobs. . . .

CASE QUESTIONS

1. Assess the truth of the statement: "But for Diane Joyce's sex, she would not have been appointed to the position."

2. Did the agency's AAP authorize "blind hiring" practices requiring the hiring of a specified number of women regardless of the number of qualified applicants?
3. Did the Court follow the principles set forth in the *Weber* decision in assessing the legality of the agency's plan?
4. Did the agency's plan unnecessarily trammel male employees' rights?

SECTION 13—REVERSE DISCRIMINATION

When an employer's affirmative action plan is not shown to be justified or when it "unnecessarily trammels" the interests of nonminority employees in regards to promotions, training, or other employment expectations, it is said that the employer's action is unlawful "reverse discrimination." In the so-called reverse discrimination cases, the courts apply the *Weber* principles, set forth in Section 12 of this text, to test the validity of the employer action in question.

In *Jurgens v. Thomas*,[28] a reverse discrimination suit brought by white male employees of the Equal Employment Opportunity Commission, the court held that the EEOC itself had acted contrary to the *Weber* decision in its promotion and hiring procedures. The court determined that clear evidence of preferences for minorities and women was found in the EEOC's affirmative action plans, its Special Hiring Plan for Hispanics, and its District Directors Selection Program. After extensive discussion and an analysis of statistics on the affirmative action plans, the court held that the evidence showed that through the process of reorganization, white male district directors were reduced from ten to two. Also, the Special Hiring Plan for Hispanics was discussed by the court in the lengthy decision. Hispanics constituted 6.8 percent of the national population but 12.9 percent of the EEOC work force, and the plan called for a 10 percent hiring goal even in field offices where the local population was less than 10 percent Hispanic. The preferences of this plan were not temporary, according to the court, because of the follow-up procedure built into the plan whereby those offices that did not meet initial hiring goals "committed" one or more positions to future recruitment of Hispanics. The court held that the affirmative action plans were not remedial because the jobs were not traditionally closed to women and minorities; nor were they temporary for the preferences appeared in slightly different form in each of the seven plans at issue. The court held that *Weber's* language should not be read to permit an employer with statistical parity in its own plant to use "status" as a basis for decisions as a means of compensating for unremedied societal discrimination elsewhere. The court held that the EEOC's affirmative action plans unnecessarily trammeled the interests of the plaintiffs and violated Title VII.

In the *San Francisco Police Officers' Association v. San Francisco* decision the U.S. court of appeals applied the *Weber* standards and found that the city's decision to rescore promotional tests in order to achieve specific and identified racial and gender percentages for promotion purposes "unnecessarily trammeled" the interests of while male police officers.

---

[28]29 FEP 1561 (1982).

●   **San Francisco Police Officers' Association v. City and County of San Francisco**
United States Court of Appeals, Ninth Circuit, 812 F.2d 1125 (1987).

[The city and county of San Francisco (City) and the Civil Service Commission (Commission) entered into a consent decree that required the City to employ good faith efforts to achieve particular goals for employment of women and minorities. The Police Officers' Association (POA) intervened in those actions and agreed to the consent decree. The consent decree specifically prohibited the City from unlawfully discriminating in any manner on the basis of sex, race, or national origin. In 1983 the City administered selection procedures for the positions of assistant inspector and sergeant. The promotional examinations had three parts: a multiple-choice test, a written examination, and an oral examination. Part way through the examination, the Commission set the weights for all three components. When the examinations were scored, the results showed an adverse impact on minorities in both ranks and a slight adverse impact on women for the assistant inspector examination. This adverse impact led the Commission to revise the scoring procedures for the examinations. The Commission regarded the multiple-choice and written examination components on a pass-fail basis and used the oral examination as the sole criterion for ranking candidates who passed the multiple-choice and written examinations. The police union brought suit, objecting to the new grading procedures. The district court ruled in favor of the City, and the union appealed.]

WIGGINS, C. J.

The critical issue in this case is whether the Commission acted lawfully in reweighing the examination components. The district court viewed this question in terms of fairness and held a fairness hearing in order to determine if the Commission's decision to reweigh was a valid affirmative action plan under *United Steelworkers of America v. Weber*, 443 U.S. 193 (1979).

In *Weber*, the Supreme Court identified four criteria that make an affirmative action plan valid under Title VII: (1) it is designed to break down old patterns of racial segregation and hierarchy; (2) it does not create an absolute bar to the advancement of nonminority employees; (3) it is a temporary measure, "not intended to maintain racial balance, but simply to eliminate a manifest racial imbalance"; and (4) it does not unnecessarily trammel the interests of nonminority employees. *Weber*, 443 U.S. at 208. *Weber*, did not hold that these criteria were absolute requirements, but did hold that these aspects of the plan in *Weber* placed it on the permissible side of the line between permissible and impermissible plans. Here, the district court found that reweighing fit all four *Weber* criteria and was therefore permissible. We reverse the district court because reweighing the examination unnecessarily trammeled the interests of the nonminority police officers.

In analyzing whether the interests of nonminorities were unnecessarily trammeled, the district court focused on what rights the candidates possessed and how those rights were affected by reweighing. It determined that the City did not overtly take into account race or sex in the decision to reweigh. . . .

We find that the district court clearly erred when it determined that the decision to reweigh was not a race and gender conscious act. . . .

Reweighing unlawfully displaced candidates on the basis of their race and gender. The information about the candidates' performance on the individual components led the Commission to choose the oral component as the sole ranking device. If the results of the examinations had been different, the written component or the multiple choice component might have been the new ranking device. Without readministering the test, the Commission examined the results from each component based on race and gender criteria and rescored the test to achieve specific and identified racial and gender percentages. This type of result-oriented scoring is offensive.

Candidates who participate in promotional examinations expect to have an equal opportunity to score well and to achieve promotion. This neutrality cannot exist if the City can rescore the examinations to achieve a particular race and gender balance after it analyzes the results. Permitting an employer to rescore examinations with knowledge of the ultimate results undermines the integrity of the examination process.

Moreover, candidates for promotion should be on notice of how their performance will be evaluated in order to prepare themselves effectively for an examination. . . .

. . . Here . . . the Commission's decision to reweigh unlawfully restricted the promotional opportunities of nonminority candidates because the tests were scored to achieve a particular racial result. It trammeled the interests of nonminorities, in that the candidates were led to believe that the promotions would be based on merit alone. This harm to nonminorities was unnecessary because a less burdensome alternative, such as administering a new selection procedure, would have better achieved the goals of the consent decree without violating Title VII.

The City was obligated under the consent decree to administer an examination that would not have an adverse effect on minorities and women. When it failed in its first attempt to achieve that goal, the City inappropriately attempted to take short-cuts to meet its obligations. It did so in order to save time. Although we are sympathetic to the City's time dilemma, using an unlawful procedure is not acceptable. The City was required either to validate its initial examination or, if it could not, to devise and administer an alternative selection procedure that did not have an adverse impact.

The City was additionally obligated under the consent decree not to practice racial or sexual discrimination—no more against white males than against others. The POA was a party to the consent decree. The POA has a right to insist that this unequivocal renunciation of all discrimination means what it says. The reweighing as practiced here violated the consent decree.

The judgment is reversed and remanded.

CASE QUESTIONS

1. Did the district court determine that the decision to rescore the components of the exam was not a race- and gender-conscious act?
2. How did the commission's decision to rescore the components of the exam unnecessarily trammel the interests of nonminorities?
3. Was the city's obligation under the consent decree not to practice racial or sexual discrimination applicable to white male police officers?

SECTION 14—EXECUTIVE ORDER 11246: AFFIRMATIVE ACTION PROGRAMS

The Civil Rights Act, federal funding laws, and federal licensing laws have provided statutory authority for requiring certain employers to take affirmative action to improve the job opportunities for women and minorities.[29] The Rehabilitation Act of 1973

---

[29]Civil Rights Act of 1964, Title VII, as amended. Federal funding laws: Title VI of the 1964 Civil Rights Act prohibits employment discrimination in any program or activity receiving federal financial assistance when the primary objective of the program is employment; sex discrimination is prohibited in HEW's aid-to-education programs by the terms of the Education Amendments of 1972. Federal licensing laws: the Federal Communications Commission has taken the position that it has authority to require licensees to take affirmative action to improve job opportunities for women and minorities; the Securities Exchange Commission has authority to require corporations registering securities to report on significant developments in their equal employment practices.

requires affirmative action by federal departments and government contractors to improve job opportunities for the handicapped. The Vietnam Veterans Readjustment Act of 1974 requires certain federal contractors to develop written affirmative action plans to hire veterans of the Vietnam War. The major source of affirmative action requirements, however, is presidential Executive Order 11246.

The Office of Federal Contract Compliance Programs

Under Executive Order 11246 the Secretary of Labor is charged with supervising and coordinating the compliance activities of the federal contracting agencies. The Secretary of Labor has established the Office of Federal Contract Compliance Programs (OFCCP) to administer the order. The OFCCP, having the responsibility to implement equal opportunity in the federal procurement area, has set forth regulations that apply to service and supply contractors and subcontractors as well as construction contractors and subcontractors. Under Executive Order 12086, issued by President Carter in 1978, the OFCCP has full responsibility for conducting service, supply, and construction compliance review for the Department of Defense, the General Services Administration, Housing and Urban Development, the Department of Transportation, the Department of Interior, the Environmental Protection Agency, the Treasury Department, the Department of Commerce, and the Small Business Administration.

Each contract that the federal government awards amounting to $10,000 or more must contain an equal employment clause that is binding on the contractor or subcontractor for the duration of the contract. The clause contains the following commitments by the contractor:

1. Not to discriminate against any employee or job applicant because of race, color, sex, religion, or national origin.
2. To state in all employment advertisements that applicants will be considered on the basis of their qualifications.
3. To advise all unions of the employer's commitments.
4. To include the same type of equal employment opportunity agreement in every subcontract or purchase order.

Whenever the director of the OFCCP has reason to believe that a contractor has violated the equal employment opportunity clause in the contract, the director may initiate administrative proceedings to seek correction of the violation. The contractor must be afforded a full hearing before an administrative law judge before a sanction can be imposed. The OFCCP has the power to cancel or suspend contracts for failure to comply with a nondiscrimination clause. The OFCCP may also require contracting agencies to refrain from entering into new contracts with "debarred" or ineligible contractors.

Service and Supply Contracts

Service and supply contractors and subcontractors having fifty or more employees and a contract exceeding $50,000 must develop written affirmative action plans for the increased utilization of women and minorities. In assessing whether a contract exceeds

$50,000, the OFCCP counts the total value of the various orders anticipated in certain blanket purchase agreements (BPAs) rather than counting each order as a single contract.

Some requirements for an acceptable affirmative action program are as follows:

1. An analysis of all major job categories at a facility must be conducted with explanations if minority group members are being underutilized in job categories.
2. Goals, timetables, and affirmative action commitments must be designed to correct any identifiable deficiencies. When deficiencies exist, the regulations require the contractor to create specific goals and a timetable as part of its written affirmative action program. [30]
3. Support data for the program and analysis shall be compiled and maintained as part of the contractor's affirmative action program.
4. Contractors shall direct special attention in their analysis and goal setting to six categories identified by the government as most likely to show underutilization of minorities—officials and managers, professionals, technicians, sales workers, office and clerical workers, and skilled craft workers.

Construction Contracts

The primary difference between affirmative action approaches for construction contractors and service and supply contractors is that minority goals and timetables for construction contractors are set periodically for "covered geographic areas" by the director of the OFCCP using Standard Metropolitan Statistical Area (SMSA) data. The service and supply contractors generate their own goals and timetables on an individual basis. The director has used the SMSA data and will use census data to set the goals for minority utilization equal to the percentage of minorities in the civilian labor force in the relevant area. The director has set a 6.9 percent nationwide goal for the utilization of women by contractors working on federally assisted construction contracts of $100,000 or more. The goal is not on a trade-by-trade basis but applies in the aggregate. In the OFCCP *Final Regulations on Affirmative Action Requirements* published in March 1983, the OFCCP stated:

> It must be emphasized that it is the policy of the OFCCP that goals are targets which the contractor must make every good fair effort to achieve. The goals called for in § 60–4.2 are not rigid quotas which the contractor must achieve regardless of employment circumstances. Rather, they are targets to be affirmatively pursued. Accordingly, no contractor will be found to have violated its obligations solely because of non-achievement of goals, nor shall such non-achievement be, in itself, a deficiency. Instead, the contractor will be measured on its good faith efforts to carry out the affirmative steps and will be found deficient if such good faith effort is not demonstrated. [31]

---

[30]The "goals and timetables" approach to affirmative action programs, required of federal contractors by the OFCCP, has been approved by several circuit courts. See Contractors Association of Eastern Pennsylvania v. Shultz, 442 F.2d 159 (3rd Cir. 1971); Southern Illinois Builders Association v. Ogilvie, 471 F.2d 680 (7th Cir. 1972); and Associated General Contractors of Massachusetts, Inc. v. Altshuler, 490 F.2d 9 (1st Cir. 1973). These cases predate the reverse discrimination cases of Regents of the University of California v. Bakke, 438 U.S. 265 (1978); Steelworkers v. Weber, 443 U.S. 193 (1979); and Fullilove v. Klutznick, 448 U.S. 448 (1980).
[31]DLR No. 144 (1983).

The "80 Percent" Rule

The revised Labor Department regulations outlining the affirmative action obligations of federal contractors under Executive Order 11246 continue to include an "80 percent" or "four-fifths" rule for determining underutilization of minorities and women. Under this rule an adverse impact is presumed if the selection rate for minorities and women from the relevant applicant pool is less than four-fifths or 80 percent of the selection rate for whites or males. The 80 percent rule has been sharply criticized for failing to account for differences in sampling size and test results in the applicant population and has had mixed acceptance by the courts. This rule is subject to modification at any time. It is considered by the EEOC and the OFCCP as a practical device for reviewing company employee profiles to see if serious discrepancies exist in the hiring and promotion policies of a company.

Sanctions for Noncompliance

Where it has been determined that a contracting firm has not made adequate good faith efforts to hire minority workers or women for federal or federally assisted projects, the OFCCP, after notice and a hearing, is authorized to debar the firm from participating in such projects.

Construction firms may apply to the OFCCP for reinstatement; however, they must show that they have made good faith efforts to increase minority hiring and must agree to additional terms set by the OFCCP. For example, a construction firm that had been debarred because of its failure to make good faith efforts to hire minorities on a federally assisted hospital project in New Haven, Connecticut, applied for reinstatement with the OFCCP. After an investigation established that the firm had made renewed efforts to comply with Executive Order 11246, it was reinstated with certain conditions.

Under the terms of the reinstatement order by the OFCCP, the firm was required to pay back wages of $13,606 to three workers who were found to have been victims of past discrimination. In addition, the company agreed to submit to the Labor Department copies of its monthly payroll records for at least two years and to employ minority apprentices and trainees at the completion of their training if employment opportunities were available.

Other terms of the agreement specified that the company was bound by any OFCCP-approved affirmative action requirements and that it must take certain specific affirmative actions. These included:

1. Maintaining a working environment free of harassment, intimidation, and coercion.
2. Developing on-the-job apprentice and trainee opportunities for minorities.
3. Conducting an inventory and evaluation of all minority personnel for promotional opportunities.
4. Establishing and maintaining a current list of minority recruitment sources and minority job applicants toward which it would direct recruitment efforts.
5. Encouraging minority employees to recruit other minority persons, including students, for summer or part-time work.

In *OFCCP v. Bruce Church, Inc.*,[32] the Secretary of Labor ordered the immediate debarment of a lettuce supplier to military bases for failure to submit its written affirmative action plan for inspection by the Labor Department. The supplier's contention that since each order was less than $50,000 it was not covered by Executive Order 11246 was rejected. The OFCCP counts the total value of the orders anticipated in assessing whether the $50,000 threshold of the executive order has been reached where blanket purchase orders are used by the government. In this case the contractor had done $3,500,000 in business with the federal government from 1981 through 1987. The contractor will remain ineligible under the debarment until it submits an affirmative action plan and satisfies the Labor Department that it is in compliance with the plan.

SECTION 15—OTHER REMEDY OPTIONS

Because of an EEOC case backlog or the desire to avoid EEOC procedures, grievants have sometimes chosen to circumvent Title VII procedures. There are three principal avenues other than the Title VII approach to remedy discriminatory employment practices: (1) district court action under the Civil Rights Act of 1866, (2) private grievance and arbitration proceedings, and (3) NLRA unfair labor practice proceedings.

The Civil Rights Act of 1866

Following the Civil War, Congress enacted the Civil Rights Act of 1866 pursuant to the congressional power to eradicate slavery provided by the Thirteenth Amendment, which had been ratified in 1865. To remove any doubt as to its constitutionality, the statute was reenacted in 1870 following ratification of the Fourteenth Amendment in 1868 and was codified as 42 USC Sections 1981 and 1982. Lawsuits under the Civil Rights Act of 1866 are commonly referred to as Section 1981 and Section 1982 lawsuits.

In *Johnson v. Railway Agency*[33] the Supreme Court held that Section 1 of the Civil Rights Act of 1866, and therefore its derivative 42 USC Section 1981, provides an independent remedy for discrimination in employment. The Court noted that filing a Section 1981 claim does not foreclose the use of EEOC procedures.

In *General Building Contractors Association v. Pennsylvania*[34] the Supreme Court considered whether discrimination under Section 1981 could be proven by establishing that the defendant's policies had a disparate impact without proving intentional discrimination. The Court decided that Section 1981 can be violated only by purposeful discrimination.

In Section 2 of this text the time limitation for filing charges concerning alleged violations of Title VII is set forth. Where an individual misses the relatively short filing deadlines under Title VII, the individual may be able to bring a race discrimination case under the longer time limits allowed under Section 1981 (formerly six years, presently two years).

---

[32]Case No. 87–OFC–7, June 30, 1987.
[33]421 U.S. 454 (1975).
[34]458 U.S. 375, 29 FEP 139 (1982).

In *Saint Francis College v. Al-Khazraji*, presented in this section, the plaintiff's Title VII claims had been dismissed as untimely, but the Supreme Court upheld his right to sue under Section 1981 alleging racial discrimination based on his Arabian ancestry. In a related case, *Shaare Tefila Congregation v. Cobb*, also presented in this section, the Supreme Court determined that Jews can, under Section 1982 of the Civil Rights Act of 1866, sue those who allegedly desecrated a synagogue since Jews were among the peoples considered to be distinct races at the time the 1866 act was passed.

Grievance and Arbitration

An employee may seek a remedy against discriminatory employment practices through the grievance and arbitration procedures in an existing collective bargaining agreement. The advantage to the grievance and arbitration process is that it can be implemented with far less delay than the Title VII procedures, a suit under the Civil Rights Act of 1866, or NLRB proceedings. A difficulty with arbitration in employment discrimination cases is that the individual grievant is often left without adequate representation in the arbitration proceedings. The Supreme Court recognized in *Vaca v. Sipes* that because the remedies of grievance arbitration are devised and controlled by the union and the employer, "they may very well prove unsatisfactory or unworkable for the individual grievant."[35] Indeed a union may often have an interest in perpetuating a discriminatory practice. A further difficulty with arbitration is that labor arbitrators are not as experienced in dealing with racial, religious, or sex discrimination grievances as the EEOC or federal judges. Indeed an arbitrator may feel bound by the collective bargaining contract and thus may never reach the substantive legal questions inherent in racial, religious, or sex discrimination charges.

In *Alexander v. Gardner-Denver Company*[36] the United States Supreme Court considered the question of whether an individual grievant's election to invoke grievance and arbitration machinery that resulted in an adverse arbitration award precludes the individual from filing a subsequent Title VII claim. The Court found that it did not. The Court held that Title VII was designed by Congress to supplement existing laws and institutions relating to employment discrimination and that the doctrine of election of remedies was inapplicable in the present context, which involved statutory rights distinctly separate from the employee's contractual rights, regardless of the fact that violation of both rights may have resulted from the same factual occurrence. The Court held, however, that the arbitral decision may be admitted as evidence at the Title VII trial in a federal court and set forth in its much-discussed footnote 21 the weight to be accorded the arbitral decision. Footnote 21 states:

> We adopt no standards as to the weight to be accorded an arbitral decision, since this must be determined in the court's discretion with regard to the facts and circumstances of each case. Relevant factors include the existence of provisions in the collective-bargaining agreement that conform substantially with Title VII, the degree of procedural fairness in the arbitral forum, adequacy of the record with respect to the issue of discrimination, and the special competence of particular arbitrators. Where an arbitral

---

[35]386 U.S. 171, 185 (1967).
[36]415 U.S. 147 (1974).

determination gives full consideration to an employee's Title VII rights, a court may properly accord it great weight. This is especially true where the issue is solely one of fact, specifically addressed by the parties and decided by the arbitrator on the basis of an adequate record. But courts should ever be mindful that Congress, in enacting Title VII, thought it necessary to provide a judicial forum for the ultimate resolution of discriminatory employment claims. It is the duty of courts to assure the full availability of this forum.

NLRA Remedies

An employer's racial discrimination is an unfair labor practice in violation of Section 8(a)(1) of the NLRA if it is found that this discrimination interferes with the affected employees' Section 7 rights to act concertedly for their own protection.[37] In *Jubilee Manufacturing Co.*[38] the Board pointed out that it was "by no means inevitable" that an employer's racial or sex discrimination would set one group of employees against the other. The Board stated that a finding of a violation of the NLRA would depend upon a showing of "the necessary direct relationship" between the alleged race or sex discrimination and interference with employee rights under Section 7.

In *King Soopers, Inc.*[39] the Board found an employer to be in violation of Section 8(a)(1) of the NLRA for suspending a Spanish-American employee for filing charges with the EEOC alleging promotional discrimination. The Board also found the union to be in violation of Section 8(b)(1)(A) for refusing to represent and process the grievances of the charging party. The Board's order held the company and the union jointly and severally liable for back pay damages. It should be pointed out that the NLRA does not protect picketing, handbilling, or other concerted activity by a group of minority employees seeking to bargain directly with an employer concerning alleged racial discrimination by the employer when the minority employees circumvented their elected bargaining representative and refused to participate in the contract grievance procedure.

In *Frank Briscoe v. NLRB*[40] twelve ironworkers were laid off in February 1979. Four of the laid-off ironworkers were black, and they filed Title VII charges of discrimination based on race. When the weather improved, the company began rehiring but refused to hire any of the twelve laid-off workers. The company stated that to rehire those who did not file charges would be evidence of discrimination. Some of the ironworkers obtained other work, and eight of the workers laid off in February, including three of the black workers who filed Title VII charges, brought unfair labor charges before the NLRB. The U.S. court of appeals held that the filing of a complaint with the Equal Employment Opportunity Commission by the black employees under Title VII could constitute "concerted activity" protected by Section 7 of the NLRA. The court determined that retaliation by the employer against those employees and the others affected thereby was an unfair practice giving rise to the remedial measures of the NLRA. The court held that the availability of a remedy from the EEOC under Title VII does not preclude a plaintiff from seeking and obtaining relief under the NLRA. Indeed a remedy under the NLRA may provide a faster resolution to a problem than under Title VII procedures.

---

[37]Tipler v. E. I. du Pont de Nemours & Co., 443 F.2d 125 (6th Cir. 1971).
[38]202 NLRB 2 (1973).
[39]222 NLRB 80 (1976).
[40]637 F.2d 946, 106 LRRM 2155 (3d Cir. 1981).

Employers are also protected from racial and religious prejudice in relation to Board election activities. In *M & M Supermarkets, Inc. v. NLRB*[41] the Eleventh Circuit Court of Appeals let it be clearly known that appeals to racial and religious prejudice have no place in our system of justice or in an NLRB-conducted election. During the course of an election campaign, the company's personnel director, Patrick, made a presentation to a small group of employees at which a union supporter began to berate the company's owners as follows:

> The damn Jews who run this Company are all alike. They pay us pennies out here in the warehouse, and take all their money to the bank. The Jews ought to remember their roots. Norton Malaver ought to remember his roots. Us blacks were out in the cotton field while they, the damned Jews, took their money from the poor hardworking people.

> As Patrick attempted to defend the reputation of Norton Malaver and his family as liberal and community-minded people, Charles Wade angrily interrupted her and continued loudly. . . .[42]

The union, which did not condone the remarks, won the election, and the Board issued a bargaining order. The court of appeals refused to enforce the order, stating that the remarks were "so inflammatory and derogatory that they inflamed racial and religious tensions against the . . . owners of the company and destroyed the laboratory conditions necessary for a free and open election."[43]

[41]125 LRRM 2918 (11th Cir. 1987).
[42]Id. at 2919.
[43]Id. at 2922.

Saint Francis College v. Al-Khazraji
Supreme Court of the United States, 43 FEP 1305 (1987).

[Respondent, a U.S. citizen born in Iraq, was an associate professor of behavioral science at St. Francis College in Pennsylvania. He filed suit in federal district court against the college and its tenure committee alleging that by denying him tenure nearly three years before, they had discriminated against him on the basis of his Arabian race in violation of 42 USC Section 1981. His Title VII claims of discrimination based on national origin, religion, and race were dismissed as untimely. The district court granted a summary judgment for the college, finding that Section 1981 does not cover claims based on Arabian ancestry. The court of appeals reversed, holding that the respondent had properly alleged racial discrimination in that, although Arabs are Caucasians under current racial classifications, Congress, when it passed what is now Section 1981, did not limit its protections to those who today would be considered members of a race different than the defendant's. The Supreme Court granted certiorari.]

WHITE, J.
Section 1981 provides:

All persons within the jurisdiction of the United States shall have the same right in every State and Territory to make and enforce contracts, to sue, be parties, give evidence, and to the full and equal benefit of all laws and proceedings for the security of persons and prop-

erty as is enjoyed by white citizens, and shall be subject to like punishment, pains, penalties, taxes, licenses, and exactions of every kind, and to no other.

Although § 1981 does not itself use the word "race," the Court has construed the section to forbid all "racial" discrimination in the making of private as well as public contracts. *Runyon v. McCrary*, 427 U.S. 160, 168, 174–175 (1976). The petitioner college, although a private institution, was therefore subject to this statutory command. There is no disagreement among the parties on these propositions. The issue is whether respondent has alleged *racial* discrimination within the meaning of § 1981.

Petitioners contend that respondent is a Caucasian and cannot allege the kind of discrimination § 1981 forbids. Concededly, *McDonald v. Sante Fe Trail Transportation Co.*, 427 U.S. 273 (1976), held that white persons could maintain a § 1981 suit; but that suit involved alleged discrimination against a white person in favor of a black, and petitioner submits that the section does not encompass claims of discrimination by one Caucasian against another. We are quite sure that the Court of Appeals properly rejected this position.

Petitioner's submission rests on the assumption that all those who might be deemed Caucasians today were thought to be of the same race when § 1981 became law in the 19th century; and it may be that a variety of ethnic groups, including Arabs, are now considered to be within the Caucasian race. The understanding of "race" in the 19th century, however, was different. Plainly, all those who might be deemed Caucasian today were not thought to be of the same race at the time § 1981 became law. . . .

Encyclopedias of the 19th century . . . described race in terms of ethnic groups, which is a narrower concept of race than petitioners urged. Encyclopedia Americana in 1858, for example, referred in 1854 to various races such as Finns, gypsies, Basques, and Hebrews. The 1863 version of the New American Cyclopaedia divided the Arabs into a number of subsidiary races,

represented the Hebrews as of the Semitic race, and identified numerous other groups as constituting races, including Swedes, Norwegians, Germans, Greeks, Finns, Italians, Spanish, Mongolians, Russians, and the like. The Ninth edition of the Encyclopedia Britannica also referred to Arabs, Jews, and other ethnic groups such as Germans, Hungarians, and Greeks, as separate races.

These dictionary and encyclopedic sources are somewhat diverse, but it is clear that they do not support the claim that for the purposes of § 1981, Arabs, Englishmen, Germans and certain other ethnic groups are to be considered a single race. We would expect the legislative history of § 1981, which the Court held in *Runyon v. McCrary* had its source in the Civil Rights Act of 1866, as well as the Voting Rights Act of 1870, to reflect this common understanding, which it surely does. The debates are replete with references to the Scandinavian races, Cong. Globe, 39th Cong., 1st Sess, 499 (1866) (remarks of Sen. Cowan), as well as the Chinese (remarks of Sen. Davis), Latin (remarks of Rep. Kasson during debate of home rule for the District of Columbia), Spanish (remarks of Sen. Davis during debate of District of Columbia suffrage) and Anglo-Saxon races (remarks of Rep. Dawson). Jews, Mexicans (remarks of Rep. Dawson), blacks, and Mongolians (remarks of Sen. Cowan), were similarly categorized. Gypsies were referred to as a race (remarks of Sen. Cowan). . . .

Based on the history of § 1981, we have little trouble in concluding that Congress intended to protect from discrimination identifiable classes of persons who are subjected to intentional discrimination solely because of their ancestry or ethnic characteristics. Such discrimination is racial discrimination that Congress intended § 1981 to forbid, whether or not it would be classified as racial in terms of modern scientific theory. The Court of Appeals was thus quite right in holding that § 1981, "at a minimum," reaches discrimination against an individual "because he or she is genetically part of an ethnically and physiognomically distinctive subgrouping of *homo sapiens*." It is clear from our holding, however, that a distinctive physiognomy is not essential to qualify for § 1981 protection. If respondent on remand can prove that he was subjected to intentional discrimination based on the fact that he was born an Arab, rather than solely on the place or nation of his origin, or his religion, he will have made out a case under § 1981.

The judgment of the Court of Appeals is accordingly

Affirmed.

CASE QUESTIONS

1. Why did the plaintiff bring a Section 1981 claim rather than rely on a Title VII claim?
2. Can a Section 1981 claim encompass a charge of discrimination by one Caucasian against another?
3. Did the plaintiff prove that St. Francis College had discriminated against him because of his Arabian ancestry?

Shaare Tefila Congregation v. Cobb
Supreme Court of the United States, 43 FEP 1309 (1987).

[*After their synagogue was painted with anti-Semitic slogans, phrases, and symbols, petitioners brought suit in federal district court alleging that the desecration by respondents violated 42 USC Section 1982. The district court dismissed petitioners' claims, and the court of appeals affirmed, holding that discrimination against Jews was not racial discrimination under Section 1982. The Supreme Court granted certiorari.*]

WHITE, J.

We agree with the Court of Appeals that a charge of racial discrimination within the meaning of § 1982 cannot be made out by alleging only that the defendants were motivated by racial animus; it is necessary as well to allege that defendants' animus was directed towards the kind of group that Congress intended to protect when it passed the statute. To hold otherwise would unacceptably extend the reach of the statute.

We agree with petitioners, however, that the Court of Appeals erred in holding that Jews cannot state a § 1982 claim against other white defendants. That view rested on the notion that because Jews today are not thought to be members of a separate race, they cannot make out a claim of racial discrimination within the mean-

ing of § 1982. That construction of the section we have today rejected in *Saint Francis College v. Al-Khazraji*. Our opinion in that case observed that definitions of race when § 1982 was passed were not the same as they are today and concluded that the section was "intended to protect from discrimination identifiable classes of persons who are subjected to intentional discrimination solely because of their ancestry or ethnic characteristics." As *St. Francis* makes clear, the question before us is not whether Jews are considered to be a separate race by today's standards, but whether, at the time § 1982 was adopted, Jews constituted a group of people that Congress intended to protect. It is evident from the legislative history of the section reviewed in *Saint Francis College*, a review that we need not repeat here, that Jews and Arabs were among the peoples then considered to be distinct races and hence within the protection of the statute. Jews are not foreclosed from stating a cause of action against other members of what today is considered to be part of the Caucasian race.

The judgment of the Court of Appeals is therefore reversed and the case is remanded for further proceedings consistent with this opinion.

CASE QUESTIONS

1. Why did the district court dismiss the congregation's Section 1982 claim?

2. Can Jews state a Section 1982 claim against other white defendants?

Part Questions and Problems

1. What remedies are available to individuals charging discriminatory employment practices?
2. What guidelines did the *Weber* Court set forth for permissible affirmative action plans?
3. On what authority do federal agencies require bidders on government contracts to formulate and carry out affirmative action plans?
4. Explain how the 80 percent rule works.
5. Manual Lerma, a Mexican-American, responded to an advertisement announcing the availability of a custodial position at the Harlingen, Texas, post office. The applications were independently rated. Lerma placed third on the hiring list with a score of 95 points out of 110. Immediately behind Lerma was a white male named Ricky Schwab with a rating of 94. Schwab had worked at the Harlingen post office on a temporary basis in the past. After interviewing the four top candidates, the postmaster appointed Schwab to the vacant custodial position. The postmaster cited the favorable recommendation of a supervisor who had observed Schwab during his temporary work at the post office as a persuasive factor in his decision to choose Schwab over the other candidates.

    Lerma brought a Title VII action against the postal service alleging that the failure to hire him was discrimination based on his race and national origin.

    The postal service contended that no discrimination took place, that Lerma failed to establish a prima facie case under Title VII, and that legitimate reasons existed for selecting Schwab over Lerma.

    On the basis of the facts given, did Lerma establish a prima facie case under Title VII? If so, what must the defendant do to avoid liability? Decide. [Lerma v. Balger, 29 FEP 1829 (5th Cir. 1982)]
6. The New Bedford Police Department required all police officers, both male and female, to satisfy a 5-foot-6-inch minimum height requirement. Marie Costa wished to become a police officer. She had passed the city's physical examination and had scored 93 percent on the state civil service examination. Costa's successful completion of these requirements gained her a ranking as the number one candidate on the eligibility list for female officers. When two vacancies for a female police officer occurred, Costa was interviewed for the position but was rejected due to her failure to satisfy the minimum height requirement. The second ranked female applicant was also rejected under the height requirement. The city hired the third and fourth ranked women, who did meet the minimum height.

    Costa brought an action under Title VII, producing undisputed evidence that less than 20 percent of women attain the height of 5 feet 6 inches. Therefore, Costa claimed that the police department's minimum height policy had a disparate impact upon women in violation of Title VII.

    The city denied this allegation by claiming that their policy did not result in a disparate impact upon women since they hired women for the vacancies.

    Does the city policy violate Title VII? Decide the case. [Costa v. Markey, 706 F.2d 1 (1st Cir. 1983)]
7. In 1985 a U.S. district court approved an affirmative action plan for the Washington, D.C. (D.C.), fire department that required that 60 percent of new hires be black. D.C. itself was predominantly black, with 65 percent of the work force and up to 75 percent of the applicants from D.C. being black. Twenty-nine percent of the entire metropolitan Washington, D.C., area, from which D.C. recruited fire fighters, was black. In 1983,

80 percent of the new hires were black. In 1982, 67.5 percent of the new hires were black. Over a four-year period an average of 75 percent of those hired were black. Between 1980 and 1984 virtually every candidate who showed up to take the test for fire fighter passed it because the cutoff score was set so low that even random answering of questions would lead to a passing mark. D.C.'s goal in its affirmative action plan was to achieve racial parity in its fire fighting force.

The plaintiffs contended that the evidence was clear that the fire department was not engaging in hiring practices that discriminated against blacks and that no dismantling of the structures of past discrimination remained for the courts. They contended that the plan and its goal were illegal.

D.C. stated that the fire department was just 38 percent black, while the working age population of D.C. was 70 percent black. D.C. contended that "plantation politics" were practiced in D.C. for over a century. It stated that the plaintiffs urged D.C. to forget the bad old days of discrimination and concentrate on the purity of current practices; however, it argued that racial parity would be lost without the 60 percent hiring goal.

What standard must a court apply in reviewing whether a city's race-conscious affirmative action quotas are permissible? On the limited evidence before you, were D.C.'s hiring practices discriminatory considering the qualified and relevant labor market? Is D.C.'s goal of achieving racial parity constitutionally valid? [Hammond v. Barry, 42 EPD ¶ 36,804 (D.C. Cir. 1987)]

8. The First Alabama Bank of Montgomery was a party to various contracts with the United States in which it agreed to be bound by the terms of Executive Order 11246. The bank formulated an affirmative action plan. The Office of Federal Contract Compliance Programs notified First Alabama that it wished to review the compliance with Executive Order 11246, Section 503 of the Rehabilitation Act of 1973, and Section 402 of the Vietnam Veterans Readjustment Assistance Act of 1974. Accordingly, the OFCCP asked the bank to submit a copy of its affirmative action plan and other supporting documentation.

The bank refused to supply the requested information or to allow a OFCCP compliance officer to conduct an on-site review. The bank stated that it had undergone three compliance reviews under Executive Order 11246 in the last ten years and had been found to be in compliance each time. Furthermore, the bank stated that it had been a defendant in a ten-year race discrimination action under Title VII during which it had filed quarterly reports with the court. The litigation had ended with a finding by the court that the bank did not discriminate against blacks in its hiring practices.

Given the bank's refusal to comply, the Department of Labor issued a complaint against the bank asking that First Alabama be debarred from receiving government contracts until it convinced the Secretary of Labor that it was in compliance with the affirmative action obligations of Executive Order 11246. After notice and hearing, the secretary's complaint was sustained and First Alabama was debarred.

Citing its compliance history and the favorable decision in the Title VII case, First Alabama sought judicial review of the debarment in district court.

Should the debarment decision be upheld as proper? If so, what must First Alabama do to renew its eligibility as a government contractor? [First Alabama Bank of Montgomery, N.A. v. Donovan, 30 FEP 4448 (11th Cir. 1982)]

9. Clara Watson, who is black, was hired by the Fort Worth Bank and Trust Co. in August 1973 and was promoted to teller in 1976. Between 1980 and 1981 Watson applied for four supervisory jobs, but white employees were selected for these positions. The bank, which had some eighty employees, had not developed formal criteria for evaluating candidates but

relied on the subjective judgment of supervisors who were acquainted with the candidates and the nature of the jobs to be filled.

In a Title VII lawsuit against the bank, the trial court, following a disparate treatment model, concluded that Watson had established a prima facie case; the bank had rebutted it by presenting legitimate, nondiscriminatory reasons for each challenged promotion decision; and Watson had failed to show that the reasons were pretexts. Watson presented evidence that showed that the bank had only one black supervisor from 1975 to 1983, and a statistician testified on her behalf that a white applicant had a four times better chance of being hired than a black applicant. Watson claimed that a disparate impact model analysis of the employer's subjective promotion policy standards indicated that she was discriminated against in violation of Title VII. The court refused to apply a disparate impact analysis to subjective promotion procedures such as job interviews and performance evaluations, saying that disparate impact analysis was meant to evaluate objective criteria such as testing or diploma requirements.

Watson contended that if an employer's undisciplined system of subjective decision making had precisely the same effect as a system pervaded by impermissible intentional discrimination, it was difficult to see why Title VII was not violated. She contended, moreover, that the *Griggs* decision would be nullified if disparate impact analysis were applied only to objective selection practices.

The bank contended that employers would have to abandon subjective methods of evaluating candidates for promotion, such as interviews or performance evaluations, if it were forced to defend disparate impact cases, and its only alternative would be to adopt a quota system in order to ensure that no plaintiff could establish a prima facie case. It stated that quota systems were clearly contrary to Title VII. Further, the bank stated that Watson had full opportunity to prove that the bank did not promote her because of her race, and she failed to prove her case.

Did the trial court err in failing to apply disparate impact analysis to Watson's claims of discrimination in promotion? [Watson v. Fort Worth Bank and Trust Co., 47 FEP 102 (U.S.S. Ct. 1988)]

3

Fair Employment Practices: III

SECTION 16—EQUAL PAY FOR EQUAL WORK

The principle of equal pay for equal work regardless of sex is set forth in the Equal Pay Act of 1963, which was enacted as Section 6(d) of the Fair Labor Standards Act (FLSA). The Equal Pay Act prohibits employers from discriminating against employees covered by the minimum wage provisions of the FLSA by paying lower wages to employees of one sex than the rate paid employees of the opposite sex for equal work in the same establishment on jobs that require equal skill, effort, and responsibility and are performed under similar working conditions.[1] The Equal Pay Act was intended as a broad charter of women's rights in the business world. The act seeks to eliminate the depressing effects on living standards caused by reduced wages for female workers. The act does not prohibit any variation in wage rates paid men and women but only those variations based solely on sex. The act sets forth four exceptions, allowing variances in wages to be based on (1) a seniority system, (2) a merit system, (3) a system that measures earnings by quantity or quality of production, or (4) a differential based on any factor other than sex.[2]

The 1974 amendments to the FLSA make the act applicable to employees of the federal, state, and local governments and their agencies.[3] Enforcement of the act is the responsibility of the Equal Employment Opportunity Commission.

Congress, in prescribing equal pay for equal work, did not require that the jobs in

---

[1] 29 USC Section 206(d)(1).
[2] Id.
[3] See Section 3(d) of the FLSA as amended in 1974, P.L., 93–259.

question be identical but only that the jobs be "substantially equal."[4] In applying this "substantially equal" test, the courts have had no difficulty finding that it is the job content, not the job description, that is controlling.[5]

The courts have uniformly found that the enforcing federal agency bears the initial burden of proving that the employer pays employees of one sex less than employees of the other sex for performing equal work. Once the enforcing agency sustains its initial burden of proof, the burden shifts to the employer to show that the differential is justified by one of the four allowable exceptions.

In *Shultz v. Wheaton Glass Co.*[6] the Third Circuit Court of Appeals found that a manufacturing plant's 10 percent pay differential for male selector-packers over the pay for female selector-packers, where the male selector-packers spent a relatively small portion of their time doing the additional tasks of "snap-up boys," a lower paying classification requiring lifting and other unskilled tasks, was a violation of the Equal Pay Act. The court did not require the skill, effort, and responsibility of the female selector-packers' work to be precisely equal to the male selector-packers' work but rather that the work be substantially equal.

In *Hodgson v. Robert Hall Clothes, Inc.*,[7] the Third Circuit Court of Appeals allowed an employer to pay male salespersons at a higher rate than female salespersons holding that the exception for "any other factor other than sex" included the greater profits that an employer received for the men's clothing department as compared to the women's clothing department.

The *Corning Glass Works* decision, presented in this section, discusses several important aspects of the Equal Pay Act. This case was brought at a time when enforcement of the act was the responsibility of the Department of Labor's Employment Standards Administration and court actions were brought in the name of the Secretary of Labor.

---

[4]Shultz v. Wheaton Glass Co., 421 F.2d 259 (3rd Cir. 1970).
[5]Brennan v. Victoria Bank & Trust Co., 493 F.2d 896 (5th Cir. 1974).
[6]421 F.2d 259 (3rd Cir. 1970).
[7]473 F.2d 589 (3rd Cir. 1973).

Corning Glass Works v. Brennan
Supreme Court of the United States, 415 U.S. 972 (1974).

MARSHALL, J.
These cases arise under the Equal Pay Act of 1963, 29 U.S.C. Section 206(d)(1), which added to the Fair Labor Standards Act the principle of equal pay for equal work regardless of sex. The principal question posed is whether Corning Glass Works violated the Act by paying a higher base wage to male night shift inspectors than it paid to female inspectors performing the same tasks on the day shift, where the higher wage was paid in addition to a separate night shift differential paid to all employees for night work. In No. 73–29, the Court of Appeals for the Second Circuit, in a case involving several Corning plants in Corning, New York, held that this practice violated the Act. 474 F.2d 226 (1973). In No.

73–695, the Court of Appeals for the Third Circuit, in a case involving a Corning plant in Wellsboro, Pennsylvania, reached the opposite conclusion. 480 F.2d 1254 (1973). We granted certiorari and consolidated the cases to resolve this unusually direct conflict between two circuits. Finding ourselves in substantial agreement with the analysis of the Second Circuit, we affirm in No. 73–29 and reverse in No. 73–695.

I

Prior to 1925, Corning operated its plants in Wellsboro and Corning only during the day, and all inspection work was performed by women. Between 1925 and 1930, the company began to introduce automatic production equipment which made it desirable to institute a night shift. During this period, however, both New York and Pennsylvania law prohibited women from working at night. As a result, in order to fill inspector positions on the new night shift, the company had to recruit male employees from among its male day workers. The male employees so transferred demanded and received wages substantially higher than those paid to women inspectors engaged on the two day shifts. During this same period, however, no plant-wide shift differential existed and male employees working at night, other than inspectors, received the same wages as their day shift counterparts. Thus a situation developed where the night inspectors were all male, the day inspectors all female, and the male inspectors received significantly higher wages.

In 1944, Corning plants at both locations were organized by a labor union and a collective-bargaining agreement was negotiated for all production and maintenance employees. This agreement for the first time established a plant-wide shift differential, but this change did not eliminate the higher base wage paid to male night inspectors. Rather, the shift differential was superimposed on the existing difference in base wages between male night inspectors and female day inspectors.

Prior to the June 11, 1964, effective date of the Equal Pay Act, the law in both Pennsylvania and New York was amended to permit women to work at night. It was not until some time after the effective date of the Act, however, that Corning initiated efforts to eliminate the differential rates for male and female inspectors. Beginning in June 1966, Corning started to open up jobs on the night shift to women. Previously separate male and female seniority lists were consolidated and women became eligible to exercise their seniority, on the same basis as men, to bid for the higher paid night inspection jobs as vacancies occurred.

On January 20, 1969, a new collective-bargaining agreement went into effect, establishing a new "job evaluation" system for setting wage rates. The new agreement abolished for the future the separate base wages for day and night shift inspectors and imposed a uniform base wage for inspectors exceeding the wage rate for the night shift previously in effect. All inspectors hired after January 20, 1969, were to receive the same base wage, whatever their sex or shift. The collective-bargaining agreement further provided, however, for a higher "red circle" rate for employees hired prior to January 20, 1969, when working as inspectors on the night shift. This "red circle" rate served essentially to perpetuate the differential in base wages between day and night inspectors.

The Secretary of Labor brought these cases to enjoin Corning from violating the Equal Pay Act and to collect back wages allegedly due female employees because of past violations. Three distinct questions are presented: (1) Did Corning ever violate the Equal Pay Act by paying male night shift inspectors more than female day shift inspectors? (2) If so, did Corning cure its violation of the Act in 1966 by permitting women to work as night shift inspectors? (3) Finally, if the violation was not remedied in 1966, did Corning cure its violation in 1969 by equalizing day and night inspector wage rates but establishing higher "red circle" rates for existing employees working on the night shift?

II

Congress' purpose in enacting the Equal Pay Act was to remedy what was perceived to be a serious and endemic problem of employment discrimination in private industry—the fact that the wage structure of "many segments of American industry has been based on an ancient but outmoded belief that a man, because of his role in society, should be paid more than a woman, even though his duties are the same." S. Rept. No. 176, 88th Cong., 1st Sess. (1963), at 1. The solution adopted was quite simple in principle: to require that "equal work be rewarded by equal wages." *Ibid.*

The Act's basic structure and operation are similarly straightforward. In order to make out a case under the Act, the Secretary must show that an employer pays different wages to employees of opposite sexes "for equal work on jobs the performance of which requires equal skill, effort, and responsibility, and which are performed under similar working conditions." Although the Act is silent on this point, its legislative history makes plain that the Secretary has the burden of proof on this issue, as both of the courts below recognized.

The Act also establishes four exceptions—three specific and one a general catchall provision—where different payment to employees of opposite sexes "is made pursuant to (i) a seniority system; (ii) a merit system; (iii) a system which measures earnings by quantity or quality of production; or (iv) a differential based on any other factor other than sex." Again, while the Act is silent on this question, its structure and history also suggest that once the Secretary has carried his burden of showing that the employer pays workers of one sex more than workers of the opposite sex for equal work, the burden shifts to the employer to show that the differential is justified under one of the Act's four exceptions. All of the many lower courts that have considered this question have so held, and this view is consistent with the general rule that the application of an exemption under the Fair Labor Standards Act is a matter of affirmative defense on which the employer has the burden of proof.

The contentions of the parties in this case reflect the Act's underlying framework. Corning argues that the Secretary has failed to prove that Corning ever violated the Act because day shift work is not "performed under similar working conditions" as night shift work. The Secretary maintains that day shift and night shift work are performed under "similar working conditions" within the meaning of the Act. . . .

Congress' intent, as manifested in [the Act's] history, was to use these terms to incorporate into the new federal act the well-defined and well-accepted principles of job evaluation so as to ensure that wage differentials based upon bona fide job evaluation plans would be outside the purview of the Act. . . .

While a layman might well assume that time of day worked reflects one aspect of a job's "working conditions," the term has a different and much more specific meaning in the language of industrial relations. As Corning's own representative testified at the hearings, the element of working conditions encompasses two subfactors: "surroundings" and "hazards." "Surroundings" measure the elements, such as toxic chemicals or fumes, regularly encountered by a worker, their intensity, and their frequency. "Hazards" take into account the physical hazards regularly encountered, their frequency, and the severity of injury they can cause. This definition of "working conditions" is not only manifested in Corning's own job evaluation plans but is also well accepted across a wide range of American industry.

Nowhere in any of these definitions is time of day worked mentioned as a relevant criterion. The fact of the matter is that the concept of "working conditions," as used in the specialized language of job evaluation systems, simply does not encompass shift differentials. Indeed, while Corning now argues that night inspection work is not equal to day inspection work, all of its own job evaluation plans, including the one now in effect, have consistently treated them as equal in all respects, including working conditions. And Corning's Manager of Job Evaluation testified in No. 73–29 that time of day worked was not considered to be a "working condition." . . .

The question remains, however, whether Corning carried its burden of proving that the higher rate paid for night inspection work, until 1966 performed solely by men, was in fact intended to serve as compensation for night work, or rather constituted an added payment based upon sex. We agree that the record amply supported the District Court's conclusion that Corning had not sustained its burden of proof. As its history revealed, "the higher night rate was in large part the product of the generally higher wage level of male workers and the need to compensate them for performing what were regarded as demeaning tasks." 474 F.2d, at 233. The differential in base wages originated at a time when no other night employees received higher pay than corresponding day workers and it was maintained long after the company instituted a separate plant-wide differential which was thought to compensate adequately for the additional burdens of night work. The differential arose simply because men would not work at the low rates paid women inspectors, and it reflected a job market in which Corning could pay women less than men for the same work. That the company took advantage of such a situation may be understandable as a matter of economics, but its differential nevertheless became illegal once Congress enacted into law the principle of equal pay for equal work.

III

We now must consider whether Corning continued to remain in violation of the Act after 1966 when, without changing the base wage rates for day and night inspectors, it began to permit women to bid for jobs on the night shift as vacancies occurred. . . .

. . . Congress required that employers pay equal pay for equal work and then specified:

Provided, *That an employer who is paying a wage differential in violation of this subsection shall not, in order to comply with the provisions of this subsection, reduce the wage rate of any employee.*

The purpose of this proviso was to ensure that to remedy violations of the Act, "the lower wage rate must be increased to the level of the higher." H.R. Rep. No. 309, *supra,* at 3. . . .

By proving that after the effective date of the Equal Pay Act, Corning paid female day inspectors less than male night inspectors for equal work, the Secretary implicitly demonstrated that the wages of female day shift inspectors were unlawfully depressed and that the fair wage for inspection work was the base wage paid to male inspectors on the night shift. The whole purpose of the Act was to require that these depressed wages be raised, in part as a matter of simple justice to the employees themselves, but also as a matter of market economics, since Congress recognized as well that discrimination in wages on the basis of sex "constitutes an unfair method of competition." Section 2(5).

We agree with Judge Friendly that:

In light of this apparent congressional understanding, we cannot hold that Corning, by allowing some—or even many—women to move into the higher paid night jobs, achieved full compliance with the Act. Corning's action still left the inspectors on the day shift— virtually all women—earning a lower base wage than the night shift inspectors because of a differential initially based on sex and still not justified by any other consideration; in effect, Corning was still taking advantage of the availability of female labor to fill its day shift at a differentially low wage rate not justified by any factor other than sex. 474 F.2d, at 235.

The Equal Pay Act is broadly remedial, and it should be construed and applied so as to fulfill the underlying purposes which Congress sought to achieve. If, as the Secretary proved, the work performed by women on the day shift was equal to that performed by men on the night shift, the company became obligated to pay the women the same base wage as their male counter-parts on the effective date of the Act. To permit the company to escape that obligation by agreeing to allow some women to work on the night shift at a higher rate of pay as vacancies occurred would frustrate, not serve, Congress' ends. . . .

The company's final contention—that it cured its violation of the Act when a new collective bargaining agreement went into effect on January 20, 1969—need not detain us long. While the new agreement provided for equal base wages for night or day inspectors hired after that date, it continued to provide unequal base wages for employees hired before that date, a discrimination likely to continue for some time into the future because of a large number of laid-off employees who had to be offered reemployment before new inspectors could be hired. . . .

The judgment in No. 73–29 is affirmed. The judgment in No. 73–695 is reversed and the case remanded to the Court of Appeals for further proceedings consistent with this opinion.

It is so ordered.

CASE QUESTIONS

1. Summarize the facts of the case.
2. Who brought the two court actions against Corning Glass Works?
3. Does the statutory term *working conditions* encompass the time of day worked?
4. Did Corning cure its violation in June 1966 when it permitted women to work as night shift inspectors?

SECTION 17—THE *GUNTHER* DECISION AND COMPARABLE WORTH

In spite of the passage of the Equal Pay Act of 1963 and Title VII of the Civil Rights Act of 1964, a substantial earnings gap exists between the average earnings of women working full time and the average earnings of men working full time. The disparity has closed from 62 percent in 1979 to 71 percent in 1987.[8] It is generally accepted that the reason the overall statistics show that women earn substantially less than men is that a large proportion of working women are employed in certain predominantly female occupations, such as nursing, secretarial work, social work, clerical work, school teaching, food service, and domestic service, that have significantly lower pay scales relative to other occupations where men are dominant. The Equal Pay Act has been very successful in remedying pay disparity between men and women performing the same work for their employer. Thus female full-time college professors earn about the same as male full-time college professors of similar qualifications; female autoworkers earn the same as male autoworkers doing the same work.

Advocates of the concept of *comparable worth* believe that female employees whose jobs are separate and distinct from jobs performed by male employees but are of comparable worth or value to the employer are entitled to wages comparable to those of male employees. Advocates of comparable worth believe that if comparable wages are not paid, female employees should be entitled to relief under Title VII of the Civil Rights Act of 1964. This theory has not been accepted in the courts.

Sex-Based Discrimination in Job Compensation

In *County of Washington v. Gunther,* presented in this section, the Supreme Court considered the claims of four women employed as matrons at the Washington County,

---

[8]Bureau of Labor Statistics, July 30, 1987.

Oregon, jail. These women claimed that the pay differential between them and male corrections officers was attributable to intentional sex discrimination even though the matron's job was not substantially the same job as that of the corrections officers. The Supreme Court set forth the narrow holding that the plaintiffs' claim of low pay because of discrimination based on sex was not barred by Section 703(h) of Title VII, the Bennett Amendment, merely because the plaintiffs did not perform work "equal" to that of the male corrections officers. The significance of the decision is that women may now bring a sex discrimination suit on the basis of low compensation even if they cannot prove that male co-workers are being paid higher wages for substantially the same job. The Court majority emphasized that its narrow holding did not require it to take a position on the issue of comparable worth.

Comparable Worth

The *Gunther* decision was widely acclaimed by advocates of comparable worth as a first step in the direction of court acceptance of that doctrine. In *AFSCME v. State of Washington (AFSCME I)*[9] a U.S. district court judge held that the state violated Title VII by its failure to pay men and women the same wages for work of comparable, but not equal, worth. The judge found that the state's practice of taking prevailing market rates into account in setting employee wages had an adverse impact on women, who have historically received lower wages than men in the labor market. The judge ordered implementation of a salary schedule based on comparable worth and ordered back pay of up to $800 million.

In *AFSCME v. State of Washington (AFSCME II)*[10] the Ninth Circuit Court of Appeals reversed the trial court's decision. The court of appeals rejected the doctrine of comparable worth, holding that reliance on market forces to set wages did not violate Title VII. The appeals court stated that the value of a job depends on factors other than just the actions performed on the job, factors such as the availability of workers and the effectiveness of unions in negotiating wages. Moreover, the court stated that the legislative history of Title VII did not indicate that Congress intended "to abrogate fundamental economic principles such as the laws of supply and demand."[11]

AFSCME and the state of Washington reached a pay equity agreement in 1986 in resolution of the comparable worth dispute. This agreement calls for the state to spend some $482.4 million between April 1, 1986, and June 30, 1992, to raise salaries of certain underpaid workers.

In *American Nurses Ass'n v. State of Illinois*,[12] a sex discrimination case brought by nurses against the state of Illinois, the Seventh Circuit Court of Appeals stated in part:

> An employer (private or public) that simply pays the going wage in each of the different types of jobs in its establishment, and makes no effort to discourage women from applying for particular jobs, would justifiably be surprised to discover that it may be violating federal law because each wage rate and therefore the ratio between them have

[9]578 F. Supp. 846 (W.D. Wash. 1983).
[10]770 F.2d 1401 (9th Cir. 1985).
[11]Id. at 1407.
[12]783 F.2d 716 (7th Cir. 1986).

been found to be determined by cultural or psychological factors attributable to the history of male domination of society; that it has to hire a consultant to find out how it must, regardless of market conditions, change the wages it pays, in order to achieve equity between traditionally male and traditionally female jobs; and that it must pay back pay to boot.[13]

In cases dealing with comparable worth issues, employers have a valid defense if they relied on market forces to set wages. The *Gunther* decision may be shown to be consistent with cases such as *AFSCME II* in that the compensation system in *Gunther* tied wages to market rates, but the violation of Title VII occurred when it did not pay the same percentage of the market rate to women as it did to men. The decision not to pay the women the full rate was attributable to intentional sex discrimination.

---

[13]Id. at 720.

County of Washington v. Gunther
Supreme Court of the United States, 452 U.S. 161 (1981).

[The plaintiffs were four women employed as matrons at the Washington County, Oregon, jail. The county also employed male corrections officers and deputy sheriffs. The matrons under Oregon law guarded female inmates, while the corrections officers and deputy sheriffs guarded male inmates. Effective February 1, 1973, the matrons were paid monthly salaries of between $525 and $668, while the salaries for the male guards ranged from $701 to $940. The plaintiffs filed suit under Title VII, alleging that they were paid unequal wages for work substantially equal to that performed by their male counterparts and, in the alternative, that part of the pay differential was attributable to intentional sex discrimination. The district court found that the male corrections officers supervised up to ten times as many prisoners per guard as did the matrons and that the females devoted much of their time to less valuable clerical duties such as processing fingerprint cards and mug shots, filing reports, keeping medical records, recording deputy sheriffs' activities, and censoring mail. The district court held that the plaintiffs' jobs were not substantially equal to those of the male guards, and the plaintiffs were thus not

entitled to equal pay. The district court also dismissed the claim based on intentional sex discrimination, holding as a matter of law that sex-based wage discrimination cannot be brought under Title VII unless it would satisfy the "equal work" standard of the Equal Pay Act. The court of appeals reversed the district court on this point, and the Supreme Court granted certiorari.]

BRENNAN, J.

The question presented is whether § 703(h) of Title VII of the Civil Rights Act of 1964, restricts Title VII's prohibition of sex-based wage discrimination to claims of equal pay for equal work.

I

We emphasize at the outset the narrowness of the question before us in this case. Respondents' claim is not based on the controversial concept of "comparable worth," under which plaintiffs might claim increased compensation on the basis of a comparison of the intrinsic worth or difficulty of their job with that of other jobs in the same organization or community. Rather, respondents seek to prove, by direct evidence, that their wages were depressed because of intentional sex discrimination, consisting of setting the wage scale for female guards, but not for male guards, at a level lower than its own survey of outside markets and the worth of the jobs warranted. The narrow question in this case is whether such a claim is precluded by the last sentence of § 703(h) of Title VII, called the "Bennett Amendment."

II

Title VII makes it an unlawful employment practice for an employer "to discriminate against any individual with respect to his compensation, terms, conditions, or privileges of employment, because of such individual's . . . sex. . . ." The Bennett Amendment to Title VII, however, provides:

"It shall not be an unlawful employment practice under this subchapter for any employer to differentiate upon the basis of sex in determining the amount of the wages or compensation paid or to be paid to employees of such employer if such differentiation is authorized by the provisions in Section 206(d) of Title 29." Section 703(h).

To discover what practices are exempted from Title VII's prohibitions by the Bennett Amendment, we must turn to § 206(d) of Title 29—the Equal Pay Act—which provides the relevant part:

"No employer having employees subject to any provisions of this section shall discriminate, within any establishment in which such employees are employed, between employees on the basis of sex by paying wages to employees in such establishment at a rate less than the rate at which he pays wages to employees of the opposite sex in such establishment for equal work on jobs the performance of which requires equal skill, effort, and responsibility, and which are performed under similar working conditions, except where such payment is made pursuant to (i) a seniority system; (ii) a merit system; (iii) a system which measures earnings by quantity or quality of production; or (iv) a differential based on any other factor other than sex." 29 U.S.C. § 206(d)(1).

On its face, the Equal Pay Act contains three restrictions pertinent to this case. First, its cov-

erage is limited to those employers subject to the Fair Labor Standards Act. Thus, the Act does not apply, for example, to certain businesses engaged in retail sales, fishing, agriculture, and newspaper publishing. Second, the Act is restricted to cases involving "equal work on jobs the performance of which requires equal skill, effort, and responsibility, and which are performed under similar working conditions." Third, the Act's four affirmative defenses exempt any wage differentials attributable to seniority, merit, quantity or quality of production, or "and other factor other than sex."

Petitioner argues that the purpose of the Bennett Amendment was to restrict Title VII sex-based wage discrimination claims to those that could also be brought under the Equal Pay Act, and thus that claims not arising from "equal work" are precluded. Respondents, in contrast, argue that the Bennett Amendment was designed merely to incorporate the four affirmative defenses of the Equal Pay Act into Title VII for sex-based wage discrimination claims. Respondents thus contend that claims for sex-based wage discrimination can be brought under Title VII even though no member of the opposite sex holds an equal but higher-paying job, provided that the challenged wage rate is not based on seniority, merit, quantity or quality of production, or "any other factor other than sex." The Court of Appeals found respondents' interpretation the "more persuasive." 623 F.2d at 1311, 20 FEP Cases, at 797. While recognizing that the language and legislative history of the provision are not unambiguous, we conclude that the Court of Appeals was correct. . . .

The legislative background of the Bennett Amendment is fully consistent with this interpretation. . . .

"Mr. BENNETT. Mr. President, after many years of yearning by members of the fair sex in this country, and after very careful study by the appropriate committees of Congress, last year Congress passed the so-called Equal Pay Act, which became effective only yesterday.

"By this time, programs have been established for the effective administration of this act. Now, when the civil rights bill is under consideration, in which the word 'sex' has been inserted in many places, I do not believe sufficient attention may have been paid to possible conflicts between the wholesale insertion of the word 'sex' in the bill and in the Equal Pay Act.

"The purpose of my amendment is to provide that in the event of conflicts, the provisions of the Equal Pay Act shall not be nullified.

"I understand that the leadership in charge of the bill have agreed to the amendment as a proper technical correction of the bill. If they will confirm that understand [sic], I shall ask that the amendment be voted on without asking for yeas and nays.

"Mr. HUMPHREY. The amendment of the Senator from Utah is helpful. I believe it is needed. I thank him for his thoughtfulness. The amendment is fully acceptable.

"Mr. DIRKSEN. Mr. President, I yield myself 1 minute.

"We were aware of the conflict that might develop, because the Equal Pay Act was an amendment to the Fair Labor Standards Act. The Fair Labor Standards Act carries out certain exceptions.

"All that the pending amendment does is recognize those exceptions, that are carried in the basic act.

"Therefore, this amendment is necessary, in the interest of clarification." 110 Cong. Rec. 13647 (1964).

As this discussion shows, Senator Bennett proposed the Amendment because of a general concern that insufficient attention had been paid to the relation between the Equal Pay Act and Title VII, rather than because of a *specific* potential conflict between the statutes. His explanation that the Amendment assured that the provisions of the Equal Pay Act "shall not be nullified" in the event of conflict with Title VII may be read as referring to the affirmative defenses of the Act. Indeed, his emphasis on the "technical" nature of the Amendment and his concern for not disrupting the "effective administration" of the Equal Pay Act are more compatible with an interpretation of the Amendment as incorporating the Act's affirmative defenses, as administratively interpreted, than as engrafting

all the restrictive features of the Equal Pay Act onto Title VII. . . .

Thus, although the few references by Members of Congress to the Bennett Amendment do not explicitly confirm that its purpose was to incorporate into Title VII the four affirmative defenses of the Equal Pay Act in sex-based wage discrimination cases, they are broadly consistent with such a reading, and do not support an alternative reading.

Our interpretation of the Bennett Amendment draws additional support from the remedial purposes of Title VII and the Equal Pay Act. . . .

Under petitioner's reading of the Bennett Amendment, only those sex-based wage discrimination claims that satisfy the "equal work" standard of the Equal Pay Act could be brought under Title VII. In practical terms, this means that a woman who is discriminatorily underpaid could obtain no relief—no matter how egregious the discrimination might be—unless her employer also employed a man in an equal job in the same establishment, at a higher rate of pay. Thus, if an employer hired a woman for a unique position in the company and then admitted that her salary would have been higher had she been male, the woman would be unable to obtain legal redress under petitioner's interpretation. Similarly, if an employer used a transparently sex-biased system for wage determination, women holding jobs not equal to those held by men would be denied the right to prove that the system is a pretext for discrimination.

III

Petitioner argues strenuously that the approach of the Court of Appeals places "the pay structure of virtually every employer and the entire economy . . . at risk and subject to scrutiny by the federal courts." It raises the spectre that "Title VII plaintiffs could draw any type of comparison imaginable concerning job duties and pay between any job predominantly performed by women and any job predominantly performed by men." But whatever the merit of petitioner's arguments in other contexts, they are inapplicable here, for claims based on the type of job comparisons petitioner describes are manifestly different from respondents' claim. Respondents contend that the County of Washington evaluated the worth of their jobs; that the county determined that they should be paid approximately 95 percent as much as the male correctional officers; that it paid them only about 70 percent as much, while paying the male officers the full evaluated worth of their jobs; and that the failure of the county to pay respondents the full evaluated worth of their jobs can be proven to be attributable to intentional sex discrimination. Thus, respondents' suit does not require a court to make its own subjective assessment of the value of the male and female guard jobs, or to attempt by statistical technique or other method to quantify the effect of sex discrimination on the wage rates.

We do not decide in this case the precise contours of lawsuits challenging sex discrimination in compensation under Title VII. It is sufficient to note that respondents' claims of discriminatory undercompensation are not barred by § 703(h) of Title VII merely because respondents do not perform work equal to that of male jail guards. The judgment of the Court of Appeals is therefore
Affirmed.

Dissenting Opinion

REHNQUIST, J., joined by BURGER, C. J., and STEWART and POWELL, J. J.
The Court today holds a plaintiff may state a claim of sex-based wage discrimination under Title VII without even establishing that she has performed "equal or substantially equal work" to that of males as defined in the Equal Pay Act. Because I believe that the legislative history of both the Equal Pay Act and Title VII clearly establish that there can be no Title VII claim of sex-based wage discrimination without proof of "equal work," I dissent. . . .

CASE QUESTIONS

1. What does the Bennett Amendment provide?
2. What did the employer argue was the purpose of the Bennett Amendment?
3. State the Supreme Court's decision.
4. If the equal work standard were to apply, could situations exist where a discriminatorily underpaid woman would be unable to obtain a remedy?

SECTION 18—AGE DISCRIMINATION

The Age Discrimination in Employment Act of 1967 (ADEA) as amended forbids discrimination against men and women over forty years of age by employers, unions, and employment agencies.[14] In 1974 the definition of *employer* was extended to include state and local governments. Executive Order 11141 has a similar purpose to the ADEA, prohibiting age discrimination by government contractors and federal agencies. The ADEA prohibits mandatory retirement for age.[15] Enforcement of the ADEA is the responsibility of the EEOC.

As stated previously, the definition of *employer* was extended to include state and local governments in 1974. In *EEOC v. Wyoming*[16] the Supreme Court upheld the constitutionality of this extension of the ADEA to state and local governments. Wyoming had forced Bill Crump, a supervisor with the state Game and Fish Department, to retire at the age of fifty-five, and he filed a complaint with the EEOC. In a suit brought by the

---

[14]29 USC Section 623.
[15]Public Law No. 99–592, Age Discrimination in Employment Act of 1986. See act for exceptions for law enforcement officers, fire fighters, and tenured professors pending studies to be concluded by 1991.
[16]103 S. Ct. 1453 (1983).

EEOC against the state, the district court found that the ADEA violated the Tenth Amendment. This contention was rejected by the Supreme Court, and Crump's complaint was reinstated. The Court majority stressed that Wyoming may assess the fitness of its game wardens on an individualized basis and may dismiss those wardens whom it reasonably finds to be unfit. The state remains free under the act to continue to do precisely what it is doing if it can demonstrate that age is a bona fide occupational qualification for the job of game warden. The dissent contended that the BFOQ defense does not adequately protect the state's ability to force unfit employees to retire. Given the state of modern medicine, it is virtually impossible to prove that substantially all persons within a class are unable to perform a particular job after a certain age.

Prohibited Practices and Remedial Procedures

Section 4(a) of the ADEA sets forth the employment practices that are unlawful under the act, including the failure to hire because of age and the discharge of employees because of age. Labor organizations are prohibited from discriminating because of age or attempting to cause employers to violate the ADEA under Section 4(b) of the act.

Most ADEA suits are brought on a disparate treatment theory of intentional discrimination because of age. Procedures are similar in many respects to those previously set fort in the text on Title VII. The burden of proof is as set forth in the *McDonnell Douglas-Burdine* model, with appropriate modifications for age in place of race or sex.

Most litigation at this writing results from reductions in force by employers where individual employees believe they have been terminated because of age. Also, suits are brought by job candidates who believe their employment applications were rejected because of age. Moreover, suits are brought by individuals who believe they were not promoted because of their age.

Defenses

Section 4(f) of the ADEA sets forth certain exemptions from the strictures of the act for employers. Thus where an individual is terminated because of a bona fide seniority plan, basic fairness and the language of the act dictate that the employer not be responsible for an ADEA violation. Also, if the employer discharges or disciplines an employee for "good cause," the employer is not in violation of the act. Thus if a sixty-year-old employee is discovered stealing from an employer, the employer may terminate that individual without being in violation of the act. Additionally, Section 4(f) provides employer defenses for "reasonable factors other than age" (RFOA) and "bona fide occupational qualifications reasonably necessary to the normal operation of a particular business" (BFOQ).

Generally the BFOQ defense is raised by employers in cases involving public safety. This was the defense in *Hodgson v. Greyhound Lines Inc.*[17] There the company had a policy of limiting new driver applicants to persons under the age of thirty-five. The district court judge held that Greyhound failed to meet its "burden of demonstrating that its policy of age limitation is reasonably necessary to the normal and safe operation of its business." However, the judge's ruling was overturned by a three-member panel of the

---

[17]499 F.2d 859, 7 FEP 817 (7th Cir. 1974).

United States court of appeals holding that Greyhound did not violate the act because of its hiring age limitation since it had a rational basis in fact to believe that elimination of its hiring policy would increase the likelihood or risk of harm to its passengers and others. The courts generally require the employer to prove that the BFOQ is reasonably necessary to the essence of its business and that the employer has a factual basis for believing that all or substantially all persons within the affected class would be unable to perform safely and efficiently the duties involved.

In recent years large scale reductions in forces (RIFs) have taken place in many industries and in public sector occupations such as school teachers, police, and fire personnel. Where the RIFs take place according to a bona fide seniority plan, no violation of the act occurs. Where no collective bargaining agreement restricts an employer as to the manner of a RIF, the employer has the right to use reasonable factors other than age (RFOA) in implementing the reduction in force. For example, the employer may consider the relative performances of employees in each classification in deciding which employee to terminate. However, the risks are high that an employer may be found to be in violation of the ADEA because statistical and other evidence of discrimination may be developed, as cost-cutting work force reduction decisions tend to encourage the termination of highly paid, experienced employees, who tend to be older employees. Often employers reduce forces of managerial employees without violating the act by offering truly voluntary retirement incentives. Also, using a combination of seniority and performance appraisal in reductions in force of older or protected workers keeps the employer within the RFOA exception. Examples of what not to do are set forth in excerpts from the *EEOC v. Liggett & Meyers Inc.* decision. In this case the employer was ordered to pay back wages and benefits plus liquidated damages to more than one hundred employees terminated between 1971 and 1973. It should be noted that Section 7(b) of the ADEA allows for the doubling of damages in cases of "willful violations" of the act. Consequently, an employer who willfully violates the ADEA is liable not only for back wages and benefits but also for "an additional equal amount as liquidated damages."

In *Trans World Airlines Inc. v. Thurston,*[18] presented in this section, the Supreme Court set forth a test for whether a successful plaintiff is entitled to liquidated damages under the ADEA. The Court held that where an employer's officers acted reasonably and in good faith in attempting to determine whether their plan would violate the act, their conduct was not "willful," and the plaintiffs were not entitled to liquidated damages.

---

[18]469 U.S. 111 (1985).

EEOC v. Liggett & Meyers Inc.
United States District Court for Eastern North Carolina, 29 FEP 1611 (1982).

MERHIGE, D. J.
Plaintiff's case rests upon its contention that pursuant to a plan or pattern, a large number of defendant's employees were discriminated against by the defendant company by reason of each being 40 years of age or older.

Defendant, on the other hand, denies any such plan or pattern and indeed that any employee has been discriminated against, by reason of age or any other reason, in either being terminated from his or her respective position or not being offered another position. . . .

The sad saga seems to have begun in February of 1971 when the Company appointed J.C. Gfeller, then 35 years of age, as its director of sales. Shortly thereafter he also became vice president in charge of the Sales Department. At the time the Company's sales had declined from a high 68.9 billion in 1952 to 33.5 billion in 1970. Cigarette sales continued to decline, as did the Company's percentage share of the market.

The sales quota for 1971 was established at 39 billion cigarettes, but it was reduced to 35 billion in September, and 32 billion was the actual amount sold in 1971.

The Hiring of New Top Management

The Company hired Ken McAllister as president of the cigarette and tobacco division, and Jack Southard as vice president of marketing. Both had consumer package goods backgrounds.

In February 1971 the Company hired John Gfeller as vice president of sales. His business background was consumer package goods. Gfeller's charge was to help turn around the decline in the Company's cigarette sales. He was expected to show a dramatic improvement in sales within 18 months.

As senior sales officer it was Gfeller's responsibility to achieve and maintain the distribution of the product line—to make sure the right amount of the product line was in the right place at the right time, properly priced and displayed. The sales responsibility ended at the retail shelf. Inducing the consumer to take the produce off the shelf once the sales department got it there was the responsibility of marketing. . . .

Manpower Planning and Analysis— Age and Minority Reports

In late February 1971, Gfeller requested an analysis of field sales personnel showing ages and minority representation. He requested for each management level an age breakout in five-year groups and the average age for each level. For minority groups he asked for a breakout showing the numbers of each level and the percentage they represented.

In April 1971, Gfeller hired Tom McMorrow as Director of Sales Planning. His job was to maximize promotion effectiveness and coordinate all promotion activities. Also he reviewed all communications between field and headquarters and put a new Headquarters Communication Program into effect.

Gfeller requested and received two updates of the age report—one dated July 31, 1971, and another dated September 30, 1971. This information showed the average age of sales representatives to be 33 and that of first-line managers to be 42. . . .

McMorrow was appointed National Field Sales Manager on June 21, 1971, and was instructed by Gfeller to find out what the problems were in the field that were causing the continuing sales decline. McMorrow went into the field and worked with all levels of the sales force and called on customers. . . .

. . . Based on his visits and investigation, McMorrow concluded that field sales had an inferior management team compared to those of companies he had formerly worked for.

Personnel Changes—Sales Department

Thus, the Company set out on an intensive program of personnel changes. Gfeller and McMorrow instructed top management personnel to move against certain older managers working under their supervision. If the top manager delayed or sought to justify keeping the older manager, he was informed that he was "not getting the message." The key phrase used was that certain individuals were "not able to adapt" to the new procedures to be used by the Company. Throughout this period, Gfeller and McMorrow emphasized that they wanted young and aggressive people, that older individuals were not able to conform or adapt to the new procedures. In specific reference to R. E. Moran, the defendant's top division manager for the year 1971, they made statements such as "he is over the hill" and "he is too old to learn." They also had a frequent saying when it was suggested that an employee had numerous years of experience: that it was not twenty years' experience, but rather one year's experience twenty times. Gfeller also commented in specific reference to L. D'Erasmo, who was 27 years of age in 1971, and who replaced R. E. Moran as area sales manager on September 1, 1972, that he was just the type of young man needed.

The terminations under Gfeller's plans to reorganize the sales force began with the region managers. They were all replaced with younger people. The first one terminated was W. F. Barrow, then 41 years of age, who had been employed in September 1954 and had been promoted to Central Region Manager in July 1970. He was terminated on September 10, 1971, when Gfeller and McMorrow told him he was no longer needed. The only reason they gave him was that he had a "human relations problem." He had no notice from defendant of any deficiency in his duties prior to his termination date. In fact, less than two months earlier Gfeller had notified him by letter dated July 15, 1971, in pertinent part, as follows:

My heartiest congratulations on your outstanding performance during the month of June in achieving and exceeding your assigned quota.

This month was particularly important to all of us in that it was the first month of our recently assigned new specific sales objectives, the first month of your new incentive compensation program and the first month, as I view it, that you were given specific directions, specific tools and you dramatically demonstrated your individual and personal ability to rise to the occasion.

Barrow, so the Court finds, had a history of outstanding performance. . . .

C. Schmidt was the second region manager to be terminated. He was then 46 years of age, had been employed for 21 years, and had in 1969 been promoted to Western Region Manager. Without prior notice, McMorrow came to his office on October 28, 1971, and read a letter to him from Gfeller stating that for the best interest of the Company he should be terminated.

McMorrow told him that he (McMorrow) felt nervous about having Schmidt as his representative. The Court finds that McMorrow told Schmidt he felt him inadequate. Schmidt did not receive a copy of the Gfeller letter. At that time his region ranked first for the year to date of the four regions, having met 97.56% of the assigned quota. The only document in his personnel file relating to his dismissal is a termination form indicating his resignation was requested for inability to perform duties. The Court finds that shortly after Schmidt's discharge, McMorrow stated he "needed younger men," and further that Schmidt "was not competent." Age obviously was a factor. Effective November 1, 1971, Hal Grant was appointed Western Region Manager.

Shortly thereafter, Grant began terminations in California. On February 7, 1972, Grant went to the office of E. W. Gardiner (age 46), the San Francisco Department Manager, and terminated him as of that date. Gardiner had no prior knowledge that he was to be terminated. Grant told him he was too old for the job and indicated that Gardiner did not fit the new youthful image the Company wanted to project. At the time, Gardiner's department had a 9% share of the market, which was substantially higher than the defendant's share of the national market. Grant never notified him of any charged deficiencies in his performance. Gardiner (age 46) was replaced by T. Jennings (age 32). Thereafter, on August 7, 1972, the date he received his final salary check, Gardiner wrote a letter to the president of Liggett & Meyers in which, among other things, he specified how Grant had informed him "I was too old for the job." He received no response to the letter. . . .

T. Jennings immediately began to complete the reorganization of the San Francisco Department. He terminated R. J. Asche (age 41) on March 7, 1972. Asche had been an employee for 17 years. There was no BDR [an evaluation of the employee, called a business development review or BDR] or evaluation prepared on Asche. The records in his personnel file reflect that he was a highly qualified employee. Jennings told him that he was to be replaced by a younger person. Jennings stated to him that many were to be replaced by younger, more qualified persons. Asche heard Jennings place an order with an employment agency for individuals under 35. Asche offered to take any other job, including sales representative, but Jennings told him that he would not fit in, he would not be happy, and they had no room for him. . . .

[Here the court sets forth the details of numerous terminations in the sales department.]

A similar pattern occurred in the terminations of older sales representatives. J. T. Owens (age 42) and V. H. Hall (age 42) were terminated as sales representatives in the Nashville division on September 15, 1972, by H. M. Clunan (age 26), who was hired as a supervisor in Nashville on July 3, 1972. Clunan and D. O. Johnson (age 25), who was hired as the assistant department manager for the Memphis district on May 29, 1972, had visited Nashville after Clunan's appointment. At the first meeting in Nashville, Johnson commented to Clunan in the presence of Owens that some of the gentlemen were too old to be in the business. Later, Johnson asked Owens what a man his age was doing in this business. At this time, the Nashville division had five sales representatives: M. D. Garner (age 37), E. V. Holt (age 34), H. Vance Owens (age 33), and Hall. Clunan kept the youngest, H. Vance, and terminated the remaining four. Clunan replaced them with K. Ingram (age 23), hired September 1, 1972, B. Marshall (age 25), hired September 1, 1972, R. Puettman (age 23), employed September 1, 1972 (transferred from Alabama), and S. Roberts (age 23), hired October 9, 1972. Clunan also hired L. Winn (age 26) on September 18, 1972.

Clunan gave Owens no reason for termination. On the termination report, Clunan gave the reason that he felt Owens "could not adapt to new configuration." On the payroll notification form, the reason given was the Owens was "not adapted to our type of work." . . .

T. T. Clarke, Jr. (age 55), who was employed as a sales representative in the Manchester, New Hampshire division, was forced to take early re-tirement on September 1, 1972. At the time, he was the oldest sales representative in that division. He had suffered a slight heart attack in 1966 but had returned to work. In 1972, he missed only two days of work up until his termination, and the Court rejects the Company's contention that health was the major factor in Clarke's forced retirement.

By letter dated May 8, 1972, the Connecticut division manager requested J. P. Duffy (age 47) to submit his resignation as a sales representative in Hartford, Connecticut effective May 12, 1972. The reason given in the letter was that "[d]uring the past months you have not met the standards of performance which indicates your inability to adapt to the change." The letter further stated that it was "this inability to change that prompts this request." In the last appraisal in his file dated February 5, 1971, he was ranked first out of six representatives; he was the second oldest. In the evaluation, the interviewer stated that he discussed with Duffy "the high level of efficiency maintained by him over the 20 years he has been in our employ." On June 26, 1972, E. Chapman (age 23) and J. Radeno (age 24), were hired in Connecticut as sales representatives. . . .

The vast majority of sales representatives hired from 1971 through 1973 were in their twenties. In 1971 the defendant hired 194 sales representatives, of whom 142 were in their twenties, 47 were in their thirties, and five were in their forties (oldest 43). In 1972, the year the major first line management changes were made, the defendant hired 180 sales representatives, of whom 162 were in their twenties, 16 in their thirties, and two in their forties (oldest 40). In 1973 the defendant hired 221 sales representatives, of whom 198 were in their twenties, 21 in their thirties, and two in their forties (oldest 42). Even more significantly, the two over 40, one hired November 16, 1973, and the other November 19, 1973, and 12 of the individuals over 30 were all hired after September 7, 1973, when the compliance officer began his investigation and the defendant had notice of possible age discrimination. Thus, from January 1, 1973, through September 7, 1973, the defendant had hired no sales representatives age 40 or above, and only nine in their thirties. . . .

Personnel Changes—Leaf Department

In April 1973, the Leaf Department, which was responsible for purchasing tobacco, was notified that for economic reasons there would have to be cost reductions which would require the termination of personnel. Initially, J. C. Burton, vice president of the Leaf Department, attempted to place selected employees in the domestic sales department. . . . [Burton was not successful, and as a result he was required to terminate 33 individuals on July 31, 1973.]

In the various employee classifications, Burton made the following selections. In supervisors, he terminated the oldest of nine. In head buyers, he terminated the oldest eight of nineteen. In buyers, he terminated 13 of 73. The 13 terminations included the seven oldest, three more in the age group 58 to 57, and three age 48. He retained everyone under the age of 48, a group of 26 employees. . . .

While the Company's explanation that it was undergoing a reduction in force for valid business reasons must be accepted, the Court is of the view that the plaintiff has borne the ultimate burden of establishing that age was a determining factor in the Company's choice of discharging or forcing retirement on the discriminatees listed in Appendix "I." The assigned reasons were pretextual. . . .

The bottom line is probably best exemplified by Burton's response to how B. P. Franklin, age 63, H. C. Chinn, age 60, and J. C. Payne, age 61, were selected for termination. Burton said,

We selected them because of their nearness to mandatory retirement. If we kept them, we would not have been able to reduce people, because we would have to pick or take people and train them to take their place in a couple of years or so.

In short, but for their age, they would not have been terminated.

Personnel Changes—Legal Department

In 1974, it was determined to move the Legal Department from New York to Durham, North Carolina. Charles B. Morganthaler, the second-ranking attorney in the department, was notified by the general counsel in January 1974 that he was being asked to relocate and that he would be entitled to three house-hunting trips to Durham. Morganthaler notified the general counsel in January that he intended to relocate. On April 4, 1974, the general counsel, F. P. Haas, informed Morganthaler that he, Morganthaler, would be retiring soon and that he was too old to make the move. Morganthaler was then forced to take early retirement effective January 1, 1975, at age 62. A contract was executed relating to his payment, but it contained no provision in regard to the age discrimination claim. Even if there had been a release, it would have been void as against public policy. . . . [The facts set forth above demonstrate that the company was in violation of the Age Discrimination in Employment Act. The court held that the company's disavowal of any discriminatory attitude on age was overcome by overwhelming evidence. It finds that although there may have been factors other than age considered, in each instance age was one of the determining factors, and that this is impermissible under the law. The court determined that the violations of the company were willful, thereby triggering liquidated damages in addition to the lost wages and benefits.]

So ordered.

CASE QUESTIONS

1. What options did the employer have at its disposal to improve the performance of the sales department other than the massive terminations of its older employees?
2. Speculate as to why Gfeller and McMorrow favored younger employees over older employees.
3. Did the employer have a valid business reason for the RIF in the legal department? Is a company immune from damages if it proves a valid business reason for a RIF?
4. If a person, wrongfully forced to take early retirement, signs a release not to sue the company for violation of the ADEA, is that release a defense in a subsequent ADEA lawsuit?

Trans World Airlines Inc. v. Thurston
Supreme Court of the United States, 469 U.S. 111 (1985).

[*Trans World Airlines had approximately three thousand employees who filled the three cockpit positions on most of its flights. The captain is the pilot and controls the aircraft. The first officer is the copilot and assists the captain. The flight engineer usually monitors a side-facing instrument panel and does not operate the flight controls unless the captain and the first officer become incapacitated. The Age Discrimination in Employment Act (ADEA) was amended in 1978 to prohibit the mandatory retirement of a protected employee because of age. Concerned that its retirement policy, at least as it applied to flight engineers, violated the ADEA, petitioner Trans World Airlines (TWA) adopted a plan permitting any employee in flight engineer status at age sixty to continue working in that capacity. The plan, however, did not give sixty-year-old captains the right to automatically begin training as flight engineers. Instead, a captain could remain with the airline only if the captain had been able to obtain flight engineer status through the bidding procedures outlined in the collective bargaining agreement between TWA and petitioner Air Line Pilots Association (ALPA). If no vacancy occurred prior to the captain's sixtieth birthday, the captain was retired. Under the collective bargaining agreement, a captain displaced for any reason besides age need not resort to the bidding procedure. Respondent former TWA captains were retired upon reaching age sixty. Each was denied an opportunity to "bump" a less senior flight engineer. They sued TWA, asserting that the ADEA was violated. The district court entered a summary judgment in favor of TWA, which was reversed by the court of appeals. The Supreme Court granted certiorari.*]

POWELL, J.

I

The ADEA "broadly prohibits arbitrary discrimination in the workplace based on age." Section 4(a)(1) of the Act proscribes differential treatment of older workers "with respect to . . . [a] privileg[e] of employment." Under TWA's transfer policy, 60-year-old captains are denied a "privilege of employment" on the basis of age. . . .

The Act does not require TWA to grant transfer privileges to disqualified captains. Nevertheless, if TWA does grant some disqualified captains the "privilege" of "bumping" less senior flight engineers, it may not deny this opportunity to others because of their age. In *Hishon v. King & Spalding*, we held that "[a] benefit that is part and parcel of the employment relationship may not be doled out in a discriminatory fashion, even if the employer would be free . . . not to provide the benefit at all." . . .

TWA contends that the [pilots] failed to make out a prima facie case of age discrimination under *McDonnell Douglas v. Green*, 441 U.S. 792 (1973), because at the time they were retired, no flight engineer vacancies existed. This argument fails, for the *McDonnell Douglas* test is inapplicable where the plaintiff presents direct evidence of discrimination. . . . In this case there is direct evidence that the method of transfer available to a disqualified captain depends upon his age. Since it allows captains who become disqualified for any reason other than age to "bump" less senior flight engineers, TWA's transfer policy is discriminatory on its face. . . .

Although we find that TWA's transfer policy discriminates against disqualified captains on the basis of age, our inquiry cannot end here. [TWA] contends that the age-based transfer policy is justified by two of the ADEA's five affirmative defenses. [TWA] first argues that the discharge of respondents was lawful because age is a "bona fide occupational qualification" (BFOQ) for the position of captain. Furthermore, TWA claims that its retirement policy is part of a "bona fide seniority system," and thus exempt from the Act's coverage.

Section 4(f)(1) of the ADEA provides that an employer may take "any action otherwise prohibited" where age is a "bona fide occupational qualification." In order to be permissible under § 4(f)(1), however, the age-based discrimination must relate to a "particular business." Every court to consider the issue has assumed that the "particular business" to which the statute refers is the job from which the protected individual is excluded. . . .

TWA's discriminatory transfer policy is not permissible under § 4(f)(1) because age is not a BFOQ for the "particular" position of flight engineer. It is necessary to recognize that the airline has two age-based policies: (i) captains are not allowed to serve in that capacity after reaching the age of 60; and (ii) age-disqualified captains are not given the transfer privileges afforded captains disqualified for other reasons. The first policy, which precludes individuals from serving as captains, is not challenged by [the pilots]. The second practice does not operate to exclude protected individuals from the position of captain; rather it prevents qualified 60-year-olds from working as flight engineers. Thus, it is the "particular" job of flight engineer from which the [pilots] were excluded by the discriminatory transfer policy. Because age under 60 is not a BFOQ for the position of flight engineer, the age-based discrimination at issue in this case cannot be justified by § 4(f)(1). . . .

TWA also contends that its discriminatory transfer policy is lawful under the Act because it is part of a "bona fide seniority system." . . . Any seniority system that includes the challenged practice is not "bona fide" under the statute. The Act provides that a seniority system may not "require or permit" the involuntary retirement of a protected individual because of his age. Although the FAA "age 60 rule" may have caused [the pilots'] retirement, TWA's seniority plan certainly

"permitted" it within the meaning of the ADEA. Moreover, because captains disqualified for reasons other than age are allowed to "bump" less senior flight engineers, the mandatory retirement was age-based. Therefore, the "bona fide seniority system" defense is unavailable to the petitioners.

In summary, TWA's transfer policy discriminates against protected individuals on the basis of age, and thereby violates the Act. The two statutory defenses raised by petitioners do not support the argument that this discrimination is justified. The BFOQ defense is meritless because age is not a bona fide occupational qualification for the position of flight engineer, the job from which the respondents were excluded. Nor can TWA's policy be viewed as part of a bona fide seniority system. A system that includes this discriminatory transfer policy permits the forced retirement of captains on the basis of age.

II

. . . As noted above, the Court of Appeals stated that a violation is "willful" if "the employer either knew or showed reckless disregard for the matter of whether its conduct was prohibited by the ADEA." Although we hold that this is an acceptable way to articulate a definition of "willful," the court below misapplied this standard. TWA certainly did not "know" that its conduct violated the Act. Nor can it fairly be said that TWA adopted its transfer policy in "reckless disregard" of the Act's requirements. The record makes clear that TWA officials acted reasonably and in good faith in attempting to determine whether their plan would violate the ADEA. . . .

There simply is no evidence that TWA acted in "reckless disregard" of the requirements of the ADEA. The airline had obligations under the collective-bargaining agreement with the Air Line Pilots Association. In an attempt to bring its retirement policy into compliance with the ADEA, while at the same time observing the terms of the collective-bargaining agreement, TWA sought legal advice and consulted with the Union. Despite opposition from the Union, a plan was adopted that permitted cockpit employees to work as "flight engineers" after reaching age 60. Apparently TWA officials and the airline's attorneys failed to focus specifically on the effect of each aspect of the new retirement policy for cockpit personnel. It is reasonable to believe that the parties involved, in focusing on the larger overall problem, simply overlooked the challenged aspect of the new plan. We conclude that TWA's violation of the Act was not willful within the meaning of § 7(b), and that respondents therefore are not entitled to liquidated damages.

III

The ADEA requires TWA to afford 60-year-old captains the same transfer privileges that it gives to captains disqualified for reasons other than age. Therefore, we affirm the Court of Appeals on this issue. We do not agree with its holding that TWA's violation of the Act was willful. We accordingly reverse its judgment that respondents are entitled to liquidated or double damages.

It is so ordered.

CASE QUESTIONS

1. Did TWA have a policy of different treatment of pilots who were disqualified on the basis of age as compared to pilots who were disqualified for reasons other than age?
2. Why did the Court find TWA's transfer policy discriminatory on its face?
3. What did TWA argue as to BFOQ, and what did the Court hold?
4. How did the Supreme Court define a willful violation of the ADEA? Did this definition help or hurt TWA?

SECTION 19—DISCRIMINATION AGAINST THE HANDICAPPED

The right of handicapped persons to enjoy equal employment opportunities was established on the federal level with the enactment of the Rehabilitation Act of 1973.[19] Although not designed specifically as an employment discrimination measure but rather as a comprehensive plan to meet many of the needs of the handicapped, the Rehabilitation Act does contain three sections that provide guarantees against discrimination in employment.

As set forth below in detail, Section 501 of the act is applicable to the federal government itself, Section 503 applies to federal contractors, and Section 504 applies to the recipients of federal funds.

Handicaps include a wide range of medical and physical disabilities. Some impairments are obvious, such as paraplegia or blindness. Others may not be readily noticeable, such as heart disease, high blood pressure, and diabetes. In some cases people have recovered from their disabilities but have encountered job discrimination because of their past medical records. Cancer and mental or emotional disorders are examples of past medical conditions that may be associated with job discrimination. Sometimes people are perceived as having handicaps when in fact they do not. One example is a facial disfigurement that causes no disability but which others regard as an impairment. All these conditions are included within the definition of *handicap* as set forth in the Rehabilitation Act.

[19]29 USC Sections 701–794.

Section 501

Section 501 of the act requires the federal government as an employer to develop and implement affirmative action plans on behalf of handicapped employees. Congress enacted Section 501 with the expectation that governmental policy regarding the employment of handicapped individuals would serve as a model for other employers. In *Mantolete v. Bolger*[20] a person with epilepsy sued the U.S. postal service under Section 501 because she was denied a position as a letter-sorting machine operator because of her handicap. The court of appeals overturned the trial court's decision in favor of the postal service and remanded the case for further consideration based on the requirement that the postal service demonstrate that the individual's handicap would result in a reasonable probability of substantial harm to Mantolete and/or her co-workers if she were to work the machine. The court made clear that employment decisions cannot be based on unsubstantiated generalizations and stereotypes but must instead be made on the basis of individual qualifications, taking into account the employee's handicap.

Section 503

Section 503 requires all federal contractors having federal contracts in excess of $2,500 to take affirmative action to employ the handicapped. Enforcement of Section 503 is carried out by the Department of Labor's Office of Federal Contract Compliance Programs (OFCCP). There is no private right of action under Section 503.[21] A handicapped individual must file a complaint with the OFCCP within 180 days of the occurrence of the alleged discriminating act in violation of Section 503. The complaint will then be investigated, and thereafter the matter may be heard at an administrative hearing. If a finding of discrimination is made and the employer disagrees with the finding, the OFCCP will initiate legal proceedings. The vast majority of Section 503 cases are resolved at or prior to the hearing before the administrative law judge.

Section 504

Section 504 of the Rehabilitation Act deals with discrimination in broader terms than the affirmative action requirements of Section 503. Section 504 prohibits federally funded programs and government agencies from excluding from employment an "otherwise qualified handicapped individual . . . solely by reason of [his or her] handicap." Enforcement of Section 504 rests with each federal agency providing financial assistance. The attorney general of the United States has responsibility for the coordination of the enforcement efforts of the agencies.[22]

Under the Rehabilitation Act a *handicapped person* is defined as one who (1) has an impairment that affects a major life activity, (2) has a history of such an impairment, or

---

[20]767 F.2d 1416, 38 FEP 1081 (9th Cir. 1985).
[21]See Auffant v. Searle and Co., 25 FEP 1254 (D.P.R. 1981) and Davis v. UAL, Inc., 622 F.2d 120, 26 FEP 1527 (2nd Cir. 1981).
[22]Executive Order No. 12250, November 2, 1980.

(3) is considered as having one. The term *major life activity* includes such functions as caring for oneself, seeing, speaking, or walking.

To be entitled to the protection of the Rehabilitation Act with respect to employment, the individual must meet the requirements set forth in the definition of a handicapped person and must be an "otherwise qualified . . . individual" as set forth in Section 504. An *otherwise qualified individual* is one who can perform "the essential functions" of the job in question.[23] When a handicapped person is not able to perform the essential functions of the job, the court must also consider whether any "reasonable accommodation" by the employer would enable the handicapped person to perform those functions. Reasonable accommodation includes making a facility accessible to the handicapped, as well as job restructuring and modification of work schedules. However, expenses and business necessity are also considered in determining what reasonable accommodation requires. The act was amended to exclude from its protection any individual who is an alcoholic or a drug abuser and whose current use of alcohol or drugs prevents the individual from performing the duties of the job or whose employment constitutes a direct threat to property or the safety of others.

Contagious Diseases

In *Nassau County, Florida v. Arline*, presented in this section, the Supreme Court determined that a person afflicted with tuberculosis may be a handicapped person as defined in Section 504, and the fact that such a person is also contagious does not remove that person from Section 504's coverage. Under *Arline* a district court must determine whether the handicapped person is "otherwise qualified" under Section 504. The district court must conduct an individualized inquiry and make appropriate findings of fact based on reasonable medical judgments, given the state of medical knowledge, about (1) the nature of the risk (e.g., how the disease is transmitted), (2) the duration of the risk (how long the carrier is infectious), (3) the severity of the risk (what is the potential harm to third parties), and (4) the probabilities that the disease will be transmitted and cause varying degrees of harm. In making these findings, courts normally should defer to the reasonable medical judgments of public health officials. Courts must then determine, in light of these findings, whether any "reasonable accommodation" can be made by the employer under the established standards for that inquiry, as set forth previously. Since the district court did not make the appropriate findings in *Arline* the case was remanded.

In *Chalk v. U.S. District Court*[24] the U.S. Court of Appeals for the Ninth Circuit relied on the *Arline v. Nassau County Board of Education* decision in concluding that discrimination on the basis of AIDS violates the Rehabilitation Act. In the *Chalk* case the court of appeals ruled that the Orange County Department of Education violated the Rehabilitation Act when it reassigned Vincent Chalk from his position as a teacher of hearing-impaired students to an administrative position after Chalk was diagnosed as having AIDS. The court ruled that Chalk, who was "handicapped" as a result of the disease, was "otherwise qualified" for classroom duty because the medical evidence indicated that the disease could not be transmitted through normal classroom contact.

---

[23]45 CFR 84.3(k), 1985.
[24] 46 FEP 279 (9th Cir. 1988).

Nassau County, Florida v. Arline

Supreme Court of the United States, 43 FEP 81 (1987).

[Respondent Gene Arline was hospitalized for tuberculosis in 1957. The disease went into remission for the next twenty years, during which time she began teaching elementary school in Florida. In 1977, March 1978, and November 1978 she had relapses. After the latter two relapses she was suspended with pay for the rest of the school year. At the end of the 1978–1979 school year, the school board discharged her after a hearing because of the continued recurrence of tuberculosis. After she was denied relief in state administrative proceedings, she brought suit in federal district court, alleging a violation of Section 504 of the Rehabilitation Act. The district court held that although Arline suffered a handicap, she was not a handicapped person under the statute since it was difficult "to conceive that Congress intended contagious diseases to be included within the definition of a handicapped person." The court of appeals reversed, and the Supreme Court granted certiorari.]

BRENNAN, J.

I

In enacting and amending the Act, Congress enlisted all programs receiving federal funds in an effort "to share with handicapped Americans the opportunities for an education, transportation, housing, health care, and jobs that other Americans take for granted." 123 Cong. Rec. 13515 (1977) (statement of Sen. Humphrey). To that end, Congress not only increased federal support for vocational rehabilitation, but also addressed the broader problem of discrimination against the handicapped by including § 504, an antidiscrimination provision patterned after Title VII of the Civil Rights Act of 1964. Section 504 of the Rehabilitation Act reads in pertinent part:

"No otherwise qualified handicapped individual in the United States, as defined in section 706(7) of

this title, shall, solely by reason of his handicap, be excluded from participation in, be denied the benefits of, or be subjected to discrimination under any program or activity receiving Federal financial assistance. . . ." 29 U.S.C. § 794.

In 1974 Congress expanded the definition of "handicapped individual" for use in § 504 to read as follows:

"[A]ny person who (i) has a physical or mental impairment which substantially limits one or more of such person's major life activities, (ii) has a record of such an impairment, or (iii) is regarded as having such an impairment." 29 U.S.C. § 706(7)(B).

The amended definition reflected Congress' concern with protecting the handicapped against discrimination stemming not only from simple prejudice, but from "archaic attitudes and laws" and from "the fact that the American people are simply unfamiliar with and insensitive to the difficulties confront[ing] individuals with handicaps." To combat the effects of erroneous but nevertheless prevalent perceptions about the handicapped, Congress expanded the definition of "handicapped individual" so as to preclude discrimination against "[a] person who has a record of, or is regarded as having, an impairment [but who] may at present have no actual incapacity at all." *Southeastern Community College v. Davis*, 442 U.S. 397, 405–406, n. 6 (1979).

In determining whether a particular individual is handicapped as defined by the Act, the regulations promulgated by the Department of Health and Human Services are of significant assistance. . . . The regulations are particularly significant here because they define two critical terms used in the statutory definition of handicapped individual. "Physical impairment" is defined as follows:

"[A]ny physiological disorder or condition, cosmetic

disfigurement, or anatomical loss affecting one or more of the following body systems: neurological; musculosketetal; special sense organs; respiratory, including speech organs; cardiovascular; reproductive, digestive, genitourinary; hemic and lymphatic; skin; and endocrine." 45 CFR § 84.3(j)(2)(i) (1985).

In addition, the regulations define "major life activities" as:

"functions such as caring for one's self, performing manual tasks, walking, seeing, hearing, speaking, breathing, learning, and working." § 84.3j(2)(ii).

II

Within this statutory and regulatory framework, then, we must consider whether Arline can be considered a handicapped individual. According to the testimony of Dr. McEuen, Arline suffered tuberculosis "in an acute form in such a degree that it affected her respiratory system," and was hospitalized for this condition. Arline thus had a physical impairment as that term is defined by the regulations, since she had a "physiological disorder or condition . . . affecting [her] . . . respiratory [system]." This impairment was serious enough to require hospitalization, a fact more than sufficient to establish that one or more of her major life activities were substantially limited by her impairment. Thus, Arline's hospitalization for tuberculosis in 1957 suffices to establish that she has a "record of . . . impairment" within the meaning of 29 U.S.C. § 706(7)(b)(ii), and is therefore a handicapped individual.

Petitioners concede that a contagious disease may constitute a handicapping condition to the extent that it leaves a person with "diminished physical or mental capabilities," and concede that Arline's hospitalization for tuberculosis in 1957 demonstrates that she has a record of a physical impairment. Petitioners maintain, however, Arline's record of impairment is irrelevant in this case, since the School Board dismissed Arline not because of her diminished physical capabilities, but because of the threat that her relapses of tuberculosis posed to the health of others.

We do not agree with petitioners that, in defining a handicapped individual under § 504, the contagious effects of a disease can be meaningfully distinguished from the disease's physical effects on a claimant in a case such as this. Arline's contagiousness and her physical impairment each resulted from the same underlying condition, tuberculosis. It would be unfair to allow an employer to seize upon the distinction between the effects of a disease on others and the effects of a disease on a patient and use that distinction to justify discriminatory treatment.*

Nothing in the legislative history of § 504 suggests that Congress intended such a result. . . .

. . . Few aspects of a handicap give rise to the same level of public fear and misapprehension as contagiousness. Even those who suffer or have recovered from such noninfectious diseases as epilepsy or cancer have faced discrimination based on the irrational fear that they might be contagious. The Act is carefully structured to replace such reflexive reactions to actual or perceived handicaps with actions based on reasoned and medically sound judgments: the definition of "handicapped individual" is broad, but only those individuals who are both handicapped *and* otherwise qualified are eligible for relief. The fact that *some* persons who have contagious diseases may pose a serious health threat to others under certain circumstances does not

---

*The United States argues that it is possible for a person to be simply a carrier of a disease, that is, to be capable of spreading a disease without having a "physical impairment" or suffering from any other symptoms associated with the disease. The United States contends that this true in the case of some carriers of the Acquired Immune Deficiency Syndrome (AIDS) virus. From this premise the United States concludes that discrimination solely on the basis of contagiousness is never discrimination on the basis of a handicap. The argument is misplaced in this case, because of the handicap here, tuberculosis, gave rise both to a physical impairment *and* to contagiousness. This case does not present, and we therefore do not reach, the questions whether a carrier of a contagious disease such as AIDS could be considered to have a physical impairment, or whether such a person could be considered, solely on the basis of contagiousness, a handicapped person as defined by the Act.

justify excluding from the coverage of the Act *all* persons with actual or perceived contagious diseases. Such exclusion would mean that those accused of being contagious would never have the opportunity to have their condition evaluated in light of medical evidence and a determination made as to whether they were "otherwise qualified." Rather, they would be vulnerable to discrimination on the basis of mythology—precisely the type of injury Congress sought to prevent. We conclude that the fact that a person with a record of a physical impairment is also contagious does not suffice to remove that person from coverage under § 504.

III

The remaining question is whether Arline is otherwise qualified for the job of elementary school teacher. To answer this question in most cases, the District Court will need to conduct an individualized inquiry and make appropriate findings of fact. Such an inquiry is essential if § 504 is to achieve its goal of protecting handicapped individuals from deprivations based on prejudice, stereotypes, or unfounded fear, while giving appropriate weight to such legitimate concerns of grantees as avoiding exposing others to significant health and safety risks. The basic factors to be considered in conducting this inquiry are well established. In the context of the employment of a person handicapped with a contagious disease, we agree with *amicus* American Medical Association that this inquiry should include:

"[findings of] facts, based on reasonable medical judgments given the state of medical knowledge, about (a) the nature of the risk (how the disease is transmitted), (b) the duration of the risk (how long is the carrier infectious), (c) the severity of the risk (what is the potential harm to third parties) and (d) the probabilities the disease will be transmitted and will cause varying degrees of harm." Brief for American Medical Association as Amicus Curiae *19.*

In making these findings, courts normally should defer to the reasonable medical judgments of public health officials. The next step in the "otherwise-qualified" inquiry is for the court to evaluate, in light of these medical findings, whether the employer could reasonably accommodate the employee under the established standards for that inquiry.

Because of the paucity of factual findings by the District Court, we, like the Court of Appeals, are unable at this stage of the proceedings to resolve whether Arline is "otherwise qualified" for her job. The District Court made no findings as to the duration and severity of Arline's condition, nor as to the probability that she would transmit the disease. Nor did the court determine whether Arline was contagious at the time she was discharged, or whether the School Board could have reasonably accommodated her. Accordingly, the resolution of whether Arline was otherwise qualified requires further findings of fact.

IV

We hold that a person suffering from the contagious disease of tuberculosis can be a handicapped person within the meaning of the § 504 of the Rehabilitation Act of 1973, and that respondent Arline is such a person. We remand the case to the District Court to determine whether Arline is otherwise qualified for her position. The judgment of the Court of Appeals is

Affirmed.

CASE QUESTIONS

1. Why did the school board terminate Arline?
2. When a person with a record of physical impairment is also contagious, is that person removed from coverage under Section 504?
3. Did Congress seek to prevent discrimination against handicapped individuals based on the fear and mythology of contagiousness when it enacted Section 504?
4. Did the Court find that Arline was otherwise qualified?

SECTION 20—SELECTED CONSTITUTIONAL ARGUMENTS ON DISCRIMINATION

Many employment discrimination problems have been approached on constitutional rather than statutory grounds. When statutory solutions, such as those provided by Title VII, are either inapplicable, inadequate, or too time-consuming, the constitutional guarantees of equal protection and due process found in the Fifth and Fourteenth Amendments have been argued in an attempt to remedy the allegedly discriminatory employment practices.

Race Discrimination

Since the passage of Title VII, cases involving alleged racially discriminatory employment practices have generally been argued in the courts on statutory, rather than constitutional, grounds. This was not the case, however, in *Washington v. Davis*[25] where the Supreme Court was faced with the question of whether a written personnel test used by the District of Columbia's police department to measure verbal skill that a higher percentage of blacks than whites failed was violative of the equal protection component of the Due Process Clause of the Fifth Amendment. The district court ruled that the test was a reliable indication of job performance and was not designed to, and did not discriminate against, otherwise qualified blacks. The court of appeals reversed, basing its decision on the standards enunciated in *Griggs v. Duke Power Co.* The court of appeals held that the lack of discriminatory intent was irrelevant, that four times as many blacks as whites failed the test, and that such disproportionate impact sufficed to establish a constitutional violation. The Supreme Court reversed the court of appeals' decision and reinstated the order of the district court upholding the use of the test. The Supreme Court held that although disproportionate impact is not irrelevant, where a law or official conduct such as the administering of a personnel test is not designed to discriminate and serves legitimate governmental interests it will not be struck down simply because it burdens blacks more than whites. It is now clear that the only remedy available to persons alleging racial discrimination in federal employment is provided by Section 717 of the Civil Rights Act of 1964.[26] Complaints formerly processed by the Civil Service Commission under Section 717 are processed by the EEOC under Presidential Reorganization Plan No. 1 of 1978.

Sex Discrimination

The *LaFleur* decision, presented in this section, was initially successful in the court of appeals utilizing Equal Protection Clause arguments against mandatory maternity leave rules for pregnant teachers. However, the Supreme Court sustained the court of appeals on the basis of the Due Process Clause, finding the challenged maternity leave rules to be violative of due process since they created a conclusive presumption that every teacher who is four or five months pregnant is physically incapable of continuing her duties,

---

[25]426 U.S. 229 (1976).
[26]See Brown v. G.S.A., 425 U.S. 820 (1976).

whereas any such teacher's inability to continue past a fixed pregnancy period is an individual matter.

Freedom of the press contentions relating to employment opportunities advertising were considered by the U.S. Supreme Court. In *Pittsburgh Press Company v. Pittsburgh Commission on Human Relations*[27] the Supreme Court upheld an order of the Pittsburgh Commission on Human Relations that forbade placing help-wanted advertisements under the headings "Jobs—Male Interest" and "Jobs—Female Interest." The majority of the Court took the position that the order came under the "commercial speech" exception to the First Amendment, while the four dissenters viewed it as a prior restraint on the press. The commission had ordered the *Pittsburgh Press* to stop using the headings in its help-wanted columns after the National Organization for Women, Inc., complained.

Speaking for the Supreme Court, Mr. Justice Powell held that the case came under the commercial speech doctrine of *Valentine v. Chrestensen*,[28] which sustained a city ordinance that banned the distribution of a handbill soliciting customers for a tour of a submarine. The Court distinguished the commercial speech cases from the holding of *New York Times v. Sullivan*,[29] a libel suit in which the Court held that paid political advertising was entitled to First Amendment protection. The help-wanted advertisements in *Pittsburgh Press*, the Court held, do not express a position on "whether as a matter of social policy, certain positions ought to be filled by members of one or the other sex. . . . Each is no more than a proposal of possible employment. The advertisements are thus classic examples of commercial speech." The Court added that nothing in its holding prevented the *Pittsburgh Press* from publishing advertisements commenting on the ordinance and the commission or its enforcement practices or the propriety of sex preferences in employment.

In his dissent Chief Justice Burger called the decision "a disturbing enlargement of the 'commercial speech' doctrine." Mr. Justice Douglas argued that the newspaper could print whatever it pleased without censorship or restraint by government. The want ads express the preference of the employer for the kind of help the employer wants, Justice Douglas said, and the commission might issue an order against the employer if discrimination in employment was shown. Mr. Justice Stewart, whose dissent Justice Douglas joined, declared that the issue was whether government "can tell a newspaper in advance what it can print and what it cannot." Mr. Justice Blackmun also dissented, substantially for the reasons stated by Mr. Justice Stewart.

---

[27]413 U.S. 376 (1973).
[28]316 U.S. 52 (1942).
[29]376 U.S. 254 (1964).

 ## Cleveland Board of Education v. LaFleur
Supreme Court of the United States, 414 U.S. 632 (1974).

STEWART, J.

The respondents in No. 72–777 and the petitioner in No. 72–1129 are female public school teachers. During the 1970–1971 school year, each informed her local school board that she was pregnant; each was compelled by a mandatory maternity leave rule to quit her job without pay several months before the expected birth of her child. These cases call upon us to decide the constitutionality of the school boards' rules.

I

Jo Carol LaFleur and Ann Elizabeth Nelson, the respondents in No. 72–777, are junior high school teachers employed by the Board of Education of Cleveland, Ohio. Pursuant to a rule first adopted in 1952, the school board requires every pregnant school teacher to take a maternity leave without pay, beginning five months before the expected birth of her child. Application for such leave must be made no later than two weeks prior to the date of departure. A teacher on maternity leave is not allowed to return to work until the beginning of the next regular school semester which follows the date when her child attains the age of three months. A doctor's certificate attesting to the health of the teacher is a prerequisite to return; an additional physical examination may be required. The teacher on maternity leave is not promised reemployment after the birth of the child; she is merely given priority in reassignment to a position for which she is qualified. Failure to comply with the mandatory maternity leave provisions is grounds for dismissal.

Neither Mrs. LaFleur nor Mrs. Nelson wished to take an unpaid maternity leave; each wanted to continue teaching until the end of the school year. Because of the mandatory maternity leave rule, however, each was required to leave her job in March of 1971. The two women then filed separate suits in the United States District Court for the Northern District of Ohio under 42 U.S.C. Section 1983, challenging the constitutionality of the maternity leave rule. The District Court tried the cases together, and rejected the plaintiffs' arguments. 326 F. Supp. 1208. A divided panel of the United States Court of Appeals for the Sixth Circuit reversed, finding the Cleveland rules in violation of the Equal Protection Clause of the Fourteenth Amendment.

The petitioner in No. 72–1129, Susan Cohen, was employed by the School Board of Chesterfield County, Virginia. The school board's maternity leave regulation requires that a pregnant teacher leave work at least four months prior to the expected birth of her child. . . .

II

This Court has long recognized that freedom of personal choice in matters of marriage and family life is one of the liberties protected by the Due Process Clause of the Fourteenth Amendment. . . . As we noted in *Eisenstadt v. Baird,* 405 U.S. 438, 453, there is a right "to be free from unwarranted governmental intrusion into matters so fundamentally affecting a person as the decision whether to bear or beget a child."

By acting to penalize the pregnant teacher for deciding to bear a child, overly restrictive maternity leave regulations can constitute a heavy burden on the exercise of these protected freedoms. Because public school maternity leave rules directly affect "one of the basic civil rights of man," *Skinner v. Oklahoma, supra,* at 541, the Due Process Clause of the Fourteenth Amendment requires that such rules must not needlessly, arbitrarily, or capriciously impinge upon this vital area of a teacher's constitutional liberty. The question before us in these cases is whether the interests advanced in support of the rules of the Cleveland and Chesterfield County School Boards can justify the particular procedures they have adopted.

The school boards in these cases have offered two essentially overlapping explanations for their mandatory maternity leave rules. First, they contend that the firm cutoff dates are necessary to maintain continuity of classroom instruction, since advance knowledge of when a pregnant teacher must leave facilitates the finding and hiring of a qualified substitute. Secondly, the school boards seek to justify their maternity rules by arguing that at least some teachers become physically incapable of adequately performing certain of their duties during the latter part of pregnancy. By keeping the pregnant teacher out of the classroom during these final months, the maternity leave rules are said to protect the health of the teacher and her unborn child, while at the same time assuring that students have a physically capable instructor in the classroom at all times.

We . . . conclude that the arbitrary cutoff dates embodied in the mandatory leave rules before us have no rational relationship to the valid state interest of preserving continuity of instruction. As long as the teacher is required to give substantial advance notice of her condition, the choice of firm dates later in pregnancy would serve the boards' objectives just as well, while imposing a far lesser burden on the women's exercise of constitutionally protected freedom.

The question remains as to whether the fifth and sixth month cutoff dates can be justified on the other ground advanced by the school boards— the necessity of keeping physically unfit teachers out of the classroom. There can be no doubt that such an objective is perfectly legitimate, both on educational and safety grounds. And, despite the plethora of conflicting medical testimony in these cases, we can assume *arguendo* that at least some teachers become physically disabled from effectively performing their duties during the latter stages of pregnancy.

The mandatory termination provisions of the Cleveland and Chesterfield County rules surely operate to insulate the classroom from the presence of potentially incapacitated pregnant teachers. But the question is whether the rules sweep too broadly. See *Shelton v. Tucker,* 364 U.S. 479. That question must be answered in the affirmative, for the provisions amount to a conclusive presumption that every pregnant teacher who reaches the fifth or sixth month of pregnancy is physically incapable of continuing. There is no individualized determination by the teacher's doctor—or the school board's—as to any particular teacher's ability to continue at her job. The rules contain an irrebuttable presumption of physical incompetency, and that presumption applies even when the medical evidence as to an individual woman's physical status might be wholly to the contrary.

As the Court noted last Term in *Vlandis v.*

Kline, 412 U.S. 441, 446, "permanent irrebuttable presumptions have long been disfavored under the Due Process Clauses of the Fifth and Fourteenth Amendments." . . .

These principles control our decision in the cases before us. While the medical experts in these cases differed on many points, they unanimously agreed on one—the ability of any particular pregnant woman to continue at work past any fixed time in her pregnancy is very much an individual matter. Even assuming *arguendo* that there are some women who would be physically unable to work past the particular cutoff dates embodied in the challenged rules, it is evident that there are large numbers of teachers who are fully capable of continuing work for longer than the Cleveland and Chesterfield County regulations will allow. Thus, the conclusive presumption embodied in these rules, like that in *Vlandis,* is neither "necessary nor universally true," and is violative of the Due Process Clause.

The school boards have argued that the mandatory termination dates serve the interest of administrative convenience, since there are many instances of teacher pregnancy, and the rules obviate the necessity for case-by-case determinations. . . .

While it might be easier for the school boards to conclusively presume that all pregnant women are unfit to teach past the fourth or fifth month or even the first month, of pregnancy, administrative convenience alone is insufficient to make valid what otherwise is a violation of due process of law. The Fourteenth Amendment requires the school boards to employ alternative administrative means, which do not so broadly infringe upon basic constitutional liberty, in support of their legitimate goals.

We conclude, therefore, that neither the necessity for continuity of instruction nor the state interest in keeping physically unfit teachers out of the classroom can justify the sweeping mandatory leave regulations that the Cleveland and Chesterfield County School Boards have adopted. While the regulations no doubt represent a good-faith attempt to achieve a laudable goal, they cannot pass muster under the Due Process Clause of the Fourteenth Amendment, because they employ irrebuttable presumptions that unduly penalize a female teacher for deciding to bear a child.

III

In addition to the mandatory termination provisions, both the Cleveland and Chesterfield County rules contain limitations upon a teacher's eligibility to return to work after giving birth. Again, the school boards offer two justifications for the return rules—continuity of instruction and the desire to be certain that the teacher is physically competent when she returns to work. As is the case with the leave provisions, the question is not whether the school board's goals are legitimate, but rather whether the particular means chosen to achieve those objectives unduly infringe upon the teachers' constitutional liberty.

Under the Cleveland rule, the teacher is not eligible to return to work until the beginning of the next regular school semester following the time when her child attains the age of three months. A doctor's certificate attesting to the teacher's health is required before return; an additional physical examination may be required at the option of the school board.

The respondents in No. 72–777 do not seriously challenge either the medical requirements of the Cleveland rule or the policy of limiting eligibility to return to the next semester following birth. The provisions concerning a medical certificate or supplemental physical examination are narrowly drawn methods of protecting the school board's interest in teacher fitness; these requirements allow an individualized decision as to teacher's condition, and thus avoid the pitfalls of the presumptions inherent in the leave rules. Similarly, the provision limiting eligibility to return to work the semester following delivery is a precisely drawn means of serving the school board's interest in avoiding unnecessary changes in classroom personnel during any one school term.

The Cleveland rule, however, does not simply contain these reasonable medical and next-semester eligibility provisions. In addition, the school board requires the mother to wait until her child reaches the age of three months before the return rules begin to operate. The school boards have offered no reasonable justification for this supplemental limitation, and we can perceive none. To the extent that the three months provision reflects the school board's thinking that no mother is fit to return until that point in time, it suffers from the same constitutional deficiencies that plague the irrebuttable presumption in the termination rules. The presumption, moreover, is patently unnecessary, since the requirement of a physician's certificate or a medical examination fully protects the school's interests in this regard. And finally, the three month provision simply has nothing to do with continuity of instruction, since the precise point at which the child will reach the relevant age will obviously occur at a different point throughout the school year for each teacher.

Thus, we conclude that the Cleveland return rule, insofar as it embodies the three months age provision, is wholly arbitrary and irrational, and hence violates the Due Process Clause of the Fourteenth Amendment. The age limitation serves no legitimate state interest, and unnecessarily penalizes the female for asserting her right to bear children. . . .

IV

For the reasons stated, we hold that the mandatory termination provisions of the Cleveland and Chesterfield County maternity regulations violate the Due Process Clause of the Fourteenth Amendment, because of their use of unwarranted conclusive presumptions that seriously burden the exercise of protected constitutional liberty. For similar reasons, we hold the three months' provision of the Cleveland return rule unconstitutional.

Accordingly, the judgment in No. 72–777 is affirmed; the judgment in No. 72–1129 is reversed, and the case is remanded to the Court of

Appeals for the Fourth Circuit for further proceedings consistent with this opinion.

It is so ordered.

CASE QUESTIONS

1. Summarize the Cleveland school board's mandatory maternity leave rule.

2. What are the principal purposes claimed to be served by the Cleveland board of education's mandatory maternity leave rule?
3. What is the gist of the Court's Due Process Clause position?
4. Did the Court allow to stand the part of the Cleveland school board's rule that prevented reemployment earlier than three months after birth?

Part Questions and Problems

1. In reviewing a claim under the Equal Pay Act, do the courts require that the jobs in question be identical?
2. As a result of the passage of the Equal Pay Act of 1963 and Title VII of the Civil Rights Act of 1964, have the overall earnings for women become roughly comparable to that of men?
3. Can an employer terminate older employees as a reduction in the employer's work force without violating the ADEA?
4. Are individuals who are perceived as having handicaps, but in fact either have recovered from the disability or are not handicapped, covered by the Rehabilitation Act?
5. Della Janich was employed as a matron at the Yellowstone County Jail in Montana. The duties of the position of matron resemble those of a parallel male position—jailer. Both employees have the responsibility for booking prisoners, showering and dressing them, and placing them in the appropriate section of the jail depending on the sex of the offender. Because 95 percent of the prisoners at the jail were men and 5 percent were women, the matron was assigned more bookkeeping duties than the jailer. At all times during Della's employment at the jail, her male counterparts received $125 more per month as jailers.

    Della brought an action under the Equal Pay Act alleging discrimination against her in her wages because of her sex. The county sheriff denied the charge.

    What factors must be considered by the court when deciding this case under the Equal Pay Act? Decide the case. [Janich v. Sheriff, 29 FEP 1195 (D.C. Mont. 1977)]
6. The Federal Aviation Administration (FAA) has promulgated a federal regulation that prohibits airlines from employing pilots or copilots past age sixty. The FAA's rule is recognized by the courts as a bona fide occupational qualification under the ADEA due to the administration's recognition that the possible onset of disease or debilitating condition would pose a flight or safety risk.

    Western Airlines maintained a policy that all flight deck personnel must retire at age sixty. Flight deck personnel include the pilot, copilot, and second officer (sometimes referred to as a flight engineer). The duties of a flight engineer are performed at a separate instrument panel, where various systems necessary for the operation of the aircraft, such as the electrical and hydraulic systems, are monitored and adjusted. The engineer does not manipulate the flight controls, and in the event of an emergency, all pilots and copilots having previously served as flight engineers are qualified to perform the necessary duties.

    Ron Douglas worked as a flight engineer for Western Airlines for over thirty years. As his sixtieth birthday approached, he informed Western management that he wished to continue working past age sixty. The airline told Ron that as a member of the flight deck, second officers were required to retire at sixty for the same reasons as pilots and copilots.

    Ron brought an action against Western under the Age Discrimination in

Employment Act, claiming that Western's mandatory retirement policy was a form of age discrimination against flight engineers. Western denied the claim.

What defenses, if any, are available to Western Airlines to support its retirement policy? Has Western engaged in age discrimination? Decide the case. [Criswell v. Western Airlines, 29 FEP 350 (D.C. C.D. Cal. 1981)]

7. Carlyle Cline, age forty-two, was employed for ten years by Roadway Express Company, most recently as a loading dock supervisor at a Roadway terminal in North Carolina. Cline had received periodic merit pay raises, and his personnel file contained an even amount of both complimentary and critical evaluations by supervisors. When R. W. Hass became vice-president for Roadway's southern division, he decided that the division needed to "upgrade" the quality of its personnel. Hass directed terminal managers to "look at" employees who had been with the company for five years without being promoted and decide whether they should be replaced with higher quality employees, preferably college graduates. Thus the ultimate decision regarding "promotability" was left to the terminal managers. They were not told that they were not to consider age when determining promotability. After the announcement of the new policy, Cline was discharged and classified "unpromotable." The terminal manager compiled a list of negative comments from Cline's file as evidence that Cline was discharged for "poor work performance." Roadway immediately replaced Cline with a man in his early thirties.

Cline brought an action against Roadway under the Age Discrimination in Employment Act, claiming he was discharged "because of his age in violation of the Act." Roadway maintained that Cline was discharged because of poor work performance.

Has Roadway violated the ADEA? Decide the case. [Cline v. Roadway Express, 29 FEP 1365 (4th Cir. 1982)]

8. Mazir Coleman drove a school bus for the Casey County, Kentucky, board of education for four years. In 1978 Coleman's left leg was amputated. Coleman was fitted with an artificial leg and underwent extensive rehabilitation to relearn driving skills. When his driving skills had been sufficiently relearned over the course of four years, Coleman applied to the county board of education for a job as a school bus driver. The county refused to accept Coleman's application. The county board said that they had no alternative but to deny Coleman a bus-driving job because a Kentucky administrative regulation required it. That regulation states in part: "No person shall drive a school bus who does not possess both of these natural bodily parts: feet, legs, hands, arms, eyes, and ears. The driver shall have normal use of the above named body parts."

Coleman brought an action under the Rehabilitation Act claiming discrimination based on his physical handicap. The county board of education denied this charge claiming that the reason they rejected Coleman was because of the requirement of the state regulation.

May Coleman maintain an action of employment discrimination in light of the state regulation on natural body parts? What factors must be proven to establish his case? Decide the case. [Coleman v. Casey County Board of Education, 26 FEP 357 (D.C. N.D. Ky. 1980)]

9. The New York City police department was a recipient of federal funds subject to the Rehabilitation Act of 1973. In 1982 Officer Heron, a three-year veteran of the department, began having attendance problems. A police psychologist suggested that Heron turn in his guns and be placed on nonpatrol duty. Despite these actions Heron's attendance problems continued, and it was eventually discovered that Heron was addicted to heroin.

The department immediately initiated disciplinary proceedings against Heron and sought to dismiss him. After a hearing Heron was dismissed and denied eligibility for continuing health or pension benefits.

Heron alleged that his condition was due to job-related stress and exposure to dangerous and violent incidents. He challenged his dismissal in federal court because the department had a policy of not dismissing alcoholic officers. He alleged that the initiation of disciplinary action against him was prohibited by Section 504 of the Rehabilitation Act of 1973 because he was an otherwise qualified person disciplined solely because of his handicap.

What factors must the court consider in evaluating Heron's claim? What result should the court reach in this case? Decide. [Heron v. McGuire, 42 FEP 31 (2d Cir. 1986)]

4

Developing Topics

SECTION 21—EMPLOYMENT AT WILL, EXCEPTIONS, AND TITLE VII/ADEA CLAIMS

The employment-at-will rule set forth in *Payne v. Western & Atlantic R.R. Co.* states:

> [M]en must be left, without interference to buy and sell where they please, and to discharge or retain employees at will for good cause or for no cause, or even for bad cause without thereby being guilty of an unlawful act per se. It is a right which an employee may exercise in the same way, to the same extent, for the same cause or want of cause as the employer.[1]

This rule, which gives an employer the right to terminate an employee for any reason—good cause, no cause, or bad cause, has been uniformly recognized throughout the country. However, judicial and, in some instances, legislative intervention has had an impact on the application of the rule in nearly 40 states. The court decisions that have carved out exceptions to the employment-at-will doctrine may be classified as follows: (1) the tort theory that a discharge violates established public policy (the so-called whistle-blowing cases also are structured on public policy), (2) the tort theory of abusive discharge, (3) the contract theory of express or implied guarantee of continued employment except for just-cause terminations, and (4) the theory of an implied covenant of good faith and fair dealing in employment contracts. Common to the court decisions on these developing exceptions to the employment-at-will doctrine are the expressions of

---

[1]82 Tenn. 507, 518–19 (1884).

judicial warnings on the narrowness of each decision. The employment-at-will doctrine continues to be a viable doctrine, subject to the developing exceptions. In several jurisdictions courts have stated that changes in the employment-at-will doctrine must await legislative action.

For unionized employees, collective bargaining agreements often contain a provision whereby the employer agrees that no employee subject to the agreement will be discharged without just cause. These agreements provide for arbitration over whether the employer had just cause for a discharge, with the burden of proof being on the employer. Over half of the approximately fifteen million workers employed in the public sector by federal, state, and local governments are protected by tenure processes or civil service against termination of employment without good cause. Also, a small number of managerial and professional employees have been successful in negotiating employment contracts in which the employer and the individual agree on a salary figure and duration of the employment relationship and further agree that the employer cannot terminate the employment during the duration of the contract unless there is good and sufficient cause. Workers with union memberships who have protection against termination without just cause constitute less than 20 percent of the nation's work force. Protected employees in the public sector and employees with employment contracts constitute less than 10 percent of the work force. Thus more than 70 percent of the nation's work force are employed "at will" or for indefinite durations and do not have the "good cause" or "just cause" protection against terminations negotiated by unions, granted by governmental bodies, or negotiated by the individuals.

Individuals are protected against discriminatory discharges principally by Title VII of the Civil Rights Act and the Age Discrimination in Employment Act. An at-will employee who is terminated may believe that there was a discriminatory motive to the discharge. Also, that employee may believe that one or more of the emerging exceptions to the employment-at-will doctrine are applicable to that employee's discharge. The result is that a terminated individual may join claims based on exceptions to the employment-at-will doctrine and a claim based on discrimination. In *Murphy v. American Home Products Corporation* the New York Court of Appeals rejected four of the plaintiff's theories of wrongful discharge based on tort and contract law and reinstated the plaintiff's fifth theory, that of age discrimination. The case is presented in this section. Difficulties exist with such a joinder because the tort and contract theories may entitle the individual to a jury trial, while Title VII claims are heard before judges only. If joinder of claims is denied, an employer must defend similar claims resulting from a single discharge in different forums.

A discussion of the four exceptions to the employment-at-will doctrine follows.

Public Policy

The courts in a number of jurisdictions have carved out an exception to the employment-at-will doctrine when the discharge is contrary to established public policy. In *Palmateer v. International Harvester,*[2] a so-called whistle-blowing case, the court awarded damages, for the wrongful discharge of an employee who was discharged in retaliation for his

---

[2]85 Ill. 2d 124, 421 NE 2d 876 (1981).

reporting to the police that a coemployee was engaged in criminal activities. The court held that the discharge violated an important public policy. In *Sheets v. Teddy's Frosted Foods*, presented in this section, the court held that a cause of action in tort exists for wrongful discharge from employment where a quality control director alleges that he has been dismissed in retaliation for his insistence that the employer comply with the Food, Drug, and Cosmetics Act.

In *Phipps v. Clark Oil & Refining Corp.*, presented in this section, the court found that an at-will employee who was discharged because he refused his supervisor's directive in violation of the Clean Air Act to pump leaded gasoline into an automobile equipped to receive only unleaded gasoline could sue for wrongful termination.

The most frequent application of the public policy exception occurs where employees are discharged in retaliation for filing a workers' compensation claim. The courts' concern in these cases is that the statute would not be effective if employees feared the consequence of their filing a compensation claim would be their discharge from employment. In most states the public policy exception to the employment-at-will doctrine is a narrow one and is applied only if the plaintiff can satisfy a two-part test: (1) the discharge must violate some well-established public policy expressed in a constitution, statutes, or regulations promulgated pursuant to the statutes and (2) there must be no other remedy available to protect the interest of the aggrieved individual or society. However, in some states the exception is broadly formulated so as to permit recovery even in the absence of a specific constitutional or statutory prohibition.[3]

Abusive Discharge

The leading case for the abusive discharge tort theory exception to the employment-at-will doctrine is *Monge v. Beebe Rubber Co.*[4] where a female employee was discharged for declining to date her supervisor. Such a discharge is against public policy. A similar fact situation today would probably not be handled as an abusive discharge tort theory since employees now have the post-*Monge* Title VII theory of sexual harassment to provide a remedy for such misconduct.

Express or Implied Guarantee of Continued Employment

Courts have begun to construe statements by employers concerning continued employment, which previously had been viewed as having no binding effect, as a contractual basis for requiring good cause for the discharge of an employee. Also, written personnel policies used as guidelines for the employer's supervisors have been interpreted as being rules restricting the employer's right to discharge at will without proof of good or just cause. In *Toussaint v. Blue Cross and Blue Shield*[5] two management employees had been told upon their hiring that they would be employed as long as they "did the job." The company's personnel policy manual represented that it was the employer's policy, applicable to all nonprobationary employees, to require good cause for discharge. The court

---

[3]Wogenseller v. Scottsdale Memorial Hospital, 147 Ariz. 370, 376 (1985) and Dabbs v. Cardiopulmonary Management, 188 Cal. App. 3d 437, 234 Cal. Rptr. 129 (1987).
[4]114 N.H. 130, 316 A.2d 549 (1974).
[5]408 Mich. 579, 292 NW 2d 880 (1980).

held that such oral and written statements could give rise to an enforceable contractual provision requiring good cause for discharge.

In *Duldulao v. St. Mary Nazareth Hospital Center*[6] an eleven-year employee, Nora Duldulao, was fired without notice for unsatisfactory performance. The hospital's *Employee Handbook* provided that an employee could be terminated for enumerated causes following "proper notice and investigation." Duldulao contended before the Supreme Court of Illinois that such a provision had a limiting effect on her at-will employment status and created an enforceable contract that barred the hospital from terminating her without following the safeguards of notice and an investigation. The Court agreed, holding that an employee handbook or other policy statement creates enforceable contractual rights if the traditional requirements for contract formation are present. The Court set forth the requirements as follows: (1) the language must contain a promise clear enough that an employee would reasonably believe that an offer has been made, (2) the statement must be disseminated to the employee in such a manner that the employee is aware of its contents and reasonably believes it to be an offer, and (3) the employee must accept the offer by continuing to work after learning of the policy statement. According to the Court, the employee's continued work constitutes consideration for the promise.

Good Faith and Fair Dealing

Another development in the law governing the employment relationship is the recognition of a covenant of good faith and fair dealing in the employment relationship. For example, in *Fortune v. National Cash Register Co.*[7] the court for the first time in Massachusetts recognized a common law contract action of "wrongful" or "bad faith" termination for an at-will employee. This case involved an employer's termination of a commission salesperson in order to deprive him of benefits and bonuses to which he was entitled. The court was offended by the overreaching and malicious acts of the company at the expense of the employee for the sole benefit of the employer. The court held that there existed an implied covenant of good faith and fair dealing in certain employment relationships.

Employer Reactions

As a result of cases such as *Toussaint* and *Duldulao*, some nonunion employers have inserted on employment applications for applicants to sign conspicuous statements that the employment offered is "at will." Employers have revised their personnel manuals and employee handbooks and issued directives to all employees that no assurances of continued employment exist and that the employers are not obligated to have good cause to terminate employees, just as employees are free to leave their positions with the employers. However, such employers have had some difficulties in hiring and retaining quality craft, professional, and managerial employees in the aftermath of such actions. Such actions have provided the impetus for the organization of employees by unions.

Most employers have no interest in terminating employees without good and suf-

---

[6]Ill. S. Ct. 505 NE 2d 314 (1987).
[7]373 Mass. 96, 364 NE 2d 1251 (1977). See also, Cleary v. American Airlines, Inc., 111 Cal. App. 3d 443, 168 Cal. Rptr. 722 (1980) and Khanna v. Microdata Corp., 170 Cal. App. 3d 250, 215 Cal. Rptr. 860 (1985).

ficient cause. They have taken steps to assure that terminations are in fact for good cause and that a solid case exists for each termination should the employee in question sue on an unjust dismissal theory. Employers have standardized their termination methods. Employers often now require that every disciplined employee be advised in writing of the infraction, the expected corrective action, and that further misconduct could lead to additional discipline up to and including discharge. When a termination appears to be warranted, most employers require that at least two supervisors be involved and that they take care to ensure that the reasons for the termination are accurate and consistent with the documentation concerning the employee's deficiencies. Moreover, employers should inform the employee of the basis of the proposed termination and give the employee an opportunity to be heard.

Murphy v. American Home Products Corp.
New York State Court of Appeals, 461 N.Y. 2d 232 (1983).

[Plaintiff, Joseph Murphy, was first employed by defendant, American Home Products Corp., in 1957. He thereafter served in various accounting positions, eventually attaining the position of assistant treasurer, but he never had a formal contract of employment. On April 18, 1980, when he was fifty-nine years old, he was discharged. Plaintiff claims that he was fired for two reasons: because of his disclosure to top management of alleged accounting improprieties on the part of corporate personnel and because of his age. As to the first ground, plaintiff asserts that his firing was in retaliation for his revelation to officers and directors of defendant corporation that he had uncovered at least $50 million in illegal account manipulations of secret pension reserves which improperly inflated the company's growth in income and allowed high-ranking officers to reap unwarranted bonuses from a management incentive plan. He contends that the company's internal regulations required him to make the disclosure. He also alleges that his termination was carried out in a humiliating manner. As to the second basis for his termination, plaintiff claims that defendant's top financial officer told him on various occasions that he wished he could fire plaintiff but that because to do so would be illegal due to plaintiff's age, he would make sure by confining
him to routine work that plaintiff did not advance in the company. Plaintiff asserts that a contributing factor to his dismissal was that he was over fifty years of age.]

JONES, J.

With respect to his first cause of action, plaintiff urges that the time has come when the courts of New York should recognize the tort of abusive or wrongful discharge of an at-will employee. To do so would alter our long settled rule that where an employment is for an indefinite term it is presumed to be a hiring at will which may be freely terminated by either party at any time for any reason or even for no reason. Plaintiff argues that a trend has emerged in the courts of other states to temper what is perceived as the unfairness of the traditional rule by allowing a cause of action in tort to redress abusive discharges. He accurately points out that this tort has elsewhere been recognized to hold employers liable for dismissal of employees in retaliation for employees' conduct that is protected by public policy. Thus, the abusive discharge doctrine has been applied to impose liability on employers where employees have been discharged for disclosing illegal activities on the part of their employers, where employees have been terminated due to their service on jury duty (*Nees v. Hocks*, 277 Or 210), and where employees have been dismissed because they have filed workers' compensation claims (*Kelsay v. Motorola, Inc.*, 74 Ill 2d 172). Plaintiff would have this Court adopt this emerging view. We decline his invitation, being of the opinion that such a significant change in our law is best left to the Legislature.

Those jurisdictions that have modified the traditional at-will rule appear to have been motivated by conclusions that the freedom of contract underpinnings of the rule have become outdated, that individual employees in the modern work force do not have the bargaining power to negotiate security for the jobs on which they have grown to rely, and that the rule yields harsh results for those employees who do not enjoy the benefits of express contractual limitations on the power of dismissal. Whether these conclusions are supportable or whether for other compelling reasons employers should, as a matter of policy, be held liable to at-will employees discharged in circumstances for which no liability has existed at common law, are issues better left to resolution at the hands of the Legislature. In addition to the fundamental question whether such liability should be recognized in New York, of no less practical importance is the definition of its configuration if it is to be recognized.

Both of these aspects of the issue, involving perception and declaration of relevant public policy are best and more appropriately explored and resolved by the legislative branch of our government. The Legislature has infinitely greater resources and procedural means to discern the public will, to examine the variety of pertinent considerations, to elicit the views of the various segments of the community that would be directly affected and in any event critically interested, and to investigate and anticipate the impact of imposition of such liability. Standards should doubtless be established applicable to the multifarious types of employment and the various circumstances of discharge. If the rule of nonliability for termination of at-will employment is to be tempered, it should be accomplished through a principled statutory scheme, adopted

after opportunity for public ventilation, rather than in consequence of judicial resolution of the partisan arguments of individual adversarial litigants.

Additionally, if the rights and obligations under a relationship forged, perhaps some time ago, between employer and employee in reliance on existing legal principles are to be significantly altered, a fitting accommodation of the competing interests to be affected may well dictate that any change should be given prospective effect only, or at least so the Legislature might conclude.

For all the reasons stated, we conclude that recognition in New York State of tort liability for what has become known as abusive or wrongful discharge should await legislative action.*

Plaintiff's [next] cause of action is for breach of contract. Although he concedes in his complaint that his employment contract was of indefinite duration (inferentially recognizing that, were there no more, under traditional principles his employer might have discharged him at any time), he asserts that in all employment contracts the law implies an obligation on the part of the employer to deal with his employees fairly and in good faith and that a discharge in violation of that implied obligation exposes the employer to liability for breach of contract. Seeking then to apply this proposition to the present case, plaintiff argues in substance that he was required by the terms of his employment to disclose accounting improprieties and that defendant's discharge of him for having done so constituted a failure by the employer to act in good faith and thus a breach of the contract of employment.

New York does recognize that in appropriate

---

*Employees in New York have already been afforded express statutory protection from firing for engaging in certain protected activities (e.g., Judiciary Law, § 519 [prohibiting discharge of employee due to absence from employment for jury service]; Executive Law, § 296[1][3] [barring discharge of employees for opposing unlawful discriminatory practices or for filing a complaint or participating in a proceeding under the Human Rights Law]; Labor Law, § 215 [proscribing discharge of employee for making a complaint about a violation of the Labor Law or for participating in a proceeding related to the Labor Law]). . . .

circumstances an obligation of good faith and fair dealing on the part of a party to a contract may be implied and, if implied, will be enforced. In such instances the implied obligation is in aid and furtherance of other terms of the agreement of the parties. No obligation can be implied, however, which would be inconsistent with other terms of the contractual relationship. Thus, in the case now before us, plaintiff's employment was at will, a relationship in which the law accords the employer an unfettered right to terminate the employment at any time. In the context of such an employment it would be incongruous to say that an inference may be drawn that the employer impliedly agreed to a provision which would be destructive of his right of termination. The parties may by express agreement limit or restrict the employer's right of discharge, but to imply such a limitation from the existence of an unrestricted right would be internally inconsistent. In sum, under New York law as it now stands, absent a constitutionally impermissible purpose, a statutory proscription, or an express limitation in the individual contract of employment, an employer's right at any time to terminate an employment at will remains unimpaired.

Of course, if there were an express limitation on the employer's right of discharge it would be given effect even though the employment contract was of indefinite duration. Thus, in *Weiner v. McGraw-Hill, Inc.* (57 NY 2d 458), cited by plaintiff, we recently held that, on an appropriate evidentiary showing, a limitation on the employer's right to terminate an employment of indefinite duration might be imported from an express provision therefor found in the employer's handbook on personnel policies and procedures.

Plaintiff's attempts on this appeal to bring himself within the beneficial scope of that holding must fail, however. There is here no evidence of any such express limitation. Although general references are to be found in his brief in our Court to an employer's "manual," no citation is furnished to any provision therein pertinent to the employer's right to terminate his employment, and the alleged manual was not submitted with his affidavit in opposition to the motion to dismiss his complaint.

As to his [last] cause of action for age discrimination, plaintiff correctly contends that in dismissing this cause of action as barred by the Statute of Limitations the courts below applied the wrong statute. . . .

. . . It was, therefore, error to dismiss plaintiff's cause of action for age discrimination as barred by the one-year period prescribed in subdivision 5 of section 297.

Plaintiff's cause of action for age discrimination reinstated.

CASE QUESTIONS

1. Did New York adopt the tort of abusive or wrongful discharge of an at-will employee?
2. What was the court's rationale for its decision on the tort of abusive or wrongful discharge for an at-will employee?
3. Did the court accept the plaintiff's argument that the employer violated the implied contractual term of "good faith and fair dealing" when it discharged him for disclosing alleged accounting improprieties?
4. Would the court give effect to a limitation on the employer's right to discharge found in a personnel handbook where the employment contract was of indefinite duration?

Sheets v. Teddy's Frosted Foods, Inc.
Supreme Court of Connecticut, 179 Conn. 471, 427 A.2d 385 (1980).

[*The complaint alleges that for a four-year period, from November 1973 to November 1977, the*

plaintiff was employed by the defendant, a producer of frozen food products, as its quality control

*director and subsequently also as operations man-
ager. In the course of his employment, the plaintiff
received periodic raises and bonuses. In his capacity as quality control director and operations
manager, the plaintiff began to notice deviations
from the specifications contained in the defendant's standards and labels, in that some vege-
tables were substandard and some meat components underweight. These deviations meant that
the defendant's products violated the express
representations contained in the defendant's
labeling. False or misleading labels violate
the provisions of General Statutes § 19–222, the
Connecticut Uniform Food, Drug, and Cosmetic Act. In May of 1977, the plaintiff com-
municated in writing to the defendant concerning
the use of substandard raw materials and underweight components in the defendant's finished
products. His recommendations for more selective
purchasing and conforming components were
ignored. On November 3, 1977, his employment
with the defendant was terminated. The plaintiff's complaint alleges that although the stated
reason for his discharge was unsatisfactory performance of his duties, he was actually dismissed
in retaliation for his efforts to ensure that the
defendant's products would comply with the applicable law relating to labeling and licensing.
The plaintiff's complaint alleges that his dismissal
by his employer was wrong.]*

PETERS, A. J.

The issue before us is whether to recognize an
exception to the traditional rules governing employment at will so as to permit a cause of action
for wrongful discharge where the discharge
contravenes a clear mandate of public policy. In
addressing that claim, we must clarify what
is not at stake in this litigation. The plaintiff does
not challenge the general proposition that contracts of permanent employment, or for an indefinite term, are terminable at will. Nor does he
argue that contracts terminable at will permit
termination only upon a showing of just cause for
dismissal. . . . There is a significant distinction
between a criterion of just cause and what the
plaintiff is seeking. "Just cause" substantially lim-

its employer discretion to terminate, by requiring
the employer, in all instances, to proffer a proper
reason for dismissal, by forbidding the employer
to act arbitrarily or capriciously. By contrast, the
plaintiff asks only that the employer be responsible in damages if the former employee can
prove a demonstrably *improper* reason for dismissal, a reason whose impropriety is derived
from some important violation of public policy.

The argument that contract rights which are
inherently legitimate may yet give rise to liability
in tort if they are exercised improperly is not
a novel one. Although private persons have the
right not to enter into contracts, failure to contract under circumstances in which others are
seriously misled gives rise to a variety of claims
sounding in tort. . . .

It would be difficult to maintain that the
right to discharge an employee hired at will is
so fundamentally different from other contract
rights that its exercise is never subject to judicial
scrutiny regardless of how outrageous, how violative of public policy, the employer's conduct
may be. The defendant does not seriously contest
the propriety of cases in other jurisdictions that
have found wrongful and actionable a discharge
in retaliation for the exercise of an employee's
right to: (1) refuse to commit perjury; *Petermann
v. International Brotherhood of Teamsters*, 174
Cal. App. 2d 184, 189, 344 P.2d 25 (1959);
(2) file a workmen's compensation claim; *Framp-
ton v. Central Indiana Gas Co.*, 260 Ind. 249,
252, 297 N.E. 2d 425 (1973). . . . While it may
be true that these cases are supported by mandates
of public policy derived directly from the applicable state statutes and constitutions, it is equally
true that they serve at a minimum to establish the
principle that public policy imposes some limits
on unbridled discretion to terminate the employment of someone hired at will. . . . No case has
been called to our attention in which, despite
egregiously outrageous circumstances, the employer's contract rights have been permitted to
override competing claims of public policy, although there are numerous cases in which the
facts were found not to support the employee's
claim.

The issue then becomes the familiar common-law problem of deciding where and how to draw the line between claims that genuinely involve the mandates of public policy and are actionable, and ordinary disputes between employee and employer that are not. We are mindful that courts should not lightly intervene to impair the exercise of managerial discretion or to foment unwarranted litigation. We are, however, equally mindful that the myriad of employees without the bargaining power to command employment contracts for a definite term are entitled to a modicum of judicial protection when their conduct as good citizens is punished by their employers.

The central allegation of the plaintiff's complaint is that he was discharged because of his conduct in calling to his employer's attention repeated violations of the Connecticut Uniform Food, Drug, and Cosmetic Act. This act prohibits the sale of mislabled food. The act, in § 19–215, imposes criminal penalties upon anyone who violates § 19–213; subsection (b) of § 19–215 makes it clear that criminal sanctions do not depend upon proof of intent to defraud or mislead, since special sanctions are imposed for intentional misconduct. The plaintiff's position as quality control director and operations manager might have exposed him to the possibility of criminal prosecution under this act. The act was intended to "safeguard the public health and promote the public welfare by protecting the consuming public from injury by product use and the purchasing public from injury by merchandising deceit. . . ." General Statutes § 19–211.

It is useful to compare the factual allegations of this complaint with those of other recent cases in which recovery was sought for retaliatory discharge. In *Geary v. United States Steel Corporation* [319 A.2d 174 (1974)], in which the plaintiff had disputed the safety of tubular steel casings, he was denied recovery because, as a company salesman, he had neither the expertise nor the corporate responsibility to "exercise independent, expert judgment in matters of product safety." By contrast, this plaintiff, unless his title is meaningless, did have responsibility for product quality control. Three other recent cases in which the plaintiff's claim survived demurrer closely approximate the claim before us. In *Trombetta v. Detroit, Toledo & Ironton Co.*, 81 Mich. App. 489, 496, 265 N.W.2d 285 (1978), a cause of action was stated when an employee alleged that he had been discharged in retaliation for his refusal to manipulate and alter sampling results for pollution control reports required by Michigan law. There as here falsified reports would have violated state law. In *Harless v. First National Bank in Fairmont*, 246 S.E.2d 270, 276 (W. Va. 1978), an employee stated a cause of action when he alleged that he had been discharged in retaliation for his efforts to ensure his employer's compliance with state and federal consumer credit protection laws. There as here the legislature had established a public policy of consumer protection. . . .

In the light of these recent cases, which evidence a growing judicial receptivity to the recognition of a tort claim for wrongful discharge, the trial court was in error in granting the defendant's motion to strike. The plaintiff alleged that he had been dismissed in retaliation for his insistence that the defendant comply with the requirements of a state statute, the Food, Drug, and Cosmetic Act. We need not decide whether violation of a state statute is invariably a prerequisite to the conclusion that a challenged discharge violates public policy. Certainly when there is a relevant state statute we should not ignore the statement of public policy that it represents. For today, it is enough to decide that an employee should not be put to an election whether to risk criminal sanction or to jeopardize his continued employment.

There is error and the case is remanded for further proceedings.

Dissenting Opinion

COTTER, C. J.
I cannot agree that, on the factual situation presented to us, we should abandon the well-established principle that an indefinite general hiring may be terminated by the will of either party without liability to the other. . . .

. . . Unlike those cases where an employer allegedly discharged employees for engaging in union activities or filing workmen's compensation claims and the discharge itself contravened a statutory mandate, in the present case the discharge itself at most only indirectly impinged on the statutory mandate. . . .

Finally, it should be reiterated that the minority of jurisdictions which have created a cause of action for retaliatory discharges have done so with caution and when the employee termination contravenes a clear mandate of public policy. It is because the majority abandons that caution and for the reason that the factual situation before us does not demonstrate a "wrongful discharge where the discharge contravenes a clear mandate of public policy" that I feel compelled to dissent.

CASE QUESTIONS

1. Did the plaintiff seek reinstatement to his job and back pay as a remedy?
2. Does the Court identify a pattern of cases in other jurisdictions that demonstrate that public policy imposes some limits on the unbridled discretion to terminate the employment of someone hired at will?
3. Was Sheets subject to the risk of criminal penalties if the company violated the Connecticut Uniform Food, Drug, and Cosmetic Act?
4. State the rule of the case.

Phipps v. Clark Oil & Refining Corp.
Court of Appeals of Minnesota, 396 N.W. 2d 588 (1986).

[The complaint stated that Mark Phipps was employed as a cashier at a Clark gas station. On November 17, 1984, a customer drove into the station and asked him to pump leaded gasoline into her 1976 Chevrolet—an automobile equipped to receive only unleaded gasoline. The station manager told Phipps to comply with the request, but he refused, believing that his dispensing leaded gasoline into the gas tank was a violation of law. Phipps stated that he was willing to pump unleaded gas into the tank, but the manager immediately fired him. Phipps sued Clark for wrongful termination, and the trial court decided the case in favor of Clark, stating that Minnesota law allowed Phipps, an employee at will, to be terminated for any reason or for no reason. Phipps appealed.]

LANSING, J.
Does Minnesota law recognize a cause of action for wrongful discharge if an employee is terminated for refusing to violate a law? . . .

Employment-at-Will Doctrine and the Public Policy Exception

The parties concede that there is no formal agreement governing the employment relationship between Phipps and Clark Oil. Thus, Phipps is an at-will employee. The at-will employment doctrine in Minnesota is generally traced to the early case of *Skagerberg v. Blandin Paper Co.,* 197 Minn. 291, 266 N.W. 872 (1936). The *Skagerberg* court interpreted a contract for permanent employment as being merely a contract for employment at will. *Skagerberg* set forth the general rule in Minnesota that employment at will "may be terminated by either party at any time, and no action can be sustained in such case for a wrongful discharge." *Id.* at 301–02, 266 N.W. at 877 (quoting *Minter v. Tootle, Campbell Dry Goods Co.,* 187 Mo.App. 16, 27–28, 173 S.W. 4, 8 (1915)).

The employer's absolute right of discharge has been tempered during the last 50 years. The majority of jurisdictions have adopted, and numerous commentators have advocated, exceptions to the employment-at-will doctrine. Three general exceptions have been judicially created to relieve employees from the strict application of the employment-at-will doctrine:

1. a contract cause of action based on implied-in-fact promises of employment conditions, generally derived from personnel manuals;
2. an implied covenant of "good faith and fair dealing" under both contract and tort theories; and
3. a "public policy" exception, based in tort, which permits recovery upon the finding that the employer's conduct undermines some important public policy.

Although the Minnesota Supreme Court has declined to imply a covenant of good faith and fair dealing into every employment contract, it has followed the modern trend in recognizing exceptions to employment at will.

In *Pine River State Bank v. Mettille*, 333 N.W.2d 622 (Minn. 1983), the supreme court recognized the implied-in-fact contract exception. The *Pine River* court held that an employee manual may constitute an employment contract with enforceable terms preventing termination at will. . . .

Among other states, the most widely adopted exception to the doctrine is the public policy exception. Simply stated, the exception provides that an employer becomes subject to tort liability if its discharge of an employee contravenes some well-established public policy. Although the adoption of this exception has not been addressed in Minnesota, the majority of jurisdictions recognize this exception to the employment-at-will doctrine.*

The exception began as a narrow rule permitting employees to sue their employers when a statute expressly prohibited their discharge. The rule later expanded to include any discharge in violation of a statutory expression of public policy. The broadest formulation of the rule permits recovery even in the absence of a specific statutory prohibition.

---

*At least 25 jurisdictions have adopted the public policy exception.

Courts have reached the public policy exception to accommodate competing interests of society, the employee, and the employer. The Illinois Court of Appeals stated:

With the rise of large corporations conducting specialized operations and employing relatively immobile workers who often have no other place to market their skills, recognition that the employer and employee do not stand on equal footing is realistic. In addition, unchecked employer power, like unchecked employee power, has been seen to present a distinct threat to the public policy carefully considered and adopted by society as a whole. As a result, it is now recognized that a proper balance must be maintained among the employer's interest in operating a business efficiently and profitably, the employee's interest in earning a livelihood, and society's interest in seeing its public policies carried out.

Palmateer v. International Harvester Co., 85 Ill.2d 124, 129, 52 Ill.Dec. 13, 15, 421 N.E.2d 876, 878 (1981) (citation omitted).

These courts have also recognized that important societal interests oppose an employer's conditioning employment on required participation in unlawful conduct:

Although employers generally are free to discharge at-will employees with or without cause at any time, they are not free to require employees, on pain of losing their jobs, to commit unlawful acts or acts in violation of a clear mandate of public policy expressed in the constitution, statutes, and regulations promulgated pursuant to statute. The at-will employment doctrine does not depend upon the employer having such a right. The employer is bound to know the public policies of the state and nation as expressed in their constitutions, statutes, judicial decisions and administrative regulations, particularly, as here, those bearing directly upon the employer's business. . . .

The at-will employment doctrine does not include, contemplate or require a privilege in the employer to subject its employees to the risks of civil and criminal liability that participation in such activities entails.

Boyle v. Vista Eyewear, Inc., 700 S.W.2d 859, 877–78 (Mo.Ct.App. 1985).

We find the reasoning of the cases adopting a public policy exception to be persuasive. An employer's authority over its employee does not include the right to demand that the employee commit a criminal act. An employer therefore is liable if an employee is discharged for reasons that contravene a clear mandate of public policy.

Employers may have a legitimate concern that such an exception will allow fraudulent or frivolous suits by disgruntled employees who are discharged for valid reasons. In order to prevent this, the employee should have the burden of proving the dismissal violates a clear mandate of public policy, either legislatively or judicially recognized. Once the employee has demonstrated that the discharge may have been motivated by reasons that contravene a clear mandate of public policy, the burden then shifts to the employer to prove that the dismissal was for reasons other than those alleged by the employee. This structure, obviously, is a tort-based analysis rather than a contract-based analysis. A significant difference between these theories is the measure of damages. From the standpoint of damages and the conceptual framework which supports the action, we believe it is properly based in tort.

We also believe the reasons supporting recognition of the public policy exception are consistent with principles expressed by the Minnesota Supreme Court. In *Lewis* [389 N.W.2d 876 (Minn. 1986)] the court characterized its decisions on exceptions to the employment-at-will doctrine as following the modern trend. Although recovery in *Lewis* was based on an implied contract theory, we believe that a public policy exception to the employment-at-will doctrine would assist in maintaining the integrity and limitations of other causes of action. Rather than attempting to reach a grievous wrong, repugnant to an ordered society, through the artificial expansion of other doctrines, it is preferable to recognize it in its individual posture.

Clark Oil argues that the decision to adopt the public policy exception should be left to the legislature, citing *Murphy v. American Home Products Corp.*, 58 N.Y.2d 293, and *Hunt v. IBM Mid America Employees Federal Credit Union*, 384 NW2d 853 (Minn. 1986). In re-

jecting the implied covenant of good faith and fair dealing, the court in *Hunt* adverted to the problem of defining the amorphous concept of bad faith and the extent of the intrusion in imposing this concept on the employment relationship.

We see a public policy exception as significantly different from a covenant of good faith and fair dealing. A public policy exception can be reasonably defined by reference to clear mandates of legislative or judicially recognized public policy. In addition, courts have historically interpreted the effect of illegality on contracts. The at-will doctrine is a creation of common law. Other exceptions to the doctrine have been considered and adopted or rejected by the courts. The judiciary may properly extend or limit a judicially created doctrine. . . .

Application of the Public Policy Exception

On appeal from a judgment on the pleadings, this court assumes as true all material facts which are well pleaded. Phipps' complaint alleges that he was terminated for refusing to violate the Federal Clean Air Act, 42 U.S.C. §§ 7401–7642.

Clark Oil argues that this is not the proper case to apply this exception because the penalty for violating this provision is imposed only upon the retailer, not the retailer's employees or agent.

We hold that Phipps has stated a cause of action for wrongful termination under the public policy exception to the at-will employment doctrine. It is not determinative that the employee would not have suffered any monetary loss by violating the law. The law clearly states:

[N]o retailer or his employee . . . shall introduce or allow the introduction of leaded gasoline into any motor vehicle which is labeled "unleaded gasoline only," or which is equipped with a gasoline tank filler inlet which is designed for the introduction of unleaded gasoline.

40 C.F.R. § 80.22(a) (1984) (emphasis added). . . .

Complaint which alleges that an at-will employee was terminated for refusing to violate a law states a cause of action in Minnesota for wrongful discharge. . . .

Reversed and remanded.

CASE QUESTIONS

1. What is the most common exception to the employment-at-will doctrine?

2. How does the court expect to cut down on frivolous lawsuits by disgruntled former employees based on the public policy exception?
3. Is the public policy exception a tort-based or contract-based analysis?
4. Did the court hold that the public policy exception would apply only to clear mandates of legislative or judicially recognized public policy?

SECTION 22—ALCOHOL ABUSE AND EMPLOYEE ASSISTANCE PROGRAMS

Alcohol abuse in the workplace is the cause of many deaths, injuries, lost workdays, and much unsatisfactory worker performance. The economic costs to employers are significant. Most employers publicize and enforce plant or company rules prohibiting the use or possession of alcoholic beverages (and drugs) while on duty or subject to duty. Through observations of an employee, such as an unsteady or staggering walk, slurred speech, bloodshot eyes, and the odor of alcohol on the breath, supervisors are often able to identify an employee who has been apparently violating the employer's no-alcohol rule. Commonly employers require two supervisors to observe the employee, and where their observations indicate a rule violation, the supervisors will confront the employee and offer the employee the opportunity to vindicate himself or herself by taking a blood-alcohol test or breatholyzer test. Employees who violate an employer's no-alcohol rule are subject to major discipline up to and including discharge.

Most employers have made major investments in the selection and training of their employees. It is in the employer's best interest to retain valuable employees by providing a rehabilitation program for those employees who suffer from alcohol abuse. Employee Assistance Programs (EAPs) exist in most major companies to help troubled employees overcome difficulties such as drug and alcohol abuse, work and family tensions, eating disorders, gambling addictions, and financial and other problems.

The recovery rate from alcohol abuse under EAPs has been determined to be as high as 80 percent. Employers, cooperating unions, and the individual participants are pleased with the success of the EAPs in dealing with alcohol problems. Instead of disciplining or discharging employees for the no-alcohol rule violation on a first offense, the matter is commonly handled through the EAP, with the employee signing a Conditional Reinstatement Agreement under which the employee, after a period of hospitalization at a rehabilitation facility, promises to abide by the rehabilitation program. Should the employee fail to do so, the employee agrees and acknowledges that she or he may be subject to termination.

Where an employee is unwilling to participate in such a program and where there is a collective bargaining agreement with a just-cause provision restricting the employer's right to discharge, the employee may be discharged for the no-alcohol rule violation. If the observations of two supervisors indicate a problem concerning the demeanor of an employee and if the odor of alcohol is present on the employee's breath, as discussed above, there is probable cause for the employer to seek a blood-alcohol or breatholyzer test. Under such circumstances no serious challenge to the decision to test can be raised at an arbitration hearing. Absent mitigating or unusual circumstances, the discharge of the employee will likely be upheld in arbitration.

Incidents such as accidents or major safety rule violations may also trigger an employer's testing program, and where impairment due to alcohol is found through a test, the EAP procedures may also be followed. In the case of serious accidents or injuries caused by alcohol or drug impairment, reinstatement to employment may not be offered, absent an agreement to the contrary.

The misconduct involved in the *Brotherhood of Locomotive Engineers* arbitration decision, presented in this section, led to the criminal conviction of the engineer. The misconduct stirred a national dialogue on the issue of alcohol and drug testing for operating employees in the transportation industries.

Brotherhood of Locomotive Engineers and Illinois Central Gulf Railroad
PLB 3538, No. 2 (NMB, July 3, 1984).

FROM THE FINDINGS OF THE
ARBITRATION BOARD:
The record before the Board indicates that on September 27, 1982, the Claimant, Engineer E. P. Robertson and crew went on duty about 7:00 p.m. at McComb, Mississippi, to take a train to Baton Rouge, Louisiana. They went off duty at 10:40 p.m. at Baton Rouge and were immediately transported to their designated lodging at the Prince Murat Inn to rest because, according to the usual routine of their assignment, they would be required after the rest period to work the return assignment back to McComb. The crew was thereafter called at 2:30 a.m., September 28, and listed for work at 3:30 a.m.

The testimony indicates that Mr. Robertson did not take his rest when he arrived at the motel; and that he and Brakeman Reeves went to the motel bar and stayed until midnight. He drank at least one drink and ordered a drink to go in a plastic cup, according to the testimony of the bartender Mr. J. D. Morales and the waitress Ms. K. M. Sword. Sometime after midnight, he and Mr. Reeves met with Clerk Janet Byrd, and it developed that he, Brakeman Reeves, and Ms. Byrd boarded the cab of the locomotive together. The crew had been called at 2:30 a.m., listed for work at 3:30 a.m., and departed Baton Rouge at 4:15 a.m. Ms. Byrd later told company officials

that Mr. Robertson invited Ms. Byrd to "run" the engine.

At approximately 5:05 a.m. on September 28, 1982, the train, Extra 9629 East (GS-2-28) derailed 43 cars on the single main track of the Hammond District in Livingston, Louisiana. Of the derailed cars, 36 were tank cars; 27 of these cars contained various regulated hazardous materials, and 5 contained flammable petroleum products. Fires broke out in the wreckage, and smoke and toxic gases were released into the atmosphere. Explosions of two tank cars that had not been punctured caused them to rocket violently. Some 3000 persons living within a five-mile radius of the derailment site were evacuated for as long as two weeks. Nineteen residences and other buildings in Livingston were destroyed or severely damaged. Toxic chemical products were spilled and absorbed into the ground requiring extensive excavation of contaminated soil and its transportation to a distant dump site. This caused the closing of the track for a year; and the derailment costs to the Carrier are presently over $25,000,000, with several lawsuits still pending.

The Carrier does not hold that Mr. Robertson caused the derailment, for its experts determined that the derailment was caused by equipment failure. The Carrier did, however, find that Mr. Robertson was responsible for three serious rule violations: (1) drinking while subject to duty [Rule G], (2) speeding at several locations during his trip, and (3) allowing an unauthorized passenger to ride in the locomotive. We find that substantial evidence of record exists to support the Carrier's findings in this case.

Two employees from the Prince Murat Inn, J. D. Morales and Kelly M. Sword, testified that two drinks were served to Mr. Robertson containing one and one-half ounces of alcohol, one he drank at the bar and the other was put in a plastic glass to go. Mr. Robertson knew full well that he was on a short layover and that he was subject to duty, after a limited rest period. When an engineer, entrusted with the responsibility for a train, and particularly when entrusted with responsibility for a train containing hazardous chemicals, spends a portion of his short layover in a bar drinking any amount of alcohol, he is guilty of the highest degree of irresponsibility. Such is a clear violation of Rule G, for that employee is "subject to duty" within the explicit language of that rule. Clearly one drink by an employee subject to duty causes some impairment of that individual, and the Carrier and the public have a right not to have a train operated by an individual impaired to any degree. Mr. Robertson acted in a most irresponsible manner by

purchasing alcoholic beverages while subject to duty and he was clearly in violation of Rule G.

The evidence of record, including the testimony of Supervisor of Communications R. L. Mont and Supervisor Instructor A. J. Puth, make it evident that Mr. Robertson's train was operated well beyond the timetable authorized at several locations during the trip. . . .

. . . Mr. Robertson's widely publicized misconduct not only caused a national embarrassment to the Illinois Central Gulf Railroad, but tarnished the high professional reputation of locomotive engineers throughout the Country. The discipline of dismissal is appropriate.

Claim denied.

CASE QUESTIONS

1. Company Rule G not only prohibits the use of alcohol or drugs while on duty but also while "subject to duty." Give your opinion as to whether an employer can properly regulate the actions of its employees when they are off duty and not being paid.
2. Refer to the CSX Drug Testing Program shown on pages 570–572. Under the "Employees Who Test Positive" language, would Engineer Robertson have been returned to service upon successful completion of the EAP?

SECTION 23—DRUG TESTING

It is estimated that some six million Americans currently use cocaine and that some twenty-three million Americans use marijuana. The outward signs of drug use and impairment are sometimes not as evident as is impairment due to the abuse of alcohol. Employee drug users themselves often believe that they are not impaired while at work. For example, in a study of ten experienced pilots who were trained for eight hours on a flight simulator for landing tasks, when each smoked a marijuana cigarette containing 19 milligrams of THC, twenty-four hours after smoking the cigarettes their mean performance on flight tasks showed trends toward impairment on all variables. Moreover, each experienced significant impairment in "distance off center" in landing and vertical and lateral deviation on approach to landing.[8] Despite these deficiencies the pilots reported no awareness of impaired performance. Such a study conducted by the Stanford University School of Medicine, and other studies, indicate that there is a need for concern

---

[8]J. A. Yesauage, M.D. et al., "Carry-over Effects of Marijuana Intoxication on Aircraft Pilot Performances: A Preliminary Report," *Am. J. Psychiatry* 142 (1985): 1325–29.

about the performance of those entrusted with complex behavioral and cognitive tasks within twenty-four hours after smoking marijuana.

Employee drug use costs the United States government alone an estimated $33 billion per year. The seriousness of the problem at all levels of government has led to efforts to combat drug use by the use of compulsory drug testing by public employers. Constitutional challenges of the testing programs have been made in courts by individual employees and public sector unions. Many public employer testing programs still are being considered by the courts, and presently legislation is pending at all levels of government concerning drug testing in the public sector. Nevertheless, certain patterns have emerged as to the legality of various types of testing.

The most common challenges to governmental employers' drug testing programs is that the tests violate the Fourth Amendment prohibition against unreasonable searches and seizures. Courts uniformly have found that requiring an individual to submit urine samples for drug analysis constitutes a search and seizure within the meaning of the Fourth Amendment. The *Patchogue-Medford Congress of Teachers v. Board of Education* decision of New York State's highest court, reported in this section, makes very clear that such testing constitutes a search. The next question for a court is whether the search was reasonable under the Fourth Amendment. This question is answered on a case-by-case basis by balancing the social and governmental need for the testing in question against the invasion of personal privacy rights that the search entails.

The outcome of cases in the public sector may turn on whether there is "individualized suspicion" in requiring testing. Different considerations exist in cases involving testing in the private sector. In both the private and public sectors, concern exists over the reliability of testing procedures and methods. These matters are presented below.

1. *Testing where there is individualized suspicion.* Testing where there is individualized suspicion of drug use is commonly considered to be a "reasonable" search and seizure. Thus, in *Turner v. Fraternal Order of Police,*[9] the court held that a police department order, which required police officers suspected of drug use to submit to urinalysis testing, did not on its face violate the Fourth Amendment. Individualized suspicion was required in *Turner,* necessitating a reasonable, objective basis for suspecting an officer of illegal drug usage before the test could be ordered. It is sufficient individualized suspicion if the employee is involved in an incident such as safety rules violations or an accident. Thus bus drivers involved in traffic accidents may be required to take drug tests under the individualized suspicion classification of drug testing.[10]

2. *Testing in the absence of individualized suspicion.* Random testing or testing in the absence of individualized suspicion has been found to be an unreasonable search and seizure. Thus mass screening of police and fire fighters was found unconstitutional in *Capua v. City of Plainfield*[11] when there were no individualized grounds for suspecting employees of drug use. The court stated that such testing "casually sweeps up the innocent with the guilty." Random drug

---

[9]500 A.2d 1005 (D.C. 1985).
[10]Division 241, Amalgamated Transit Union v. Suscy, 538 F.2d 1264 (7th Cir. 1986).
[11]643 F. Supp. 1507 (D. N.J. 1986). But see Policemen's Union v. Township of Washington, 851 F.2d 133 (3rd Cir. 1988), where it was held that drug testing for all police officers during annual physical exams did not violate the Fourth Amendment since police officers belong to a pervasively regulated profession that reduces their expectation of privacy.

testing of school bus attendants and employees in critical positions with the army has also been found to be an unreasonable search.[12]

Situations exist, however, where testing in the absence of individualized suspicion has been held to be reasonable based on the compelling governmental interest involved and reduced employee expectations of privacy. Thus employees working in a nuclear power plant, where there is pervasive government regulation, have a reduced expectation of privacy and, coupled with the compelling governmental interest in safety, may properly be subject to random urine testing for drugs.[13] In *National Treasury Employees Union v. Von Raab,* presented in this section, the U.S. Court of Appeals for the Fifth Circuit found that the drug testing of all employees who seek a transfer to sensitive positions in the U.S. Customs Service, without any individualized suspicion, is not an unreasonable search. The court reached the decision after weighing all factors involving the public interest and the rights of the individuals.

3. *Testing in the private sector.* The federal constitutional protections of privacy, to whatever extent they exist, apply only to the actions of the state.[14] Thus constitutional defenses may be raised against public employers, as set forth previously. Private sector employers may have collective bargaining agreements that restrict employer testing to "reasonable cause" situations. These employers may have to meet just-cause standards in disciplinary matters. However, unless restricted or prohibited by collective bargaining contracts or state or local law, private employers have a right to require employees to submit to drug testing.

It is common for private sector employers to test applicants for employment for drug use as one of the numerous tests given in a preemployment physical examination. Past drug users may be protected by certain state and federal laws from discrimination; however, if they test positive for drugs in a preemployment drug test, they are not protected under the handicap discrimination laws. Job applicants ordinarily have no protection under collective bargaining contracts. Government regulations may require notice of testing. However, private sector employers generally have wide latitude in testing job applicants for drug use. Job applicants who test positively for drug use simply do not get a position offered to them. Commonly they are not told that they either were subject to drug testing or that they tested positive for drug use. The are simply rejected in a generic fashion or on other grounds that may exist, such as lack of appropriate experience or qualifications.

Private sector employers have an obligation to bargain with their unions about new drug testing programs for their current employees unless the employers have expressly reserved rights to make changes in these programs in their current

---

[12]Jones v. McKenzie, 628 F. Supp. 875 (D. D.C. 1986) and AFGE v. Weinberger, No. CV486–353 (S.D. Ga. Dec. 2, 1986).

[13]Rushton v. Nebraska Public Power District, 653 F. Supp. 1513 (D. Neb. 1987).

[14]Jackson v. Metropolitan Edison Co., 419 U.S. 345 (1974).

[15]Upon request an employer must bargain in good faith with the union about a decision to institute drug testing and the content, procedures, and effect of such a program. A union's failure to object to drug testing "for cause" does not constitute a waiver of the union's right to bargain over random drug testing. The NLRB will seek injunctive relief under Section 10(j) of the NLRA to block unilateral implementation of drug testing programs for current employees. See Memorandum GC 87–5, "NLRB General Counsel's Memorandum On Drug and Alcohol Testing," 8 September, 1987, DLR NO. 184, D-1 (1987).

collective bargaining contracts.[15] Changes in drug testing programs, where testing is required other than "for cause" or for individualized suspicion, will inevitably lead to arbitration on the matter. In *National Football League Players Association v. NFL Management Council*[16] an arbitrator rejected the commissioner's order for "unscheduled" or random testing that he unilaterally promulgated based on an asserted residual management right to discipline where the employers and employees had bargained for an existing testing program limited to reasonable-cause testing. The arbitrator found that the commissioner's authority was supplanted by the specific agreement language on testing.

While legislation is now pending that may allow for random drug and alcohol testing of certain operating employees working in the transportation industries, including rail, air, and over-the-road trucks and buses, significant opposition exists to the "reasonableness" of such proposed searches. In general, testing in the private sector is carried out based on individualized suspicion or on a "for cause" basis with the presence of objective evidence of impairment, such as dilated or bloodshot eyes coupled with an unsteady walk and other specified erratic behavior, or a triggering incident, such as an accident or major safety rules violation. Employees who test positive for drugs are often offered help and rehabilitation through Employee Assistance Programs. First-time offenders are commonly offered Conditional Reinstatement Agreements on the same basis as alcohol abusers.

4. *Reliability of testing procedures and methods.* Questions may be raised at an arbitration or in a wrongful-discharge lawsuit as to the integrity of the chain of custody of the test sample, the accuracy of the type of test(s) performed, and the reliability of the testing laboratory. Some employers and unions have reached agreements on testing protocols, which help eliminate these issues. Thus the Teamsters and a committee of employers have reached a reasonable-cause testing agreement as part of a Master Freight Agreement. The agreement designates the testing laboratory and procedures and covers such details as the amount of urine to be taken and the type of tests to be performed. The CSX Transportation and United Transportation Union—Brotherhood of Locomotive Engineers Testing Agreement, which is set forth in this section, is an example of a comprehensive alcohol and drug testing agreement. The *National Treasury Employees Union v. Von Raab* decision, which is presented in this section, dealt in part with the reliability of the testing program in question and gives some insight into the problems to be addressed.

---

[16]NFL Players Association v. NFL Management Council (R. Kasher, October 25, 1986).

Alcohol and Drug Testing Agreements

Parties To Agreements:
   The CSX Transportation rail units and their employees represented by the United Transportation Union (including its Yardmasters Division) and Brotherhood of Locomotive Engineers.

Date Signed:
   August 6, 1987.

Duration of Agreements:
   The agreements remain in effect through

June 30, 1990 and thereafter until changed in accordance with the Railway Labor Act.

Recognition Of The Problem:

The parties, in their agreements, recognize that the use of alcohol and/or drugs by employees on duty or subject to call is a serious problem and that the safety of the general public as well as that of all employees is jeopardized by the use of drugs and alcohol; further, employees found to have alcohol and/or drugs in their systems will not be allowed to perform service.

When Testing Is Permissible:

The agreements permit drug and alcohol testing when the following events occur:

• Any FRA reportable accident under 49 CFR, Part 225, in which a minimum of $5,200 damage occurs but which does not reach the thresholds as defined in Subpart C of 49 CFR, Part 219, for mandatory testing.

Exclusions:

—Grade crossing accidents.

—Accidents caused by an act of God.

—Accidents caused by track and mechanical failures which are not coupled with Operating Rules violations.

• Any FRA Group A reportable injury.

Exceptions:

—An employee will not be tested when it is determined that the employee is merely a passive participant in circumstances leading to the injury, such as bee stings, snake bites, employees injured as a result of vandalism, and other enumerated events.

• When reasonable suspicion exists that the employee has been using alcohol or drugs, based upon appearance, behavior, speech, or body odors. For urine testing, a determination must be made by two supervisory employees, one of whom must have attended the Company's drug training program.

• As a part of all reinstatement physical examinations.

• As a part of all return from furlough physical examinations.

• As a part of all other Company-sponsored examinations for individuals who have been out of service for more than 90 days.

Refusal To Provide Samples Of Urine:

If an employee refuses to provide samples as required by the agreements, he/she will be taken out of service immediately and charged with insubordination; a hearing will be conducted under the terms of applicable labor agreements.

Employees Who Test Positive:

Employees who have positive tests will be medically disqualified, and will be required to participate in the Employee Assistance Program for evaluation. He/she must successfully complete the prescribed program prior to being considered for return to service.

Exception:

—Former employees being considered for reinstatement to service who are required to take physical examinations must, within 45 days of receipt of notification of positive drug or alcohol finding, begin to participate in the Employee Assistance Program; he/she must successfully complete the prescribed program prior to being considered for return to service.

Procedure For Resolving Disputes:

Disputes over interpretation or application of the agreements will be submitted for final and binding determination through the "minor" disputes machinery established by the Railway Labor Act. Disputes over the evaluation or treatment recommendations of the Company's Employee Assistance Counselors will be resolved by a joint medical board.

Oversight Committee:

An Oversight Committee is established to review the overall results of the testing conducted pursuant to the agreements, identify and make recommendations to resolve any implementation difficulties, and assure quality control of the testing facilities and procedures. Membership on the Committee includes a representative from the Unions and the Company's Transportation and Labor Relations Departments, Chief Medical Officer, and the Director-Employee Assistance Program.

Testing Procedures:

• Employee provides urine sample. At his/her option, blood samples may also be provided; however, a positive urine test will be conclusive for drugs notwithstanding the results of the blood test.

• Employees will not be screened for alcohol and/drugs after 8 hours from the event which would have triggered the testing, nor after having been relieved from duty.

• Drugs for which the Company will screen an employee's urine sample include, but are not limited to: amphetamines, barbituates, benzodiazepines, cannabinoids, cocaine, methadone, methaqualone, opiates, and phencyclidine.

• Method of screening for drugs will be by the EM method (an immunoassay method); all positives will be confirmed by gas chromatography/mass spectroscopy (GC/MS)

and reported quantitatively. Cannabinoids will be screened with a detection limit of 100 ng/ml, and will be confirmed by use of the GC/MS detecting the Delta 9 fractions, at a confirmation detection limit of 20 ng/ml.

• Alcohol screening of urine will be performed via enzyme kinetic methods and positive results will be confirmed by gas chromatography (GC). Urine tests will not be considered positive at levels less than 20 mg/dl.

• Testing laboratories used by the Company will be of high quality. They must observe the chain of custody requirements established by the FRA, and have appropriate safeguards for the handling of samples. Should standards and certification be established by the National Institute of Drug Abuse, the laboratory selected by the Company must be able to satisfy these criteria.

Patchogue-Medford Congress of Teachers v. Board of Education
New York State Court of Appeals, 517 N.Y. 2d 456 (1987).

[On May 3, 1985, the Patchogue-Medford School District notified all of its twenty-two teachers completing their probationary terms that they must submit to urinalysis examination. The letter stated that "the district is requiring a urine sample for all employees eligible for tenure." The sample would be collected by the school nurse and then forwarded to a laboratory for testing. It was conceded that the sole purpose of this examination was to determine whether any of the teachers were using drugs illegally. The teachers' union challenged the testing, and an injunction against the testing was issued. The action of the lower court was affirmed by the Appellate Division of the New York Supreme Court.]

WACHTLER, C. J.
. . . It is unrealistic to argue, as the School District and the United States Attorney General do,

that a person has no reasonable expectation of privacy with respect to urine because it is a waste product periodically eliminated from the body. Although it is a waste product, it is not generally eliminated in public or in such a way that the public or government officials can gain access to it in order to "read" its contents. That is why the School District is requiring the teachers to preserve it and deliver it for inspection. It is settled that a person can have no reasonable expectation of privacy in things which are intentionally abandoned or discarded. But it does not follow from this rule that a person has no privacy interests in a waste product before it is abandoned and therefore no right to dispose of it in a way which maintains privacy. If that were true, documents which individuals and businesses periodically destroy would be entitled to no constitutional protection from government scrutiny.

We also reject the School District's contention that no search is involved when a person is required to provide a urine sample because urine, unlike blood, may be obtained without invading the person's body. That is not the only privacy interest the Constitution protects. The act of discharging urine is a private, indeed intimate, one and the product may contain revealing information concerning an individual's personal life and habits for those capable of analyzing it. There is no question that requiring a person to disrobe and expose his body or body cavities, or to empty the contents of his pockets, involves a sufficient intrusion on privacy to constitute a search (*Bell v Wolfish*, 441 US 520, 558). Requiring a person to urinate in the presence of a government official or agent, as is sometimes required in these cases, is at least as intrusive as a strip search. Even when the individual is permitted to perform the act in private, at the command and supervision of a person designated by the State, privacy interests are implicated. Ordering a person to empty his or her bladder and produce the urine in a container for inspection and analysis by public officials is no less offensive to personal dignity than requiring an individual to empty his pockets and produce a report containing the results of a urinalysis examination. In short, we conclude that the government's act of requiring a person to submit to urinalysis for drug abuse constitutes a search and seizure. The remaining question is what standard of reasonableness the State must meet before it can require an employee to submit to such a test.

Reasonableness generally requires that the State have probable cause and obtain a warrant before conducting a search and seizure. Under certain special circumstances, however, it may be reasonable to permit the government to search without a warrant on grounds not amounting to probable cause. In such instances the court must assess the reasons for the search and the extent to which it intrudes on legitimate privacy interests to determine whether, on balance, the government's action is reasonable.

. . . The School District has an interest in seeing that its teachers are fit and that drug abuse does not impair their ability to deal with the students. Teachers in this state are generally required to submit to an examination to determine their physical and mental fitness to perform their duties (Education Law, § 613). They therefore have a diminished expectation of privacy with respect to State inquiries into their physical fitness to perform as teachers, and it is not unreasonable to require teachers to submit to further testing when school authorities have reason to suspect that they are currently unfit for teaching duties. Thus we agree with the courts below that reasonable suspicion is an appropriate standard, and that probable cause and a warrant are not required before school officials can demand that a teacher submit to a urinalysis for potential drug abuse. . . .

The School District concededly did not have reasonable suspicion to believe that all or any of its probationary teachers was engaged in drug abuse. It claims, however, that reasonable suspicion is not required when a public employer chooses to test all employees in a particular category for potential drug abuse. . . .

The State has a legitimate interest in seeing that its employees are physically fit and that their performance is not impaired by illegal drug usage. The State also has a manifest interest in preventing crime and seeing that those who violate the law are brought to justice. There is little question that these goals would be more attainable if the State were able to search everyone periodically in an all inclusive dragnet. If random searches of those apparently above suspicion were not effective, there would be little need to place constitutional limits upon the government's power to do so. By restricting the government to reasonable searches, the State and Federal Constitutions recognize that there comes a point at which searches intended to serve the public interest, however effective, may themselves undermine the public's interest in maintaining the privacy, dignity and security of its members. Thus random searches conducted by the State without reasonable suspicion are closely scrutinized, and generally only permitted when the privacy interests implicated are minimal, the government's interest is substantial, and safeguards are provided to insure that the individual's reasonable expectation of privacy is not subjected to unregulated discretion (*People v. Scott, supra*). In this case those requirements have not been satisfied. . . .

Accordingly, the order of the Appellate Division should be

Affirmed.

CASE QUESTIONS

1. Was the testing required by the school district individualized-suspicion testing?
2. Did the court find that the testing constituted a search and seizure?
3. Must there be probable cause and a warrant before school officials can demand that an individual teacher submit to urinalysis for suspected drug abuse?
4. Why would a court prohibit random testing when it is an effective method of protecting the public interest against drug abuse?

National Treasury Employees Union v. Commissioner Von Raab USCS
United States Court of Appeals, 808 F.2d 1057 (5th Cir. 1987).

[The commissioner of the United States Customs Service implemented a urinalysis drug testing program for employees transferring or being promoted to sensitive positions in the Customs Service. The union challenged the constitutionality of the testing program in the district court, which court permanently enjoined the drug testing as violative of the Fourth and Fifth Amendments. The matter was appealed to the Fifth Circuit Court of Appeals.]

RUBIN, C. J.

I.

. . . At the test site, an observer gives the employee a form on which he may list any medications he has taken or any other legitimate reasons for his having been exposed to potentially illicit drugs in the preceding thirty days. The form is sealed in an envelope that will not be opened unless the urine test is positive.

After the employee surrenders his outer garments and personal belongings, the observer gives the employee a bottle for the specimen. The employee then enters a restroom stall and produces the urine sample. In order to prevent tam-

pering, the observer remains in the restroom to listen for the normal sounds of urination and to collect the sample immediately after urination, but the observer does not visually observe the act of urination. The employee then leaves the stall and presents the bottle containing the specimen to the observer. To ensure that a previously collected sample has not been proffered, the observer is instructed to reject an unusually hot or cold sample.

The Service uses strict chain-of-custody procedures after collection. The observer applies a tamper-proof seal to the bottle, the employee initials a label affixed to the seal and signs a chain-of-custody form, and the observer signifies that the procedures have been correctly followed. The observer then seals the sample in a bag together with other samples and mails the bag to a laboratory where both a tracking system and chain-of-custody record are maintained.

Laboratory employees test the samples for marijuana, cocaine, opiates, amphetamines, and phencyclidine (PCP). Initially, all samples are screened by the enzyme-multiplied-immunoassay technique (EMIT). Because

EMIT yields a significant rate of positive results even in the absence of drug use, all positive samples are then screened by gas chromatography/mass spectrometry (GC/MS). Both parties agree that GC/MS provides a highly accurate test for the presence of drugs, assuming proper handling, storage, and testing techniques. If the GC/MS test is positive, the employee may designate a laboratory to test the original sample independently. Because EMIT will generally report the test for drug use as negative when five days have elapsed between the last use of drugs and the testing date, the test may fail to detect the prior use of drugs by persons who have abstained for five days. . . .

II.
The fourth amendment states

The right of the people to be secure in their persons, houses, papers and effects, against unreasonable searches and seizures, shall not be violated.

. . . [B]y its express text, the amendment prohibits only those searches and seizures that are unreasonable in the particular circumstances in which they are performed. In determining the constitutionality of the testing program, therefore, we look first to whether the urinalysis program is such a significant intrusion as to constitute a search or seizure, or both search and seizure, in the sense in which those terms are used in the Constitution, and, if we determine it to be a search or seizure, then decide its reasonableness.

. . . In several ways, drug screening by urinalysis infringes the employee's reasonable expectation of privacy and thereby constitutes a search under the fourth amendment. There are few activities in our society more personal or private than the passing of urine. Most people describe it by euphemisms if they talk about it at all. It is a function traditionally performed without public observation; indeed, its performance in public is generally prohibited by law as well as social custom. . . .

Urine testing may disclose not only the presence of drug traces but much additional personal information about an employee—whether the employee is under treatment for depression or epilepsy, suffering from diabetes, or, in the case of a female, pregnant. Even tests limited to the detection of controlled substances will reveal the use of medications prescribed for relief of pain or other medical symptoms. . . .

For these reasons, and in accordance with the other courts that have decided the question, we hold that compulsory urine testing by the government constitutes a search for purposes of the fourth amendment. While compulsory urine testing is less aptly characterized as a seizure because the individual is not held against his will and the urine excreted cannot be considered meaningful property, the remainder of our analysis would apply equally whether the test is considered only a search, only a seizure, or both.

III.

Because the fourth amendment proscribes only searches and seizures that are unreasonable, we now analyzed the Customs Service's urine testing programs to determine whether it is a forbidden search. As the Supreme Court emphasized in *Bell v. Wolfish*, that determination cannot be precisely made or decided by general rules susceptible of mechanical application. The validity of each different kind of search must be assessed by balancing the social and government need for it against the risk that the search will itself undermine the social order by unduly invading personal rights of privacy. "Courts must consider the scope of the particular intrusion, the manner in which it is conducted, the justification for initiating it, and the place in which it is conducted," the Court said in *Wolfish*. . . . In certain limited situations, "the balance of interest precludes insistence upon 'some quantum of individualized suspicion.' " The Union concedes that the Customs Service might test employees who seek transfers if there were some degree of individualized suspicion, so we must balance the factors involved when tests are conducted in the absence of any such suspicion. The determination of fourth-amendment reasonableness requires consideration of the totality of circumstances in a particular case, weighing all of the factors suggesting constitutional violation against all of those indicating validity. . . .

ADMINISTRATIVE NATURE
OF THE SEARCH

The Customs Service program has been adopted solely for an administrative purpose. While the fourth amendment protects against invasions for civil as well criminal investigatory purposes, the need for protection against governmental intrusion diminishes if the investigation is neither designed to enforce criminal laws nor likely to be used to bring criminal charges against the person investigated. Thus, when the police undertake "routine administrative caretaking functions" like inventory searches, particularly when they are not subterfuge for criminal investigations, "[t]he probable-cause approach" and its concomitant requirement of a warrant are "unhelpful." Similarly, visits by government officials to the homes of welfare recipients for the purpose of evaluating their eligibility for benefits do not abridge the fourth amendment.

Even a search solely for an administrative purpose is not per se reasonable. The ubiquitous balancing test applies in this determination as well, entailing a weighing of the need for the search against its intrusiveness. Urine testing serves primarily the administrative function of assessing suitability for employment in a sensitive position, but it does so by searching for evidence of improper behavior. Such screening is not therefore as far removed from criminal investigation as routine inventory searches of an arrestee's personal effects to guard against claims of theft. Consequently, it is important that the government has demonstrated a need to test applicants for sensitive positions in order to assure both the integrity of the Customs Service and the absence of possible moral risk in the performance of their new duties by these applicants.

ANALOGY TO REGULATED INDUSTRY

The Supreme Court has also recognized that, to ensure compliance with a regulatory scheme applicable to highly regulated industries, the government may undertake inspections of the premises occupied by those industries without a warrant and without any degree of individualized suspicion. The exception occurs when warrantless searches are necessary to accomplishment of the regulatory scheme and when the very existence of the federal regulatory program diminishes the reasonable expectations of privacy of those involved in the industry. While this case does not involve a highly regulated private industry, it calls for the same kind of balance between the need for the search and the invasion of the individual's expectation of privacy. Individuals seeking employment in drug interception know that inquiry may be made concerning their off-the-job use of drugs and that the tolerance usually extended for private activities does not extend to them if investigation discloses their use of drugs.

IV.

Testing urine for the presence of drugs does not violate the privilege against self-incrimination. The privilege applies only to evidence that is testimonial. Like blood samples, voice exemplars, or line-up identifications, urine samples reveal "physical characteristics" only, not "any knowledge [the person tested] might have."

When the employee lists the medications taken and any circumstances involving legitimate contact with illicit drugs in the preceding thirty days, testimonial evidence is involved. The fifth amendment, however, protects compelled disclosure of incriminating information, not information that is merely private. Questions about medications or legitimate contact with illicit drugs do not, by their nature, seek incriminating information. Like income tax returns, the Customs Service pre-testing forms may elicit incriminating information, but in the great majority of cases, they will not. Indeed, the information will more likely exculpate the employee. . . . Our decision not to strike the pre-test forms on fifth amendment grounds does not intimate any opinion about whether a particular employee may invoke the privilege against self-incrimination and refuse to fill out the forms. . . .

V.

The drug-testing program is not so unreliable as to violate due process of law. While the initial screening test, EMIT, may have too high a rate of false-positive results for the presence of drugs, the union does not dispute the evidence that the follow-up test, GC/MS, is almost always accurate, assuming proper storage, handling, and measurement techniques. Customs also employs elaborate chain-of-custody procedures to minimize the possibility of falsely positive readings. Moreover, the employee may resubmit a specimen pronounced positive to a laboratory of his own choosing for retesting. Finally, the Customs Service program includes a quality-assurance feature. Control samples will be intermingled with those of the employees to measure the incidence of false-positive results. Quality-assurance reports will be provided to the Union. Hence, if the quality-assurance program indicates that false-positive results occur, employees

may challenge the validity of their own positive tests on that basis. . . .

VI.

. . . Considering all of the circumstances involved, we hold that the Customs Service testing program constitutes a search within the meaning of the fourth amendment, but, because of the strong governmental interest in employing individuals for key positions in drug enforcement who themselves are not drug users and the limited intrusiveness of this particular program, it is reasonable and, therefore, is not unconstitutional. . . .

For these reasons, we VACATE the district court's permanent injunction against the Customs Service's drug screening program. . . .

CASE QUESTIONS

1. Summarize the testing procedures set forth in Part I of the opinion.
2. Is the GC/MS test almost always accurate?
3. What factors are considered by the court in applying the *Wolfish* balancing test?
4. Did the appeals court find that the testing violated the privilege against self-incrimination?

SECTION 24—POLYGRAPH EXAMINATIONS

Law enforcement and security agencies do not want to hire individuals who have sold or who use illegal drugs because drug-impaired judgment would adversely affect law enforcement duties and may lead to compromised operations. A large segment of society believes that there is an inherent contradiction in law breakers being hired to enforce the law. Some law enforcement and security agencies believe that preemployment polygraph testing is an effective tool in finding out whether certain applicants should be disqualified for employment. The applicants may truthfully admit drug sales or drug use during the polygraph examination, or where no admissions are made during the examination, the polygraph examiners may find that certain applicants are "deceptive."

Employers believe that polygraph examinations are one of the best tools that management has at its disposal to investigate thefts and related workplace misconduct. The problem is that there is no widely accepted evidence establishing the scientific validity of polygraph testing, and the utility of such testing is debatable and, indeed, is much debated.[17] In a polygraph examination a relative increase in heart rate, respiration, and perspiration when theft or economic loss related questions are asked is interpreted as a

---

[17]See Anderson v. Philadelphia, 845 F. 2d 1216 (3rd Cir. 1988).

sign of guilt. Opponents of polygraph testing point out that errors may result when an innocent person, who believes that the test could be wrong, out of fear exhibits an increase in heart rate, respiration, and perspiration when asked such incident-related questions.[18]

State Laws

Some twenty-five states and the District of Columbia either prohibit or restrict the use of polygraphs in employment matters. In the *Anderson v. Philadelphia* decision, presented in this section, the United States court of appeals rejected employment applicants' constitutional challenges to a state law that forbade preemployment polygraph testing except for public law enforcement agencies. The court deferred to the state legislature's judgment to allow polygraph testing in the limited circumstances of law enforcement. Where a state statute prohibits requiring a polygraph as a condition of employment, an employer who terminates or adversely affects employees who refuse to take such examinations may be found liable under a "public policy" tort theory for back pay, damages for emotional distress, and punitive damages.[19]

Federal Laws

The federal Employee Polygraph Protection Act of 1988 (EPPA)[20] makes it unlawful for private employers to use preemployment lie detector (polygraph) tests while screening applicants for employment or to take any disciplinary action or deny employment or promotion to any individual who refuses to take a polygraph test. However, federal, state, and local government employers are exempt from any restrictions on the use of polygraph tests, and the federal government may also test private consultants under contract to the Defense Department, CIA, FBI, the National Security Agency, or the Department of Energy. The law also permits private security firms and drug companies to administer polygraph tests to job applicants and employees.

Under the law a limited exemption exists that allows employers to request an employee to submit to a polygraph test if (1) the test is administered in connection with an ongoing investigation involving economic loss or injury to an employer's business, such as theft or embezzlement; (2) the employee had access to the property in question; (3) the employer has "reasonable suspicion" of the employee; and (4) the employer gives a written statement to the employee of the basis for its reasonable suspicion.

The EPPA also deals with a number of objections to the testing process itself. To avoid short, incomplete, and unfair tests, the law requires that tests last at least ninety minutes.[21] Because examiners have sometimes asked offensive questions about sexual preferences and practices, racial matters, religious beliefs, or political or union affiliations or beliefs, the law prohibits questions on such topics.[22] Section 8 of the EPPA sets forth detailed procedures that must be followed prior to, during, and following any lie detector test permitted under the limited exception for "ongoing investigations."

---

[18]P. Ekman, *Telling Lies* (New York: Berkley, 1985), 201–206.
[19]Moniodis v. Cook, 1 ITER Cases 441 (Md. Ct. Spec. App. 1985).
[20]Public Law No. 100–347, signed into law on June 27, 1988.
[21]Section 8(b)(5).
[22]Section 8(b)(11)(C).

The law authorizes civil suits to enforce the act and to make whole adversely affected individuals, including the payment of lost wages and benefits. An employer who violates the act may also be assessed a civil penalty of up to $10,000 as determined by the Secretary of Labor.[23]

The law does not preempt any state or local law or collective bargaining agreement that prohibits lie detector tests or is more restrictive than the federal law.

---

[23]Section 6(a).

Anderson v. Philadelphia
United States Court of Appeals, 845 F.2d 1216 (3rd Cir. 1988).

[Pennsylvania law forbids the use of polygraph testing for preemployment screening by any private or public employer. An exception exists, however, for public law enforcement agencies. The city of Philadelphia police and prison departments base their hiring on the results of a competitive civil service examination with individuals passing this test being placed on a certified eligibility list. As openings occur, individuals ranked high on the eligibility lists are notified and must then pass a number of additional tests before being found qualified for employment. These additional tests include a medical examination, a psychiatric examination, a background investigation, and, usually last in the process, a polygraph test. As part of the background investigation, candidates must fill out a Personal Data Questionnaire (PDQ), which includes questions about family and financial status; driving record; educational and employment history; criminal record; use of alcoholic beverages; and the use, sale, and possession of illicit drugs. Candidates are given prior notification of the content of the PDQ, including the questions relating to illicit drugs. Candidates are also informed that deception or falsification in answering PDQ/polygraph questions may result in rejection. The police and prison departments will hire otherwise qualified individuals who admit that they have used or possessed drugs over six months before completing the PDQ and taking the polygraph. The plaintiffs claim that the use of the polygraph test results in order to deny them employment deprives them of their constitutional rights to procedural and substantive due process and equal protection of law. After a bench trial the district court held in favor of the plaintiffs, and the city appealed.]

STAPLETON, C. J.

I.

. . . The polygraph testing procedures currently used by both the police and prison departments were developed in 1983 in the course of settling class actions by blacks and Hispanics who had brought suit alleging that the Philadelphia Police Department's hiring and promotion policies were discriminatory. These settlements require the above-described prior notification concerning the PDQ/polygraph questions, and require that if during the test the polygraph examiner finds the applicant "deceptive", the applicant must be told immediately and given a chance to explain, deny, or admit the deception. If the applicant denies being deceptive, or if the explanation is found unsatisfactory by the examiner, the applicant must have the opportunity to retake the test with a second examiner. The second examiner does not review the results of the first prior to readministering the polygraph. If the second examiner finds no deception, the applicant is considered to have passed; if the second examiner also finds the applicant deceptive, that finding is ordinarily final and preclusive of employment. The applicant may, however, appeal to either the Police Department's Review Panel or to the Superintendent of Prisons or the prison review panel, and the reviewers may decide to give the applicant the opportunity to take a third test. If the applicant is found deceptive on a third test, he or she will not be hired. Deception is found on about half of all the tests given.

During a pre-test interview, applicants are asked if there is any other information they would like to provide. During a post-test review, if deception is indicated, they are asked again if there is any information they are withholding. Admissions to disqualifying information were made during these interviews by 315 of the 1028 applicants for positions with the Police Department in 1985, and 251 of the 619 applicants in 1986.

. . . The results of the tests are not made public, but are used only within the departments for evaluating the suitability of the applicant for employment.

There is considerable controversy about the validity and reliability of polygraph testing. The polygraph measures stress or anxiety, which in many cases may not correlate very well with deception. In 1983, Congress' Office of Technology Assessment put out a Technical Memorandum on polygraph testing, which read in part as follows:

There are two major reasons why an overall measure of validity is not possible. First, the polygraph test is, in reality, a very complex process that is much more than the instrument. Although the instrument is essentially the same for all applications, the types of individuals tested, training of the examiner, purpose of the test, and types of questions asked, among other factors, can differ substantially. A polygraph test requires that the examiner infer deception or truthfulness based on a comparison of the person's physiological responses to various questions. . . . Second, the research on polygraph validity varies widely in terms of not only results, but also in the quality of research design and methodology. Thus, conclusions about scientific validity can be made only in the context of specific applications and even then must be tempered by the limitations of available research evidence.

. . . OTA concluded that the available research evidence does not establish the scientific validity of the polygraph test for personnel security screening.

. . . [D]espite many decades of judicial, legislative, and scientific discussion, no consensus has emerged about the accuracy of polygraph tests.

App. at 618, 652. Professor Leonard Saxe, who headed the OTA group, testified as an expert witness for the plaintiffs. According to Professor Saxe, polygraph tests are likely to find many truthful applicants deceptive (false positives) and some unknown lesser, though "potentially large", number of deceptive applicants truthful (false negatives). App. at 344. When polygraphs are used for pre-employment screening, the risk of false positive results is generally thought to be higher than that of false negative results.

The City's law enforcement departments consider polygraph tests reliable and valid. An additional advantage of using the polygraph test, in the departments' view, is that it encourages applicants to be candid in responding to questions on the PDQ. The departments do not believe that this secondary advantage can be separated from the trustworthiness that they consider to be the main advantage of the polygraph. Both advantages, the departments believe, enable them to acquire necessary information about potential employees.

The departments' experts do admit that polygraph testing is not perfect. While they recognize the impossibility of conducting error-free polygraph testing, however, they correctly point out that there is no evidence establishing that the polygraph is not valid. Moreover, they point out that there must be some method of acquiring the information necessary to make choices among applicants and stress that the decision to utilize a polygraph examination must be evaluated in light of the available alternatives. One of the departments' experts, Dr. Frank Horvath, noted that

there is also little scientific support for many of the procedures which are used in employment screening. There is little "scientific" evidence, for instance, to show that background investigations actually yield accurate information or that psychiatric interviews accurately discriminate between "good" and "bad" candidates. On the other hand, there is considerable scientific data to show that personal interviews as generally used in employment screening are unreliable; yet, employers continue to carry out such interviews. Written psychological tests, moreover, have received considerable research attention which, according to many, shows little scientific support for their use.

App. at 398. . . .

II.

. . . In *Board of Regents v. Roth*, the Supreme Court made it clear that "[t]he requirements of procedural due process apply only to the deprivation of interests encompassed by the Fourteenth Amendment's protection of liberty and property." 408 U.S. 564, 569 (1972). According to the Court, "to determine whether due process requirements apply in the first place, we must look . . . to the *nature* of the interest at stake." *Id.* at 571. In this case, the plaintiffs have alleged that they have been deprived of both property and liberty interests by the City departments' use of the polygraph test to disqualify them from employment.

Property Interest

. . . While the departments were bound to consider the plaintiffs for employment, they were by no means bound to hire the plaintiffs. The plaintiffs can cite to no section of the Pennsylvania statutes which sets an objective standard for the hiring or rejection of applicants from the eligibility lists, and which might thereby create a legitimate claim of entitlement to employment. On the contrary, under the state law applicable here, agencies such as the defendant departments may and do exercise broad discretion in hiring. . . .

[W]e find nothing in the departmental hiring practices or in Pennsylvania law that establishes a legitimate claim of entitlement to employment in applicants like the plaintiffs. We therefore conclude that the plaintiffs' interest in the civil service positions they sought did not rise to the level of a property interest protected by the Constitution.

Liberty Interest

On the subject of liberty interests in employment, this court has stated that

[a]n employment action implicates a fourteenth amendment liberty interest only if it (1) is based on a "charge against [the individual] that might seriously damage his standing and associations in the community . . . for example, [by implying] that he had been guilty of dishonesty, or immorality," or (2) "impose[s] on him a stigma or other disability that forecloses his freedom to take advantage of other employment opportunities."

Robb, 733 F.2d at 294 (citing *Roth,* 408 U.S. at 573). . . .

In this case, plaintiffs assert that they have been "branded as liars" on account of their failure to pass the polygraph examination. While the polygraph results might conceivably be viewed as stigmatizing the plaintiffs or damaging their reputations, the plaintiffs have not alleged that any of their polygraph test results were made public. Rather, the departments' assertion that the polygraph results are kept confidential and undisclosed stands unchallenged. Given that, we find untenable the plaintiffs' claim that they have been deprived of a liberty interest.

We conclude that the City's polygraph requirement does not violate the plaintiffs' right to procedural due process, since no protected property or liberty interest of the plaintiffs is at stake.

III.

We next address the plaintiffs' argument that they have been denied equal protection of the law. . . . The plaintiffs bear the burden of proof on this issue, and so must show that the requirements imposed by law or regulation "so lack rationality that they constitute a constitutionally impermissible denial of equal protection." *Rogin v. Bensalem Township,* 616 F.2d 680, 688 (3d Cir. 1980). In considering this issue, we bear in mind the Court's statement that a statute or regulation should not be overturned on equal protection grounds "unless the varying treatment of different groups or persons is so unrelated to the achievement of any combination of legitimate purposes that we can only conclude that the legislature's actions were irrational." *Vance v. Bradley*, 440 U.S. 93, 97 (1979).

The defendants stress, and the plaintiffs acknowledge, that the public has a legitimate and, indeed, compelling interest in hiring applicants who are qualified for employment as public law enforcement officers. It is this interest that the polygraph requirement is said to serve. The key question we confront here, therefore, is whether the requirement that applicants pass a polygraph test can arguably be said to result in a better-qualified group of new employees. The defendant City departments need not show that the polygraph requirement does in fact result in the selection of better-qualified group of new employees. Rather, the burden is on the plaintiff applicants to show that the departments' use of the polygraph could not reasonably be believed to produce a better-qualified group of new hires than would be chosen absent the polygraph requirement.

It is clear that the district court placed the burden on the wrong party in this case, since a necessary stepping-stone to that court's holding was its conclusion that "[t]he testimony, exhibits and evidence presented at the trial failed to prove the reliability of polygraph tests in general." App. at 706, 709. . . .

Professor Saxe's testimony supports the proposition that the validity and reliability of polygraph testing as a device to screen prospective employees have not been scientifically established. It does not demonstrate, however, that it is irrational to believe that the polygraph has utility in connection with the selection of law enforcement officers. First, Professor Saxe acknowledges that "virtually no research has been conducted on the validity of polygraph tests to screen prospective employees." App. at 354, and it is, accordingly, apparent that such testing has not been empirically established as invalid or unreliable. Moreover, Professor Saxe does not dispute that pre-employment polygraph screening is widely used by intelligence and law enforcement agencies which consider it useful in eliminating unqual-

ified candidates. The record indicates that such screening is used by the National Security Administration, the Central Intelligence Agency, and approximately 50% of police departments throughout the nation. Finally, Professor Saxe does not dispute Dr. Horvath's assertion that "both proponents and opponents maintain that such testing can distinguish between truthful and deceptive persons with an accuracy greater than chance." App. at 394. . . .

. . . As Dr. Horvath put it,

the important practical issue is not whether polygraph testing is 95% or 90% or even 70% accurate but whether relative to other methods it yields a reasonable degree of accuracy and whether there is another more suitable method of accomplishing the same objective.

App. at 397. The record in this case provides no basis for concluding that superior alternatives are available.

. . . [W]e think it rational for the departments to believe that the polygraph requirement results in fuller, more candid disclosures on the PDQ and thus provides additional information that is helpful in selecting qualified law enforcement officers.

In sum, from the plaintiffs' perspective, the most that can be said on the basis of this record is that the utility of polygraph testing in the pre-employment screening of candidates for law enforcement positions is a debatable and much-debated issue. In such situations, legislators and administrators are free to exercise their judgment regarding the manner in which the public interest will best be served. *Ginsberg v. New York*, 390 U.S. 629, 642–43 (1967) (where causal link between pornography and impaired ethical and moral development of youth is debatable, courts "do not demand of legislatures 'scientifically certain criteria of legislation' " and will not overturn the legislative judgment). Accordingly, we conclude that in the absence of a scientific consensus, reasonable law enforcement administrators may choose to include a polygraph requirement in their hiring process without offending the equal protection clause. . . .

IV.

For the foregoing reasons, we reverse the judgment of the district court and remand with instructions that judgment be entered for the defendants.

CASE QUESTIONS

1. Did the congressional Office of Technology Assessment (OTA) Memorandum conclude that the evidence established the scientific validity of polygraph tests for personnel security screening?
2. Does the city believe that polygraph tests encourage applicants to be candid in responding to questions on the PDQ?
3. Did the court conclude that the city's polygraph test requirement violated the plaintiffs' right to procedural due process having been deprived of a "liberty interest"?
4. Was it important to the outcome of this case that the plaintiffs had the burden of proof?

SECTION 25—EMPLOYER-RELATED IMMIGRATION LAWS: INTRODUCTION

The Immigration Reform and Control Act of 1986 (IRCA) became law on November 6, 1986.[24] This act granted amnesty to illegal aliens who had lived in the United States prior to January 1, 1982, and established a system for the legalization of the residency of certain foreign seasonal agricultural workers (SAWs). The IRCA sets forth criminal and civil penalties against employers who knowingly hire illegal aliens. It is the design of the IRCA to discourage aliens from coming illegally to the United States by eliminating job opportunities for them through employer sanctions. A special counsel's office was established by the IRCA to enforce the law's antidiscrimination provision. On November 10, 1986, the Immigration Marriage Fraud Amendments[25] to the Immigration and Nationality Act (INA) became law, allowing aliens married to U.S. citizens conditional permanent residence status reviewable at the end of a two-year period, at which time the condition would be lifted if the marriage had not been legally terminated. Criminal penalties of up to five years in prison and fines up to $250,000 may be applied to those who knowingly arrange or participate in fraudulent marriage for immigration benefits.

SECTION 26—LEGALIZATION UNDER THE IRCA

To qualify for legalization under the IRCA, an alien (1) must have continuous and unlawful residence in the United States since January 1, 1982; (2) must have continuous presence since November 6, 1986; and (3) must meet the admissibility requirements of an immigrant. A conviction of a felony or three or more misdemeanors makes an individual ineligible for legalization. Persons who lack financial responsibility and are likely to become a public charge will also be denied legalization.

Foreign SAWs are protected under a separate legalization program created by the IRCA, where, if the undocumented person has worked at least ninety man-hours during the twelve-month period ending May 1, 1986, in seasonal field work related to the growing and harvesting of perishable farm commodities, then that person may apply for temporary, and later permanent, residency status.

---

[24]Public Law No. 99–603, also known as the Simpson-Rodino Act.
[25]Public Law No. 99–639.

SECTION 27—EMPLOYER SANCTIONS AND VERIFICATION RESPONSIBILITIES

The availability of jobs and the higher pay scales in the United States have been a principal factor in drawing illegal immigrants to the United States. The premise upon which the IRCA is structured is that if employer sanctions are applied and employers are enlisted to help enforce the immigration laws, employment opportunities for illegal immigrants will be drastically diminished and so will illegal immigration. The employer sanctions and verification responsibilities under the law are covered below.

Employer Sanctions

Section 101 of the IRCA makes it illegal to hire, recruit, or hire for a fee unauthorized aliens. The law also makes it illegal for an employer to employ an alien in the United States knowing that the alien is (or has become) an unauthorized alien with respect to employment. An employer who violates the law is subject to civil penalties of $250 to $2,000 for each unauthorized alien. This penalty is increased to $2,000 to $5,000 for each alien for a second violation.[26] Criminal penalties where a "pattern or practice" of unlawful hiring exists can include a fine of not more than $3,000 for each unauthorized alien and imprisonment for up to six months.[27]

Employer Verification

The law requires employers to verify that each new employee hired after November 6, 1986, is authorized to work in the United States. The Immigration and Naturalization Service (INS) has designated Form I–9, Immigration Eligibility Verification Form, as the official verification form to comply with the IRCA.

The prospective employee must complete the initial portion of Form I–9 attesting under the penalty of perjury that the prospective employee is a U.S. citizen or is authorized by the INS to work in the United States and that the verification document(s) presented to the employer are genuine and relate to the signer. The employer must then review the documents that support the individual's right to work in the United States. Documents that both identify and support an individual's eligibility to work are a U.S. passport, a certificate of U.S. citizenship, a certificate of naturalization, an unexpired foreign passport with attached visa authorizing U.S. employment, or an Alien Registration Card with photograph. Where the individual does not have one of the above documents, the individual may provide a document evidencing his or her identity and another document evidencing the right to employment. Thus a state-issued driver's license is sufficient to provide identify and a social security card or official birth certificate issued by a municipal authority is sufficient to prove employment eligibility. Numerous other documents exist that will satisfy the identity and employment eligibility documentation requirements.

The employer, after examining all documents, signs the following certification:

---

[26]IRCA § 101(a)(1), 8 USC § 1324 A(e)(4).
[27]IRCA § 101(a)(1), 8 USC § 1324 A(f).

CERTIFICATION: I attest, under penalty of perjury, that I have examined the documents presented by the above individual, that they appear to be genuine, relate to the individual named, and that the individual, to the best of my knowledge, is authorized to work in the United States.

The employer has three days to complete the I–9s. I–9s must be completed for all employees hired after November 6, 1986, including employees who are U.S. citizens. I–9s must be kept for three years after the date of hire.[28] Fines of between $100 and $1,000 may be assessed for each individual employee for failure to comply with the paperwork verification requirements.[29]

Burden of Proof and Affirmative Defenses

The employer is obligated to examine documents and to complete and retain the I–9 forms for all new employees after November 6, 1986. The employer has no other obligations to conduct further inquiries. In an action against the employer under the IRCA, the government must establish that the employer had "actual knowledge" that the employee was unauthorized to work in the United States. This standard is one of the highest standards of proof under law.

The IRCA provides an affirmative defense for an employer if the employer, in good faith, simply complies with the verification requirements of the act, and this is accomplished "if the document reasonably appears on its face to be genuine."[30]

SECTION 28—EMPLOYER DISCRIMINATION

Under Section 102 of the IRCA and Title VII of the Civil Rights Act, it is an unfair practice to discriminate against a person in employment situations on the basis of national origin. Additionally, Section 102 of the IRCA makes it an unfair immigration-related practice to discriminate against an individual in hiring, discharging, or recruiting or referring for a fee because of an individual's national origin or, in the case of a citizen or intending citizen, because of that individual's citizenship status.

Since the IRCA imposes employer sanctions for violations of the act, Congress was concerned that the IRCA might lead to employment discrimination against "foreign looking" or "foreign sounding" persons or against persons who, although not citizens, are legally in the United States. In order to prevent the occurrence of such practices, Congress enacted Section 102 and established enforcement measures including the creation of a "Special Counsel for Immigration-Related Unfair Employment Practices" within the Department of Justice. Among the special counsel's statutory responsibilities is the investigation of unfair immigration-related employment practices either on the counsel's own initiative or in response to charges filed with the Office of Special Counsel by aggrieved individuals, their representatives, or officers of the Immigration and Naturalization Service. The Department of Justice Regulations explicitly prohibit only those employment practices where a person or entity has "knowingly and intentionally"

---

[28] *52 Fed. Reg.* 8765 (March 19, 1987).
[29] IRCA § 101(a)(1), 8 USC § 1324 A(e)(5).
[30] IRCA § 101(a)(1) and 8 USC § 1324 A(b)(1)(A).

discriminated or has engaged in a "pattern or practice of knowing and intentional discrimination."[31]

After the enactment of the IRCA, the EEOC has taken the position that Title VII continues to protect undocumented aliens. The EEOC filed a brief in the case of *Patel v. Quality Inn South*, presented in Section 151 of this chapter, stating that it has explicitly directed its investigators since 1981 to accept Title VII charges from undocumented aliens. The EEOC asserted before the court that the IRCA contains no indication of intent to change this coverage of Title VII. In the *Patel* case the U.S. court of appeals held that following passage of the IRCA, an undocumented alien continues to have the right to sue an employer for violations of the minimum wage and overtime provisions of the Fair Labor Standards Act.

The *League of United Latin American Citizens v. Pasadena Independent School District* decision, reported in this section, was the first case interpreting the antidiscrimination provisions of the IRCA.

---

[31]28 CFR, 44 200(a), March 23, 1987.

League of United Latin American Citizens v. Pasadena Independent School District
United States District Court, 43 EPD ¶ 37,089 (S.D. Tex. 1987).

[*Plaintiff, League of United Latin American Citizens (LULAC), is the oldest national organization of persons of Hispanic descent in the United States and was founded for the express purpose of protecting, defending, and preserving the civil rights of Hispanics. Plaintiffs Maria Olympia Hernandez, Reina Raquel Guillen, Blanca Lopez, and Maria Garza (the individual plaintiffs) are undocumented aliens, each of whom entered the United States before January 1, 1982. As undocumented aliens, the individual plaintiffs are currently unable to obtain valid social security numbers. At no time have any of the plaintiffs been arrested or convicted of a criminal offense. The individual plaintiffs were employed by the Pasadena Independent School District (PISD) prior to November 6, 1986. At the time they applied for employment, each individual plaintiff inserted an invalid social security number on her application form. The testimony showed that they were "good people" who had performed their jobs satisfactorily, some for as long as seven years. The*

individual plaintiffs are eligible for the legalization program under the IRCA. Each testified that she intends to submit an application for legalization. The continued employment of the plaintiffs is permitted under the "Grandfather Clause" of the IRCA, Section 101(a)(3). Upon approval of their legalization applications, each individual plaintiff will be authorized to secure a valid social security number. On February 18, 1987, each of the individual plaintiffs was terminated from her employment as a custodial worker by PISD on the ground that she had provided false information on the employment application by giving an invalid social security number. The defendant maintains a policy that falsifying information on an application constitutes grounds for refusal to hire or for termination. The plaintiffs contend that such a termination violates the IRCA.]

MCDONALD, J.
On November 6, 1986, the Immigration Reform and Control Act of 1986 ("IRCA") became law.

This legislation was designed, in part, to allow hundreds of thousands of undocumented aliens now present in the United States to become citizens by proceeding through a several-step legalization process. In enacting this law Congress recognized that:

The United States has a large undocumented alien populated living and working within its borders. Many of these people have been here for a number of years and have become a part of their communities. Many have strong family ties here which include U.S. citizens and lawful residents. They have built social networks in this country. They have contributed to the United States in myriad ways, including providing their talents, labor and tax dollars. However, because of their undocumented status, these people live in fear, afraid to seek help when their rights are violated, when they are victimized by criminals, employers or landlords or when they become ill.

Continuing to ignore this situation is harmful to both the United States and the aliens themselves.

H.R. Conf. Rep. No. 99–682(I), at 49, U.S. Code Cong. & Admin. News, p. 5653.

Only those undocumented aliens who can demonstrate that they have lived in the United States since prior to January 1, 1982, are protected under the Act and are eligible for legalization. IRCA also makes it illegal to hire unauthorized aliens after November 6, 1986, and provides for sanctions against an employer to enforce this provision. The period between November 6, 1986, and June 1, 1987, is to be a public information period during which the employer sanction provisions will not be enforced. Individuals cannot apply for legalization until May 5, 1987.

The Act also contains provisions against discrimination based on national origin or citizenship status that might result from the new law. The instant action calls upon the Court to determine, among other things, whether Defendant's termination of Plaintiffs violated these anti-discrimination provisions. . . .

There is a substantial likelihood . . . that Plaintiffs will prevail on their claim that actions taken by PISD in terminating Plaintiffs violate the anti-discrimination provision of IRCA Section 274B(a). Since this is a case of first impression, it is the Court's duty "to find that interpretation which can most fairly be said to be imbedded in the statute, in the sense of being most harmonious with its scheme and with the general purposes that Congress manifested." C.I.R. v. Engle, 464 U.S. 206, 217 (1984).

The relevant portion of Section 102 states:

It is an unfair immigration-related employment practice for a person or other entity to discriminate against any individual (other than an unauthorized alien) with respect to the hiring, or recruitment or referral for a fee, of the individual for employment or the discharging of the individual from employment—

(A) because of such individual's national origin, or

(B) in the case of a citizen or intending citizen . . . because of such individual's citizenship status.

When applied to those who are qualified for legalization, and who intend to become citizens, a policy of terminating undocumented aliens for no other reason than that they have given employers a false social security number constitutes an unfair immigration-related employment practice under § 274B(a) of the Act. Only because of Plaintiffs' citizenship status have they been unable to secure valid social security numbers. . . .

. . . Similarly, the Act would be manifestly unjust if it encouraged qualified aliens to come forward and reveal their undocumented status only to have that very information serve as grounds for termination by employers. Under IRCA undocumented workers are given an opportunity to come forward, reveal their status, and apply for temporary residency, permanent residency and ultimately citizenship. The proposed application for legalization requires that candidates list *inter alia* their aliases, social security numbers used and employers. It seems only logical that the Immigration and Naturalization Service will seek to verify this information with the employers of undocumented workers. Such verification will inform employers of falsifications that these workers have made, and, in the case of

PISD, the result will be that the workers will be automatically terminated. In short, the application for legalization will lead to a revelation of falsifications made by undocumented aliens. Such revelations will in many cases lead to terminations. Clearly, Congress did not intend to force qualified aliens to make the choice between exercising this right and risking termination of their employment. This Hobson's choice, however, is precisely the peril that Defendant and others with similar policies would have the intended beneficiaries of this new law face.

Though not before the Court, it is undoubtedly true that most employers have a policy of terminating employees who falsify their applications. Under ordinary circumstances, such a policy is justifiable and valid. It is an extraordinary circumstance, however, to have so many undocumented aliens working in the United States under false names and with invalid social security numbers. In the coming months and years, the administrative process established under Section 102 of the Act will have to reconcile many current employment practices with the new rights established under IRCA. . . .

The second criterion in reviewing the request for preliminary injunction is the substantial likelihood of irreparable injury to Plaintiffs. . . .

. . . The Plaintiffs have demonstrated that they would likely suffer irreparable injury in the absence of an injunction. Leonel Castillo, a former Commissioner of the Immigration and Naturalization Service, testified that it has long been the policy of the United States to reject as candidates for citizenship aliens who are likely to become a public charge. That policy is modified by, but continues under Section 245A(d)(2)(B)(iii). He also testified that the more income that an applicant for legalization brings in support of his or her petition, the more favorably that petition will be viewed. . . .

In balancing the relative harm to the parties under the third prong of the criteria, the Court finds that the threatened injury to the Plaintiffs outweighs the potential harm to Defendant. . . .

Finally, the Court finds that the granting of the injunction will not disserve the public interest, but rather will advance it. The school district has urged that it has a legitimate and important role in inculcating and upholding the virtue of honesty to its students. *See Bethel School District No. 403 v. Frazier*, 106 S. Ct. 3159 (1986). The citizens, however, through their elected officials in Congress, have determined that the presence of large numbers of illegal aliens can no longer be ignored. Congress has determined that it can neither turn back the hands of time nor ignore reality. The purpose of the Act is to extend a welcome hand to those undocumented aliens who have lived in the United States for the requisite number of years and can meet the other requirements for citizenship. At the same time, the law seeks to discourage unregulated immigration by providing for future sanctions against employers who hire unauthorized aliens.

If Defendant's employment practice is allowed to stand, Plaintiffs and many others similarly situated would be placed in the unfortunate and untenable position of deciding between prospective citizenship and present employment. In order to qualify for legalization, they must come forward and reveal their past misdeeds, misstatements and falsifications. Once made, these revelations will automatically result in the termination of any qualified alien now working with PISD. Other similarly situated individuals run the risk of being fired from their jobs, either for falsifying their employment applications or for having invalid social security numbers. . . .

. . . Defendant's actions have the effect of jeopardizing Plaintiffs' rights under IRCA before they have had an opportunity to exercise those rights. If the Act is to be given force and effect, obvious impediments to securing its benefits should not be sanctioned.

Accordingly, it is ORDERED, ADJUDGED, and DECREED that Plaintiffs' Motion for a Preliminary Injunction be and hereby is GRANTED.

It is further ORDERED that:

1. Defendant shall immediately reinstate Plaintiffs Maria Olympia Hernandez, Reina

Raquel Guillen, Blanca Lopez, and Maria Garza to the positions they occupied in Defendant's employ immediately prior to their dismissal. Plaintiffs shall receive at least the same wages, benefits and other terms and conditions of employment that they received prior to their dismissals.

2. Upon issuance of a permanent injunction, Defendant shall pay Plaintiffs back wages from the date of their individual terminations.

3. Defendant is hereby enjoined from dismissing any employee who is an undocumented alien qualified for legalization under the Immigration Reform and Control Act of 1986 because he or she has provided a false social security number.

4. A hearing will be held to determine Plaintiffs' entitlement to reasonable attorney's fees and the amount thereof. . . .

CASE QUESTIONS

1. State the issue before the court.
2. Did Congress intend to force aliens qualified for legalization under the IRCA to make the choice between exercising their legalization rights and risking termination from their jobs when employers find out that they have falsified their employment applications?
3. Is income a factor in the legalization process under the IRCA?
4. Were the identified plaintiffs illegal aliens when they were terminated?

SECTION 29—BUSINESS VISAS

The IRCA did not affect business visas. Nonimmigrant B–1 business visas are issued by a U.S. consular office abroad after it has been shown that (1) the visitor has an unabandoned foreign residence, (2) intends to enter the United States for a limited period of time, and (3) will engage solely in legitimate business activities for which the visitor will not be paid in the United States.[32] Thus aliens may qualify for a B–1 visa to perform after-sale warranty work on equipment sold by a foreign company to a United States purchaser.

Certain investors qualify for E–2 business visas. Principal foreign investors responsible for development and direction of an enterprise in the United States are granted such a visa. An E visa is very desirable because it is issued for extended periods of time, usually four to five years, and may be renewed indefinitely so long as the alien maintains her or his role with respect to the investment.

L–1 visas allow qualifying multinational businesses to make intracompany transfers of foreign persons to the United States when the individuals are employed in management or have "specialized knowledge."[33] L–1 visas are good for an initial period of up to three years, with a possible extension not to exceed two years. The alien must then depart the country and reside outside of it for a year before again being eligible for L–1 status.[34]

H–1 classification visas allow aliens of "distinguished merit and ability" to enter and work in the United States for an initial period of up to three years, with extensions in increments of two years. These persons include architects, engineers, lawyers, physicians, surgeons, and teachers in elementary and secondary schools and colleges.[35]

---

[32]Department of State, 9 *Foreign Affairs Manual*, § 41.25.
[33]Some 66,000 individuals were issued L-1 visas in 1986, up from 6,000 in 1972. AILA Capital Conference, Washington, D.C., November 21, 1986.
[34]8 CFR, § 214(1)(12).
[35]INA § 101(a)(32).

Seasonal, temporary workers may obtain H–2 visas for an initial period of one year, with extensions allowing for a total length of stay not to exceed three years.

The *International Union of Bricklayers v. Meese* decision, presented in this section, is an example of the complicated employment issues an employer faces in meeting the needs of its business.

International Union of Bricklayers v. Meese
United States District Court, 616 F. Supp. 1387 (D.C. Cal. 1985).

[The International Union of Bricklayers (Union) brought an action against U.S. Attorney General Edwin Meese, Secretary of State George Shultz, the INS, and the Homestake Mining Co., which owned the McLaughlin Gold Project in Lake County, California. The Union challenges the INS instruction that allowed B–1 "temporary visitor for business" visas to be issued to ten West Germans to come to the United States temporarily to do certain bricklaying and other work. The Union contends that the instruction is in violation of the INA. The defendants disagree.]

LEGGE, D. J.

I.

Statutory and Regulatory Overview
The Act generally charges the Attorney General and the Secretary of State with the administration and enforcement of the immigration laws of the United States. *See* 8 U.S.C. §§ 1103(a), 1104(a). Primary responsibility, however, rests with the Attorney General, and his "determination and ruling . . . with respect to all questions of [immigration] law [is] controlling." 8 U.S.C. § 1103(a).

Under the Act, an alien seeking to enter the United States is categorized either as an "immigrant" or "nonimmigrant." In most instances, an immigrant seeks permanent residence, and a nonimmigrant seeks only a temporary stay. . . . The distinction between immigrant and nonimmigrant aliens is significant. The Act contains numerical limitations and strict documentary

requirements for certain classes of immigrant aliens. In contrast, there are no numerical limitations placed upon the classes of nonimmigrant aliens.

The dispute in the present case centers on the Act's provisions regarding nonimmigrant aliens. Section 101(a)(15) of the Act, 8 U.S.C. § 1101(a)(15), sets forth thirteen classes of aliens entitled to nonimmigrant status. The parties have stipulated, however, that only two of those classes are germane to this case.

A.

Temporary Visitors for Business
The first class of nonimmigrant aliens relevant here is the "temporary visitor for business" class. Section 101(a)(15)(b) of the Act defines a "temporary visitor for business" as:

an alien (other than one coming for the purpose of study or of performing skilled or unskilled labor or as a representative of foreign press, radio, film, or other foreign information media coming to engage in such vocation) having a residence in a foreign country which he has no intention of abandoning and who is visiting the United States temporarily for business. . . .

8 U.S.C. § 1101(a)(15)(B). An alien qualifying for this nonimmigrant status is entitled to receive a "B–1" visa. *See* 8 U.S.C. § 1201(a)(2).

Pursuant to his authority under the Act, *see* 8 U.S.C. § 1104(a), the Secretary of State has promulgated a regulation defining the term "business" for purposes of the B–1 "temporary visitor for business" class:

The term "business", as used in section 101(a)(15)(B) of the Act, refers to legitimate activities of a commercial or professional character. It does not include purely local employment or labor for hire. An alien seeking to enter as a nonimmigrant for employment or labor pursuant to a contract or other prearrangement shall be required to qualify under the provisions of [22 C.F.R.] § 41.55.

22 C.F.R. § 41.25(b)(1985). *See also* 22 C.F.R. § 41.25(a) (1985) (specifying factors considered by consular officer in determining whether an alien is classifiable as a "temporary visitor for business").

Among the criteria utilized to determine an alien's eligibility for B–1 "temporary visitor for business" status is INS Operations Instruction 214.2(b)(5), an INS internal agency guideline that is the subject of this dispute. The Operations Instruction provides:

Each of the following may also be classified as a B–1 nonimmigrant if he/she is to receive no salary or other remuneration from a United States source (other than an expense allowance or other reimbursement for expenses incidental to the temporary stay): . . .

(5) An alien coming to install, service, or repair commercial or industrial equipment or machinery purchased from a company outside the U.S. or to train U.S. workers to perform such service, provided: the contract of sale specifically requires the seller to perform such services or training, the alien possesses specialized knowledge essential to the seller's contractual obligation to provide services or training, the alien will receive no remuneration from a U.S. source, and the trip is to take place within the first year following the purchase.

Pursuant to the Operations Instruction, B–1 visas have been issued to the foreign laborers who came to the United States to work on the project owned by Homestake, and to foreign laborers to do other work throughout the United States. The central issue in this case is whether the Operations Instruction violates the Act and the regulations promulgated under the Act.

B.

Temporary Workers

The second class of nonimmigrant aliens involved here is the "temporary worker" class. Section 101(a)(15)(H)(ii) of the Act defines a "temporary worker" as:

an alien having a residence in a foreign country which he has no intention of abandoning . . . [and] who is coming temporarily to the United States to perform temporary services of labor, if unemployed persons capable of performing such service or labor cannot be found in this country. . . .

8 U.S.C. § 1101(a)(15)(H)(ii). An alien qualifying for this nonimmigrant status is entitled to receive an "H–2" visa. *See* 8 U.S.C. § 1201(a)(2).

The Attorney General is authorized to make the determination concerning the admissibility of an H–2 "temporary worker" applicant after consulting with other government agencies. . . .

II.

The Present Case

Factual Background

Homestake began construction in early 1984 on its McLaughlin Gold Project in order to open a new gold mine. Due to metallurgical problems in the Lake County region, Homestake concluded that it was necessary to employ technology not used previously in the gold mining industry. Davy McKee Corporation ("Davy McKee"), Homestake's construction manager, therefore conducted a search to locate the appropriate technology.

On behalf of Homestake, Davy McKee agreed to purchase a newly-designed gold ore processing system from Didier-Werke ("Didier"), a West German manufacturing company. Although the purchase agreement required Didier to supply an integrated processing system, it was not possible to premanufacture the entire system in West Germany. The purchase agreement was therefore made contingent upon Didier's West German employees completing the work on the system at the project site in Lake County.

In September 1984, Didier submitted B–1 "temporary visitor for business" visa petitions on behalf of ten of its West German employees to United States consular officers in Bonn, West Germany. Relying upon INS Operations Instruction 214.2(b)(5), consular officers approved the petitions and issued B–1 visas to the West Germans. In January 1985, the West Germans entered the United States to work on the processing system. The work involves the installation of the interior linings of the system's autoclaves, and requires certain technical bricklaying skills. . . .

III.

The Validity of the Operations Instruction Under the Act

Plaintiffs contend that INS Operations Instruction 214.2(b)(5) violates the Act, because the Operations Instruction is inconsistent with specific provisions of the Act, and with the legislative intent underlying those provisions.

In testing the Operations Instruction against the Act, the court's task is to interpret the Act in light of the purposes Congress sought to achieve in enacting it. *Dickerson v. New Banner Institute, Inc.*, 460 U.S. 103 (1983). The starting point must be the language employed by Congress. *I.N.S. v. Phinpathya*, 464 U.S. 183 (1984). Absent a clearly expressed legislative intention to the contrary, the statutory language is to be regarded as conclusive. *Escondido Mutual Water Co. v. Mission Indians*, 466 U.S. 765 (1984).

The Language of the Act and the Operations Instruction

The court must begin its analysis by comparing the language of the Act with the language of the Operations Instruction. In particular, the court must focus on the nonimmigrant visa provisions in sections 101(a)(15)(B) and 101(a)(15)(H)(ii) of the Act.

Section 101(a)(15)(B) of the Act defines a "temporary visitor for business" nonimmigrant as:

an alien (other than one coming for the purpose of *study or of* performing skilled or unskilled labor *or as*

a representative of foreign press, radio, film, or other foreign information media coming to engage in such vocation) having a residence in a foreign country which he has no intention of abandoning and who is visiting the United States temporarily for business. . . .

8 U.S.C. § 1101(a)(15)(B) (emphasis added). A "temporary visitor for business" nonimmigrant is entitled to receive a B–1 visa. *See* 8 U.S.C. § 1201(a)(2). Under section 101(a)(15)(B), however, an alien coming to the United States for the purpose of "performing skilled or unskilled labor" is expressly *excluded* from the "temporary visitor for business" class.

Section 101(a)(15)(H)(ii) of the Act defines a "temporary worker" nonimmigrant as:

an alien *having a residence in a foreign country which he has no intention of abandoning . . . [and] who is* coming temporarily to the United States to perform temporary services or labor, if unemployed persons capable of performing such service or labor cannot be found in this country. . . .

8 U.S.C. § 1101(a)(15)(H)(ii) (emphasis added). A "temporary worker" nonimmigrant is entitled to receive an H–2 visa.

INS Operations Instruction 214.2(b)(5) provides that an alien may be classified as a "temporary visitor for business" nonimmigrant if:

he/she is *to receive no salary or other remuneration from a United States source (other than an expense allowance or other reimbursement for expenses incidental to the temporary stay) . . . [and is]* coming to install, service, or repair commercial or industrial equipment or machinery purchased from a company outside the U.S. *or to train U.S. workers to perform such service.* . . .

A comparison of the language of section 101(a)(15)(B) of the Act with the language of INS Operations Instruction 214.2(b)(5) demonstrates that the Operations Instruction contravenes that section of the Act. Section 101(a)(15)(B) unequivocally excludes from the B–1 "temporary visitor for business" classification an alien who is "coming for the purpose of . . . performing skilled or unskilled labor." 8 U.S.C. § 1101(a)(15)(B). . . .

INS Operations Instruction 214.2(b)(5), however, does not contain an exclusion for an alien seeking to enter the United States to perform skilled or unskilled labor. The Operations Instruction provides that an alien may be classified as a "temporary visitor for business" if the alien is "coming to install, service, or repair commercial or industrial equipment or machinery." The effect of this language is to authorize the issuance of a B–1 visa to an alien coming to this country to perform skilled or unskilled labor. In the present case, for example, the West Germans undeniably are performing labor—whether it be deemed skilled or unskilled—in connection with the installation of the gold ore processing system at the McLaughlin Gold Project.

Similarly, a comparison of the language of section 101(a)(15)(H)(ii) of the Act with the language of INS Operations Instruction 214.2(b)(5) shows that the Operations Instruction also contravenes that section of the Act. Section 101(a)(15)(H)(ii) classifies an H–2 "temporary worker" as an alien "coming . . . to perform temporary services or labor, if unemployed persons capable of performing such service or labor cannot be found in this country." 8 U.S.C. § 1101(a)(15)(H)(ii). Because the Act requires the Attorney General to consult other agencies of the government concerning "temporary worker" visas, *see* 8 U.S.C. § 1184(c), the Attorney General has established H–2 labor certification procedures. Thus, an H–2 visa petition cannot be approved unless the alien's employer obtains either "*[a] certification from the Secretary of Labor . . . stating that qualified persons in the United States are not available and that the employment* of the beneficiary *will not adversely affect wages and working conditions of workers in the United States* similarly employed . . . [or]* notice that such certification *cannot* be made." 8 C.F.R. § 214.2(h)(3) (1985) (emphasis added).

In contrast, INS Operations Instruction 214.2(b)(5) does not require an alien to seek labor certification prior to obtaining a nonimmigrant visa. More importantly, the Operations Instruction authorizes the issuance of a nonimmigrant visa to a person performing skilled or unskilled labor, though qualified Americans may be available to perform the work involved. The Operations Instruction therefore lacks the safeguards contained in section 101(a)(15)(H)(ii) of the Act and the regulation promulgated under that section. Again, the present case illustrates this point, because the parties have stipulated that neither the West Germans nor their employer was required to seek labor certification from the Secretary of Labor prior to the issuance of the visas to the West Germans.

In summary, it is apparent that the language of INS Operations Instruction 214.2(b)(5) is inconsistent with the language of sections 101(a)(15)(B) and 101(a)(15)(H)(ii) of the Act. First, the Operations Instruction ignores the provision in section 101(a)(15)(B) *excluding* skilled or unskilled labor. Second, the Operations Instruction ignores the provision in section 101(a)(15)(H)(ii) concerning the availability of qualified American workers. . . .

The court concludes from both the language and legislative intent of the Act that the federal defendants' interpretation embodied in the Operations Instruction contravenes the Act. The court therefore decides that INS Operations Instruction 214.2(b)(5) violates sections 101(a)(15)(B) and 101(a)(15)(H)(ii) of the Act. . . .

It is so ordered.

CASE QUESTIONS

1. Summarize the facts of this case.
2. What rule of statutory construction did the court follow in assessing the validity of the INS instruction in question?
3. Was INS Operations Instruction 214.2(b)(5) consistent with the law that provides for "temporary visitor for business" B–1 visas?
4. May an H–2 visa be obtained as easily as a B–1 visa?

SECTION 30—DEVELOPING LAW REGULATING WAGES AND HOURS

On January 3, 1938, President Franklin Roosevelt declared in his annual message to Congress:

> The people of this country by an overwhelming vote are in favor of having Congress—this Congress—put a floor below which individual wages shall not fall, and a ceiling beyond which the hours of individual labor shall not rise.

Within six months of the president's message, Congress passed a federal wage and hour law called the Fair Labor Standards Act (FLSA). It was signed into law on June 25, 1938.[36] The FLSA has three broad objectives:

1. The establishment of minimum wages, a floor under which wages would not fall that would provide a basic minimum standard of living for workers.
2. The encouragement of a ceiling on the number of hours of labor for individual workers in a workweek, the ultimate purpose of which was to put financial pressure on employers to spread employment opportunities and hire additional workers to avoid the extra pay required for overtime hours (time worked in excess of forty hours per week).[37]
3. The discouragement of "oppressive child labor."[38]

The original FLSA provided that the statutory minimum wage would be set at 30 cents per hour beginning October 24, 1939, with increases to take effect on subsequent dates. The present minimum wage provisions of the FLSA require that covered nonexempt workers are entitled to a minimum wage of not less than $3.35 an hour in 1989.[39]

Coverage and Exemptions

Workers at enterprises engaged in interstate commerce are covered by the FLSA. Moreover, the act has been amended to cover domestic service workers, including day workers such as housekeepers, chauffeurs, cooks, and full-time baby-sitters. The FLSA applies to most federal employees as well as to state and local government workers.[40]

Some workers are exempt from both the minimum wage and overtime provisions of the law, including executive, administrative, and professional employees and outside salespersons. Also exempt are employees of certain small farmers and casual baby-sitters.

Certain highly paid commissioned employees of retail and service businesses are exempt from the overtime pay provision, as are domestic service workers residing in their employer's homes and farmworkers.

The Wage and Hour Division (Wage-Hour Office) of the U.S. Department of Labor administers and enforces the FLSA. Detailed information about coverage and exemp-

---

[36]Public Law No. 718, 75th Cong., 52 Stat. 1060.
[37]See Section 7(a) of the FLSA and Overnight Motor Transportation Co. v. Missel, 316 U.S. 572 (1942).
[38]See Section 12(a) of the FLSA.
[39]A bill (S. 837), which would have raised the minimum wage to $4.55 per hour by 1992, was withdrawn from further consideration by the U.S. Senate in 1988 after five days of debate.
[40]See Garcia v. San Antonio Metropolitan Transit Authority, 469 U.S. 528 (1985).

tions is beyond the scope of this section but is available at local Wage-Hour Offices.

The *Patel v. Quality Inn South* decision, presented in this section, shows the far-reaching scope of coverage of the FLSA and upheld an undocumented alien's right to sue an employer for violations of the minimum wage and overtime provisions of the FLSA.

Subminimum Wage Provisions

The FLSA provides for the employment of certain individuals at wage rates below the statutory minimum, including full-time students at institutions of higher education.

Individuals whose productive capacity is impaired by age or physical or mental deficiency or injury may also be employed at less than the minimum wage in order to prevent the curtailment of work opportunities for these individuals. However, such employment is permitted only under certificates issued by the appropriate Wage-Hour Office. Compliance officers closely scrutinize practices in regards to the issuance and reissuance of certificates allowing subminimum wages.

Basic Wage Standards

Wages required by the FLSA are due on the regular payday for the period covered. Deductions made from wages for such items as cash or merchandise shortages, employer-required uniforms, and tools of a trade are not legal if they reduce wages below the minimum wage or reduce the amount of overtime pay due under the FLSA. Moreover, should an employer require employees to provide uniforms or tools on their own, to the extent that they reduce wages below the minimum wage such is also a violation of the law. Thus nursing homes that require their nurse's aides to wear either white dresses or white pantsuits to work each day but pay these individuals the minimum wage are in violation of the FLSA. The employer nursing homes must, in addition to the minimum wage, compensate these employees for the value of such uniforms.

Overtime Pay

Overtime must be paid at a rate of at least 1½ times the employee's regular rate of pay for each hour worked in a workweek in excess of forty hours. Thus an employee whose regular rate of pay is $10 per hour who works forty-four hours in a workweek is entitled to $400 for the first forty hours plus $15 for each of the four hours over forty—the overtime hours—for a total of $460 pay for the workweek.

The Wage-Hour Office provides regulations for employers to guide them in the calculation of overtime for piecework and salaried workers.

Under the Portal-to-Portal Act,[41] activities of employees that take place either before an employee begins or after the employee completes the productive activities for which the employee was hired are not to be included in "working time" for compensation purposes unless required by a collective bargaining contract or by past practice.

---

[41]Public Law No. 49, 80th Cong., 29 USC § 251–263.

Child Labor Provisions

The FLSA child labor provisions are designed to protect the educational opportunities of minors and prohibit their employment in occupations detrimental to their health and well-being. The FLSA restricts hours of work for minors under 16 and lists hazardous occupations too dangerous for minors to perform.

Record Keeping

Employers are required by the act to keep records on wages and hours for each employee for three years from the date of last entry.[42] Should an employer have to defend a wage or overtime suit under the FLSA, adequate records are essential for the employer's defense.

Enforcement

Enforcement of the FLSA is carried out by wage-hour compliance officers. Wage-hour officers may supervise the recovery and payment of back wages. Either the Secretary of Labor or an employee may file suit for back wages plus an equal amount as liquidated damages against employers who violate the FLSA. A two-year statute of limitations applies to the recovery of back pay except in the case of willful violations in which a three-year statute applies.

In *McLaughlin v. Richland Shoe Co.*, presented in this section, the Supreme Court held that a violation of the FLSA is "willful" for purposes of triggering the three-year statute of limitations if the employer either knew that or showed reckless disregard for whether the employer's conduct was prohibited by the FLSA.

---

[42]Section 11(c) of the FLSA and regulations 29 CFR, Ch. V, Sec. 516.5.

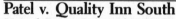

Patel v. Quality Inn South
United States Court of Appeals, 846 F.2d 700 (8th Cir. 1988).

[On June 1, 1982, Rajni Patel came to the United States from India on a visitor's visa. Although the visa expired after six weeks, Patel remained in the United States. In July 1983 he began working for the Sumani Corporation's Quality Inn South in Birmingham, Alabama. Patel performed maintenance and janitorial work at the hotel until October 1985. In August 1986 Patel brought an FLSA suit against the hotel seeking to recover unpaid back wages of $47,132 and an equivalent amount as liquidated damages plus

attorney's fees. The district court granted the defendants' motion from summary judgment, holding that undocumented aliens could not recover for violations of the FLSA. Patel appealed.]

VANCE, C. J.

A.

. . . In deciding whether undocumented aliens are entitled to the protections of the FLSA we begin by examining the act itself. Congress enacted the FLSA in 1938 to eliminate substandard working conditions. *See* 29 U.S.C. § 202. It requires covered employers to pay their employees a statutorily prescribed minimum wage, *Id.* § 206, and prohibits employers from requiring their employees to work more than forty hours per week unless the employees are compensated at one and one half times their regular hourly rate. *Id.* § 207(a)(1). For violations of its provisions the FLSA imposes criminal sanctions and allows employees to bring an action to recover any unpaid minimum wages and overtime plus liquidated damages and attorney's fees. *Id.* § 216(a), (b).

In section 3(e) of the FLSA, *Id.* § 203(e), Congress defined the term "employee" for the purpose of determining who would be covered by the act. It would be difficult to draft a more expansive definition. The term "employee" was defined to include "any individual employed by an employer." *Id.* § 203(e)(1). . . . This definitional framework—a broad general definition followed by several specific exceptions—strongly suggests that Congress intended an all encompassing definition of the term "employee" that would include all workers not specifically excepted.

That Congress intended a broad definition of the term "employee" is also apparent from the FLSA's legislative history. One representative described the act as "the most momentous and far-reaching measure that [Congress has] considered for many years." 83 Cong. Rec. 9262 (1938) (statement of Rep. Fish). The remarks of then Senator Hugo Black, the FLSA's chief legislative sponsor, are even more instructive. During debate over the act Senator Black declared that its "definition of employee . . . is the broadest definition that has ever been included in any one act. . . ." 81 Cong. Rec. 7656–57 (1937).

Given the unequivocal language of the FLSA and its legislative history, it is not surprising that the Supreme Court has adopted an expansive definition of the term "employee" in its decisions under the act. Although it has never faced the question of whether undocumented aliens are covered by the FLSA, the Court consistently has refused to exempt from coverage employees not within a specific exemption. As the Court explained in *Powell v. United States Cartridge Co.*, 339 U.S. 497, 70 S. Ct. 755, 94 L.Ed. 1017 (1950):

Breadth of coverage was vital to [the FLSA's] mission. . . . Where exceptions were made, they were narrow and specific. [Congress] included as employees "any individual employed by an employer" § 3(e), and . . . devoted § 13 to listing exemptions of specific classes of employees. . . . Such specificity in stating exemptions strengthens the implication that employees not thus exempted . . . remain within the Act.

. . . In *Sure-Tan, Inc. v. NLRB*, 467 U.S. 883, 104 S. Ct. 2803, 81 L.Ed.2d 732 (1984), the Court used similar reasoning when it held that undocumented aliens are "employees" within the meaning of the National Labor Relations Act (NLRA). The Court stated:

The breadth of § 2(3)'s definition is striking: the Act squarely applies to "any employee." The only limitations are specific exemptions. . . . Since undocumented aliens are not among the few groups of workers expressly exempted by Congress, they plainly come within the broad statutory definition of "employee."

. . . The Department of Labor also supports Patel's position. It first interpreted the FLSA to cover undocumented aliens in 1942, when the Wage and Hour Administrator opined that alien prisoners of war were covered by the act and therefore were entitled to be paid the minimum wage. Since that time the Department of Labor has enforced the FLSA on behalf of undocumented workers on numerous occasions. *See, e.g., Donovan v. Burgett Greenhouses, Inc.*, 759 F.2d 1483 (10th Cir. 1985); *Brennan v. El San Trading Corp.*, 73 Lab. Cas. (CCH) ¶ 33,032 (W.D. Tex. 1973). To be sure, we are not bound by the Department of Labor's interpretation of the FLSA. As the agency charged with implementing the act, however, the Department's interpretation is entitled to considerable deference. . . .

In short, the defendants' contention that Congress did not intend to protect undocumented workers when it passed the FLSA is contrary to the overwhelming weight of authority. Nothing in the FLSA or its legislative history suggests that Congress intended to excluded undocumented workers from the act's protections. The defendants conceded as much during oral argument. The defendants, however, . . . argue that in light of the IRCA undocumented aliens are no longer entitled to the protections of the FLSA. . . .

B.

We first consider the effect of the IRCA on the rights of undocumented aliens under the FLSA. As we noted earlier, the district court relied heavily on the IRCA in granting the defendants' motion for summary judgment.

We begin our analysis by noting the familiar principle that amendments by implication are disfavored. Only when Congress' intent to repeal or amend is clear and manifest will we conclude that a later act implicitly repeals or amends an earlier one. *See, e.g., Rodriguez v. United States*, 107 S. Ct. 1391, 1392, 94 S. Ct. 1391 (1987). Here, nothing in the IRCA or its legislative history suggests that Congress intended to limit the rights of undocumented aliens under the FLSA. To the contrary, the FLSA's coverage of undocumented aliens is fully consistent with the IRCA and the policies behind it. . . .

[T]he FLSA's coverage of undocumented aliens goes hand in hand with the policies behind the IRCA. Congress enacted the IRCA to reduce illegal immigration by eliminating employers'

economic incentive to hire undocumented aliens. To achieve this objective the IRCA imposes an escalating series of sanctions on employers who hire such workers. *See* 8 U.S.C. § 1324a. The FLSA's coverage of undocumented workers has a similar effect in that it offsets what is perhaps the most attractive feature of such workers—their willingness to work for less than the minimum wage. If the FLSA did not cover undocumented aliens, employers would have an *incentive* to hire them. Employers might find it economically advantageous to hire and underpay undocumented workers and run the risk of sanctions under the IRCA. . . .

. . . Nothing in the FLSA suggests that undocumented aliens cannot recover unpaid minimum wages and overtime under the act, and we can conceive of no other reason to adopt such a rule. We therefore conclude that Patel is entitled to the full range of available remedies under the FLSA without regard to his immigration status.

Reversed and remanded.

CASE QUESTIONS

1. Did the court agree with Quality Inn's contention that Congress did not intend to protect illegal aliens when it passed the FLSA? Explain.
2. Is it true that in light of the Immigration Reform and Control Act of 1966, undocumented aliens are not entitled to the protection of the FLSA?
3. Could the FLSA's coverage of undocumented aliens go hand in hand with the policies behind the IRCA?

McLaughlin v. Richland Shoe Co.
Supreme Court of the United States, 108 S. Ct. 1677 (1988).

[*The respondent, a manufacturer of shoes and boots, employed seven mechanics to maintain and repair its equipment. In 1984 the Secretary of Labor (Secretary) filed a complaint alleging that*

"in many workweeks" the respondent had failed to pay those employees the overtime compensation required by the FLSA. As an affirmative defense the respondent pleaded the two-year statute of

limitations. The district court rejected the respondent's claim that the two-year statute of limitations applied, finding the three-year exception applicable under the standard of Coleman v. Jiffy June Farms, Inc., 458 F.2d 1139, whereby an action is "willful" if there is substantial evidence that the employer "knew or suspected that his actions might violate the FLSA," i.e., if the employer merely knew that the FLSA was "in the picture." Vacating the judgment against the respondent and remanding, the court of appeals rejected the Jiffy June standard in favor of the test employed in Trans World Airlines, Inc. v. Thurston, 469 U.S. 111. The Supreme Court granted certiorari to resolve the conflict between the circuit courts regarding the meaning of the word willful *in the FLSA.]*

STEVENS, J.

. . . Because no limitations period was provided in the original 1938 enactment of the FLSA, civil actions brought thereunder were governed by state statutes of limitations. In the Portal-to-Portal Act of 1947, 61 Stat. 84, 29 U.S.C. §§ 216, 251–262, however, as part of its response to this Court's expansive reading of the FLSA, Congress enacted the 2-year statute to place a limit on employers' exposure to unanticipated contingent liabilities. As originally enacted, the 2-year limitations period drew no distinction between willful and nonwillful violations.

In 1965, the Secretary proposed a number of amendments to expand the coverage of the FLSA, including a proposal to replace the 2-year statute of limitations with a 3-year statute. The proposal was not adopted, but in 1966, for reasons that are not explained in the legislative history, Congress enacted the 3-year exception for willful violations.

The fact that Congress did not simply extend the limitations period to three years, but instead adopted a two-tiered statute of limitations, makes it obvious that Congress intended to draw a significant distinction between ordinary violations and willful violations. It is equally obvious to us that the *Jiffy June* standard of willfulness—a

standard that merely requires that an employer knew that the FLSA "was in the picture"— virtually obliterates any distinction between willful and nonwillful violations. As we said in *Trans World Airlines, Inc. v. Thurston, supra,* at 128, "it would be virtually impossible for an employer to show that he was unaware of the Act and its potential applicability." Under the *Jiffy June* standard, the normal 2-year statute of limitations would seem to apply only to ignorant employers, surely not a state of affairs intended by Congress.

In common usage the word "willful" is considered synonymous with such words as "voluntary," "deliberate," and "intentional." See Roget's International Thesaurus § 622.7, p. 479; § 653.9, p. 501 (4th ed. 1977). The word "willful" is widely used in the law, and, although it has not by any means been given a perfectly consistent interpretation, it is generally understood to refer to conduct that is not merely negligent. The standard of willfulness that was adopted in *Thurston*—that the employer either knew or showed reckless disregard for the matter of whether its conduct was prohibited by the statute—is surely a fair reading of the plain language of the Act. . . .

Ordinary violations of the FLSA are subject to the general 2-year statute of limitations. To obtain the benefit of the 3-year exception, the Secretary must prove that the employer's conduct was willful as that term is defined in both *Thurston* and this opinion.*

The judgment of the Court of Appeals is *Affirmed.*

---

*Of course, we express no view as to whether, under the proper standard, respondent's violation was "willful." That determination is for the District Court to make on remand from the Court of Appeals.

CASE QUESTIONS

1. Summarize the *Jiffy June* standard of "willfulness."
2. What did the Supreme Court find to be wrong with the *Jiffy June* standard of "willfulness"?
3. State the rule of the case.

Part Questions and Problems

1. Why does the law differ between public sector employers and private sector employers in their testing of employees for drug use?

2. List the four types of exceptions to the classic employment-at-will rule.

3. Under IRCA verification procedures, may an employer insist that a prospective employee with a foreign accent produce either a certificate of naturalization or an Alien Registration Card?

4. Local 1 of the Association of Western Pulp and Paper Workers was the bargaining representative for employees at Boise-Cascade Corporation's paper mill in St. Helen's, Oregon. Workers at the mill worked with heavy equipment, pressurized vessels, and hazardous chemicals. As a result, injuries were common.

   The labor agreement in effect between Local 1 and Boise-Cascade allowed the company unilaterally to introduce work rules that were consistent with the agreement. The union could challenge the reasonableness of a rule through grievance arbitration. In an effort to combat on-the-job injuries, Boise-Cascade unilaterally implemented a drug and alcohol testing program. The company announced that the testing program would apply to employees suspected by their supervisor of being under the influence of drugs or alcohol, employees who suffered on-the-job injuries that required more than first aid, and all employees involved in accidents at the mill. A positive result could result in discipline or discharge. In addition, refusal to submit to a test under the circumstances outlined above would result in discipline.

   The union objected to the drug and alcohol testing program as "illegal" and "unconstitutional." The union has asked you for advice on how to challenge the testing program.

   Should the union bring the issue to arbitration? The NLRB? The courts? Advise the union and explain. [Paper Workers v. Boise-Cascade Corp., 1 ITER Cases 1072 (D. Oregon 1986)]

5. Five years after Kathy Small began her employment with Spring Industries, the company distributed an employee handbook to all employees setting forth the company's termination procedure. It outlined a four-step disciplinary process consisting of a verbal reprimand, a written warning, a final written warning, and discharge. Small was discharged after only one written warning and sued the company for breach of contract.

   Small contended that the company was bound by the plain language of the handbook and that it would be unjust for an employer to issue a handbook and not be held to its contents. Moreover, she contended that if company policies were not worth the paper on which they were printed, then it would be better not to mislead employees by distributing them.

   The company contended that Small did not present evidence that the parties agreed the handbook was to become part of her employment contract and that if Small were to succeed, it would result in the removal of employee handbooks from the work force and stifle economic growth in the state.

   Did Small have an enforceable contract? Comment on whether handbooks will be removed from the workplace because of cases like this. What can an employer do to avoid liability under similar circumstances? [Small v. Spring Industries, Inc., Sup. Ct. S.C., 357 SE 2d 452 (1987)]

6. The Nebraska Public Power District (NPPD) operated the Cooper Nuclear Station and instituted a "fitness for duty" program in 1985 that required all employees who had access to protected areas at the Cooper plant to undergo random annual urine tests for drugs.

The employees challenged the testing program on the grounds that it was contrary to the Fourth Amendment's ban on unreasonable searches and seizures since there was no individualized suspicion. They also argued that through tampering or mistakes in the testing process, employees could be wrongly accused of drug use.

The NPPD stated that its testing program was "reasonable" and that its "chain of custody" rules and confirmatory tests protected employees from mistakes in the test results.

Decide. [Rushton v. Nebraska Public Power District, 653 F. Supp. 1513 (D. Neb. 1987)]

7. Under an oral contract of indefinite duration, Marlene S. Gates worked as a cashier for Life of Montana Insurance Company for over three years prior to October 19, 1979, when she was called in to meet with her supervisor, Roger Syverson. Without any prior warnings, she was given the option of resigning or being fired. She testified that while in a distraught condition and under duress, she signed a letter of resignation that was handed to her by Syverson. Gates stated that she signed the letter of resignation because she thought it would be better for her record and because Syverson told her he would give her a letter of recommendation so that she could be reemployed. Gates went home and discussed the situation with her husband who advised her to retrieve the letter of resignation and inform her supervisor that she was not resigning. Appellant stated that she immediately called Mr. Syverson and demanded the letter be returned and that he promised to do so. Syverson testified that she only requested a photocopy of the letter. Syverson testified that he offered to give Gates a letter of recommendation if she resigned. However, he testified that he only planned to give her a letter that would state that appellant was employed by Life of Montana Insurance Company; he never intended to provide appellant with a favorable letter of recommendation. There was evidence from which a jury might infer that Gates understood she was to receive a favorable letter of recommendation and that Syverson allowed her to resign on this basis. The company contended that Gates was discharged for incompetency and insubordination. The evidence indicated that a resignation rather than a discharge may protect an employer from immediately becoming liable for unemployment compensation benefits in Montana and by obtaining a letter of resignation an employer may be insulating itself against a claim for wrongful discharge.

Montana law allows for the litigation of the question of whether there was a breach of an implied convenant of fair dealing where an employee is discharged without warning and an opportunity for a hearing. Montana law holds that a breach of the covenant of fair dealing is imposed by operation of law; therefore, its breach should find a remedy in tort for which punitive damages can be recovered if the defendant's conduct is sufficiently culpable, that is, if there was fraud, oppression, or malice.

The company contended that it was a legislative rather than a judicial function to create a cause of action that would apply a just-cause standard for the discharge of at-will employees and that, in any event, the company should not be liable for punitive damages if new legal rights are granted Gates, which rights could not have been known by the company at the time it terminated her.

Did the company breach its implied covenant of fair dealing to Gates when it terminated her? Should the company be held liable for punitive damages? [Gates v. Life of Montana Insurance Co., 668 P.2d 213 Mont., DLR No. 162 (1983)]

8. Knifepersons performed butchering operations at the King Packing Co. Various knives and three types of electric saws were used in the butchering operation. Some of the knives were furnished by the employees. The saws and the more expensive knives were furnished by the employer. All the knives, as well as the saws, had to be razor-sharp for the proper

performance of work. A dull knife slowed down production, which was conducted on an assembly line basis; affected the appearance of the meat, as well as the quality of the hides; and caused waste and accidents. The knifepersons were required to sharpen their own knives outside the scheduled shift of eight hours, and they were not paid for the time so spent.

The Secretary of Labor contended that the time spent sharpening knives was compensable working time under the FLSA. King Packing Co. contended that such is noncompensable preliminary activity under the Portal-to-Portal Act. Decide. [Mitchell v. King Packing Co., 350 U.S. 260 (1956)]

9. Prior to 1988 Marguerite Cook and other former employees of Rite Aid of Maryland Inc. were directed to submit to polygraph examinations regarding inventory shortages or "shrinkage" at certain Rite Aid stores. Cook and others refused to take the examination. After her refusal Cook had her hours cut, her store keys taken away, and was transferred to a distant store. When Cook refused to comply with the transfer and schedule changes, she was terminated for refusing the directives of management. The state polygraph statute prohibits employers from requiring individuals or employees to take polygraph examinations and authorizes the attorney general to bring suit on behalf of "any aggrieved applicant for employment."

Cook brought a common-law tort action for "discharge contrary to public policy" against Rite Aid, seeking compensatory and punitive damages from Rite Aid. Cook contended that Rite Aid improperly challenged her trustworthiness by ordering her to take a polygraph and then aggravated the injury by attempting to force her to resign by giving her undesirable work hours at an undesirable work location. She stated that when she refused the new assignment, she was wrongfully discharged.

Rite Aid contended that the common-law action must be dismissed because the polygraph statute includes a civil remedy, and such is Cook's exclusive remedy. Rite Aid contended that while the polygraph statute prohibits the discharge of employees who refuse to take a polygraph test, it did not prohibit a transfer or a reduction in hours for an employee who refused to take such an examination. Rite Aid contended that it terminated Cook because she failed to follow a proper directive of management, which was its right, and that chaos would result if an employer were not allowed to terminate insubordinate employees.

Was Cook precluded from bringing a wrongful discharge case on her own rather than seeking a remedy under the polygraph statute? Will the EPPA of 1988 preclude similar public policy wrongful discharge actions? Did the employer have a right to terminate Cook for failure to comply with the assignment and hours given to her? [Moniodis v. Cook, 64 Md. App. 1 (1985)]

Appendixes

Uniform Guidelines on Employee Selection Procedures (1978)[1]

To meet the need for a uniform set of principles concerning the use of tests and other selection procedures, the EEOC, the Civil Service Commission, the Department of Labor, and the Department of Justice jointly adopted in 1978 the Uniform Guidelines on Employee Selection Procedures (called the Uniform Guidelines).[2] These guidelines are designed to provide a framework for the proper, nondiscriminatory use of tests and other selection procedures. The Uniform Guidelines endorse the standard of the best-qualified candidate for the job.[3]

The Uniform Guidelines are not administrative "regulations" promulgated by Congress. However, the Second Circuit Court of Appeals views the weight to be accorded the guidelines as follows:

> While courts are not bound by the EEOC Guidelines, the Supreme Court (in *Griggs*) has declared that the guidelines should be shown "great deference."[4]

---

[1] Through September 28, 1984.
[2] 29 CFR 1607 *et seq.* (1979).
[3] 29 CFR 1607.2(c) (1979).
[4] Bushey v. N.Y. Civ. Serv. Comm., 733 F.2d 220 at 225 (2d Cir. 1984).

COMPREHENSIVE TABLE OF CONTENTS

(2) Problem and Setting

(3) Job Analysis or Review of Job Information

(4) Job Titles and Codes

(5) Criterion Measures

(6) Sample Description

(7) Description of Selection Procedure

(8) Techniques and Results

(9) Alternative Procedures Investigated

(10) Uses and Applications

(11) Source Data

(12) Contact Person

(13) Accuracy and Completeness

C. Content Validity Studies

(1) User(s), Location(s), and Date(s) of Study

(2) Problem and Setting

(3) Job Analysis—Content of the Job

(4) Selection Procedure and its Content

(5) Relationship Between Selection Procedure and the Job

(6) Alternative Procedures Investigated

(7) Uses and Applications

(8) Contact Person

(9) Accuracy and Completeness

D. Construct Validity Studies

(1) User(s), Location(s), and Date(s) of Study

(2) Problem and Setting

(3) Construct Definition

(4) Job Analysis

(5) Job Titles and Codes

(6) Selection Procedure

(7) Relationship to Job Performance

(8) Alternative Procedures Investigated

(9) Uses and Applications

(10) Accuracy and Completeness

(11) Source Data

(12) Contact Person

E. Evidence of Validity from Other Studies

(1) Evidence from Criterion-Related Validity Studies

(a) Job Information

(b) Relevance of Criteria

(c) Other Variables

(d) Use of the Selection Procedure

(e) Bibliography

(2) Evidence from Content Validity Studies

(3) Evidence from Construct Validity Studies

F. Evidence of Validity from Cooperative Studies

G. Selection for Higher Level Jobs

H. Interim Use of Selection Procedures

Definitions

1607.16. Definitions

Appendix

1607.17. Policy Statement on Affirmative Action (see Section 13B)

1607.18. Citations

AUTHORITY: Secs. 709 and 713, Civil Rights Act of 1964 (78 Stat. 265) as amended by the Equal Employment Opportunity Act of 1972 (Pub. L. 92–261); 42 U.S.C. 2000e-8, 2000e-12.

SOURCE: 43 FR 38295 and 43 FR 38312, Aug. 25, 1978, unless otherwise noted.

GENERAL PRINCIPLES

§ 1607.1 Statement of purpose.

A. *Need for uniformity—Issuing agencies.* The Federal government's need for a uniform set of principles on the question of the use of tests and other selection procedures has long been recognized. The Equal Employment Opportunity Commission, the Civil Service Commission, the Department of Labor, and the Department of Justice jointly have adopted these uniform guidelines to meet that need, and to apply the same principles to the Federal Government as are applied to other employers.

B. *Purpose of guidelines.* These guidelines incorporate a single set of principles which are designed to assist employers, labor organizations, employment agencies, and licensing and certification boards to comply with requirements of Federal law prohibiting employment practices which discriminate on grounds of race, color, religion, sex, and national origin. They are designed to provide a framework for determining the proper use of tests and other selection procedures. These guidelines do not require a user to conduct validity studies of selection procedures where no adverse impact results. However, all users are encouraged to use selection procedures which are valid, especially users operating under merit principles.

C. *Relation to prior guidelines.* These guidelines are based upon and supersede previously issued guidelines on employee selection procedures. These guidelines have been built upon court decisions, the previously issued guidelines of the agencies, and the practical experience of the agencies, as well as the standards of the psychological profession. These guidelines are intended to be consistent with existing law.

§ 1607.2 Scope.

A. *Application of guidelines.* These guidelines will be applied by the Equal Employment Opportunity Commission in the enforcement of Title VII of the

Civil Rights Act of 1964, as amended by the Equal Employment Opportunity Act of 1972 (hereinafter "Title VII"), by the Department of Labor, and the contract compliance agencies until the transfer of authority contemplated by the President's Reorganization Plan No. 1 of 1978, in the administration and enforcement of Executive Order 11246, as amended by Executive Order 11375 (hereinafter "Executive Order 11246"); by the Civil Service Commission and other Federal agencies subject to section 717 of Title VII; by the Civil Service Commission in exercising its responsibilities toward State and local governments under section 208(b)(1) of the Intergovernmental-Personnel Act; by the Department of Justice in exercising its responsibilities under Federal law; by the Office of Revenue Sharing of the Department of the Treasury under the State and Local Fiscal Assistance Act of 1972, as amended; and by any other Federal agency which adopts them.

B. *Employment decisions.* These guidelines apply to tests and other selection procedures which are used as a basis for any employment decision. Employment decisions include but are not limited to hiring, promotion, demotion, membership (for example, in a labor organization), referral, retention, and licensing and certification, to the extent that licensing and certification may be covered by Federal equal employment opportunity law. Other selection decisions, such as selection for training or transfer, may also be considered employment decisions if they lead to any of the decisions listed above.

C. *Selection procedures.* These guidelines apply only to selection procedures which are used as a basis for making employment decisions. For example, the use of recruiting procedures designed to attract members of a particular race, sex, or ethnic group, which were previously denied employment opportunities or which are currently underutilized, may be necessary to bring an employer into compliance with Federal law, and is frequently an essential element of any effective affirmative action program; but recruitment practices are not considered by these guidelines to be selection procedures. Similarly, these guidelines do not pertain to the question of the lawfulness of a seniority system within the meaning of section 703(h), Executive Order 11246 or other provisions of Federal law or regulation, except to the extent that such systems utilize selection procedures to determine qualifications or abilities to perform the job. Nothing in these guidelines is intended or should be interpreted as discouraging the use of a selection procedure for the purpose of determining qualifications or for the purpose of selection on the basis of relative qualifications, if the selection procedures had been validated in accord with these guidelines for each such purpose for which it is to be used.

D. *Limitations.* These guidelines apply only to persons subject to Title VII, Executive Order 11246, or other equal employment opportunity requirements of Federal law. These guidelines do not apply to responsibilities under the Age Discrimination in Employment Act of 1967, as amended, not to discriminate on the basis of age, or under sections 501, 503, and 504 of the Rehabilitation Act of 1973, not to discriminate on the basis of handicap.

E. *Indian preference not affected.* These guidelines do not restrict any obligation imposed or right granted by Federal law to users to extend a preference in employment to Indians living on or near an Indian reservation in connection with employment opportunities on or near an Indian reservation.

§ 1607.3 Discrimination defined: Relationship between use of selection procedures and discrimination.

A. *Procedure having adverse impact constitutes discrimination unless justified.* The use of any selection procedure which has an adverse impact on the hiring, promotion, or other employment or membership opportunities of members of any race, sex, or ethnic group will be considered to be discriminatory and inconsistent with these guidelines, unless the procedure has been validated in accordance with these guidelines, or the provisions of section 6 below are satisfied.

B. *Consideration of suitable alternative selection procedures.* Where two or more selection procedures are available which serve the user's legitimate interest in efficient and trustworthy workmanship, and which are substantially equally valid for a given purpose, the user should use the procedure which has been demonstrated to have the lesser adverse impact. Accordingly, whenever a validity study is called for by these guidelines, the user should include, as a part of the validity study, an investigation of suitable alternative selection procedures and suitable alternative methods of using the selection procedure which have as little adverse impact as possible, to determine the appropriateness of using or validating them in accord with these guidelines. If a user has made a reasonable effort to become aware of such alternative procedures and validity has been demonstrated in accord with these guidelines, the use of the test or other selection procedure may continue until such time as it should reasonably be reviewed for currency. Whenever the user is shown an alternative selection procedure with evidence of less adverse impact and substantial evidence of validity for the same job in similar circumstances, the user should investigate it to determine the appropriateness of using or validating it in accord with these guidelines. This subsection is not intended to preclude the combination of procedures into a significantly more valid procedure, if the use of such a combination has been shown to be in compliance with the guidelines.

§ 1607.4 Information on impact.

A. *Records concerning impact.* Each user should maintain and have available for inspection records or other information which will disclose the impact which its tests and other selection procedures have upon employment opportunities of persons by identifiable race, sex, or ethnic group as set forth in subparagraph B below in order to determine compliance with these guidelines. Where there are large numbers of applicants and procedures are administered frequently, such information may be retained on a sample basis, provided that the sample is appropriate in terms of the applicant population and adequate in size.

B. *Applicable race, sex, and ethnic groups for record keeping.* The records called for by this section are to be maintained by sex, and the following races and ethnic groups: Blacks (Negroes), American Indians (including Alaskan Natives), Asians (including Pacific Islanders), Hispanic (including persons of Mexican, Puerto Rican, Cuban, Central or South American, or other Spanish origin or culture regardless of race), whites (Caucasians) other than Hispanic, and totals. The race, sex, and ethnic classifications called for by this section are consistent with the Equal Employment Opportunity Standard Form 100, Employer Information Report EEO-1 series of reports. The user should adopt safeguards to insure that the records required by this paragraph are used for appropriate purposes such as determining adverse impact, or (where required) for developing and monitoring affirmative action programs, and that such records are not used improperly. See sections 4E and 17(4), below.

C. *Evaluation of selection rates. The "bottom line."* If the information called for by sections 4A and B above shows that the total selection process for a job has an adverse impact, the individual components of the selection process should be evaluated for adverse impact. If this information shows that the total selection process does not have an adverse impact, the Federal enforcement agencies, in the exercise of their administrative and prosecutorial discretion, in usual circumstances, will not expect a user to evaluate the individual components for adverse impact, or to validate such individual components, and will not take enforcement action based upon adverse impact of any component of that process, including the separate parts of a multipart selection procedure or any separate procedure that is used as an alternative method of selection. However, in the following circumstances the Federal enforcement agencies will expect a user to evaluate the individual components for adverse impact and may, where appropriate, take enforcement action with respect to the individual components: (1) Where the selection procedure is a significant factor in the continuation of patterns of assignments of incumbent employees caused by prior discriminatory employment practices, (2) where the weight of court decisions or administrative interpretations hold that a specific procedure (such as height or weight requirements or no-arrest records) is not job related in the same or similar circumstances. In unusual circumstances, other than those listed in (1) or (2) above, the Federal enforcement agencies may request a user to evaluate the individual components for adverse impact and may, where appropriate, take enforcement action with respect to the individual component.

D. *Adverse impact and the "four-fifths rule."* A selection rate for any race, sex, or ethnic group which is less than four-fifths ($\frac{4}{5}$) (or eighty percent) of the rate for the group with the highest rate will generally be regarded by the Federal enforcement agencies as evidence of adverse impact, while a greater than four-fifths rate will generally not be regarded by Federal enforcement agencies as evidence of adverse impact. Smaller differences in selection rate may nevertheless constitute adverse impact, where they are significant in both statistical and practical terms or where a user's actions have discouraged applicants disproportionately on grounds of race, sex, or ethnic group. Greater differences in selection rate may not constitute adverse impact where the differences are based on small numbers and are not statistically significant, or where special recruiting or other programs cause the pool of minority or female candidates to be atypical of the normal pool of applicants from that group. Where the user's evidence concerning the impact of a selection procedure indicates adverse impact but is based upon numbers which are too small to be reliable, evidence concerning the impact of the procedure over a longer period of time and/or evidence concerning the impact which the selection procedure had when used in the same manner in similar circumstances elsewhere may be considered in determining adverse impact. Where the user has not maintained data on adverse impact as required by the documentation section of applicable guidelines, the Federal enforcement agencies may draw an inference of adverse impact of the selection process from the failure of the user to maintain such data, if the user has an underutilization of a group in the job category, as compared to the group's representation in the relevant labor market or, in the case of jobs filled from within, the applicable work force.

E. *Consideration of user's equal employment opportunity posture*. In carrying out their obligations, the Federal enforcement agencies will consider the general posture of the user with respect to equal employment opportunity for the job or group of jobs in question. Where a user has adopted an affirmative action program, the Federal enforcement agencies will consider the provisions of that program, including the goals and timetables which the user has adopted and the progress which the user has made in carrying out that program and in meeting the goals and timetables. While such affirmative action programs may in design and execution be race, color, sex, or ethnic conscious, selection procedures under such programs should be based upon the ability or relative ability to do the work.

(Approved by the Office of Management and Budget under control number 3046-0017)
(Pub. L. No. 96–511, 94 Stat. 2812 (44 U.S.C. 3501 et seq.))
[43 FR 38295, 38312, Aug. 25, 1978, as amended at 46 FR 63268, Dec. 31, 1981]

§ 1607.5 General standards for validity studies.

A. *Acceptable types of validity studies*. For the purposes of satisfying these guidelines, users may rely upon criterion-related validity studies, content validity studies or construct validity studies, in accordance with the standards set forth in the technical standards of these guidelines, section 14 below. New strategies for showing the validity of selection procedures will be evaluated as they become accepted by the psychological profession.

B. *Criterion-related, content, and construct validity*. Evidence of the validity of a test or other selection procedure by a criterion-related validity study should consist of empirical data demonstrating that the selection procedure is predictive of or significantly correlated with important elements of job performance. See section 14B below. Evidence of the validity of a test or other selection procedure by a content validity study should consist of data showing that the content of the selection procedure is representative of important aspects of performance on the job for which the candidates are to be evaluated. See 14C below. Evidence of the validity of a test or other selection procedure through a construct validity study should consist of data showing that the procedure measures the degree to which candidates have identifiable characteristics which have been determined to be important in successful performance in the job for which the candidates are to be evaluated. See section 14D below.

C. *Guidelines are consistent with professional standards*. The provisions of these guidelines are intended to be consistent with generally accepted professional standards for evaluating standardized tests and other selection procedures, such as those described in the Standards for Educational and Psychological Tests prepared by a joint committee of the American Psychological Association, the American Educational Research Association, and the National Council on Measurement in Education (American Psychological Association, Washington, D.C., 1974) (hereinafter "A.P.A. Standards") and standard textbooks and journals in the field of personnel selection.

D. *Need for documentation of validity*. For any selection procedure which is part of a selection process which has an adverse impact and which selection procedure has an adverse impact, each user should maintain and have available such documentation as is described in section 15 below.

E. *Accuracy and standardization*. Validity studies should be carried out under conditions which assure insofar as possible the adequacy and accuracy of the research and the report. Selection procedures should be administered and scored under standardized conditions.

F. *Caution against selection on basis of knowledges, skills, or ability learned in brief orientation period*. In general, users should avoid making employment decisions on the basis of measures of knowledges, skills, or abilities which are normally learned in a brief orientation period, and which have an adverse impact.

G. *Method of use of selection procedures*. The evidence of both the validity and utility of a selection procedure should support the method the user chooses for operational use of the procedure, if that method of use has a greater adverse impact than another method of use. Evidence which may be sufficient to support the use of a selection procedure on a pass/fail (screening) basis may be insufficient to support the use of the same procedure on a ranking basis under these guidelines. Thus, if a user decides to use a selection procedure on a ranking basis, and that method of use has a greater adverse impact than use on an appropriate pass/fail basis (see section 5H below), the user should have sufficient evidence of validity and utility to support the use on a ranking basis. See sections 3B, 14B(5) and (6), and 14C(8) and (9).

H. *Cutoff scores.* Where cutoff scores are used, they should normally be set so as to be reasonable and consistent with normal expectations of acceptable proficiency within the work force. Where applicants are ranked on the basis of properly validated selection procedures and those applicants scoring below a higher cutoff score than appropriate in light of such expectations have little or no chance of being selected for employment, the higher cutoff score may be appropriate, but the degree of adverse impact should be considered.

I. *Use of selection procedures for higher level jobs.* If job progression structures are so established that employees will probably, within a reasonable period of time and in a majority of cases, progress to a higher level, it may be considered that the applicants are being evaluated for a job or jobs at the higher level. However, where job progression is not so nearly automatic, or the time span is such that higher level jobs or employees' potential may be expected to change in significant ways, it should be considered that applicants are being evaluated for a job at or near the entry level. A "reasonable period of time" will vary for different jobs and employment situations but will seldom be more than 5 years. Use of selection procedures to evaluate applicants for a higher level job would not be appropriate:

(1) If the majority of those remaining employed do not progress to the higher level job;

(2) If there is a reason to doubt that the higher level job will continue to require essentially similar skills during the progression period; or

(3) If the selection procedures measure knowledges, skills, or abilities required for advancement which would be expected to develop principally from the training or experience on the job.

J. *Interim use of selection procedures.* Users may continue the use of a selection procedure which is not at the moment fully supported by the required evidence of validity, provided: (1) The user has available substantial evidence of validity, and (2) the user has in progress, when technically feasible, a study which is designed to produce the additional evidence required

by these guidelines within a reasonable time. If such a study is not technically feasible, see section 6B. If the study does not demonstrate validity, this provision of these guidelines for interim use shall not constitute a defense in any action, nor shall it relieve the user of any obligations arising under Federal law.

K. *Review of validity studies for currency.* Whenever validity has been shown in accord with these guidelines for the use of a particular selection procedure for a job or group of jobs, additional studies need not be performed until such time as the validity study is subject to review as provided in section 3B above. There are no absolutes in the area of determining the currency of a validity study. All circumstances concerning the study, including the validation strategy used, and changes in the relevant labor market and the job should be considered in the determination of when a validity study is outdated.

§ 1607.6 **Use of selection procedures which have not been validated.**

A. *Use of alternate selection procedures to eliminate adverse impact.* A user may choose to utilize alternative selection procedures in order to eliminate adverse impact or as part of an affirmative action program. See section 13 below. Such alternative procedures should eliminate the adverse impact in the total selection process, should be lawful and should be as job related as possible.

B. *Where validity studies cannot or need not be performed.* There are circumstances in which a user cannot or need not utilize the validation techniques contemplated by these guidelines. In such circumstances, the user should utilize selection procedures which are as job related as possible and which will minimize or eliminate adverse impact, as set forth below.

(1) *Where informal or unscored procedures are used.* When an informal or unscored selection procedure which has an adverse impact is utilized, the user should eliminate the adverse impact, or modify the procedure to one which is a formal, scored or quantified measure or combination of measures and then validate the procedure in accord with these guidelines, or otherwise justify continued use of the procedure in accord with Federal law.

(2) *Where formal and scored procedures are used.* When a formal and scored selection procedure is used which has an adverse impact, the validation techniques contemplated by these guidelines usually should be

followed if technically feasible. Where the user cannot or need not follow the validation techniques anticipated by these guidelines, the user should either modify the procedure to eliminate adverse impact or otherwise justify continued use of the procedure in accord with Federal law.

§ 1607.7 Use of other validity studies.

A. *Validity studies not conducted by the user.* Users may, under certain circumstances, support the use of selection procedures by validity studies conducted by other users or conducted by test publishers or distributors and described in test manuals. While publishers of selection procedures have a professional obligation to provide evidence of validity which meets generally accepted professional standards (see section 5C above), users are cautioned that they are responsible for compliance with these guidelines. Accordingly, users seeking to obtain selection procedures from publishers and distributors should be careful to determine that, in the event the user becomes subject to the validity requirements of these guidelines, the necessary information to support validity has been determined and will be made available to the user.

B. *Use of criterion-related validity evidence from other sources.* Criterion-related validity studies conducted by one test user, or described in test manuals and the professional literature, will be considered acceptable for use by another user when the following requirements are met:

(1) *Validity evidence.* Evidence from the available studies meeting the standards of section 14B below clearly demonstrates that the selection procedure is valid;

(2) *Job similarity.* The incumbents in the user's job and the incumbents in the job or group of jobs on which the validity study was conducted perform substantially the same major work behaviors, as shown by appropriate job analyses both on the job or group of jobs on which the validity study was performed and on the job for which the selection procedure is to be used; and

(3) *Fairness evidence.* The studies include a study of test fairness for each race, sex, and ethnic group which constitutes a significant factor in the borrowing user's relevant labor market for the job or jobs in question. If the studies under consideration satisfy (1) and (2) above but do not contain an investigation of test fairness, and it is not technically feasible for the borrowing user to conduct an internal study of test fairness, the borrowing user may utilize the study until

studies conducted elsewhere meeting the requirements of these guidelines show test unfairness, or until such time as it becomes technically feasible to conduct an internal study of test fairness and the results of that study can be acted upon. Users obtaining selection procedures from publishers should consider, as one factor in the decision to purchase a particular selection procedure, the availability of evidence concerning test fairness.

C. *Validity evidence from multiunit study.* If validity evidence from a study covering more than one unit within an organization satisfies the requirements of section 14B below, evidence of validity specific to each unit will not be required unless there are variables which are likely to affect validity significantly.

D. *Other significant variables.* If there are variables in the other studies which are likely to affect validity significantly, the user may not rely upon such studies, but will be expected either to conduct an internal validity study or to comply with section 6 above.

§ 1607.8 Cooperative studies.

A. *Encouragement of cooperative studies.* The agencies issuing these guidelines encourage employers, labor organizations, and employment agencies to cooperate in research, development, search for lawful alternatives, and validity studies in order to achieve procedures which are consistent with these guidelines.

B. *Standards for use of cooperative studies.* If validity evidence from a cooperative study satisfies the requirements of section 14 below, evidence of validity specific to each user will not be required unless there are variables in the user's situation which are likely to affect validity significantly.

§ 1607.9 No assumption of validity.

A. *Unacceptable substitutes for evidence of validity.* Under no circumstances will the general reputation of a test or other selection procedure, its author or its publisher, or casual reports of its validity be accepted in lieu of evidence of validity. Specifically ruled out are: assumptions of validity based on a procedure's name or descriptive labels; all forms of promotional literature; data bearing on the frequency of a procedure's usage; testimonial statements and credentials of sellers, users, or consultants; and other nonempirical or anecdotal accounts of selection practices or selection outcomes.

B. *Encouragement of professional supervision.* Professional supervision of selection activities is encouraged but is not a substitute for documented evidence of validity. The enforcement agencies will take into account the fact that a thorough job analysis was conducted and that careful development and use of a selection procedure in accordance with professional standards enhance the probability that the selection procedure is valid for the job.

§ 1607.10 Employment agencies and employment services.

A. *Where selection procedures are devised by agency.* An employment agency, including private employment agencies and State employment agencies, which agrees to a request by an employer or labor organization to devise and utilize a selection procedure should follow the standards in these guidelines for determining adverse impact. If adverse impact exists the agency should comply with these guidelines. An employment agency is not relieved of its obligation herein because the user did not request such validation or has requested the use of some lesser standard of validation than is provided in these guidelines. The use of an employment agency does not relieve an employer or labor organization or other user of its responsibilities under Federal law to provide equal employment opportunity or its obligations as a user under these guidelines.

B. *Where selection procedures are devised elsewhere.* Where an employment agency or service is requested to administer a selection procedure which has been devised elsewhere and to make referrals pursuant to the results, the employment agency or service should maintain and have available evidence of the impact of the selection and referral procedures which it administers. If adverse impact results the agency or service should comply with these guidelines. If the agency or service seeks to comply with these guidelines by reliance upon validity studies or other data in the possession of the employer, it should obtain and have available such information.

§ 1607.11 Disparate treatment.

The principles of disparate or unequal treatment must be distinguished from the concepts of validation. A selection procedure—even though validated against job performance in accordance with these guidelines—cannot be imposed upon members of a race or sex, or ethnic group where other employees, applicants, or members have not been subjected to that standard. Disparate treatment occurs where members of a race, sex, or ethnic group have been denied the same employment, promotion, membership, or other employment opportunities as have been available to other employees or applicants. Those employees or applicants who have been denied equal treatment, because of prior discriminatory practices or policies, must at least be afforded the same opportunities as had existed for other employees or applicants during the period of discrimination. Thus, the persons who were in the class of persons discriminated against during the period the user followed the discriminatory practices should be allowed the opportunity to qualify under less stringent selection procedures previously followed, unless the user demonstrates that the increased standards are required by business necessity. This section does not prohibit a user who has not previously followed merit standards from adopting merit standards which are in compliance with these guidelines; nor does it preclude a user who has previously used invalid or unvalidated selection procedures from developing and using procedures which are in accord with these guidelines.

§ 1607.12 Retesting of applicants.

Users should provide a reasonable opportunity for retesting and reconsideration. Where examinations are administered periodically with public notice, such reasonable opportunity exists, unless persons who have previously been tested are precluded from retesting. The user may however take reasonable steps to preserve the security of its procedures.

§ 1607.13 Affirmative action.

A. *Affirmative action obligations.* The use of selection procedures which have been validated pursuant to these guidelines does not relieve users of any obligations they may have to undertake affirmative action to assure equal employment opportunity. Nothing in these guidelines is intended to preclude the use of lawful selection procedures which assist in remedying the effects of prior discriminatory practices, or the achievement of affirmative action objectives.

B. *Encouragement of voluntary affirmative action programs.* These guidelines are also intended to encourage the adoption and implementation of voluntary affirmative action programs by users who have no obligation under Federal law to adopt them; but are not intended to impose any new obligations in that regard. The agencies issuing and endorsing these guidelines endorse for all private employers and reaffirm for all governmental employers the Equal Employment Opportunity Coordinating Council's "Policy Statement on Affirmative Action Programs for State and Local Government Agencies" (41 FR 38814, September 13,

1976). That policy statement is attached hereto as appendix, section 17.

TECHNICAL STANDARDS

§ 1607.14 Technical standards for validity studies.

The following minimum standards, as applicable, should be met in conducting a validity study. Nothing in these guidelines is intended to preclude the development and use of other professionally acceptable techniques with respect to validation of selection procedures. Where it is not technically feasible for a user to conduct a validity study, the user has the obligation otherwise to comply with these guidelines. See section 6 and 7 above.

A. *Validity studies should be based on review of information about the job.* Any validity study should be based upon a review of information about the job for which the selection procedure is to be used. The review should include a job analysis except as provided in section 14B(3) below with respect to criterion-related validity. Any method of job analysis may be used if it provides the information required for the specific validation strategy used.

B. *Technical standards for criterion-related validity studies.* (1) *Technical feasibility.* Users choosing to validate a selection procedure by a criterion-related validity strategy should determine whether it is technically feasible (as defined in section 16) to conduct such a study in the particular employment context. The determination of the number of persons necessary to permit the conduct of a meaningful criterion-related study should be made by the user on the basis of all relevant information concerning the selection procedure, the potential sample and the employment situation. Where appropriate, jobs with substantially the same major work behaviors may be grouped together for validity studies, in order to obtain an adequate sample. These guidelines do not require a user to hire or promote persons for the purpose of making it possible to conduct a criterion-related study.

(2) *Analysis of the job.* There should be a review of job information to determine the measures of work behavior(s) or performance that are relevant to the job or group of jobs in question. These measures or criteria are relevant to the extent that they represent critical or important job duties, work behaviors or work outcomes as developed from the review of job information. The possibility of bias should be considered both in selection of the criterion measures and their application. In

view of the possibility of bias in subjective evaluations, supervisory rating techniques and instructions to raters should be carefully developed. All criterion measures and the methods for gathering data need to be examined for freedom from factors which would unfairly alter scores of members of any group. The relevance of criteria and their freedom from bias are of particular concern when there are significant differences in measures of job performance for different groups.

(3) *Criterion measures.* Proper safeguards should be taken to insure that scores on selection procedures do not enter into any judgments of employee adequacy that are to be used as criterion measures. Whatever criteria are used should represent important or critical work behavior(s) or work outcomes. Certain criteria may be used without a full job analysis if the user can show the importance of the criteria to the particular employment context. These criteria include but are not limited to production rate, error rate, tardiness, absenteeism, and length of service. A standardized rating of overall work performance may be used where a study of the job shows that it is an appropriate criterion. Where performance in training is used as a criterion, success in training should be properly measured and the relevance of the training should be shown either through a comparison of the content of the training program with the critical or important work behavior(s) of the job(s), or through a demonstration of the relationship between measures of performance in training and measures of job performance. Measures of relative success in training include but are not limited to instructor evaluations, performance samples, or tests. Criterion measures consisting of paper and pencil tests will be closely reviewed for job relevance.

(4) *Representativeness of the sample.* Whether the study is predictive or concurrent, the sample subjects should insofar as feasible be representative of the candidates normally available in the relevant labor market for the job or group of jobs in question, and should insofar as feasible include the races, sexes, and ethnic groups normally available in the relevant job market. In determining the representativeness of the sample in a concurrent validity study, the user should take into account the extent to which the specific knowledges or skills which are the primary focus of the test are those which employees learn on the job. Where samples are combined or compared, attention should be given to see that such samples are comparable in terms of the actual job they perform, the length of time on the job where time on the job is likely to affect performance,

and other relevant factors likely to affect validity differences; or that these factors are included in the design of the study and their effects identified.

(5) *Statistical relationships.* The degree of relationship between selection procedure scores and criterion measures should be examined and computed, using professionally acceptable statistical procedures. Generally, a selection procedure is considered related to the criterion, for the purposes of these guidelines, when the relationship between performance on the procedure and performance on the criterion measure is statistically significant at the 0.05 level of significance, which means that it is sufficiently high as to have a probability of no more than one (1) in twenty (20) to have occurred by chance. Absence of a statistically significant relationship between a selection procedure and job performance should not necessarily discourage other investigations of the validity of that selection procedure.

(6) *Operational use of selection procedures.* Users should evaluate each selection procedure to assure that it is appropriate for operational use, including establishment of cutoff scores or rank ordering. Generally, if other factors remain the same, the greater the magnitude of the relationship (e.g., correlation coefficient) between performance on a selection procedure and one or more criteria of performance on the job, and the greater the importance and number of aspects of job performance covered by the criteria, the more likely it is that the procedure will be appropriate for use. Reliance upon a selection procedure which is significantly related to a criterion measure, but which is based upon a study involving a large number of subjects and has a low correlation coefficient will be subject to close review if it has a large adverse impact. Sole reliance upon a single selection instrument which is related to only one of many job duties or aspects of job performance will also be subject to close review. The appropriateness of a selection procedure is best evaluated in each particular situation and there are no minimum correlation coefficients applicable to all employment situations. In determining whether a selection procedure is appropriate for operational use the following considerations should also be taken into account: The degree of adverse impact of the procedure, the availability of other selection procedures of greater or substantially equal validity.

(7) *Overstatement of validity findings.* Users should avoid reliance upon techniques which tend to overestimate validity findings as a result of capitalization on chance unless an appropriate safeguard is taken. Reliance upon a few selection procedures or criteria of successful job performance when many selection procedures or criteria of performance have been studied, or the use of optimal statistical weights for selection procedures computed in one sample are techniques which tend to inflate validity estimates as a result of change. Use of a large sample is one safeguard; cross-validation is another.

(8) *Fairness.* This section generally calls for studies of unfairness where technically feasible. The concept of fairness or unfairness of selection procedures is a developing concept. In addition, fairness studies generally require substantial numbers of employees in the job or group of jobs being studied. For these reasons, the Federal enforcement agencies recognize that the obligation to conduct studies of fairness imposed by the guidelines generally will be upon users or groups of users with a large number of persons in a job class, or test developers; and that small users utilizing their own selection procedures will generally not be obligated to conduct such studies because it will be technically infeasible for them to do so.

(a) *Unfairness defined.* When members of one race, sex, or ethnic group characteristically obtain lower scores on a selection procedure than members of another group, and the difference in scores are not reflected in differences in a measure of job performance, use of the selection procedure may unfairly deny opportunities to members of the group that obtains the lower scores.

(b) *Investigation of fairness.* Where a selection procedure results in an adverse impact on a race, sex, or ethnic group identified in accordance with the classifications set forth in section 4 above and that group is a significant factor in the relevant labor market, the user generally should investigate the possible existence of unfairness for that group if it is technically feasible to do so. The greater the severity of the adverse impact on a group, the greater the need to investigate the possible existence of unfairness. Where the weight of evidence from other studies shows that the selection procedure predicts fairly for the group in question and for the same or similar jobs, such evidence may be relied on in connection with the selection procedure at issue.

(c) *General considerations in fairness investigations.* Users conducting a study of fairness should review the A.P.A. Standards regarding investigation of possible bias in testing. An investigation of fairness of a selection procedure depends on both evidence of validity and the manner in which the selection procedure is to be used in a particular employment context. Fairness of a selection procedure cannot necessarily be specified in advance without investigating these factors. Investigation of fairness of a selection procedure in samples where the range of scores on selection procedures or criterion measures is severely restricted for any subgroup sample (as compared to other subgroup samples) may produce misleading evidence of unfairness. That factor should accordingly be taken into account in conducting such studies and before reliance is placed on the results.

(d) *When unfairness is shown*. If unfairness is demonstrated through a showing that members of a particular group perform better or poorer on the job than their scores on the selection procedure would indicate through comparison with how members of other groups perform, the user may either revise or replace the selection instrument in accordance with these guidelines, or may continue to use the selection instrument operationally with appropriate revisions in its use to assure compatibility between the probability of successful job performance and the probability of being selected.

(e) *Technical feasibility of fairness studies*. In addition to the general conditions needed for technical feasibility for the conduct of a criterion-related study (see section 16, below) an investigation of fairness requires the following:

(i) An adequate sample of persons in each group available for the study to achieve findings of statistical significance. Guidelines do not require a user to hire or promote persons on the basis of group classifications for the purpose of making it possible to conduct a study of fairness; but the user has the obligation otherwise to comply with these guidelines.

(ii) The samples for each group should be comparable in terms of the actual job they perform, length of time on the job where time on the job is likely to affect performance, and other relevant factors likely to affect validity differences; or such factors should be included in the design of the study and their affects identified.

(f) *Continued use of selection procedures when fairness studies not feasible*. If a study of fairness should otherwise be performed, but is not technically feasible, a selection procedure may be used which has otherwise met the validity standards of these guidelines, unless the technical infeasibility resulted from discriminatory employment practices which are demonstrated by facts other than past failure to conform with requirements for validation of selection procedures. However, when it becomes technically feasible for the user to perform a study of fairness and such a study is otherwise called for, the user should conduct the study of fairness.

C. *Technical standards for content validity studies—(1) Appropriateness of content validity studies*. Users choosing to validate a selection procedure by a content validity strategy should determine whether it is appropriate to conduct such a study in the particular employment context. A selection procedure can be supported by a content validity strategy to the extent that it is a representative sample of the content of the job. Selection procedures which purpose to measure knowledges, skills, or abilities may in certain circumstances be justified by content validity, although they may not be representative samples, if the knowledge, skill, or ability measured by the selection procedure can be operationally defined as provided in section 14C(4) below, and if that knowledge, skill, or ability is a necessary prerequisite to successful job performance.

A selection procedure based upon inferences about mental processes cannot be supported solely or primarily on the basis of content validity. Thus, a content strategy is not appropriate for demonstrating the validity of selection procedures which purport to measure traits or constructs, such as intelligence, aptitude, personality, common sense, judgment, leadership, and spatial ability. Content validity is also not an appropriate strategy when the selection procedure involves knowledges, skills, or abilities which an employee will be expected to learn on the job.

(2) *Job analysis for content validity*. There should be a job analysis which includes an analysis of the important work behavior(s) required for successful performance and their relative importance and, if the behavior results in work product(s), an analysis of the work product(s). Any job analysis should focus on the work behavior(s) and the tasks associated with them. If work behavior(s) are not observable, the job analysis should identify and analyze those aspects of the behavior(s) that can be observed and the observed work products. The work behavior(s) selected for measurement should be critical work behavior(s) and/or important work behavior(s) constituting most of the job.

(3) *Development of selection procedures*. A selection procedure designed to measure the work behavior may be developed specifically from the job and job analysis in question, or may have been previously developed by the user, or by other users or by a test publisher.

(4) *Standards for demonstrating content validity*. To demonstrate the content validity of a selection procedure, a user should show that the behavior(s) demon-

strated in the selection procedure are a representative sample of the behavior(s) of the job in question or that the selection procedure provides a representative sample of the work product of the job. In the case of a selection procedure measuring a knowledge, skill, or ability, the knowledge, skill or ability being measured should be operationally defined. In the case of a selection procedure measuring a knowledge, the knowledge being measured should be operationally defined as that body of learned information which is used in and is a necessary prerequisite for observable aspects of work behavior of the job. In the case of skills or abilities, the skill or ability being measured should be operationally defined in terms of observable aspects of work behavior of the job. For any selection procedure measuring a knowledge, skill, or ability the user should show that (a) the selection procedure measures and is a representative sample of that knowledge, skill, or ability; and (b) that knowledge, skill, or ability is used in and is a necessary prerequisite to performance of critical or important work behavior(s). In addition, to be content valid, a selection procedure measuring a skill or ability should either closely approximate an observable work behavior, or its product should closely approximate an observable work product. If a test purports to sample a work behavior or to provide a sample of a work product, the manner and setting of the selection procedure and its level and complexity should closely approximate the work situation. The closer the content and the context of the selection procedure are to work samples or work behaviors, the stronger is the basis for showing content validity. As the content of the selection procedure less resembles a work behavior, or the setting and manner of the administration of the selection procedure less resemble the work situation, or the result less resembles a work product, the less likely the selection procedure is to be content valid, and the greater the need for other evidence of validity.

(5) *Reliability.* The reliability of selection procedures justified on the basis of content validity should be a matter of concern to the user. Whenever it is feasible, appropriate statistical estimates should be made of the reliability of the selection procedure.

(6) *Prior training or experience.* A requirement for or evaluation of specific prior training or experience based on content validity, including a specification of level or amount of training or experience, should be justified on the basis of the relationship between the content of the training or experience and the content of the job for which the training or experience is to be required or evaluated. The critical consideration is the resemblance between the specific behaviors, products, knowledges, skills, or abilities in the experience or training and the specific behaviors, products, knowledges, skills, or abilities required on the job, whether or not there is close resemblance between the experience or training as a whole and the job as a whole.

(7) *Content validity of training success.* Where a measure of success in a training program is used as a selection procedure and the content of a training program is justified on the basis of content validity, the use should be justified on the relationship between the content of the training program and the content of the job.

(8) *Operational use.* A selection procedure which is supported on the basis of content validity may be used for a job if it represents a critical work behavior (i.e., a behavior which is necessary for performance of the job) or work behaviors which constitute most of the important parts of the job.

(9) *Ranking based on content validity studies.* If a user can show, by a job analysis or otherwise, that a higher score on a content valid selection procedure is likely to result in better job performance, the results may be used to rank persons who score above minimum levels. Where a selection procedure supported solely or primarily by content validity is used to rank job candidates, the selection procedure should measure those aspects of performance which differentiate among levels of job performance.

D. *Technical standards for construct validity studies—(1) Appropriateness of construct validity studies.* Construct validity is a more complex strategy than either criterion-related or content validity. Construct validation is a relatively new and developing procedure in the employment field, and there is at present a lack of substantial literature extending the concept to employment practices. The user should be aware that the effort to obtain sufficient empirical support for construct validity is both an extensive and arduous effort involving a series of research studies, which include criterion related validity studies and which may include content validity studies. Users choosing to justify use of a selection procedure by this strategy should therefore take particular care to assure that the validity study meets the standards set forth below.

(2) *Job analysis for construct validity studies.* There should be a job analysis. This job analysis should show the work behavior(s) required for successful performance of the job, or the groups of jobs being studied, the critical or important work behavior(s) in the job or group of jobs being studied, and an identification of

the construct(s) believed to underlie successful performance of these critical or important work behaviors in the job or jobs in question. Each construct should be named and defined, so as to distinguish it from other constructs. If a group of jobs is being studied the jobs should have in common one or more critical or important work behaviors at a comparable level of complexity.

(3) *Relationship to the job.* A selection procedure should then be identified or developed which measures the construct identified in accord with subparagraph (2) above. The user should show by empirical evidence that the selection procedure is validly related to the construct and that the construct is validly related to the performance of critical or important work behavior(s). The relationship between the construct as measured by the selection procedure and the related work behavior(s) should be supported by empirical evidence from one or more criterion-related studies involving the job or jobs in question which satisfy the provisions of section 14B above.

(4) *Use of construct validity study without new criterion-related evidence—(a) Standards for use.* Until such time as professional literature provides more guidance on the use of construct validity in employment situations, the Federal agencies will accept a claim of construct validity without a criterion-related study which satisfies section 14B above only when the selection procedure has been used elsewhere in a situation in which a criterion-related study has been conducted and the use of a criterion-related validity study in this context meets the standards for transportability of criterion-related validity studies as set forth above in section 7. However, if a study pertains to a number of jobs having common critical or important work behaviors at a comparable level of complexity, and the evidence satisfies subparagraphs 14B (2) and (3) above for those jobs with criterion-related validity evidence for those jobs, the selection procedure may be used for all the jobs to which the study pertains. If construct validity is to be generalized to other jobs or groups of jobs not in the group studied, the Federal enforcement agencies will expect at a minimum additional empirical research evidence meeting the standards of subparagraphs section 14B (2) and (3) above for the additional jobs or groups of jobs.

(b) *Determination of common work behaviors.* In determining whether two or more jobs have one or more work behavior(s) in common, the user should compare the observed work behavior(s) in each of the jobs and should compare the observed work product(s) in each of the jobs. If neither the observed work behavior(s) in each of the jobs nor the observed work product(s) in each of the jobs are the same, the Federal enforcement agencies will presume that the work behavior(s) in each job are different. If the work behaviors are not observable, then evidence of similarity of work products and any other relevant research evidence will be considered in determining whether the work behavior(s) in the two jobs are the same.

DOCUMENTATION OF IMPACT AND VALIDITY EVIDENCE

§ 1607.15 Documentation of impact and validity evidence.

A. *Required information.* Users of selection procedures other than those users complying with section 15A(1) below should maintain and have available for each job information on adverse impact of the selection process for that job and, where it is determined a selection process has an adverse impact, evidence of validity is set forth below.

(1) *Simplified record keeping for users with less than 100 employees.* In order to minimize record keeping burdens on employers who employ one hundred (100) or fewer employees, and other users not required to file EEO-1, et seq., reports, such users may satisfy the requirements of this section 15 if they maintain and have available records showing, for each year:

(a) The number of persons hired, promoted, and terminated for each job, by sex, and where appropriate by race and national origin;

(b) The number of applicants for hire and promotion by sex and where appropriate by race and national origin; and

(c) The selection procedures utilized (either standardized or not standardized).

These records should be maintained for each race or national origin group (see section 4 above) constituting more than two percent (2%) of the labor force in the relevant labor area. However, it is not necessary to maintain records by race and/or national origin (see § 4 above) if one race or national origin group in the relevant labor area constitutes more than ninety-eight percent (98%) of the labor force in the area. If the user has reason to believe that a selection procedure has an adverse impact, the user should maintain any available evidence of validity for that procedure (see sections 7A and 8).

(2) *Information on impact—(a) Collection of information on impact.* Users of selection procedures

other than those complying with section 15A(1) above should maintain and have available for each job records or other information showing whether the total selection process for that job has an adverse impact on any of the groups for which records are called for by sections 4B above. Adverse impact determinations should be made at least annually for each such group which constitutes at least 2 percent of the labor force in the relevant labor area or 2 percent of the applicable work force. Where a total selection process for a job has an adverse impact, the user should maintain and have available records or other information showing which components have an adverse impact. Where the total selection process for a job does not have an adverse impact, information need not be maintained for individual components except in circumstances set forth in subsection 15A(2)(b) below. If the determination of adverse impact is made using a procedure other than the "four-fifths rule," as defined in the first sentence of section 4D above, a justification, consistent with section 4D above, for the procedure used to determine adverse impact should be available.

(b) *When adverse impact has been eliminated in the total selection process.* Whenever the total selection process for a particular job has had an adverse impact, as defined in section 4 above, in any year, but no longer has an adverse impact, the user should maintain and have available the information on individual components of the selection process required in the preceding paragraph for the period in which there was adverse impact. In addition, the user should continue to collect such information for at least two (2) years after the adverse impact has been eliminated.

(c) *When data insufficient to determine impact.* Where there has been an insufficient number of selections to determine whether there is an adverse impact of the total selection process for a particular job, the user should continue to collect, maintain and have available the information on individual components of the selection process required in section 15(A)(2)(a) above until the information is sufficient to determine that the overall selection process does not have an adverse impact as defined in section 4 above, or until the job has changed substantially.

(3) *Documentation of validity evidence—(a) Types of evidence.* Where a total selection process has an adverse impact (see section 4 above) the user should maintain and have available for each component of that process which has an adverse impact, one or more of the following types of documentation evidence:

(i) Documentation evidence showing criterion-related validity of the selection procedure (see section 15B, below).

(ii) Documentation evidence showing content validity of the selection procedure (see section 15C, below).

(iii) Documentation evidence showing construct validity of the selection procedure (see section 15D, below).

(iv) Documentation evidence from other studies showing validity of the selection procedure in the user's facility (see section 15E, below).

(v) Documentation evidence showing why a validity study cannot or need not be performed and why continued use of the procedure is consistent with Federal law.

(b) *Form of report.* This evidence should be compiled in a reasonably complete and organized manner to permit direct evaluation of the validity of the selection procedure. Previously written employer or consultant reports of validity, or reports describing validity studies completed before the issuance of these guidelines are acceptable if they are complete in regard to the documentation requirements contained in this section, or if they satisfied requirements of guidelines which were in effect when the validity study was completed. If they are not complete, the required additional documentation should be appended. If necessary information is not available the report of the validity study may still be used as documentation, but its adequacy will be evaluated in terms of compliance with the requirements of these guidelines.

(c) *Completeness.* In the event that evidence of validity is reviewed by an enforcement agency, the validation reports completed after the effective date of these guidelines are expected to contain the information set forth below. Evidence denoted by use of the word "(Essential)" is considered critical. If information denoted essential is not included, the report will be considered incomplete unless the user affirmatively demonstrates either its unavailability due to circumstances beyond the user's control or special circumstances of the user's study which make the information irrelevant. Evidence not so denoted is desirable but its absence will not be a basis for considering a report incomplete. The user should maintain and have available the information called for under the heading "Source Data" in sections 15B(11) and 15D(11). While it is a necessary part of the study, it need not be submitted with the report. All statistical results should be organized and presented in tabular or graphic form to the extent feasible.

B. *Criterion-related validity studies.* Reports of criterion-related validity for a selection procedure should include the following information:

(1) *User(s), location(s), and date(s) of study.* Dates and location(s) of the job analysis or review of job information, the date(s) and location(s) of the administration of the selection procedures and collection of criterion data, and the time between collection of data on selection procedures and criterion measures should be provided (Essential). If the study was conducted at several locations, the address of each location, including city and state, should be shown.

(2) *Problem and setting.* An explicit definition of the purpose(s) of the study and the circumstances in which the study was conducted should be provided. A description of existing selection procedures and cutoff scores, if any, should be provided.

(3) *Job analysis or review of job information.* A description of the procedure used to analyze the job or group of jobs, or to review the job information should be provided (Essential). Where a review of job information results in criteria which may be used without a full job analysis (see section 14B(3)), the basis for the selection of these criteria should be reported (Essential). Where a job analysis is required a complete description of the work behavior(s) or work outcome(s), and measures of their criticality or importance should be provided (Essential). The report should describe the basis on which the behavior(s) or outcome(s) were determined to be critical or important, such as the proportion of time spent on the respective behaviors, their level of difficulty, their frequency of performance, the consequences of error, or other appropriate factors (Essential). Where two or more jobs are grouped for a validity study, the information called for in this subsection should be provided for each of the jobs, and the justification for the grouping (see section 14B(1) should be provided (Essential).

(4) *Job titles and codes.* It is desirable to provide the user's job title(s) for the job(s) in question and the corresponding job title(s) and code(s) from U.S. Employment Service's *Dictionary of Occupational Titles.*

(5) *Criterion measures.* The bases for the selection of the criterion measures should be provided, together with references to the evidence considered in making the selection of criterion measures (Essential). A full description of all criteria on which data were collected and means by which they were observed, recorded, evaluated, and quantified, should be provided (Essential). If rating techniques are used as criterion measures, the appraisal form(s) and instructions to the rater(s) should be included as part of the validation evidence, or should be explicitly described and available (Essential). All steps taken to insure that criterion measures are free from the factors which would unfairly alter the scores of members of any group should be described (Essential).

(6) *Sample description.* A description of how the research sample was identified and selected should be included (Essential). The race, sex, and ethnic composition of the sample, including those groups set forth in section 4A above, should be described (Essential). This description should include the size of each subgroup (Essential). A description of how the research sample compares with the relevant labor market or work force, the method by which the relevant labor market or work force was defined, and a discussion of the likely effects on validity of differences between the sample and the relevant labor market or work force, are also desirable. Descriptions of educational levels, length of service, and age are also desirable.

(7) *Description of selection procedures.* Any measure, combination of measures, or procedure studied should be completely and explicitly described or attached (Essential). If commercially available selection procedures are studied, they should be described by title, form, and publisher (Essential). Reports of reliability estimates and how they were established are desirable.

(8) *Techniques and results.* Methods used in analyzing data should be described (Essential). Measures of central tendency (e.g., means) and measures of dispersion (e.g., standard deviations and ranges) for all selection procedures and all criteria should be reported for each race, sex, and ethnic group which constitutes a significant factor in the relevant labor market (Essential). The magnitude and direction of all relationships between selection procedures and criterion measures investigated should be reported for each relevant race, sex, and ethnic group and for the total group (Essential). Where groups are too small to obtain reliable evidence of the magnitude of the relationship, results need not be reported separately. Statements regarding the statistical significance of results should be made (Essential). Any statistical adjustments, such as for less than perfect reliability or for restriction of score range in the selection procedure or criterion should be described and explained; and uncorrected correlation coefficients should also be shown (Essential). Where the statistical technique categorizes continuous data,

such as biserial correlation and the phi coefficient, the categories and the bases on which they were determined should be described and explained (Essential). Studies of test fairness should be included where called for by the requirements of section 14B(8)(Essential). These studies should include the rationale by which a selection procedure was determined to be fair to the group(s) in question. Where test fairness or unfairness has been demonstrated on the basis of other studies, a bibliography of the relevant studies should be included (Essential). If the bibliography includes unpublished studies, copies of these studies, or adequate abstracts or summaries, should be attached (Essential). Where revisions have been made in a selection procedure to assure compatability between successful job performance and the probability of being selected, the studies underlying such revisions should be included (Essential). All statistical results should be organized and presented by relevant race, sex, and ethnic group (Essential).

(9) *Alternative procedures investigated.* The selection procedures investigated and available evidence of their impact should be identified (Essential). The scope, method, and findings of the investigation, and the conclusions reached in light of the findings, should be fully described (Essential).

(10) *Uses and applications.* The methods considered for use of the selection procedure (e.g., as a screening device with a cutoff score, for grouping or ranking, or combined with other procedures in a battery) and available evidence of their impact should be described (Essential). This description should include the rationale for choosing the method for operational use, and the evidence of the validity and utility of the procedure as it is to be used (Essential). The purpose for which the procedure is to be used (e.g., hiring, transfer, promotion) should be described (Essential). If weights are assigned to different parts of the selection procedure, these weights and the validity of the weighted composite should be reported (Essential). If the selection procedure is used with a cutoff score, the user should describe the way in which normal expectations of proficiency within the work force were determined and the way in which the cutoff score was determined (Essential).

(11) *Source data.* Each user should maintain records showing all pertinent information about individual sample members and raters where they are used, in studies involving the validation of selection procedures. These records should be made available upon request of a compliance agency. In the case of

individual sample members these data should include scores on the selection procedure(s), scores on criterion measures, age, sex, race, or ethnic group status, and experience on the specific job on which the validation study was conducted, and may also include such things as education, training, and prior job experience, but should not include names and social security numbers. Records should be maintained which show the ratings given to each sample member by each rater.

(12) *Contact person.* The name, mailing address, and telephone number of the person who may be contacted for further information about the validity study should be provided (Essential).

(13) *Accuracy and completeness.* The report should describe the steps taken to assure the accuracy and completeness of the collection, analysis, and report of date and results.

C. *Content validity studies.* Reports of content validity for a selection procedure should include the following information:

(1) *User(s), location(s) and date(s) of study.* Dates and location(s) of the job analysis should be shown (Essential).

(2) *Problem and setting.* An explicit definition of the purpose(s) of the study and the circumstances in which the study was conducted should be provided. A description of existing selection procedures and cutoff scores, if any, should be provided.

(3) *Job analysis—Content of the job.* A description of the method used to analyze the job should be provided (Essential). The work behavior(s), the associated tasks, and, if the behavior results in a work product, the work products should be completely described (Essential). Measures of criticality and/or importance of the work behavior(s), and the method of determining these measures should be provided (Essential). Where the job analysis also identified the knowledges, skills, and abilities used in work behavior(s), an operational definition for each knowledge in terms of a body of learned information and for each skill and ability in terms of observable behaviors and outcomes, and the relationship between each knowledge, skill, or ability and each work behavior, as well as the method used to determine this relationship, should be provided (Essential). The work situation should be described, including the setting in which work behavior(s) are performed, and where appropriate, the manner in which knowledges, skills, or abilities are used, and the complexity and difficulty of the knowledge, skill, or ability as used in the work behavior(s).

(4) *Selection procedure and its content.* Selection

procedures, including those constructed by or for the user, specific training requirements, composites of selection procedures, and any other procedure supported by content validity, should be completely and explicitly described or attached (Essential). If commercially available selection procedures are used, they should be described by title, form, and publisher (Essential). The behaviors measured or sampled by the selection procedure should be explicitly described (Essential). Where the selection procedure purports to measure a knowledge, skill, or ability, evidence that the selection procedure measures and is a representative sample of the knowledge, skill, or ability should be provided (Essential).

(5) *Relationship between the selection procedure and the job.* The evidence demonstrating that the selection procedure is a representative work sample, a representative sample of the work behavior(s), or a representative sample of a knowledge, skill, or ability as used as a part of a work behavior and necessary for that behavior should be provided (Essential). The user should identify the work behavior(s) which each item or part of the selection procedure is intended to sample or measure (Essential). Where the selection procedure purports to sample a work behavior or to provide a sample of a work product, a comparison should be provided of the manner, setting and the level of complexity of the selection procedure with those of the work situation (essential). If any steps were taken to reduce adverse impact on a race, sex, or ethnic group in the content of the procedure or in its administration these steps should be described. Establishment of time limits, if any, and how these limits are related to the speed with which duties must be performed on the job, should be explained. Measures of central tendency (e.g., means) and measures of dispersion (e.g., standard deviations) and estimates of reliability should be reported for all selection procedures if available. Such reports should be made for relevant race, sex, and ethnic subgroups, at least on a statistically reliable sample basis.

(6) *Alternative procedures investigated.* The alternative selection procedures investigated and available evidence of their impact should be identified (Essential). The scope, method, and findings of the investigation, and the conclusions reached in light of the findings, should be fully described (Essential).

(7) *Uses and applications.* The methods considered for use of the selection procedure (e.g., as a screening device with a cutoff score, for grouping or ranking, or combined with other procedures in a battery) and available evidence of their impact should be described (Es-

sential). This description should include the rationale for choosing the method for operational use, and the evidence of the validity and utility of the procedure as it is to be used (Essential). The purpose for which the procedure is to be used (e.g., hiring, transfer, promotion) should be described (Essential). If the selection procedure is used with a cutoff score, the user should describe the way in which normal expectations of proficiency within the work force were determined and the way in which the cutoff score was determined (Essential). In addition, if the selection procedure is to be used for ranking, the user should specify the evidence showing that a higher score on the selection procedure is likely to result in better job performance.

(8) *Contact person.* The name, mailing address, and telephone number of the person who may be contacted for further information about the validity study should be provided (Essential).

(9) *Accuracy and completeness.* The report should describe the steps taken to assure the accuracy and completeness of the collection, analysis, and report of data and results.

D. *Construct validity studies.* Reports of construct validity for a selection procedure should include the following information:

(1) *User(s), location(s), and date(s) of study.* Date(s) and location(s) of the job analysis and the gathering of other evidence called for by these guidelines should be provided (Essential).

(2) *Problem and setting.* An explicit definition of the purpose(s) of the study and the circumstances in which the study was conducted should be provided. A description of existing selection procedures and cutoff scores, if any, should be provided.

(3) *Construct definition.* A clear definition of the construct(s) which are believed to underlie successful performance of the critical or important work behavior(s) should be provided (Essential). This definition should include the levels of construct performance relevant to the job(s) for which the selection procedure is to be used (Essential). There should be a summary of the position of the construct in the psychological literature, or in the absence of such a position, a description of the way in which the definition and measurement of the construct was developed and the psychological theory underlying it (Essential). Any quantitative data which identify or define the job constructs, such as factor analyses, should be provided (Essential).

(4) *Job analysis.* A description of the method used to analyze the job should be provided (Essential). A

complete description of the work behavior(s) and, to the extent appropriate, work outcomes and measures of their criticality and/or importance should be provided (Essential). The report should also describe the basis on which the behavior(s) or outcomes were determined to be important, such as their level of difficulty, their frequency of performance, the consequences of error or other appropriate factors (Essential). Where jobs are grouped or compared for the purposes of generalizing validity evidence, the work behavior(s) and work product(s) for each of the jobs should be described, and conclusions concerning the similarity of the jobs in terms of observable work behaviors or work products should be made (Essential).

(5) *Job titles and codes.* It is desirable to provide the selection procedure user's job title(s) for the job(s) in question and the corresponding job title(s) and code(s) from the United States Employment Service's *Dictionary of Occupational Titles.*

(6) *Selection procedure.* The selection procedure used as a measure of the construct should be completely and explicitly described or attached (Essential). If commercially available selection procedures are used, they should be identified by title, form and publisher (Essential). The research evidence of the relationship between the selection procedure and the construct, such as factor structure, should be included (Essential). Measures of central tendency, variability and reliability of the selection procedure should be provided (Essential). Whenever feasible, these measures should be provided separately for each relevant race, sex and ethnic group.

(7) *Relationship to job performance.* The criterion-related study(ies) and other empirical evidence of the relationship between the construct measured by the selection procedure and the related work behavior(s) for the job or jobs in question should be provided (Essential). Documentation of the criterion-related study(ies) should satisfy the provisions of section 15B above or section 15E(1) below, except for studies conducted prior to the effective date of these guidelines (Essential). Where a study pertains to a group of jobs, and, on the basis of the study, validity is asserted for a job in the group, the observed work behaviors and the observed work products for each of the jobs should be described (Essential). Any other evidence used in determining whether the work behavior(s) in each of the jobs is the same should be fully described (Essential).

(8) *Alternative procedures investigated.* The alternative selection procedures investigated and available evidence of their impact should be identified (Essen-

tial). The scope, method, and findings of the investigation, and the conclusions reached in light of the findings should be fully described (Essential).

(9) *Uses and applications.* The methods considered for use of the selection procedure (e.g., as a screening device with a cutoff score, for grouping or ranking, or combined with other procedures in a battery) and available evidence of their impact should be described (Essential). This description should include the rationale for choosing the method for operational use, and the evidence of the validity and utility of the procedure as it is to be used (Essential). The purpose for which the procedure is to be used (e.g., hiring, transfer, promotion) should be described (Essential). If weights are assigned to different parts of the selection procedure, these weights and the validity of the weighted composite should be reported (Essential). If the selection procedure is used with a cutoff score, the user should describe the way in which normal expectations of proficiency within the work force were determined and the way in which the cutoff score was determined (Essential).

(10) *Accuracy and completeness.* The report should describe the steps taken to assure the accuracy and completeness of the collection, analysis, and report of data and results.

(11) *Source data.* Each user should maintain records showing all pertinent information relating to its study of construct validity.

(12) *Contact person.* The name, mailing address, and telephone number of the individual who may be contacted for further information about the validity study should be provided (Essential).

E. *Evidence of validity from other studies.* When validity of a selection procedure is supported by studies not done by the user, the evidence from the original study or studies should be compiled in a manner similar to that required in the appropriate section of this section 15 above. In addition, the following evidence should be supplied:

(1) *Evidence from criterion-related validity studies—a. Job information.* A description of the important job behavior(s) of the user's job and the basis on which the behaviors were determined to be important should be provided (Essential). A full description of the basis for determining that these important work behaviors are the same as those of the job in the original study (or studies) should be provided (Essential).

b. *Relevance of criteria.* A full description of the basis on which the criteria used in the original studies are determined to be relevant for the user should be provided (Essential).

c. *Other variables.* The similarity of important applicant pool or sample characteristics reported in the original studies to those of the user should be described (Essential). A description of the comparison between the race, sex and ethnic composition of the user's relevant labor market and the sample in the original validity studies should be provided (Essential).

d. *Use of the selection procedure.* A full description should be provided showing that the use to be made of the selection procedure is consistent with the findings of the original validity studies (Essential).

e. *Bibliography.* A bibliography of reports of validity of the selection procedure for the job or jobs in question should be provided (Essential). Where any of the studies included an investigation of test fairness, the results of this investigation should be provided (Essential). Copies of reports published in journals that are not commonly available should be described in detail or attached (Essential). Where a user is relying upon unpublished studies, a reasonable effort should be made to obtain these studies. If these unpublished studies are the sole source of validity evidence they should be described in detail or attached (Essential). If these studies are not available, the name and address of the source, an adequate abstract or summary of the validity study and data, and a contact person in the source organization should be provided (Essential).

(2) *Evidence from content validity studies.* See section 14C(3) and section 15C above.

(3) *Evidence from construct validity studies.* See sections 14D(2) and 15D above.

F. *Evidence of validity from cooperative studies.* Where a selection procedure has been validated through a cooperative study, evidence that the study satisfies the requirements of sections 7, 8 and 15E should be provided (Essential).

G. *Selection for higher level job.* If a selection procedure is used to evaluate candidates for jobs at a higher level than those for which they will initially be employed, the validity evidence should satisfy the documentation provisions of this section 15 for the higher level job or jobs, and in addition, the user should provide: (1) a description of the job progression structure, formal or informal; (2) the data showing how many employees progress to the higher level job and the length of time needed to make this progression; and (3) an identification of any anticipated changes in the higher level job. In addition, if the test measures a knowledge, skill or ability, the user should provide

evidence that the knowledge, skill or ability is required for the higher level job and the basis for the conclusion that the knowledge, skill or ability is not expected to develop from the training or experience on the job.

H. *Interim use of selection procedures.* If a selection procedure is being used on an interim basis because the procedure is not fully supported by the required evidence of validity, the user should maintain and have available (1) substantial evidence of validity for the procedure, and (2) a report showing the date on which the study to gather the additional evidence commenced, the estimated completion date of the study, and a description of the date to be collected (Essential).

(Approved by the Office of Management and Budget under control number 3046-0017)
(Pub. L. No. 96–511, 94 Stat. 2812 (44 U.S.C. 3501 et seq.))
[43 FR 38295, 38312, Aug. 25, 1978, as amended at 46 FR 63268, Dec. 31, 1981]

DEFINITIONS

§ 1607.16 Definitions.

The following definitions shall apply throughout these guidelines:

A. *Ability.* A present competence to perform an observable behavior or a behavior which results in an observable product.

B. *Adverse impact.* A substantially different rate of selection in hiring, promotion, or other employment decision which works to the disadvantage of members of a race, sex, or ethnic group. See section 4 of these guidelines.

C. *Compliance with these guidelines.* Use of a selection procedure is in compliance with these guidelines if such use has been validated in accord with these guidelines (as defined below), or if such use does not result in adverse impact on any race, sex, or ethnic group (see section 4, above), or, in unusual circumstances, if use of the procedure is otherwise justified in accord with Federal law. See section 6B, above.

D. *Content validity.* Demonstrated by data showing that the content of a selection procedure is representative of important aspects of performance on the job. See section 5B and section 14C.

E. *Construct validity.* Demonstrated by data showing that the selection procedure measures the degree to which candidates have identifiable characteristics which have been determined to be important for successful job performance. See section 5B and section 14D.

F. *Criterion-related validity.* Demonstrated by empirical data showing that the selection procedure is predictive of or significantly correlated with important elements of work behavior. See sections 5B and 14B.

G. *Employer.* Any employer subject to the provisions of the Civil Rights Act of 1964, as amended, including state or local governments and any Federal agency subject to the provisions of section 717 of the Civil Rights Act of 1964, as amended, and any Federal contractor or subcontractor or federally assisted construction contractor or subcontractor covered by Executive Order 11246, as amended.

H. *Employment agency.* Any employment agency subject to the provisions of the Civil Rights Act of 1964, as amended.

I. *Enforcement action.* For the purposes of section 4 a proceeding by a Federal enforcement agency such as a lawsuit or an administrative proceeding leading to debarment from or withholding, suspension, or termination of Federal Government contracts or the suspension or withholding of Federal Government funds; but not a finding of reasonable cause or a conciliation process or the issuance of right to sue letters under Title VII or under Executive Order 11246 where such finding, conciliation, or issuance of notice of right to sue is based upon an individual complaint.

J. *Enforcement agency.* Any agency of the executive branch of the Federal Government which adopts these guidelines for purposes of the enforcement of the equal employment opportunity laws or which has responsibility for securing compliance with them.

K. *Job analysis.* A detailed statement of work behaviors and other information relevant to the job.

L. *Job description.* A general statement of job duties and responsibilities.

M. *Knowledge.* A body of information applied directly to the performance of a function.

N. *Labor organization.* Any labor organization subject to the provisions of the Civil Rights Act of 1964, as amended, and any committee subject thereto controlling apprenticeship or other training.

O. *Observable.* Able to be seen, heard, or otherwise perceived by a person other than the person performing the action.

P. *Race, sex, or ethnic group.* Any group of persons identifiable on the grounds of race, color, religion, sex, or national origin.

Q. *Selection procedure.* Any measure, combination of measures, or procedure used as a basis for any employment decision. Selection procedures include the full range of assessment techniques from traditional paper and pencil tests, performance tests, training programs, or probationary periods and physical, educational, and work experience requirements through informal or casual interviews and unscored application forms.

R. *Selection rate.* The proportion of applicants or candidates who are hired, promoted, or otherwise selected.

S. *Should.* The term "should" as used in these guidelines is intended to connote action which is necessary to achieve compliance with the guidelines, while recognizing that there are circumstances where alternative courses of action are open to users.

T. *Skill.* A present, observable competence to perform a learned psychomotor act.

U. *Technical feasibility.* The existence of conditions permitting the conduct of meaningful criterion-related validity studies. These conditions include: (1) An adequate sample of persons available for the study to achieve findings of statistical significance; (2) having or being able to obtain a sufficient range of scores on the selection procedure and job performance measures to produce validity results which can be expected to be representative of the results if the ranges normally expected were utilized; and (3) having or being able to devise unbiased, reliable and relevant measures of job performance or other criteria of employee adequacy. See section 14B(2). With respect to investigation of possible unfairness, the same considerations are applicable to each group for which the study is made. See section 14B(8).

V. *Unfairness of selection procedure.* A condition in which members of one race, sex, or ethnic group characteristically obtain lower scores on a selection procedure than members of another group, and the differences are not reflected in differences in measures of job performance. See section 14B(7).

W. *User.* Any employer, labor organization, employment agency, or licensing or certification board, to the extent it may be covered by Federal equal employment opportunity law, which uses a selection procedure as a basis for any employment decision. Whenever an employer, labor organization, or employment agency is required by law to restrict recruitment for any occupation to those applicants who have met licensing or certification requirements, the licensing or certifying authority to the extent it may be covered by Federal equal employment opportunity law will be considered the user with respect to those licensing or certification requirements. Whenever a state employment agency or service does no more than administer or monitor a procedure as permitted by Department of Labor regulations, and does so without making referrals or taking any other action on the basis of the results, the state employment agency will not be deemed to be a user.

X. *Validated in accord with these guidelines or properly validated*. A demonstration that one or more validity study or studies meeting the standards of these guidelines has been conducted, including investigation and, where appropriate, use of suitable alternative selection procedures as contemplated by section 3B, and has produced evidence of validity sufficient to warrant use of the procedure for the intended purpose under the standards of these guidelines.

Y. *Work behavior*. An activity performed to achieve the objectives of the job. Work behaviors involve observable (physical) components and unobservable (mental) components. a work behavior consists of the performance of one or more tasks. Knowledges, skills, and abilities are not behaviors, although they may be applied in work behaviors.

APPENDIX

§ 1607.17 Policy statement on affirmative action (see section 13B).

The Equal Employment Opportunity Coordinating Council was established by act of Congress in 1972, and charged with responsibility for developing and implementing agreements and policies designed, among other things, to eliminate conflict and inconsistency among the agencies of the Federal Government responsible for administering Federal law prohibiting discrimination on grounds of race, color, sex, religion, and national origin. This statement is issued as an initial response to the requests of a number of state and local officials for clarification of the Government's policies concerning the role of affirmative action in the overall equal employment opportunity program. While the Coordinating Council's adoption of this statement expresses only the views of the signatory agencies concerning this important subject, the principles set forth below should serve as policy guidance for other Federal agencies as well.

(1) Equal employment opportunity is the law of the land. In the public sector of our society this means that all persons, regardless of race, color, religion, sex, or national origin shall have equal access to positions in the public service limited only by their ability to do the job. There is ample evidence in all sectors of our society that such equal access frequently has been denied to members of certain groups because of their sex, racial, or ethnic characteristics. The remedy for such past and present discrimination is twofold.

On the one hand, vigorous enforcement of the laws against discrimination is essential. But equally, and perhaps even more important are affirmative, voluntary efforts on the part of public employers to assure that positions in the public service are genuinely and equally accessible to qualified persons, without regard to their sex, racial, or ethnic characteristics. Without such efforts equal employment opportunity is no more than a wish. The importance of voluntary affirmative action on the part of employers is underscored by Title VII of the Civil Rights Act of 1964, Executive Order 11246, and related laws and regulations—all of which emphasize voluntary action to achieve equal employment opportunity.

As with most management objectives, a systematic plan based on sound organizational analysis and problem identification is crucial to the accomplishment of affirmative action objectives. For this reason, the Council urges all state and local governments to develop and implement results oriented affirmative action plans which deal with the problems so identified.

The following paragraphs are intended to assist state and local governments by illustrating the kinds of analyses and activities which may be appropriate for a public employer's voluntary affirmative action plan. This statement does not address remedies imposed after a finding of unlawful discrimination.

(2) Voluntary affirmative action to assure equal employment opportunity is appropriate at any stage of the employment process. The first step in the construction of any affirmative action plan should be an analysis of the employer's work force to determine whether percentages of sex, race, or ethnic groups in individual job classifications are substantially similar to the percentages of those groups available in the relevant job market who possess the basic job-related qualifications.

When substantial disparities are found through such analyses, each element of the overall selection process should be examined to determine which elements operate to exclude persons on the basis of sex, race, or ethnic group. Such elements include, but are not limited to, recruitment, testing, ranking certification, interview, recommendations for selection, hiring, promotion, etc. The examination of each element of the selection process should at a minimum include a determination of its validity in predicting job performance.

(3) When an employer has reason to believe that its selection procedures have the exclusionary effect described in paragraph 2 above, it should initiate affirmative steps to remedy the situation. Such steps, which in design and execution may be race, color, sex, or ethnic "conscious," include, but are not limited to, the following:

(a) The establishment of a long-term goal, and short-range, interim goals and timetables for the specific job classifications, all of which should take into account the availability of basically qualified persons in the relevant job market;

(b) A recruitment program designed to attract qualified members of the group in question;

(c) A systematic effort to organize work and redesign jobs in ways that provide opportunities for persons lacking "journeyman" level knowledge or skills to enter and, with appropriate training, to progress in a career field;

(d) Revamping selection instruments or procedures which have not yet been validated in order to reduce or eliminate exclusionary effects on particular groups in particular job classifications;

(e) The initiation of measures designed to assure that members of the affected group who are qualified to perform the job are included within the pool of persons from which the selecting official makes the selection;

(f) A systematic effort to provide career advancement training, both classroom and on-the-job, to employees locked into dead end jobs; and

(g) The establishment of a system for regularly monitoring the effectiveness of the particular affirmative action program, and procedures for making timely adjustments in this program where effectiveness is not demonstrated.

(4) The goal of any affirmative action plan should be achievement of genuine equal employment opportunity for all qualified persons. Selection under such plans should be based upon the ability of the applicant(s) to do the work. Such plans should not require the selection of the unqualified, or the unneeded, nor should they require the selection of persons on the basis of race, color, sex, religion, or national origin. Moreover, while the Council believes that this statement should serve to assist state and local employers, as well as Federal agencies, it recognizes that affirmative action cannot be viewed as a standardized program which

must be accomplished in the same way at all times in all places.

Accordingly, the Council has not attempted to set forth here either the minimum or maximum voluntary steps that employers may take to deal with their respective situations. Rather, the Council recognizes that under applicable authorities, state and local employers have flexibility to formulate affirmative action plans that are best suited to their particular situations. In this manner, the Council believes that affirmative action programs will best serve the goal of equal employment opportunity.

Respectfully submitted,

> Harold R. Tyler, Jr.,
> Deputy Attorney General and
> Chairman of the Equal
> Employment Coordinating Council.
> Michael H. Moskow,
> Under Secretary of Labor
> Ethel Bent Walsh,
> Acting Chairman, Equal
> Employment Opportunity Commission.
> Robert E. Hampton,
> Chairman, Civil Service Commission.
> Arthur E. Flemming,
> Chairman, Commission on Civil Rights.

Because of its equal employment opportunity responsibilities under the State and Local Government Fiscal Assistance Act of 1972 (the revenue sharing act), the Department of Treasury was invited to participate in the formulation of this policy statement; and it concurs and joins in the adoption of this policy statement.

Done this 26th day of August 1976.

> Richard Albrecht,
> General Counsel,
> Department of the Treasury.

§ 1607.18 Citations.

The official title of these guidelines is "Uniform Guidelines on Employee Selection Procedures (1978)." The Uniform Guidelines on Employee Selection Procedures (1978) are intended to establish a uniform Federal position in the area of prohibiting discrimination in employment practices on grounds of race, color, religion, sex, or national origin. These guidelines have been adopted by the Equal Employment Opportunity Commission, the Department of

Labor, the Department of Justice, and the Civil Service Commission.

The official citation is:

"Section _____ , Uniform Guidelines on Employee Selection Procedure (1978); 43 FR (August 25, 1978)."

The short form citation is:

"Section _____ , U.G.E.S.P. (1978); 43 FR _____ (August 25, 1978)."

When the guidelines are cited in connection with the activities of one of the issuing agencies, a specific citation to the regulations of that agency can be added at the end of the above citation. The specific additional citations are as follows:

Equal Employment Opportunity Commission
29 CFR Part 1607
Department of Labor

Office of Federal Contract Compliance
Programs
41 CFR Part 60–3
Department of Justice
28 CFR 50.14
Civil Service Commission
5 CFR 300.103(c)

Normally when citing these guidelines, the section number immediately preceding the title of the guidelines will be from these guidelines series 1–18. If a section number from the codification for an individual agency is needed it can also be added at the end of the agency citation. For example, section 6A of these guidelines could be cited for EEOC as follows: "Section 6A, Uniform Guidelines on Employee Selection Procedures (1978); 43 FR _____ , (August 25, 1978); 29 CFR Part 1607, section 6A."

Title VII of the Civil Rights Act of 1964 as Amended by the Equal Employment Opportunity Act of 1972

DEFINITIONS

Section 701. For the purposes of this title—

(a) The term "person" includes one or more individuals, governments, governmental agencies, political subdivisions, labor unions, partnerships, associations, corporations, legal representatives, mutual companies, joint-stock companies, trusts, unincorporated organizations, trustees, trustees in bankruptcy, or receivers. (As amended by P.L. No. 92–261, eff. March 24, 1972.)

(b) The term "employer" means a person engaged in an industry affecting commerce who has fifteen or more employees for each working day in each of twenty or more calendar weeks in the current or preceding calendar year, and any agent of such a person, but such term does not include (1) the United States, a corporation wholly owned by the Government of the United States, an Indian tribe, or any department or agency of the District of Columbia subject by statute to procedures of the competitive service (as defined in section 2102 of title 5 of the United States Code), or (2) a bona fide private membership club (other than a labor organization) which is exempt from taxation under section 501 (c) of the Internal Revenue Code of 1954, except that during the first year after the date of enactment of the Equal Employment Opportunity Act of 1972, persons having fewer than twenty-five employees (and their agents) shall not be considered employers. (As amended by P.L. No. 92–261, eff. March 24, 1972.)

(c) The term "employment agency" means any person regularly undertaking with or without compensation to procure employees for an employer or to procure for employees opportunities to work for an employer and includes an agent of such a person. (As amended by P.L. No. 92–261, eff. March 24, 1972.)

(d) The term "labor organization" means a labor organization engaged in an industry affecting commerce, and any agent of such an organization, and includes any organization of any kind, any agency, or employee representation committee, group, association, or plan so engaged in which employees participate and which exists for the purpose, in whole or in part, of dealing with employers concerning grievances, labor disputes, wages, rates of pay, hours, or other terms or conditions of employment, and any conference, general committee, joint or system board, or joint council so engaged which is subordinate to a national or international labor organization.

(e) A labor organization shall be deemed to be engaged in an industry affecting commerce if (1) it maintains or operates a hiring hall or hiring office which procures employees for an employer or procures for employees opportunities to work for an employer, or (2) the number of its members (or, where it is a labor organization composed of other labor organizations or their representatives, if the aggregate number of the members of such labor organization) is (A) twenty-five or more during the first year after the date of enactment of the Equal Employment Opportunity Act of 1972, or (B) fifteen or more thereafter, (As amended by P.L. No. 92–261, eff. March 24, 1972.)

(1) is the certified representative of employees under the provisions of the National Labor Relations Act, as amended, or the Railway Labor Act, as amended;

(2) although not certified, is a national or international labor organization or a local labor organization recognized or acting as the representative of employees of an employer or employers engaged in an industry affecting commerce; or

(3) has chartered a local labor organization or subsidiary body which is representing or actively seeking to represent employees of employers within the meaning of paragraph (1) or (2); or

(4) has been chartered by a labor organization representing or actively seeking to represent employees within the meaning of paragraph (1) or (2) as the local or subordinate body through which such employees may enjoy membership or become affiliated with such labor organization; or

(5) is a conference, general committee, joint or system board, or joint council subordinate to a national or international labor organization, which includes a labor organization engaged in an industry affecting commerce within the meaning of any of the preceding paragraphs of this subsection.

(f) the term "employee" means an individual employed by an employer, except that the term "employee" shall not include any person elected to public office in any State or political subdivision of any State by the qualified voters thereof, or any person chosen by such officer to be on such officer's personal staff, or an appointee on the policy making level or an immediate adviser with respect to the exercise of the constitutional or legal powers of the office. The exemption set forth in the preceding sentence shall not include employees subject to the civil service laws of a State government, governmental agency or political subdivision. (As amended by P.L. 92–261, eff. March 24, 1972.)

(g) The term "commerce" means trade, traffic, commerce, transportation, transmission, or communication among the several States; or between a State and any place outside thereof; or within the District of Columbia, or a possession of the United States; or between points in the same State but through a point outside thereof.

(h) The term "industry affecting commerce" means any activity, business, or industry in commerce or in which a labor dispute would hinder or obstruct commerce or the free flow of commerce and includes any activity or industry "affecting commerce" within the meaning of the Labor-Management Reporting and Disclosure Act of 1959, and further includes any governmental industry, business, or activity. (As amended by P.L. No. 92–261, eff. March 24, 1972.)

(i) The term "State" includes a State of the United States, the District of Columbia, Puerto Rico, the Virgin Islands, American Samoa, Guam, Wake Island, the Canal Zone, and Outer Continental Shelf lands defined in the Outer Continental Shelf Lands Act.

(j) The term "religion" includes all aspects of religious observance and practice, as well as belief, unless an employer demonstrates that he is unable to reasonably accommodate to an employee's or prospective employee's religious observance or practice without undue hardship on the conduct of the employer's business. (As amended by P.L. 92–261, eff. March 24, 1972.)

(k) The terms "because of sex" or "on the basis of sex" include, but are not limited to, because of or on the basis of pregnancy, childbirth or related medical conditions; and women affected by pregnancy, childbirth, or related medical conditions shall be treated the same for all employment-related purposes, including receipt of benefits under fringe benefit programs, as other persons not so affected but similar in their ability or inability to work, and nothing in section 703(h) of this title shall be interpreted to permit otherwise. This subsection shall not require an employer to pay for health insurance benefits for abortion, except where the life of the mother would be endangered if the fetus were carried to term, or except where medical complications have arisen from an abortion: *Provided,* That nothing herein shall preclude an employer from providing abortion benefits or otherwise affect bargaining agreements in regard to abortion.

EXEMPTION

Section 702. This title shall not apply to an employer with respect to the employment of aliens outside any State, or to a religious corporation, association, educational institution, or society with respect to the employment of individuals of a particular religion to perform work connected with the carrying on by such corporation, association, educational institution, or society of its activities. (As amended by P.L. 92–261, eff. March 24, 1972.)

DISCRIMINATION BECAUSE OF RACE, COLOR, RELIGION, SEX, OR NATIONAL ORIGIN

Section 703. (a) It shall be an unlawful employment practice for an employer—

(1) to fail or refuse to hire or to discharge any individual, or otherwise to discriminate against any individual with respect to his compensation, terms, conditions, or privileges of employment, because of such individual's race, color, religion, sex, or national origin; or

(2) to limit, segregate, or classify his employees or applicants for employment in any way which would deprive or tend to deprive any individual of employment opportunities or otherwise adversely affect his status as an employee, because of such individual's race, color, religion, sex, or national origin. (As amended by P.L. 92–261, eff. March 24, 1972.)

(b) It shall be an unlawful employment practice for an employment agency to fail or refuse to refer for employment, or otherwise to discriminate against, any individual because of his race, color, religion, sex, or national origin, or to classify or refer for employment any individual on the basis of his race, color, religion, sex, or national origin.

(c) It shall be an unlawful employment practice for a labor organization—

(1) to exclude or to expel from its membership, or otherwise to discriminate against, any individual because of his race, color, religion, sex, or national origin;

(2) to limit, segregate, or classify its membership or applicants for membership or to classify or fail or refuse to refer for employment any individual, in any way which would deprive or tend to deprive any individual of employment opportunities, or

would limit such employment opportunities or otherwise adversely affect his status as an employee or as an applicant for employment, because of such individual's race, color, religion, sex, or national origin; or

(3) to cause or attempt to cause an employer to discriminate against an individual in violation of this section.

(d) It shall be an unlawful employment practice for any employer, labor organization, or joint labor-management committee controlling apprenticeship or other training or retraining, including on-the-job training programs to discriminate against any individual because of his race, color, religion, sex, or national origin in admission to, or employment in, any program established to provide apprenticeship or other training.

(e) Notwithstanding any other provision of this title, (1) it shall not be an unlawful employment practice for an employer to hire and employ employees, for an employment agency to classify, or refer for employment any individual, for a labor organization to classify its membership or to classify or refer for employment any individual, or for an employer, labor organization, or joint labor-management committee controlling apprenticeship or other training or retraining programs to admit or employ any individual in any such program, on the basis of his religion, sex, or national origin in those certain instances where religion, sex, or national origin is a bona fide occupational qualification reasonably necessary to the normal operation of that particular business or enterprise, and (2) it shall not be an unlawful employment practice for a school, college, university, or other educational institution or institution of learning to hire and employ employees of a particular religion if such school, college, university, or other educational institution or institution of learning is, in whole or in substantial part, owned, supported, controlled, or managed by a particular religion or by a particular religious corporation, association, or society, or if the curriculum of such school, college, university, or other educational institution or institution of learning is directed toward the propagation of a particular religion.

(f) As used in this title, the phrase "unlawful employment practice" shall not be deemed to include any action or measure taken by an employer, labor organization, joint labor-management committee, or employment agency with respect to an individual who is a member of the Communist Party of the United States

or of any other organization required to register as a Communist-action or Communist-front organization by final order of the Subversive Activities Control Board pursuant to the Subversive Activities Control Act of 1950.

(g) Notwithstanding any other provision of this title, it shall not be an unlawful employment practice for an employer to fail or refuse to hire and employ any individual for any position, for an employer to discharge an individual from any position, or for an employment agency to fail or refuse to refer any individual for employment in any position, or for a labor organization to fail or refuse to refer any individual for employment in any position, if—

(1) the occupancy of such position, or access to the premises in or upon which any part of the duties of such position is performed or is to be performed, is subject to any requirement imposed in the interest of the national security of the United States under any security program in effect pursuant to or administered under any statute of the United States or any Executive order of the President; and

(2) such individual has not fulfilled or has ceased to fulfill that requirement.

(h) Notwithstanding any other provision of this title, it shall not be an unlawful employment practice for an employer to apply different standards of compensation, or different terms, conditions, or privileges of employment pursuant to a bona fide seniority or merit system, or a system which measures earnings by quantity or quality of production or to employees who work in different locations, provided that such differences are not the result of an intention to discriminate because of race, color, religion, sex, or national origin; nor shall it be an unlawful employment practice for an employer to give and to act upon the results of any professionally developed ability test provided that such test, its administration or action upon the results is not designed, intended, or used to discriminate because of race, color, religion, sex, or national origin. It shall not be an unlawful employment practice under this title for any employer to differentiate upon the basis of sex in determining the amount of the wages or compensation paid to employees of such employer if such differentiation is authorized by the provisions of Section 6(d) of the Fair Labor Standards Act of 1938 as amended (29 USC 206(d)).

(i) Nothing contained in this title shall apply to any business or enterprise on or near an Indian reservation with respect to any publicly announced employment practice of such business or enterprise under which a preferential treatment is given to any individual because he is an Indian living on or near a reservation.

(j) Nothing contained in this title shall be interpreted to require any employer, employment agency, labor organization, or joint labor-management committee subject to this title to grant preferential treatment to any individual or to any group because of the race, color, religion, sex, or national origin of such individual or group on account of an imbalance which may exist with respect to the total number or percentage of persons of any race, color, religion, sex, or national origin employed by any employer, referred or classified for employment by any employment agency or labor organization, admitted to membership or classified by any labor organization, or admitted to, or employed in, any apprenticeship or other training program, in comparison with the total number or percentage of persons of such race, color, religion, sex, or national origin in any community, State, section, or other area, or in the available work force in any community, State, section, or other area. (As amended by P.L. 92–261, eff. March 24, 1972.)

OTHER UNLAWFUL EMPLOYMENT PRACTICES

Section 704. (a) It shall be an unlawful employment practice for an employer to discriminate against any of his employees or applicants for employment, for an employment agency or joint labor-management committee controlling apprenticeship or other training or retraining, including on-the-job training programs, to discriminate against any individual, or for a labor organization to discriminate against any member thereof or applicant for membership, because he has opposed any practice, made an unlawful employment practice by this title, or because he has made a charge, testified, assisted, or participated in any manner in an investigation, proceeding, or hearing under this title. (As amended by P.L. No. 92–261, eff. March 24, 1972.)

(b) It shall be an unlawful employment practice for an employer, labor organization, employment agency, or joint labor-management committee controlling apprenticeship or other training or retraining, including on-the-job training programs, to print or cause to be printed or published any notice or advertisement relating to employment by such an employer or membership in or any classification or referral for employ-

ment by such a labor organization, or relating to any classification or referral for employment by such an employment agency, or relating to admission to, or employment in, any program established to provide apprenticeship or other training by such a joint labor-management committee indicating any preference, limitation, specification, or discrimination, based on race, color, religion, sex, or national origin, except that such a notice or advertisement may indicate a preference, limitation, specification or discrimination based on religion, sex or national origin when religion, sex, or national origin is a bona fide occupational qualification for employment. (As amended by P.L. No. 92–261, eff. March 24, 1972.)

EQUAL EMPLOYMENT OPPORTUNITY COMMISSION

Section 705. (a) There is hereby created a Commission to be known as the Equal Employment Opportunity Commission, which shall be composed of five members, not more than three of whom shall be members of the same political party. Members of the Commission shall be appointed by the President by and with the advice and consent of the Senate for a term of five years. Any individual chosen to fill a vacancy shall be appointed only for the unexpired term of the member whom he shall succeed, and all members of the Commission shall continue to serve until their successors are appointed and qualified, except that no such member of the Commission shall continue to serve (1) for more than sixty days when the Congress is in session unless a nomination to fill such vacancy shall have been submitted to the Senate, or (2) after the adjournment *sine die* of the session of the Senate in which such nomination was submitted. The President shall designate one member to serve as Chairman of the Commission, and one member to serve as Vice Chairman. The Chairman shall be responsible on behalf of the Commission for the administrative operations of the Commission, and, except as provided in subsection (b), shall appoint, in accordance with the provisions of title 5, United States Code, governing appointments in the competitive service, such officers, agents, attorneys, hearing examiners, and employees as he deems necessary to assist it in the performance of its functions and to fix their compensation in accordance with the provisions of chapter 51 and subchapter III of chapter 53 of title 5, United States Code, relating to classification and General Schedule pay rates: *Provided,* That assignment, removal, and compensation of administrative law judges shall be in accordance with sections 3105, 3344, 5362, and 7521 of title 5, United States Code.

(b)(1) There shall be a General Counsel of the Commission appointed by the President, by and with the advice and consent of the Senate, for a term of four years. The General Counsel shall have responsibility for the conduct of litigation as provided in sections 706 and 707 of this title. The General Counsel shall have such other duties as the Commission may prescribe or as may be provided by law and shall concur with the Chairman of the Commission on the appointment and supervision of regional attorneys. The General Counsel of the Commission on the effective date of this Act shall continue in such position and perform the functions specified in this subsection until a successor is appointed and qualified.

(2) Attorneys appointed under this section may, at the direction of the commission, appear for and represent the Commission in any case in court, provided that the Attorney General shall conduct all litigation to which the Commission is a party in the Supreme Court pursuant to this title. (As amended by P.L. No. 92–261, eff. March 24, 1972.)

(c) A vacancy in the Commission shall not impair the right of the remaining members to exercise all the powers of the Commission and three members thereof shall constitute a quorum.

(d) The Commission shall have an official seal which shall be judicially noticed.

(e) The Commission shall at the middle and at the close of each fiscal year report to the Congress and to the President concerning the action it has taken; the names, salaries, and duties of all individuals in its employ and the moneys it has disbursed; and shall make such further reports on the cause of and means of eliminating discrimination and such recommendations for further legislation as may appear desirable.

(f) The principal office of the Commission shall be in or near the District of Columbia, but it may meet or exercise any or all its powers at any other place. The Commission may establish such regional or State offices as it deems necessary to accomplish the purpose of this title.

(g) The Commission shall have power—

(1) to cooperate with and, with their consent, utilize regional, State, local, and other agencies, both public and private, and individuals;

(2) to pay to witnesses whose depositions are taken or who are summoned before the Commis-

sion or any of its agents the same witness and mileage fees as are paid to witnesses in the courts of the United States;

(3) to furnish to persons subject to this title such technical assistance as they may request to further their compliance with this title or an order issued thereunder;

(4) upon the request of (i) any employer, whose employees or some of them, or (ii) any labor organization, whose members or some of them, refuse or threaten to refuse to cooperate in effectuating the provisions of this title, to assist in such effectuation by conciliation or such other remedial action as it is provided by this title;

(5) to make such technical studies as are appropriate to effectuate the purposes and policies of this title and to make the results of such studies available to the public;

(6) to intervene in a civil action brought under section 706 by an aggrieved party against a respondent other than a government, governmental agency or political subdivision. (As amended by P.L. No. 92–261, eff. March 24, 1972.)

(h) The Commission shall, in any of its educational or promotional activities, cooperate with other departments and agencies in the performance of such educational and promotional activities.

(i) All officers, agents, attorneys and employees of the Commission, including the members of the Commission, shall be subject to the provisions of section 9 of the act of August 2, 1939, as amended (Hatch Act), notwithstanding any exemption contained in such section.

PREVENTION OF UNLAWFUL EMPLOYMENT PRACTICES

Section 706. (a) The Commission is empowered, as hereinafter provided, to prevent any person from engaging in any unlawful employment practice as set forth in section 703 or 704 of this title.

(b) Whenever a charge is filed by or on behalf of a person claiming to be aggrieved, or by a member of the Commission, alleging that an employer, employment agency, labor organization, or joint labor-management committee controlling apprenticeship or other training or retraining including on-the-job training programs, has engaged in an unlawful employment practice, the Commission shall serve a notice of the charge (including the date, place and circumstances of the alleged unlawful employment practice) on such employer, employment agency, labor organization, or joint labor-management committee (hereinafter referred to as the 'respondent') within ten days and shall make an investigation thereof. Charges shall be in writing under oath or affirmation and shall contain such information and be in such form as the Commission requires. Charges shall not be made public by the Commission. If the Commission determines after such investigation that there is not reasonable cause to believe that the charge is true, it shall dismiss the charge and promptly notify the person claiming to be aggrieved and the respondent of its action. In determining whether reasonable cause exists, the Commission shall accord substantial weight to final findings and orders made by State or local authorities in proceedings commenced under State or local law pursuant to the requirements of subsections (c) and (d). If the Commission determines after such investigation that there is reasonable cause to believe that the charge is true, the Commission shall endeavor to eliminate any such alleged unlawful employment practice by informal methods of conference, conciliation, and persuasion. Nothing said or done during and as a part of such informal endeavors may be made public by the Commission, its officers or employees, or used as evidence in a subsequent proceeding without the written consent of the persons concerned. Any person who makes public information in violation of this subsection shall be fined not more than $1,000 or imprisoned for not more than one year, or both. The Commission shall make its determination on reasonable cause as promptly as possible and, so far as practicable, not later than one hundred and twenty days from the filing of the charge or, where applicable under subsection (c) or (d), from the date upon which the Commission is authorized to take action with respect to the charge.

(c) In the case of an alleged unlawful employment practice occurring in a State, or political subdivision of a State, which has a State or local law prohibiting the unlawful employment practice alleged and establishing or authorizing a State or local authority to grant or seek relief from such practice or to institute criminal proceedings with respect thereto upon receiving notice thereof, no charge may be filed under subsection (a) by the person aggrieved before the expiration of sixty days after proceedings have been commenced under the State or local law, unless such proceedings have been earlier terminated, provided that such sixty-day period

shall be extended to one hundred and twenty days during the first year after the effective date of such State of local law. If any requirement for the commencement of such proceedings is imposed by a State or local authority other than a requirement of the filing of a written and signed statement of the facts upon which the proceeding is based, the proceeding shall be deemed to have been commenced for the purposes of this subsection at the time such statement is sent by registered mail to the appropriate State or local authority.

(d) In the case of any charge filed by a member of the Commission alleging an unlawful employment practice occurring in a State or political subdivision of a State which has a State or local law prohibiting the practice alleged and establishing or authorizing a State or local authority to grant or seek relief from such practice or to institute criminal proceedings with respect thereto upon receiving notice thereof, the Commission shall, before taking any action with respect to such charge, notify the appropriate State or local officials and, upon request, afford them a reasonable time, but not less than sixty days (provided that such sixty-day period shall be extended to one hundred and twenty days during the first year after the effective day of such State or local law), unless a shorter period is requested, to act under such State or local law to remedy the practice alleged.

(e) A charge under this section shall be filed within one hundred and eighty days after the alleged unlawful employment practice occurred and notice of the charge (including the date, place and circumstances of the alleged unlawful employment practice) shall be served upon the person against whom such charge is made within ten days thereafter, except that in a case of an unlawful employment practice with respect to which the person aggrieved has initially instituted proceedings with a State or local agency with authority to grant or seek relief from such practice or to institute criminal proceedings with respect thereto upon receiving notice thereof, such charge shall be filed by or on behalf of the person aggrieved within three hundred days after the alleged unlawful employment practice occurred, or within thirty days after receiving notice that the State or local agency has terminated the proceedings under the State or local law, whichever is earlier, and a copy of such charge shall be filed by the Commission with the State or local agency.

(f)(1) If within thirty days after a charge is filed with the Commission or within thirty days after expiration of any period of reference under subsection (c) or (d), the Commission has been unable to secure from the respondent a conciliation agreement acceptable to the Commission, the Commission may bring a civil action against any respondent not a government, governmental agency, or political subdivision named in the charge. In the case of a respondent which is a government, governmental agency, or political subdivision, if the Commission has been unable to secure from the respondent a conciliation agreement acceptable to the Commission, the Commission shall take no further action and shall refer the case to the Attorney General who may bring a civil action against such respondent in the appropriate United States district court. The person or persons aggrieved shall have the right to intervene in a civil action brought by the Commission or the Attorney General in a case involving a government, governmental agency, or political subdivision. If a charge filed with the Commission pursuant to subsection (b) is dismissed by the Commission, or if within one hundred and eighty days from the filing of such charge or the expiration of any period of reference under subsection (c) or (d), whichever is later, the Commission has not filed a civil action under this section or the Attorney General has not filed a civil action in a case involving a government, governmental agency, or political subdivision, or the Commission has not entered into a conciliation agreement to which the person aggrieved is a party, the Commission, or the Attorney General in a case involving a government, governmental agency, or political subdivision, shall so notify the person aggrieved and within ninety days after the giving of such notice a civil action may be brought against the respondent named in the charge (A) by the person claiming to be aggrieved or (B) if such charge was filed by a member of the Commission, by any person whom the charge alleges was aggrieved by the alleged unlawful employment practice. Upon application by the complainant and in such circumstances as the court may deem just, the court may appoint an attorney for such complainant and may authorize the commencement of the action without the payment of fees, costs, or security. Upon timely application, the court may, in its discretion, permit the Commission, or the Attorney General in a case involving a government, governmental agency, or political subdivision, to intervene in such civil action upon certification that the case is of general public importance. Upon request, the court may, in its discretion, stay further proceedings for not more than sixty days pending the termi-

nation of State or local proceedings described in subsections (c) or (d) of this section or further efforts of the Commission to obtain voluntary compliance.

(2) Whenever a charge is filed with the Commission and the Commission concludes on the basis of a preliminary investigation that prompt judicial action is necessary to carry out the purpose of this Act, the Commission, or the Attorney General in a case involving a government, governmental agency, or political subdivision, may bring an action for appropriate temporary or preliminary relief pending final disposition of such charge. Any temporary restraining order or other order granting preliminary or temporary relief shall be issued in accordance with rule 65 of the Federal Rules of Civil Procedure. It shall be the duty of a court having jurisdiction over proceedings under this section to assign cases for hearing at the earliest practicable date and to cause such cases to be in every way expedited.

(3) Each United States district court and each United States court of a place subject to the jurisdiction of the United States shall have jurisdiction of actions brought under this title. Such an action may be brought in any judicial district in the State in which the unlawful employment practice is alleged to have been committed, in the judicial district in which the employment records relevant to such practice are maintained and administered, or in the judicial district in which the aggrieved person would have worked but for the alleged unlawful employment practice, but if the respondent is not found within any such district, such an action may be brought within the judicial district in which the respondent has his principal office. For purposes of sections 1404 and 1406 of title 28 of the United States Code, the judicial district in which the respondent has his principal office shall in all cases be considered a district in which the action might have been brought.

(4) It shall be the duty of the chief judge of the district (or in his absence, the acting chief judge) in which the case is pending immediately to designate a judge in such district to hear and determine the case. In the event that no judge in the district is available to hear and determine the case, the chief judge of the district, or the acting chief judge, as the case may be, shall certify this fact to the chief judge of the circuit (or in his absence, the acting chief judge) who shall then designate a district or circuit judge of the circuit to hear and determine the case.

(5) It shall be the duty of the judge designated

pursuant to this subsection to assign the case for hearing at the earliest practicable date and to cause the case to be in every way expedited. If such judge has not scheduled the case for trial within one hundred and twenty days after issue has been joined that judge may appoint a master pursuant to rule 53 of the Federal Rules of Civil Procedure.

(g) If the court finds that the respondent has intentionally engaged in or is intentionally engaging in an unlawful employment practice charged in the complaint, the court may enjoin the respondent from engaging in such unlawful employment practice, and order such affirmative action as may be appropriate, which may include, but is not limited to, reinstatement or hiring of employees, with or without back pay (payable by the employer, employment agency, or labor organization, as the case may be, responsible for the unlawful employment practice), or any other equitable relief as the court deems appropriate. Back pay liability shall not accrue from a date more than two years prior to the filing of a charge with the Commission. Interim earnings or amounts earnable with reasonable diligence by the person or persons discriminated against shall operate to reduce the back pay otherwise allowable. No order of the court shall require the admission or reinstatement of an individual as a member of a union, or the hiring, reinstatement, or promotion of an individual as an employee, or the payment to him of any back pay, if such individual was refused admission, suspended, or expelled, or was refused employment or advancement or was suspended or discharged for any reason other than discrimination on account of race, color, religion, sex, or national origin or in violation of section 704(a). (As amended by P.L. No. 92–261, eff. March 24, 1972.)

(h) The provisions of the Act entitled "An Act to amend the Judicial Code and to define and limit the jurisdiction of courts sitting in equity, and for other purposes," approved March 23, 1932 (29 U.S.C. 101–115), shall not apply with respect to civil actions brought under this section.

(i) In any case in which an employer, employment agency, or labor organization fails to comply with an order of a court issued in a civil action brought under this section the Commission may commence proceedings to compel compliance with such order. (As amended.)

(j) Any civil action brought under this section and any proceedings brought under subsection (j) shall be subject to appeal as provided in sections 1291 and 1292, title 28, United States Code. (As amended by P.L. 92–261, eff. March 24, 1972.)

(k) In any action or proceeding under this title the court, in its discretion, may allow the prevailing party, other than the Commission or the United States, a reasonable attorney's fee as part of the costs, and the Commission and the United States shall be liable for costs the same as a private person.

Section 707. (a) Whenever the Attorney General has reasonable cause to believe that any person or group of persons is engaged in a pattern or practice of resistance to the full enjoyment of any of the rights secured by this title, and that the pattern or practice is of such a nature and is intended to deny the full exercise of the rights herein described, the Attorney General may bring a civil action in the appropriate district court of the United States by filing with it a complaint (1) signed by him (or in his absence the Acting Attorney General), (2) setting forth facts pertaining to such pattern or practice, and (3) requesting such relief, including an application for a permanent or temporary injunction, restraining order or other order against the person or persons responsible for such pattern or practice, as he deems necessary to insure the full enjoyment of the rights herein described.

(b) The district courts of the United States shall have and shall exercise jurisdiction of proceedings instituted pursuant to this section, and in any such proceeding the Attorney General may file with the clerk of such court a request that a court of three judges be convened to hear and determine the case. Such request by the Attorney General shall be accompanied by a certificate that, in his opinion, the case is of general public importance. A copy of the certificate and request for a three-judge court shall be immediately furnished by such clerk to the chief judge of the circuit (or in his absence, the presiding circuit judge of the circuit) in which the case is pending. Upon receipt of such request it shall be the duty of the chief judge of the circuit or the presiding circuit judge, as the case may be, to designate immediately three judges in such circuit, of whom at least one shall be a circuit judge and another of whom shall be a district judge of the court in which the proceeding was instituted, to hear and determine such case, and it shall be the duty of the judges so designated to assign the case for hearing at the earliest practicable date, to participate in the hearing and determination thereof, and to cause the case to be in every way expedited. An appeal from the final judgment of such court will lie to the Supreme Court.

In the event the Attorney General fails to file such a request in any such proceeding, it shall be the duty of the chief judge of the district (or in his absence, the acting chief judge) in which the case is pending immediately to designate a judge in such district to hear and determine the case. In the event that no judge in the district is available to hear and determine the case, the chief judge of the district, or the acting chief judge, as the case may be, shall certify this fact to the chief judge of the circuit (or in his absence, the acting chief judge) who shall then designate a district or circuit judge of the circuit to hear and determine the case.

It shall be the duty of the judge designated pursuant to this section to assign the case for hearing at the earliest practicable date and to cause the case to be in every way expedited.

(c) Effective two years after the date of enactment of the Equal Employment Opportunity Act of 1972, the functions of the Attorney General under this section shall be transferred to the Commission, together with such personnel, property, records, and unexpended balances of appropriations, allocations, and other funds employed, used, held, available, or to be made available in connection with such functions unless the President submits, and neither House of Congress vetoes, a reorganization plan pursuant to chapter 9 of title 5, United States Code, inconsistent with the provisions of this subsection. The Commission shall carry out such functions in accordance with subsections (d) and (e) of this section.

(d) Upon the transfer of functions provided for in subsection (c) of this section, in all suits commenced pursuant to this section prior to the date of such transfer, proceedings shall continue without abatement, all court orders and decrees shall remain in effect, and the Commission shall be substituted as a party for the United States of America, the Attorney General, as appropriate.

(e) Subsequent to the date of enactment of the Equal Employment Opportunity Act of 1972, the Commission shall have authority to investigate and act on a charge of a pattern or practice of discrimination, whether filed by or on behalf of a person claiming to be aggrieved or by a member of the Commission. All such actions shall be conducted in accordance with the procedures set forth in section 706 of this Act. (As last amended by P.L. No. 92–261, eff. March 24, 1972.)

EFFECT OF STATE LAWS

Section 708. Nothing in this title shall be deemed to exempt or relieve any person from any liability, duty, penalty, or punishment provided by any present or future law of any State or political subdivision of a State, other than any such law which purports to require or permit the doing of any act which would be an unlawful employment practice under this title.

INVESTIGATIONS, INSPECTIONS, RECORDS, STATE AGENCIES

Section 709. (a) In connection with any investigation of a charge filed under section 706, the Commission or its designated representative shall at all reasonable times have access to, for the purposes of examination, and the right to copy any evidence of any person being investigated or proceeded against that relates to unlawful employment practices covered by this title and is relevant to the charge under investigation.

(b) The Commission may cooperate with State and local agencies charged with the administration of State fair employment practices laws and, with the consent of such agencies, may, for the purpose of carrying out its functions and duties under this title and within the limitation of funds appropriated specifically for such purpose, engage in and contribute to the cost of research and other projects of mutual interest undertaken by such agencies, and utilize the services of such agencies and their employees, and notwithstanding any other provision of law, pay by advance or reimbursement such agencies and their employees for services rendered to assist the Commission in carrying out this title. In furtherance of such cooperative efforts, the Commission may enter into written agreements with such State or local agencies and such agreement may include provisions under which the Commission shall refrain from processing a charge in any cases or class of cases specified in such agreements or under which the Commission shall relieve any person or class of persons in such State or locality from requirements imposed under this section. The Commission shall rescind any such agreement whenever it determines that the agreement no longer serves the interest of effective enforcement of this title.

(c) Every employer, employment agency, and labor organization subject to this title shall (1) make and keep such records relevant to the determinations of whether unlawful employment practices have been or are being committed, (2) preserve such records for such periods, and (3) make such reports therefrom as the Commission shall prescribe by regulation or order, after public hearing, as reasonable, necessary, or appropriate for the enforcement of this title or the regulations or orders thereunder. The Commission shall, by regulation, require each employer, labor organization, and joint labor-management committee subject to this title which controls an apprenticeship or other training program to maintain such records as are reasonably necessary to carry out the purposes of this title, including, but not limited to, a list of applicants who wish to participate in such program, including the chronological order in which applications were received, and to furnish to the Commission upon request, a detailed description of the manner in which persons are selected to participate in the apprenticeship or other training program. Any employer, employment agency, labor organization, or joint labor-management committee which believes that the application to it of any regulation or order issued under this section would result in undue hardship may apply to the Commission for an exemption from the application of such regulation or order, and, if such application for an exemption is denied, bring a civil action in the United States district court for the district where such records are kept. If the Commission or the court, as the case may be, finds that the application of the regulation or order to the employer, employment agency, or labor organization in question would impose an undue hardship, the Commission or the court, as the case may be, may grant appropriate relief. If any person required to comply with the provisions of this subsection fails or refuses to do so, the United States district court for the district in which such person is found, resides, or transacts business, shall, upon application of the Commission, or the Attorney General in a case involving a governmental agency or political subdivision, have jurisdiction to issue to such person an order requiring him to comply.

(d) In prescribing requirements pursuant to subsection (c) of this section, the Commission shall consult with other interested State and Federal agencies and shall endeavor to coordinate its requirements with those adopted by such agencies. The Commission shall furnish upon request and without cost to any State or local agency charged with the administration of a fair employment practice law information obtained pursuant to subsection (c) of this section from any employer, employment agency, labor organiza-

tion, or joint labor-management committee subject to the jurisdiction of such agency. Such information shall be furnished on condition that it not be made public by the recipient agency prior to the institution of a proceeding under State or local law involving such information. If this condition is violated by a recipient agency, the Commission may decline to honor subsequent requests pursuant to this subsection. (As amended by P.O. 92–261, eff. March 24, 1972.)

(e) It shall be unlawful for any officer or employee of the Commission to make public in any manner whatever any information obtained by the Commission pursuant to its authority under this section prior to the institution of any proceeding under this title involving such information. Any officer or employee of the Commission who shall make public in any manner whatever any information in violation of this subsection shall be guilty of a misdemeanor and upon conviction thereof, shall be fined not more than $1,000, or imprisoned not more than one year.

INVESTIGATORY POWERS

Section 710. For the purpose of all hearings and investigations conducted by the Commission or its duly authorized agents or agencies, section 11 of the National Labor Relations Act (49 Stat. 455; 29 U.S.C. 161) shall apply. (As amended by P.L. 92–261, eff. March 24, 1972.)

NOTICES TO BE POSTED

Section 711. (a) Every employer, employment agency and labor organization, as the case may be, shall post and keep posted in conspicuous places upon its premises where notices to employees, applicants for employment and members are customarily posted a notice to be prepared or approved by the Commission setting forth excerpts from, or summaries of, the pertinent provisions of this title and information pertinent to the filing of a complaint.

(b) A willful violation of this section shall be punishable by a fine of not more than $100 for each separate offense.

VETERANS' PREFERENCE

Section 712. Nothing contained in this title shall be construed to repeal or modify any Federal, State, territorial, or local law creating special rights or preference for veterans.

RULES AND REGULATIONS

Section 713. (a) The Commission shall have authority from time to time to issue, amend, or rescind suitable procedural regulations to carry out the provisions of this title. Regulations issued under this section shall be in conformity with the standards and limitations of the Administrative Procedure Act.

(b) In any action or proceeding based on any alleged unlawful employment practice, no person shall be subject to any liability or punishment for or on account of (1) the commission by such person of an unlawful employment practice if he pleads and proves that the act of omission complained of was in good faith, in conformity with, and in reliance on any written interpretation or opinion of the Commission, or (2) the failure of such person to publish and file any information required by any provision of this title if he pleads and proves that he failed to publish and file such information in good faith, in conformity with the instructions of the Commission issued under this title regarding the filing of such information. Such a defense, if established, shall be a bar to the action or proceeding, notwithstanding that (A) after such act or omission, such interpretation or opinion is modified or rescinded or is determined by judicial authority to be invalid or of no legal effect, or (B) after publishing or filing the description and annual reports, such publication or filing is determined by judicial authority not to be in conformity with the requirements of this title.

FORCIBLY RESISTING THE COMMISSION OR ITS REPRESENTATIVES

Section 714. The provisions of sections 111 and 1114, title 18, United States Code, shall apply to officers, agents, and employees of the Commission in the performance of their official duties. Notwithstanding the provisions of sections 111 and 1114 of title 18, United States Code, whoever in violation of the provisions of section 1114 of such title kills a person while engaged in or on account of the performance of his official functions under this Act shall be punished by imprisonment for any term of years or for life. (As amended by P.L. 92–261, eff. March 24, 1972.)

SPECIAL STUDY BY SECRETARY OF LABOR

Section 715. There shall be established an Equal Employment Opportunity Coordinating Council (hereinafter referred to in this section as the Council) composed of the Secretary of Labor, the Chairman of the Equal Employment Opportunity Commission, the Attorney General, the Chairman of the United States Civil Service Commission, and the Chairman of the United States Civil Rights Commission, or their respective delegates. The Council shall have the responsibility for developing and implementing agreements, policies and practices designed to maximize effort, promote efficiency, and eliminate conflict, competition, duplication and inconsistency among the operations, functions and jurisdictions of the various departments, agencies and branches of the Federal Government responsible for the implementation and enforcement of equal employment opportunity legislation, orders and policies. On or before July 1 of each year, the Council shall transmit to the President and to the Congress a report of its activities, together with such recommendations for legislative or administrative changes as it concludes are desirable to further promote the purposes of this section. (As amended by P.L. No. 92–261, eff. March 24, 1972.)

EFFECTIVE DATE

Section 716. (a) This title shall become effective one year after the date of its enactment. (The effective date thus is July 2, 1965.)

(b) Notwithstanding subsection (a), sections of this title other than sections 703, 704, 706, and 707 shall become effective immediately.

(c) The President shall, as soon as feasible after the enactment of this title, convene one or more conferences for the purpose of enabling the leaders of groups whose members will be affected by this title to become familiar with the rights afforded and obligations imposed by its provisions, and for the purpose of making plans which will result in the fair and effective administration of this title when all of its provisions become effective. The President shall invite the participation in such conference or conferences of (1) the members of the President's Committee on Equal Employment Opportunity, (2) the members of the Commission on Civil Rights, (3) representatives of State and local agencies engaged in furthering equal employment opportunity, (4) representatives of private agencies engaged in furthering equal employment opportunity, and (5) representatives of employers, labor organizations, and employment agencies who will be subject to this title.

NON DISCRIMINATION IN FEDERAL GOVERNMENT EMPLOYMENT

Section 717. (a) All personnel actions affecting employees or applicants for employment (except with regard to aliens employed outside the limits of the United States) in military departments as defined in section 102 of title 5, United States Code in executive agencies (other than the General Accounting Office) as defined in section 105 of title 5, United States Code (including employees and applicants for employment who are paid from nonappropriated funds), in the United States Postal Service and the Postal Rate Commission, in those units of the Government of the District of Columbia having positions in the competitive service, and in those units of the legislative and judicial branches of the Federal Government having positions in the competitive service, and in the Library of Congress shall be made free from any discrimination based on race, color, religion, sex, or national origin.

(b) Except as otherwise provided in this subsection, the Civil Service Commission shall have authority to enforce the provisions of subsection (a) through appropriate remedies, including reinstatement or hiring of employees with or without back pay, as will effectuate the policies of this section, and shall issue such rules, regulations, orders and instructions as it deems necessary and appropriate to carry out its responsibilities under this section. The Civil Service Commission shall—

(1) be responsible for the annual review and approval of a national and regional equal employment opportunity plan which each department and agency and each appropriate unit referred to in subsection (a) of this section shall submit in order to maintain an affirmative program of equal employment opportunity for all such employees and applicants for employment;

(2) be responsible for the review and evaluation of the operation of all agency equal employment opportunity programs, periodically obtaining and publishing (on at least a semi-annual basis) progress reports from each such department, agency, or unit; and

(3) consult with and solicit the recommendations of interested individuals, groups, and organizations relating to equal employment opportunity.

The head of each such department, agency, or unit shall comply with such rules, regulations, orders, and instructions which shall include a provision that an employee or applicant for employment shall be notified of any final action taken on any complaint of discrimination filed by him thereunder. The plan submitted by each department, agency, and unit shall include, but not be limited to—

(1) provision for the establishment of training and education programs designed to provide a maximum opportunity for employees to advance so as to perform at their highest potential; and

(2) a description of the qualifications in terms of training and experience relating to equal employment opportunity for the principal and operating officials of each such department, agency, or unit responsible for carrying out the equal employment opportunity program and of the allocation of personnel and resources proposed by such department, agency, or unit to carry out its equal employment opportunity program.

With respect to employment in the Library of Congress, authorities granted in this subsection to the Civil Service Commission shall be exercised by the Librarian of Congress.

(c) Within thirty days of receipt of notice of final action taken by a department, agency, or unit referred to in subsection 717(a), or by the Civil Service Commission upon an appeal from a decision or order of such department, agency, or unit on a complaint of discrimination based on race, color, religion, sex, or national origin, brought pursuant to subsection (a) of this section, Executive Order 11478 or any succeeding executive orders, or after one hundred and eighty days from the filing of the initial charge with the department, agency, or unit or with the Civil Service Commission on appeal from a decision or order of such department, agency, or unit until such time as final action may be taken by a department, agency, or unit, an employee or applicant for employment, if aggrieved by the final disposition of this complaint, or by the failure to take final action on his complaint, may file a civil action as provided in section 706, in which civil action the head of the department, agency, or unit, as appropriate, shall be the defendant.

(d) The provisions of section 706 (f) through (k), as applicable, shall govern civil actions brought hereunder.

(e) Nothing contained in this Act shall relieve any Government agency or official of its or his primary responsibility to assure nondiscrimination in employment as required by the Constitution and statutes or of its or his responsibilities under Executive Order 11478 relating to equal employment opportunity in the Federal Government. (As amended by 92–261, eff. March 24, 1972).

SPECIAL PROVISION WITH RESPECT TO DENIAL, TERMINATION AND SUSPENSION OF GOVERNMENT CONTRACTS

Section 718. No Government contract, or portion thereof, with any employer, shall be denied, withheld, terminated, or suspended, by any agency or officer of the United States under any equal employment opportunity law or order, where such employer has an affirmative action plan which has previously been accepted by the Government for the same facility within the past twelve months without first according such employer full hearing and adjudication under the provisions of title 5, United States Code, section 554, and the following pertinent sections: *Provided*, That if such employer has deviated substantially from such previously agreed to affirmative action plan, this section shall not apply: *Provided further*, That for the purposes of this section an affirmative action plan shall be deemed to have been accepted by the Government at the time the appropriate compliance agency has accepted such plan unless within forty-five days thereafter the Office of Federal Contract Compliance has disapproved such plan. (As added by P.L. 92–261, eff. March 24, 1972.)

Index of Cases*

A

AFGE v. Weinberger, 147n.12
AFSCME I, 103
AFSCME II, 103, 104
AFSCME v. State of Washington
   AFSCME I, 103
   AFSCME II, 103, 104
Albemarle Paper Company v. Moody, 35, 63,
   64–66
Alexander v. Gardner-Denver Company, 88
American Nurses Ass'n v. State of Illinois, 103
American Tobacco Company v. Patterson, 36
Anderson v. Philadelphia, 155n, 156, **157–61**
Ansonia Board of Education v. Philbrick, 14
Arizona Annuity Plans v. Norris, 20
Arnold v. Burger King Corporation, 64
Associated General Contractors of Massachusetts,
   Inc. v. Altshuler, 85n.30
Audra Sommers, a/k/a Timothy K. Cornish v.
   Budget Marketing Inc., 20, **21–22**
Auffant v. Searle and Co., 117n.21

B

Barnes v. Costle, 23
Blum v. Gulf Oil Corp., 20n.27
Board of Trustees of Keene State College v.
   Sweeney, 50
Boyd v. Ozark Airlines, 19
Brennan v. Victoria Bank & Trust Co., 98
Brotherhood of Locomotive Engineers and Illinois
   Central Gulf Railroad, **144–45**
Brown v. D.C. Transit, 7n.14
Brown v. G.S.A., 122n.26
Bundy v. Jackson, 23–24

C

Capua v. City of Plainfield, 146
Castaneda v. Partida, 61–62
Chalk v. U.S. District Court, 118
Christiansburg Garment Co. v. EEOC, 63–64
City of Los Angeles v. Manhart, 20
Cleary v. American Airlines, Inc., 134n.7
Cleveland Board of Education v. LaFleur, 122,
   123–27
Connecticut v. Teal, 51, **55–59**
Contractors Association of Eastern Pennsylvania v.
   Shultz, 85n.30
Corning Glass Works v. Brennan, **98–102**
County of Washington v. Gunther, 102–3, **104–7**
Craig v. Y&Y Snacks, Inc., 23n.34
Crown Corke Seal Co. v. Parker, 5

D

Dabbs v. Cardiopulmonary Management, 133n.3
Dathard v. Rawlinson, 34
David Huebschen v. Department of Health and
   Social Services, 23n.31
Davis v. County of Los Angeles, 33n.44
Davis v. UAL, Inc., 117n.21
Diaz v. Pan American World Airways, Inc., 34,
   37–39
Division 241, Amalgamated Transit Union v.
   Suscy, 146n.10
Duldulao v. St. Mary Nazareth Hospital Center,
   134

E

EEOC v. Liggett & Meyers Inc., **109–13**
EEOC v. Sage Realty Corp., 27

*Note: Where the case decision is reported in the text, the case name and page reference(s) appear in boldface.

Index of Subjects